DATE DUE

GAYLORD			PRINTED IN U.S.A.

Related Titles from Potomac Books, Inc.

America and Europe After 9/11 and Iraq: The Great Divide, Revised and Updated Edition—Sarwar A. Kashmeri

Human Intelligence, Counterterrorism, and National Leadership: A Practical Guide—Gary Berntsen

European Security Institutions: Ready for the Twenty-First Century?—John R. Galvin

WMD

PROLIFERATION

Reforming the Security Sector to Meet the Threat

Fred Schreier

Potomac Books, Inc.
Washington, D.C.

Library of Congress Cataloging-in-Publication Data
Schreier, Fred.
  WMD proliferation : reforming the security sector to meet the threat / Fred Schreier. — 1st ed.
    p. cm.
  Includes bibliographical references and index.
  ISBN 978-1-59797-421-9 (hardcover : alk. paper) – ISBN 978-1-59797-422-6 (pbk. : alk. paper)
  1. Weapons of mass destruction—Government policy—United States. 2. Arms race—United States. 3. National security—United States. 4. United States—Defenses. I. Title. II. Title: Weapons of mass destruction proliferation.
  U793.S37 2009
  358'.30973–dc22

                                        2008055630

Printed in the United States of America on acid-free paper that meets the American National Standards Institute Z39-48 Standard.

Potomac Books, Inc.
22841 Quicksilver Drive
Dulles, Virginia 20166

First Edition

10 9 8 7 6 5 4 3 2 1

Contents

Preface

The term weapons of mass destruction (WMD) is used to describe weapons with the capacity to indiscriminately kill a large number of human beings. There is controversy over when the term was first used, either in 1937—in reference to the mass destruction at Guernica in the Spanish Civil War by aerial bombardment—or in August 1945, with reference to the nuclear weapons that devastated Hiroshima and Nagasaki. WMD is a political term that is used and abused in various ways. Most often, WMD is taken to mean what are also referred to as unconventional weapons. Terms used by the military began with atomic, biological, and chemical warfare (ABC warfare), which changed to nuclear, biological, and chemical warfare (NBC warfare) after the invention of the hydrogen bomb, to what is now called chemical, biological, radiological, and nuclear warfare (CBRN warfare), recognizing the threat of sub-critical radiological weapons. However, these four classes of weapons have radically different effects—some would have little effect if used by terrorists and others would have catastrophic effects. Yet, understanding of the nature of the threats is not high, in part because of imprecise usage of the term by politicians and the media.

The two most influential actors in international politics today have put the idea of WMD terrorism at the heart of their security thinking. The U.S. National Security Strategy of 2002 sees the United States "menaced less by fleets and armies than by catastrophic technologies in the hands of the embittered few." The Strategy Against the Proliferation of WMD of the European Union (EU) states that proliferation is "a growing threat to international peace and security," and that "the risk that terrorists will acquire chemical, biological, radiological, or fissile materials, and their means of delivery, adds a new critical dimension to this threat." Asia Pacific Economic Cooperation (APEC) leaders have also acknowledged the need for action on proliferation. In 2003 they committed APEC member economies to take all essential actions to eliminate what was described as the "severe and growing danger" posed by the proliferation of WMD and their means of delivery. The need to confront these challenges has equally been recognized by the United Nations Security Council (UNSC). In April 2004, in a historic and major achievement, it unanimously adopted the United Nations Security Council Resolution (UNSCR) 1540, which requires all UN members to take action to prevent the proliferation of WMD and their means of delivery, particularly to non-state actors.

The threat of terrorists using WMD is not new. The disperal of the nerve agent sarin in an attack on the Tokyo underground in 1995 by Aum Shinrikyo, a Japanese religious cult, alerted the world to the dire consequences of WMD-related materials falling into the hands of terrorists. Al Qaeda has declared its ambitions to acquire and use WMD. Terrorist groups in the Asia-Pacific region, such as Jemaah Islamiyah, have similar ambitions. Expansion of these groups' regional networks means that no state can consider itself immune from the threat of terrorist attack or proliferation activity.

But why have terrorists not used unconventional weapons more than they have so far? The answer lies in understanding both the capability and the motivational dimensions that would be involved, and how both of these factors limit the likelihood of terrorist attacks with unconventional weapons. The different types of WMD need different skills to build and use. Generally, the more dangerous the weapon, the more difficult it is for terrorist groups to obtain those weapons. An approximate guide to the difficulty in producing and using such weapons is as follows:

Radiological Dispersal Device

A radiological dispersal device (RDD)—or "dirty bomb"—is radioactive material packed around a conventional explosive. There are hundreds of different radioactive sources that could potentially be found in industry, hospitals, university laboratories, and many other places, making this the most likely form of an unconventional weapons attack. While RDDs are easy to deploy, it is very difficult to immediately administer a lethal dose of radiation. Therefore, the bomb part of a dirty bomb would likely kill more people than the device's "dirty"—radiological—component. Fortunately, many radioactive sources do not present great risks if used in an RDD. The highly radioactive sources that would be dangerous in an RDD are much more difficult for terrorists to get and to handle safely. However, actual engagement of an RDD would result in evacuations and could require a lengthy and expensive decontamination process. Because of this, RDDs are referred to as "weapons of mass disruption" rather than WMD.

Chemical Weapons

A chemical attack at its simplest could be the release of toxic gas caused by attacking an industrial facility, a chemical storage site, a tanker car, or engaging a chemical that has been stolen from its legitimate users—as the Liberation Tigers of Tamil Eelam (LTTE) did in the early 1990s when they stole chlorine from a paper factory and used it against the Sri Lankan military. While such an attack could release enough of a deadly chemical to kill many people, most people would be evacuated before they could receive a lethal dose, as industrial accidents in the past have demonstrated. Such an attack would be messy, but would be more likely to cause panic and mass evacuations rather than mass casualties. The dispersion of a chemical agent is no easy feat. The failure by jihadists in Iraq to use chlorine effectively in their attacks underscores the problem of using improvised chemical weapons. While non-state groups have made more advanced chemical weapons—most notably Aum Shinrikyo's attack on the Tokyo underground with sarin—this was a product of millions of dollars spent on research by technically skilled cult members, but they still failed to find a way to disperse it effectively. Chemical weapons are expensive, difficult to produce and use, and have proven to be largely ineffective in real-world applications. A comparison of the Aum Shinrikyo attacks with the March 2004 jihadist attacks in Madrid clearly demonstrates that explosives are far cheaper, easier to use, and more effective at killing people.

Biological Weapons

Assessing the risks of obtaining and engaging biological weapons by terrorists is more difficult. The anthrax used in the attacks in the United States in the fall of 2001 appears to have come from the U.S. government biological weapons research program. This shows the ever present possibility of weapons being diverted by an "insider." But non-state groups' attempts at using bioweapons have been less successful so far. Aum Shinrikyo failed to weaponize anthrax despite spending millions of dollars on research and being undisturbed by law enforcement as well as intelligence services. Weaponization and dispersion are the main hurdles. Among the few successful uses of biological weapons by a non-state group before the 2001 anthrax attacks was in 1984 by the Bhagwhan Shree Rajneesh cult in Oregon that spread food poisoning in a town by contaminating salad bars with salmonella. However, the rapid advances in the biosciences in the last years, including new understandings of genes and proteins, could eventually outpace national and international efforts to prevent, control, and manage the hostile uses of biology. So many vulnerabilities exist that biodefense will remain problematic for the foreseeable future. In addition to potentially substantial economic costs associated with such an attack, the psychological impact on the population could also prove attractive to terrorists. Humans, obviously, are highly vulnerable, but agricultural assets such as livestock, crops, soil, and water are also at risk. Thus, for bioweapons, the past may no longer be a good indicator of future trends.

Nuclear Weapons

Nuclear weapons are unique in their capacity to inflict instant loss of life on a massive scale, which gives them special appeal to terrorists. Senior al Qaeda members have threatened to use WMD and have demonstrated the will to carry out attacks with them. The engineering skills and equipment needed to build the simplest form of a nuclear weapon—a "gun style" bomb using highly enriched uranium—are theoretically within the ability of a well organized group. That terrorists could build a working improvised nuclear device themselves cannot be totally excluded. But getting highly enriched uranium is very difficult. A number of state programs have either failed or made very slow progress. Also, the amount of infrastructure, time, and resources necessary seems to put this way out of reach of any non-state group. This leaves terrorists with the possibility of either buying or stealing a nuclear weapon. The high security surrounding nuclear weapons arsenals protects against the possibility of terrorists stealing a ready-made weapon. Even if a nuclear warhead could be stolen or acquired with the help of insiders or organized crime, there are several different types of safety and security systems incorporated into the weapon, ensuring that no unwanted nuclear explosion can take place and that successful use of a stolen weapon would be unlikely. The danger remains that terrorists could attack nuclear facilities, provoking a nuclear incident, or use hazardous radioactive materials, spent nuclear fuel, or attack nuclear materials in transit, which is a serious problem, calling for high standards of physical protection.

Factors that May Determine the Use of WMD

The factors that would determine a non-state group's decision to seek or not to seek WMD can be tactical, strategic, ideological, or theological.

Among the tactical factors is the fact that certain types of unconventional weapons might be used purely because the opportunity presents itself, or because the situation leaves few other options. This was the case when the LTTE Tamil Tigers used chlorine; they were simply running short of conventional weapons. Also, an attack on an industrial chemical facility, for instance, could be made as a way of amplifying a conventional attack. Another tactical reality is that a government simply cannot protect every potential target. While insights gained from al Qaeda's targeting criteria have helped authorities protect high-value targets, there are far too many potential targets to protect them all. At the same time, tactical considerations may well dissuade terrorist groups from trying to use more exotic weapons as they may prefer to follow tactics that they know are likely to succeed. The Madrid rail bombings of March 2004 showed what terrorists have the ability to achieve with cheap and easily available conventional explosives. The ease with which an attack can be conducted may also play a role. Virginia Tech shooter Cho Seung Hui recently demonstrated this in the United States: he killed more people with handguns than Jemaah Islamiyah killed in Jakarta, Indonesia, in the August 2003 bombings against the Marriott Hotel and the Australian Embassy combined.

There are strategic considerations that help explain why we have not seen al Qaeda execute more follow-on attacks. The first is that strategic attacks are difficult to pull off. Most strategic targets are large and well constructed, and therefore difficult to destroy. Many such attacks have failed. Even when a plot against a strategic target is successfully executed, it might not produce the desired results. For example, despite the detonation of a massive truck bomb in a parking garage of the World Trade Center in 1993, that attack failed to achieve the jihadists' aims of toppling the two towers and producing mass casualties. What a terrorist group aims to achieve will affect its choice of weapon. Terrorism is ultimately symbolic violence; even groups that are identified as "religious" have political agendas, and the level of violence is selected to try and achieve these aims without creating a damaging response. Often this response could be the loss of support from what the group sees as its natural constituency. Particularly nationalist and separatist terrorist groups have clearly shown this. A good example was the Omagh bombing of August 1998 in Northern Ireland where the number of people killed was so high that the dissident republican group that carried out the attack lost virtually all support, even from the strongly republican. The potentially huge casualties that could be caused by some kind of WMD attack could have similar effects. Indeed, al Qaeda decided not to attack a nuclear power station with a plane on September 11 because they could not be sure what the ultimate results would be.

Among the ideological factors, one major driving force for using WMD seems to be a fascination with the weapons themselves. This was clearly the case with the leader of the Aum Shinrikyo cult, Shoko Asahara, who believed that just the use of nerve gas would hasten Armageddon. There may also be theological considerations for jihadi groups as to whether the use of WMD can be justified according to the Quran. At least one radical Saudi scholar has written a fatwa legitimizing the use of nuclear weapons against the United States, although many Muslims do not regard the fatwa as valid. According to bin Laden's deputy, Ayman al-Zawahiri, al Qaeda became interested in unconventional weapons as a result of the fears continually expressed by American officials and experts of the danger of terrorists using WMD. Up to this point, it was clear that al Qaeda saw traditional methods as the most appropriate for reaching their goals. Jihadists see suicide attacks as martyrdom and, hence, the ultimate demonstration of the strength of their faith. They believe that it is the demonstration of this faith that will awaken the Umma—the Muslim nation—not necessarily the effects of the attack. Suicide attacks using conventional explosives or hijacked planes have suited al Qaeda's ideology and world view so far: easy and reliable to organize, they show the strength of their faith to other Muslims and encourage them to join the jihad while simultaneously creating fear among their enemies. In this sense, al Qaeda and related groups have not needed to use WMD. Whether this will endure is unclear. Abu Musab al-Suri, a dual Syrian/Spanish citizen who has served as both an ideologue and an instructor for al Qaeda in Afghanistan and who is linked to the group that carried out the Madrid bombings, is highly critical of bin Laden for not using WMD. His call for the use of WMD and for highly targeted attacks where the outcome of the attack is more important than a willingness to martyr oneself in the process might be appealing to a new generation of European or Europeanized Muslims who have been attracted to radical jihadi ideology, yet whose experiences in individualistic western societies makes them less keen on martyrdom. The bottom line remains that a nuclear device is the only element of the threat of WMD that would create mass casualties and guarantee the success of a strategic strike.

Preparing the Security Sector for the Preeminent Threats

In order to be optimally prepared and organized to counter the preeminent threats posed by the unholy trinity of proliferation of WMD, terrorism, and organized crime, a state must have:

- A centralized national security decision making structure that is able to consolidate and coordinate the various aspects of decision making as well as master crisis management
- Most effective intelligence services as the first line of defense
- Updated national legislation that fulfils the obligations contained in the international conventions to counter proliferation and terrorism ratified by the state, details offenses in effectively enforceable penal law, and establishes appropriate penalties for all activities banned by the conventions
- Clearly defined National Interests, an adequate National Security Policy, and a sound National Security Strategy that find acceptance and support by the majority of the population and the international community
- A comprehensively reformed, fully accountable, well coordinated and led, interoperable, modern security sector that is well prepared and ready to cope with all major contingencies
- A layered, in-depth homeland defense providing adequate protection of the critical national infrastructure and the population, with a sufficient emergency preparedness and response potential that can also cope with all health aspects that may result from the preeminent threats
- Enhanced foreign, intergovernmental, and interagency cooperation with a vastly improved information exchange.

Most important of all, the national contribution to building a more secure world requires strong national leadership; national resources commensurate with the scale of the strategic challenges ahead; a sophisticated public information policy that does not feed the population's insecurities; full cooperation and coordinated input from all ministries, government agencies, regional and local authorities and their agencies, as well as from the private sector, where these are essential and relevant for countering the preeminent threats.

Guide to Abbreviations

ABM	Anti-Ballistic Missile Treaty
AC	Prussic Acid Chemical Warfare Agent
ACTD	U.S. Advanced Concept Technology Demonstration
BDL	EU Bureau de Liaison
BICE	Battlefield Information Collection and Exploitation System of NATO
BTWC	Convention on the Prohibition of the Development, Production, and Stockpiling of Bacteriological (Biological) and Toxin Weapons and their Destruction
BW	Biological Weapons
CATS	Article 36 Committee of the EU
CBRN	Chemical, Biological, Radiological, and Nuclear Weapons
CBW	Chemical Biological Weapons
CCWP	Customs Cooperation Working Party of the EU
CdB	Club de Berne
CDC	U.S. Centers for Disease Control and Prevention
CE	California Encephalitis Virus
CFSP	Common Foreign and Security Policy of the EU
CIA	Central Intelligence Agency
CN	CAP Chemical Warfare Agent
CNE	Computer Network Exploitation
COMINT	Communications Intelligence
COSI	Standing Committee on Internal Security of the EU
COTER	Working Party on Terrorism of the EU

CPPNM	Convention on the Physical Protection of Nuclear Material
CRYPTINT	Cryptology Intelligence
CSI	Container Security Initiative
CSNT	International Convention for the Suppression of Acts of Nuclear Terrorism
CTBT	Comprehensive Nuclear-Test-Ban Treaty
CTG	Counter Terrorist Group of the Club de Berne
CW	Chemical Weapons
CWC	Convention on the Prohibition of the Development, Production, Stockpiling, and Use of Chemical Weapons
DARPA	U.S. Defense Advanced Research Projects Agency
DM	Adamsite Chemical Warfare Agent
DNA	Deoxyribonucleic acid molecule containing the genetic instructions used in the development and functioning of all living organisms
DOD	U.S. Department of Defense
DOE	U.S. Department of Energy
DHS	U.S. Department of Homeland Security
EC	European Community
ELINT	Electronic Intelligence
EOC	Emergency Operations Center
ESDP	European Security and Defense Policy
EU	European Union
EUPAN	European Public Administration Network
FAO	Food and Agricultural Organization of the UN
FDA	U.S. Food and Drug Administration
FISINT	Foreign Instrumentation Signals Intelligence
FMCT	Fissile Materials Cut-Off Treaty
FRONTEX	European Agency for the Management of Operational Cooperation at the External Borders of the EU
GA	Tabun Chemical Warfare Agent
GAO	Government Accountability Office
GB	Sarin Chemical Warfare Agent

GC	Phosgene Chemical Warfare Agent
GD	Soman Chemical Warfare Agent
GIS	Geographic Information System
GPS	Global Positioning System
HCOC	Hague Code of Conduct Against Ballistic Missile Proliferation
HCN	Prussic Acid Chemical Warfare Agent
HD	Distilled Mustard Chemical Warfare Agent
HEU	Highly Enriched Uranium
HN3	Nitrogen Mustard Chemical Warfare Agent
HUMINT	Human Intelligence
IAEA	International Atomic Energy Agency
ICAO	International Civil Aviation Organization
ICRC	International Committee of the Red Cross
IED	Improvised Explosive Device
IMF	International Monetary Fund
IMINT	Imagery Intelligence
IMSMA	Information Management System for Mine Action
INF	Intermediate-Range Nuclear Forces Treaty
INTDIV	Intelligence Division of the EU Military Staff
IRA	Irish Republican Army
ISR	Intelligence Surveillance and Reconnaissance
IT	Information Technology
JOIIS	Joint Operations Information and Intelligence System of NATO
LOCE	Linked Operations-Intelligence Centers Europe of NATO
LSD	The best known and most researched psychedelic
MACC	Mine Action Coordination Center
MAD	Mutual Assured Destruction
MASINT	Measurement and Signatures Intelligence
MDR-TB	Multi-Drug-Resistant Tuberculosis
MEC	Middle European Conference
MOD	Ministry of Defense

MTCR	Missile Technology Control Regime
MW	Megawatt
NATO	North Atlantic Treaty Organization
NBC	Nuclear Biological Chemical
NGO	Non-Governmental Organization
NIAID	U.S. National Institute of Allergy and Infectious Diseases
NPT	Treaty on the Non-Proliferation of Nuclear Weapons
NRC	U.S. Nuclear Regulatory Commission
NSC	National Security Council
NSG	Nuclear Suppliers Group
NWFZ	Nuclear Weapon Free Zones
OECD	Organization for Economic Cooperation and Development
OLAF	European Anti-Fraud Office
OPCW	Organization for the Prohibition of Chemical Weapons
OSCE	Organization for Security and Cooperation in Europe
OSINT	Open-Source Intelligence
PAL	Permissive-Action Link
PAP(T)	Partnership Action Plan against Terrorism of NATO
PGSG	Permanent Government Strategy Group
PHOTINT	Photography Intelligence
PPEWU	Policy Planning and Early Warning Unit of the EU
PSC	Political and Security Committee of the EU
PSI	Proliferation Security Initiative
R&D	Research and Development
RDD	Radiological Dispersion Device
RFID	Radio Frequency Identification
RMA	Revolution in Military Affairs
RPV	Remotely Piloted Vehicle
SATCEN	Satellite Center of the EU
SCADA	Supervisory Control and Data Acquisition
SEB	Staphylococcal Enterotoxin
SIGINT	Signals Intelligence
SITCEN	Joint Situation Center in the EU Secretariat General

SPMU	OSCE Strategic Police Matters Unit
SSR	Security Sector Reform
SWAT	Special Weapons and Tactics
TECS	Europol Computer System
TELINT	Telemetry Intelligence
TNT	Conventional Explosives
TSA	U.S. Transportation Security Administration
TTIU	Terrorist Threat Intelligence Unit of NATO
TWG	Terrorism Working Group of the EU
TV	Television
UAV	Unmanned Aerial Vehicle
UK	United Kingdom
UN	United Nations
UNSC	United Nations Security Council
UNSCOM	United Nations Special Commission for Inspections of Iraq's WMD
UNSCR	United Nations Security Council Resolution
USEUCOM	United States European Command
USSR	Union of Soviet Socialist Republics
VEE	Venezuelan Equine Encephalitis Virus
VX	Chemical Warfare Agent of the Nerve Type
WHO	World Health Organization of the UN
WMD	Weapons of Mass Destruction
WMDC	Weapons of Mass Destruction Committee
WMO	World Meteorological Organization of the UN
WNV	West Nile Virus
YF	Yellow Fever Virus
ZC	Zangger Committee

Part I: The WMD Threat

1

Weapons of Mass Destruction

WMD are:[1]

- Nuclear weapons—fission devices that utilize a critical mass of uranium (U-238)[2] or plutonium (Pu-239),[3] fusion devices utilizing deuterium and tritium with nuclear or alternative fuses, or neutron bombs, a fission-fusion enhanced radiation and reduced blast weapon
- Chemical weapons—toxic gases and other chemical agents causing death or damage to humans and animals through chemical action on life processes
- Biological weapons—biological agents designed to cause fatal or disabling disease in victims, ranging from "traditional" diseases such as anthrax to less known and less treatable ones
- Radiological weapons—devices that incorporate some quantity of a radioisotope that is distributed with the help of conventional high explosives or other dispersing devices

Weapons in these categories vary significantly in terms of their potential lethality as well as the difficulty in actually developing or otherwise obtaining operational capabilities.

Nuclear, biological, and chemical arms are the most inhumane of all weapons. Designed to terrify as well as to destroy, they can, in the hands of either state or non-state actors, cause destruction on a vastly greater scale than conventional weapons. Their impact is more indiscriminate and long-lasting, and their effects may persist for an extended time in the environment and in the population.

On January 31, 1992, the United Nations Security Council (UNSC) issued a Presidential Statement that declared, "the proliferation of all weap-

3

Comparative Effects of the Three Major WMD Technologies[4]

USING MISSILE WARHEADS	AREA COVERED IN KM^2	DEATHS ASSUMING 3,000-10,000 PEOPLE PER KM^2
Chemical: 300 kg of Sarin nerve gas with a density of 70 mg per m^3	0.22	60-200
Biological: 30 kg of Anthrax spores with a density of 0.1 mg per m^3	10	30,000-100,000
Nuclear: 12.5 kiloton device that achieves 5 lbs per in^2 over-pressure	7.8	23,000-80,000
1 megaton hydrogen bomb	190	570,000-1,900,000

ons of mass destruction constitutes a threat to international peace and security." The global proliferation of nuclear weapons actually poses a wide spectrum of threats to regional and global security. These threats multiply as more countries acquire such weapons and as WMD are becoming easier to acquire, build, hide, and transport.

Preventing proliferation of weapons in general, and of WMD in particular, is a long-standing policy goal of UN member states that are committed to arms control—an umbrella term for restrictions on the development, production, stockpiling, proliferation, and usage of weapons. It comprises efforts, unilateral or cooperative, to limit the costs and other harmful consequences of the continued existence of arms. Mainly exercised through the use of diplomacy, arms control seeks to impose such limitations through international treaties and agreements, although it may also involve efforts by a nation or a group of nations to enforce limitations upon a non-consenting country. In principle, the existing international legal and moral norms against proliferation of WMD are stronger, have a much wider coverage and adherence than the norms against the proliferation of conventional weaponry.

A vast majority of UN member states have signed international conventions that seek to prevent proliferation—the spread of weapons and technologies that have negative consequences for local, regional, and global security interests. Horizontal proliferation is the transfer of weapons to additional governments or non-state actors. Vertical proliferation is an increase in the total numbers of weapons, or a significant qualitative modernization of these weapons held by a particular government or non-state group. Of particular concern is the proliferation of WMD, related materials, technology, and expertise from suppliers to additional states or non-state actors. The spread of missile technology adds a further element of instability that could put the world at increased risks.

The UN Conventions to prevent proliferation are:

- The Treaty on the Non-Proliferation of Nuclear Weapons (NPT) of 1968. In force since 1970, it was extended indefinitely in 1995 and has 193 parties. India, Israel, and Pakistan have not joined, and, by 2003, North Korea had announced its withdrawal from the treaty. The NPT imposes obligations on all states, including the five "official" nuclear weapon states—the United States, the United Kingdom, France, Russia, and China—to not transfer nuclear weapons or technology to others, or assist, encourage, or induce their manufacture or acquisition. The other signatories of the NPT have agreed not to acquire nuclear weapons and to accept monitoring of their civil nuclear programs by the International Atomic Energy Agency (IAEA) to prevent proliferation. Article VI of the NPT commits all state parties to conduct in good faith negotiations of a treaty on general and complete nuclear disarmament.
- The Convention on the Prohibition of the Development, Production, and Stockpiling of Bacteriological (Biological) and Toxin Weapons and their Destruction (BTWC) of 1972. It is the first multilateral treaty banning the acquisition and retention of an entire category of WMD. It builds on the ban on the use of such weapons contained in the 1925 Geneva Protocol and has 155 state parties. Another sixteen states have signed, but not ratified, the treaty. In force since 1975, it bans the development, production, stockpiling, and acquisition of bacteriological or biological and toxin weapons, and provides for the destruction of existing weapons. It does not apply to non-state actors and it prohibits only creation and storage, but not the usage, of these weapons. Furthermore, it does not require elimination of production facilities for bioweapons because the consensus among militaries is

that biological warfare is of little military use, except in the context of bioterrorism—though recent advances in science may change that assumption. No agreement has been reached on a verification regime to monitor compliance with the Convention.

- The Convention on the Prohibition of the Development, Production, Stockpiling, and Use of Chemical Weapons (CWC) of 1993 was designed to prevent proliferation and to achieve disarmament. It is the first disarmament agreement to require the elimination of an entire category of WMD under universally applied international control. In force since 1997, it has 179 state parties. Eight states, including Israel, have signed, but not ratified, the treaty. Another seven states, including Egypt, Libya, and Syria, have not yet signed the Convention. The parties are required to declare any chemical weapons-related activities, prevent their transfer, secure and destroy any stockpiles of chemical weapons within stipulated deadlines, and inactivate and eliminate any chemical weapons production capacity within their jurisdiction. Its operative functions are carried out by the Organization for the Prohibition of Chemical Weapons (OPCW).

In addition to these Conventions, and several United States–Russian bilateral agreements, there are a number of other treaties:

- Nuclear Weapons Free Zones (NWFZ). Presently, four such zones have been created: in Latin America and the Caribbean by the Treaty of Tlatelolco in 1967; in the South Pacific by the Treaty of Rarotonga in 1986; in Africa by the Treaty of Pelindaba (which has still not entered into force) in 1996; and in Southeast Asia by the Treaty of Bangkok in 1997. The number of states covered by the NWFZ regime now exceeds one hundred. Moreover, work is being completed on formation of a NWFZ in Central Asia.
- Antarctic Treaty of 1959. This treaty was entered into force in 1961 and has forty-five parties. It declares the Antarctic an area to be used exclusively for peaceful purposes, prohibits any measure of a military nature, and bans testing of any type of weapon—including nuclear explosion—as well as the disposal of radioactive waste.
- Treaty Banning Nuclear Weapon Tests in the Atmosphere, in Outer Space, and Under Water (Partial Test-Ban Treaty, PTBT) of 1963. This treaty was entered into force the same year and has 125 parties.

- Treaty on the Prohibition of the Emplacement of Nuclear Weapons and other Weapons of Mass Destruction on the Seabed and the Ocean Floor and in the Subsoil thereof (Seabed Treaty) of 1971. This treaty was entered into force in 1972 and has ninety-four parties.
- Treaty on Principles Governing the Activities of States in the Exploration and Use of Outer Space, Including the Moon and Other Celestial Bodies (Outer Space Treaty) of 1967. This treaty was entered into force in the same year and has 106 parties.
- Convention on the Physical Protection of Nuclear Material (CPPNM) of 1980. This treaty was entered into force in 1987 and amended in 2005. It obligates the 116 parties to protect nuclear material for peaceful purposes while in international transport.

Complementing these treaties are multilateral arrangements by a number of countries that have agreed on further arrangements and have set up informal groups to work together against the threat of proliferation of WMD, drawing up common lists of goods and technologies considered relevant to the activities of proliferators, and agreeing to control the exports of these:

- The Zangger Committee (ZC) was founded in 1971 and now unites thirty-five states for the technical interpretation of Article III, Point 2, NPT, according to which each state party undertakes not to provide nuclear materials or equipment to any state unless they shall be subject to IAEA safeguards. The ZC maintains a Trigger List.
- The Nuclear Suppliers Group (NSG) was set up in 1974 and unites the main exporters and producers of nuclear materials, equipment, and technologies, and non-nuclear materials for reactors, including states that were not NPT members at the time of the founding of the NSG. In 1992 a Regime for Control of Transfers of Dual-Use Items was set up in the group that today includes forty-five nations.
- The Australian Group unites thirty-nine states and is an informal voluntary export control regime with the purpose to limit the proliferation of chemical and biological weapons by monitoring transfers of dual-use items and corresponding technologies.
- The Missile Technology Control Regime (MTCR) was set up in 1987 and unites thirty-four nations. It is counteracting proliferation of missile

assets for delivering WMD by exercising export control over transfers of dual-use items and technologies to nonmember states.

- The Wassenaar Arrangement was established in 1996 and unites forty nations to promote transparency and greater responsibility in transfers of conventional arms, dual-use goods, and technologies, thus preventing destabilizing accumulations. It replaced the voluntary Coordinating Committee for Multilateral Export Controls (COCOM) that was set up in the 1950s and directed against Communist states.

- The Hague Code of Conduct Against Ballistic Missile Proliferation (HCOC) opened for membership in 2002 and now unites 123 nations. It is a corpus of basic principles of conduct in the field of missile nonproliferation. It declares general intentions to deter and prevent proliferation of ballistic missiles capable of delivering WMD and provides for measures of transparency: submission of annual declarations of missile activity and notification of launches to the Central Contact Point—the Austrian Ministry of the Interior.

In addition, there are ad hoc arrangements such as:

- The UN Security Council Resolution 1540[5] was adopted by unanimity in 2004 and imposes far-reaching obligations on all states to take a series of steps to prevent WMD and their means of delivery and related material from getting into the hands of non-state actors and especially terrorists.

- The Proliferation Security Initiative (PSI) was launched by the United States in March 2003 and involves more than sixty-five nations. It focuses on intercepting shipments of WMD, their means of delivery, and equipment and materials used in their construction, being sent to or from countries or entities of concern.

- The Container Security Initiative (CSI) was launched in 2002 by the United States and is now operational in forty-seven foreign ports. Its purpose is to increase security for container cargo shipped to the United States. In 2002 the World Customs Organization unanimously passed a resolution that will enable ports in all 161 of the member nations to begin to develop programs along the CSI model. On April 22, 2004, the EU and the U.S. Department of Homeland Security (DHS) signed an agreement that calls for the prompt expansion of CSI throughout the European Committee (EC).

The Role of the EU

The role of the EU in the fight against proliferation has been substantially strengthened by the European Council's adoption of the EU Strategy against the Proliferation of WMD in 2003.[6]

The Role of the G8

The goal of the work done in the context of the G8 is to prevent terrorists and those who support them from gaining access to WMD and the materials that would make it possible to build them. In June 2002 the G8 launched the Global Partnership against the Spread of Weapons and Materials of Mass Destruction and committed members to devote up to $20 billion over the next ten years to support projects in this area.

These arrangements differ as to their legal status, enforcement, assistance competencies, and their moral and legal standing in the world. They comprise a variety of mechanisms. With the exception of the Organization for the Prohibition of Chemical Weapons (OPCW) none are really comprehensive and they have several loopholes, or lacunae. Moreover, there are some initiatives that may not enter into force, such as the Comprehensive Nuclear-Test-Ban Treaty (CTBT) of 1996, signed by 176 and ratified by 135 states, which prohibits the carrying out of any nuclear weapon test or any other nuclear explosion and could make a significant contribution to the strengthening of the nuclear weapons non-proliferation regime. Also, there is the Fissile Materials Cut-Off Treaty (FMCT), a proposal of the Conference on Disarmament with little prospect of success.

The rationale behind these agreements is two-fold:

1. To reduce the risks inherent in the proliferation of WMD to new states, which may lead to more instability, less predictability, higher risk of accidental use, and greater risk of a local conflict developing into catastrophic war
2. To reduce the existing arsenals—sometimes radically, as in the case of chemical weapons, sometimes gradually, as in the case of nuclear weapons

The ultimate goal is to avoid the devastating impact of attacks with WMD, which, in the case of nuclear war, have the potential of putting an end to the existence of civilization. In the case of chemical weapons, they could conceivably result in thousands of deaths. In the case of biological weapons, they could possibly cause even millions of deaths as well as severe disruptions to societies and economies of belligerent and non-belligerent states alike. Since states are legally bound by these treaties, all relevant branches of government are obliged to adopt the necessary measures in accordance with their legislative procedures to prevent proliferation.

Over the past fifteen years, there has been some loss of momentum and direction in disarmament, but globally, the nonproliferation regime has been reinforced while a new wave of proliferation threatened. The new problem is now that unilateral enforcement action is increasingly advocated.

2

Nuclear Weapons

Nuclear weapons kill by the effects of heat, blast, radiation, and radioactive fallout. The attacks on Hiroshima and Nagasaki killed an estimated 200,000 people.[1] The nuclear weapons in one strategic missile submarine have a combined explosive force several times greater than all the conventional bombs dropped in World War II.[2]

Eight states possess almost 12,200 operational nuclear weapons, over 90 percent of those are in the arsenals of the United States and Russia. Several thousand nuclear weapons are kept on high alert. If all nuclear weapons are counted—operational warheads, spares, and those in both active and inactive storage—the United States, Russia, the United Kingdom, France, China, India, Pakistan, and Israel together possess a total of more than 25,000 warheads.[3] Some 150 to 240 non-strategic U.S. nuclear bombs are forward-deployed at six airbases in five European countries.[4] All these states have significant nuclear weapon modernization programs under way. Russia, China, France, the United States, and with a delay of some years the United Kingdom, are in the process of fielding a new class of ballistic missile submarines.[5]

The lack of precision in the numbers of these weapons, of those in active and inactive storage, spares, and fissile material stocks, reflects the fragmentary nature of the published information about existing nuclear arsenals. This limited transparency has many implications, including the difficulties it creates for measuring progress in achieving disarmament goals and ensuring accountability.

Delivery means for these warheads are land-based ballistic[6] and cruise missiles[7]; submarine launched ballistic and cruise missiles; and air launched missiles, cruise missiles, bombs, and unmanned aerial vehicles (UAVs).[8]

Nuclear Weapons

COUNTRY	STRATEGIC WARHEADS	NON-STRATEGIC WARHEADS	TOTAL NUMBER OF WARHEADS
USA	4,545	500	5,045
Russia	3,284	2,330	5,614
UK	~160		~160
France	348		348
China	~145		~145
India			~50
Pakistan			~60
Israel			≤100
Total			**~11,530**

Around forty states are known to have acquired or developed ballistic missiles and some thirty states have cruise missiles. Most states have only short-range (<1,000 km) delivery capabilities. Fewer than a dozen states possess medium-range (1,000–5,500 km) missiles. Only the five NPT-defined nuclear-weapon states have long-range, intercontinental, missiles.

Defense of ballistic missiles[9] poses particularly demanding technological, military, and financial challenges for the detection of attacking missiles, the tracking of missiles and, where relevant, re-entry vehicles, the discrimination between warheads and decoys, and the destruction of attacking missiles and warheads. In addition to smaller theater missile defense systems already existing,[10] strategic missile defense calls for systems with land, sea, air, and space components for mid-course interception, and for sea-based or airborne lasers for boost-phase interception.[11] Cruise missiles pose an equally significant threat and a particular challenge to air defenses. After launching from aircraft, mobile ground launchers, ships, or submarines, cruise missiles can follow erratic flight paths, actively evade air defenses, and attack targets from unpredictable directions. Continued advances in guidance and control systems, as well as propulsion and warhead design, will make cruise missiles more lethal and affordable in the years ahead. In the future, UAVs may become more attractive as delivery means than bombers or ballistic missiles, owing to their lower cost ($50,000 to $64 million),[12] ease of acquisition, growing accuracy, and reliability.

The Threats from Nuclear Weapons

The threat posed by nuclear weapons relates to the risks of deliberate use. During the Cold War, the concept of nuclear deterrence was at the heart of nuclear doctrines. Deterrence theory is based on the idea that states will avoid fighting wars if they see the costs of war outweigh the benefits. To dissuade a possible attacker by showing that the state will survive such an attack and retain the will and capability to launch a devastating nuclear counterstrike was seen as the most reliable means for a nuclear power to prevent a nuclear attack. This situation of "balance-of-terror" that prevailed between the United States and the Union of Soviet Socialist Republics (USSR) during the last three decades of the Cold War was known as mutual assured destruction (MAD). It originated in the efforts to avert the danger of war in a bipolar nuclear world that no longer exists. While nuclear deterrence still remains intact between the United States and Russia[13] and may also work between India and Pakistan, deterrence has become increasingly questionable in the post-Cold War situational development. Even though governments frequently invoke deterrence as a rationale for retaining nuclear weapons, its relevance has diminished. Invoking it in a very changed world tends to keep mistrust alive and inhibit the closer international cooperation necessary to address common global security problems. Furthermore, deterrence is no longer likely to prevent actual use by governments acting recklessly, and nuclear deterrence will not work against terrorists.

Each state that has acquired nuclear weapons has also devised principles, military doctrines, and plans on how its nuclear forces are to be configured and employed. These influence the choices of weapons to develop and produce, the capabilities needed to deliver them, and the various constraints on their use. Principles, doctrines, and plans also have an impact on the planning and postures of other countries that are trying to protect their own security interests. Thus, the five nuclear states continue to watch each other while modernizing their strategic nuclear capabilities. There has long been a close relationship between Soviet and U.S. nuclear doctrines. Now, Russia and China are closely watching the United States to see whether it will bank on missile defense as a more prominent part of its strategic doctrine, possibly affecting the deterrent capacity of their nuclear forces.[14] The United States continues to pursue an expansive array of weapon and sensor programs for active defenses against short-, medium-, and long-range ballistic missiles. It has given high priority to deploying an integrated, multilayer defense system to protect U.S. territory and allies from perceived emerging threats posed by adversaries with missiles potentially armed with nuclear weapons. It also has bilateral ballistic missile defense development programs under way with Israel and Japan, which involve significant defense-industrial cooperation.[15] Israel, a full-fledged though officially undeclared[16] nuclear power, is affecting the security thinking of its neighbors with its doctrine of nuclear ambiguity. Whenever a nuclear weapon state declares that all options are on the table, that it reserves the option of using nuclear weapons also against a non-nuclear weapon state, or that nuclear weapons are essential or vital for its security, other states take note and act accordingly.

Moreover, there is the fact that intentions, like governments, may change over time. After 9/11, high representatives of nuclear-armed states have alluded in precisely calculated ambiguity to a readiness actually to use nuclear weapons.[17] Strategically, the United States has reacted against the new threats and challenges with a new National Security Strategy[18] that calls for preemptive use of military and covert force before an enemy unleashes weapons of mass destruction—underscoring U.S. willingness to retaliate with nuclear weapons also against chemical or biological attacks on U.S. soil or American troops overseas, even if the time, place, and scale of such WMD attack were uncertain and not imminent. This represented a fundamental shift from a policy of reaction to a new policy of initiation—from wars of necessity to wars of choice. Preemption is also the strategic doctrine adopted by Russia[19] and France.[20] Even Australia[21] and Japan,[22] which have no nuclear weapons yet, have reserved the right of preemptive defense. Nor does the North Atlantic Treaty Organization (NATO) exclude preemption.[23] And in essence, we find the same diagnosis in the European Security Strategy calling for enlargement—building security in the European neighborhood.[24] The future may show whether the text contains only a different choice of words, resulting from different military capabilities. It might well be that "prevention through enlargement" is just the regional equivalent of the global U.S. strategy of preemption. Only China has formally renounced the first use of nuclear weapons.

Military doctrines providing for first, preventive, or preemptive use of nuclear weapons,[25] or for use in retaliation for attacks with weapons other than nuclear, all tend to widen the license in the doctrine of nuclear deterrence for actual nuclear war fighting. They all risk lowering the threshold for the engagement of nuclear weapons, expand the range of scenarios for military use of such weapons, and are an incentive to develop new nuclear weapons, all to the detriment of international security.[26] One problem is that some states view nuclear weapons as a way of balancing an overwhelming conventional superiority of an adversary. NATO long used this balance-of-terror rationale to counter the Soviet Union's perceived superiority in conventional forces. The same logic is now followed by Russia, which maintains that tactical or intermediate-range nuclear weapons are needed to balance a perceived superiority of NATO's conventional forces, and also views them as a hedge against some future or emerging security threats on its southern rim, from central Asia or the Middle East.[27]

Nuclear doctrines also dictate how nuclear weapons will be employed and their readiness for use. American and Russian strategic nuclear warheads are deployed in a so-called triad consisting of submarine-launched missiles, ground-based intercontinental ballistic missiles, and long-range bombers.[28] Continuing a triad policy leads to redundancy and may fuel the nuclear arms race. Some such weapons still remain on hair-trigger alert,[29] assigned as they are for retaliatory use on short notice—even before the warheads of one side reach the other's territory. Since the flight time of land-based ballistic missiles is between twenty-five and thirty-five minutes, and significantly less for sea-based missiles, such nuclear postures risk causing nuclear exchanges by faulty intelligence, technical malfunction, accident, or strategic miscalculation.

There is always a possibility that, as a result of accidental circumstances, an explosion will take place inadvertently. Though all conceivable precautions are taken to prevent them, such accidents might occur in areas where weapons are assembled and stored, during the course of loading and transportation on the ground, or when actually in the delivery vehicle.[30] The list of nuclear weapon accidents and technical malfunction is long[31] and their history as old as the introduction of such weapons into the arsenals of armed forces of nuclear weapon states. There have been dozens of serious nuclear accidents and hundreds of nuclear related incidents[32] involving explosions, burning or other spread of fissile material, high explosive detonation with no spread of fissile material, and other incidents that generated pollution, contamination, and resulted in numerous deaths, injuries, and at least sixty nuclear weapons lost.[33] Known are also at least four cases of false warning of a Soviet nuclear launch against the United States due to early-warning system malfunction.[34]

Additional dangers can arise as a result of unauthorized use or theft.

Nuclear weapons should be taken off high-alert status to reduce the risk of launching by error and they should be withdrawn from foreign soil. The risk of diversion or theft may be greater for non-strategic nuclear weapons designed to be used on the battlefield. Today, Russia has some 3,000–4,000 operational weapons and the United States retains some 500 active non-strategic nuclear warheads, and another 1,155 in inactive storage.[35] These are smaller and more robust than strategic weapons, and their security and safety systems—or permissive-action link—may be less advanced than for strategic weapons, and thus would be easier for outsiders to use. And there is a greater risk of theft or diversion during transport or storage in the field.

The Threats from Nuclear Proliferation

Nuclear proliferation is the spread of nuclear weapons, production technology, and knowledge to nations, or worse, to non-state actors, that do not already have such capabilities. The fundamental danger is that proliferation will increase the risk of use and could seriously enhance the danger of nuclear war. As long as nuclear weapons remain in any state's arsenal, there is a risk that they will one day be used, whether it be by design or accident. Any such use would be catastrophic. Moreover, global proliferation of nuclear weapons poses a wide spectrum of threats to regional and global security. These threats multiply as more states or non-state actors acquire such weapons. Every new case of horizontal proliferation has a high potential of generating more proliferation. And more fingers on more nuclear triggers result in a more dangerous world.

The NPT, while recognizing the first wave of five nuclear-weapon states, succeeded in attracting a vast number of adherents. It did not, however, prevent Israel, India, and Pakistan from forming a second wave of proliferation. Moreover, it was violated by Iraq, Libya, and North Korea in a third wave. The IAEA safeguards system, created to verify that no nuclear material is diverted from peaceful uses, proved inadequate to discover the Iraqi and Libyan violations of the NPT. And Iran failed for many years in its duty to declare important nuclear programs. If Iran and North Korea do not reliably renounce nuclear weapons, pressure could build for a fourth wave of proliferation of nuclear weapons.

The second wave of proliferation has met with forceful reaction. But as long as any state has nuclear weapons, others may want them too. Efforts to induce these states to roll back their programs—as South Africa, Brazil, and others[36] did—have gradually been weakened, and risk now to be abandoned. As none of the nations of the second wave of proliferation is a party to the NPT, they cannot be charged with violation of a treaty. Dissuading potential proliferators from moving further along the path of nuclear weapon development and maintaining support by the global community for nonproliferation is made more difficult as long as the nuclear weapon states fail in their duty to achieve nuclear disarmament through negotiation. Explanations by nuclear weapon states that these weapons are indispensable to defend their sovereignty are not the best way to convince other sovereign states to renounce the option. The single most hopeful step to revitalize nonproliferation and disarmament today would be the ratification of the CTBT by all states that have nuclear weapons.[37] The CTBT would make a significant contribution to strengthening the nuclear weapons nonproliferation regime. In 2006 it had been ten years since the CTBT was opened for signature; however, prospects are uncertain that it will become effective. So far, the treaty has been signed by 176 states and ratified by 135. Of the forty-four states that must join the treaty as a mandatory condition for it to become effective, the CTBT has not been ratified by the United States, China, Egypt, Iran, Israel, India, Pakistan, North Korea, Indonesia, and Colombia.

Weapon designs and related technology can spread from one country to another, either directly from state to state, from state to non-state actor, from non-state actor to state, or through clandestine or criminal supplier networks—such as the notorious activities of Abdul Qadeer Khan,[38] the "father" of the Pakistani nuclear bomb who was at the center of two illicit supplier networks: one bringing sensitive technology into Pakistan and another one transferring it from Pakistan to Iran, Libya, North Korea, and elsewhere. Thus, threats may arise from the illicit transfer or theft of sensitive design information. For example, a Chinese bomb design sold by the Khan network to Libya.[39] Furthermore, multilateral arrangements may be misused, as can proliferation-resistant technologies. In addition, international control may be rejected because the NPT does not provide for any consequences for non-nuclear weapon states parties that withdraw from it after having acquired nuclear material and fuel cycle technologies for peaceful purposes.

Threats also arise from vertical proliferation: the expansion or refinement of nuclear weapon capabilities already existing. Though generally less dangerous than horizontal proliferation, the appearance of a new nuclear weapon program could have a domino effect, producing fear, alarm, and possibly countermeasures involving WMD in neighboring states or in the region. One countermeasure is intervention to destroy the capability, as Israel did with the attack on Iraq's Osirak reactor[40] and again on September 6, 2007, with the destruction of a Syrian nuclear installation in the Deir ez Zor region believed to have been under construction with the help of North Korea to produce plutonium. Even suspicion of such a program can trigger severe actions, as illustrated by the invasion of Iraq. An endless competition to produce improved weapons may foster suspicion over military intentions and capabilities. In such a climate, what one state might claim is a prudent safety improvement, another state might view in a more sinister light. Thus, controversies have arisen in recent years over demands of the U.S. administration to develop nuclear weapons against targets that are well hardened or located deep underground—"mini-nukes" and "bunker busters"—both initiatives that are likely to lower the threshold for using nuclear weapons. Under such conditions, some nations begin to speculate about the nuclear option as a means to deter aggression and also as a factor in the enhancement of their own international status, a tool for gaining superiority over their neighbors, and acquiring economic advantages. This is of particular significance in some states under conditions of territorial disputes, political, economic, ethnic, and regional problems. According to the IAEA, there are about twenty nations that are potential nuclear powers. For some of these, the nuclear choice is merely a question of political will under conditions of a weakening NPT regime.

Considerable concern was expressed at the 2005 NPT Review Conference by some states about the consequences of a paradigmatic shift, led by the United States, from treaty-based disarmament to ad hoc counter-proliferation approaches involving self-selecting coalitions of the willing. This shift was criticized as intruding on the sovereign rights of individual states as well as undermining the existing legal and normative foundations of international efforts for combating the spread of WMD.[41]

Another threat exists with weapons-grade fissile materials being stored in hundreds of military and civilian sites located in nearly sixty countries. The total worldwide stockpile of highly enriched uranium (HEU)[42] is some 1,600 tons, theoretically enough to build 130,000 nuclear weapons. The stockpile of plutonium[43] separated from spent fuel is over 480 tons, enough to fabricate 110,000 nuclear bombs. However, fissile material used in nuclear reactors cannot easily be used to produce nuclear weapons. Less than a quarter of these stockpiles is secured according to the "gold standard."[44] Some sixty tons of HEU, theoretically enough to build over 1,000 nuclear weapons, is in civilian use or storage throughout the world, most of it associated with research reactors, and about half of it outside of the United States and Russia.[45] Today, roughly 135 operating research reactors in some forty countries still use HEU as their fuel, and an unknown number of shut-down or converted research reactors still have HEU fuel on-site.[46] Most of these facilities do not have enough HEU on-site for a bomb, but some facilities with 20 kg of HEU or more do. Most of these installations have very modest security—in some cases, no more than a night watchman and a chain-link fence. Some of these are located on university campuses where providing serious security against attack would be difficult.

The physical protection of fissile materials refers to controls designed to prevent sabotage, attacks, thefts, and other criminal acts. This is most important for "military" fissile materials. By ensuring detection, prevention, and recovery of missing materials, physical security controls also seek to discourage illicit uses. But physical protection involves far more than just guards, gates, and fences at particular facilities. It also requires reliable personnel to design and implement such controls, employing people who have both technical competence and professionalism, which entails extensive background checks and vetting before recruitment and thorough training after. This is lacking in many countries, even in the United States where some personnel of private security companies, among them also Israeli companies, that are responsible for the security of nuclear power plants recently have been found that have not been vetted.

Because all states apply and implement their own standards, their chain of physical security is only as strong as its weakest link. This is why the concerns that the theft of fissile material somewhere could jeopardize security elsewhere have inspired international initiatives in this area. However, many obstacles hinder progress in strengthening physical security. More international cooperation is inhibited by governmental concerns over the erosion of sovereignty, legal liability, budgetary constraints, etc. Such obstacles also hinder the development of stronger multilateral standards or expanded roles for international institutions. The lack of serious consequences for non-compliance with existing standards further erodes both the effectiveness and credibility of those standards.

While some consider the uranium enrichment route less likely for pro-liferation than the plutonium option, the latter is definitely more difficult to realize. There is considerable HEU held by nuclear powers, and those interested in assembling a weapon[47] might well look to gathering HEU from these sources through stealth, bribe, and other illegal efforts. Russia has endorsed the goal of nuclear nonproliferation, recognizing that it could be a target of potential proliferators. Security for Russia's nuclear warheads and materials has improved substantially over the last years. Nuclear experts and workers are now paid a living wage, on time, reducing the incentives to divert material or sell knowledge. And Russian security services are more pervasive than they were a decade ago, also at nuclear sites. Far more daunting, however, is the prospect of tracking unknown quantities of weapons-grade material—which even Russian and other authorities have been unable to account for with accuracy—and the international movement of experts from countries of the former USSR, South Africa, Iraq, and Libya. The end of the privileged status these scientists once enjoyed are incentives to would-be proliferators and terrorist groups alike.

There is an additional concern. It is widely expected that global reliance on nuclear power will increase in the next decades, as the price of fossil oil and gas goes up and the greenhouse gas-free nuclear energy becomes more attractive. If so, there will be a greater demand for uranium and plutonium fuel, possibly leading to expanded use of enrichment. As reprocessing of spent fuel will allow a drastically better use of the energy content of the original uranium or plutonium fuel, there may be a demand for more reprocessing plants. An increased flow of fissile material may increase the risk of misuse and diversion.[48] Technically, all twelve countries possessing an enrichment or reprocessing capability can produce reactor fuel or bomb-grade material or both.[49] This is particularly true for Brazil and Japan. In Japan, a large plant for the reprocessing of spent nuclear fuel was opened in 2006, which will further increase an already large stockpile of plutonium, and thus the risk that it might be diverted to weapons. The larger the existing stocks, the greater the danger of leakage and misuse.

Other concerns challenging the intelligence services are the buyers of uranium ore, the activities of shipping companies that might be transporting weapons parts or fissionable materials, and the governments of powers known to sell missiles and related material. Until recently, the major concern was the movement of material and expertise from Russia's cooperation in the development of Iran's nuclear weapons and missile programs, and China's sale of missiles to Pakistan and Iran. Today, the most immediate concerns are North Korea's sales, and Iranian delivery of missiles and related technology.

Presently, more than twenty-five nations have rocket systems with ballistic missiles capable of delivering WMD, or have the scientific potential for making them. At the same time, many states need rocket assets to carry out their plans and programs of peaceful use of outer space. In contrast to nuclear, chemical, and biological weapons, where legally binding agreements exist that limit their proliferation, or ban them out-right, there are no such agreements on rocket assets for the delivery of WMD. Moreover, differentiation between means of delivery of WMD and legitimate conventional weapons—conventionally armed ballistic and cruise missiles, UAVs, as well as space-launch vehicles—is extremely difficult. Conventional armament like aircraft, missiles, UAVs, multiple rocket launchers, and artillery can also be used to deliver WMD.

Today, multilateral efforts on nonproliferation of rocket means of delivery of WMD are being carried out under the auspices of the Missile Technology Control Regime (MTCR) and the Hague Code of Conduct Against Ballistic Missile Proliferation (HCOC). They unite what is now a limited number of nations with missile potential, but cannot entirely stop the spread of missiles. The lack of an international convention regulating the use of missiles is a factor conducive to proliferation of missiles,[50] and technologies, including those necessary for producing intercontinental ballistic missiles, which may be built under the pretext of developing or updating space-launch vehicles. Some states aspire to acquire missile technologies, legitimate subsystems, and components—control systems, mixed fuels, engine casings, electronics, etc.—and also to purchase antiquated models of missile equipment for the purpose of using them as a basis for developing systems with improved performance, primarily GPS guidance, greater payload and range. There are even cases of export of missiles, and missile technologies from MTCR member nations, in particular by Ukraine.

The Threats from Nuclear Terrorism

In the past, the essence of terrorism was to make a political statement through violence. It was a political act designed to influence an audience. Levels of violence were carefully calculated so as to draw attention, but not to be so high as to alienate potential supporters or to trigger overwhelming response from the authorities. That continues to be a main theme of conventional or national terrorism. However, with the advent of transnational or fourth generation terrorism we witnessed with 9/11, the

Bali, Madrid, London, and other recent attacks, the aim is to maximize the number of casualties.[51] This reflects a shift in the goal of the new terrorists from trying to make a political statement through violence to maximizing damage to the target as an end in itself. Of all the terrorist groups, religiously motivated ones are the most likely to resort to mass destructive terrorism. Because such groups perceive violence to be part of an all-encompassing struggle between good and evil, religious extremism is converging with three other factors: the deliberate quest to acquire or develop WMD, a willingness to accept martyrdom, and a perception that the only "audience" of worth is that of a deity—with the result that jihadist groups, in particular, lack the moderating influence of an external "audience" or constituency, are more detached from "moral norms" and other social constraints, and thus are less constrained in using WMD, and more difficult to deter.

Nuclear weapons are unique in their capacity to inflict instant loss of life on a massive scale, which gives them special appeal to terrorists. Senior al Qaeda members have threatened to use, and have demonstrated the will to carry out attacks with WMD.[52] This is also the desire of various other terrorist groups.[53] There is also a prestige factor that must be taken into account with nuclear devices: that their possession, threatened use, or outright use will elevate a group to a very high standing, and draw enormous attention to it and its goals. This is why the international community has long focused on the prevention of terrorism with WMD. One way to do this is through measures to prevent proliferation of WMD and their means of delivery. However, the most direct and reliable tool for preventing nuclear terrorism is by keeping nuclear weapons or materials from being stolen in the first place. Once such items have disappeared, the problem of finding them, or stopping terrorists from using them, multiplies enormously.

Presently, the greatest cause for fear from terrorist attack is the prospect that some terrorists come into possession of an operational nuclear weapon. Current nuclear programs in Iran and North Korea,[54] and the nuclear arsenal existing in a potentially destabilizing Pakistan,[55] are of major concern, as well as the prospects of weapons and fissile materials from existing nuclear powers falling into terrorist hands. Nuclear weapons would not be for deterrence: they would be utilized. Since the new terrorists are seeking spectacular results with as much death and destruction as possible, nuclear devices are an ideal choice, offering the prospects of far greater damage than with chemical or conventional explosive devices.

However, nuclear weapons are generally located at well protected and guarded weapons emplacements or in nuclear weapons storage facilities. A theft would involve many risks and great efforts in terms of personnel, finances, and organization. Without the support of insiders with local and specialized knowledge, such a theft is improbable. But even if a nuclear warhead could be stolen or acquired with the help of organized crime, there are several different types of safety and security systems incorporated in a weapon, ensuring that no unwanted nuclear explosion can take place, and that successful use of a stolen weapon would be unlikely.[56] Such systems will destroy critical components or render them useless if someone handles the weapon improperly or tries to open it.

The other option, that terrorists could build a working improvised nuclear device[57] themselves, cannot be totally excluded. Even a crude nuclear device is likely to produce enormous casualties. Used in an urban environment, casualties are likely to be in the order of tens to hundreds of thousands of deaths.[58] Many more would be injured, burned, or irradiated, requiring immediate medical help—but most of the area's medical facilities would have been obliterated. The heart of the targeted city would be destroyed by blast and fire, with any hope of rebuilding in doubt by lingering radiation. Many police, fire department, and emergency responder personnel would be killed in the initial blast, and much of their equipment destroyed.[59]

Terrorist groups, being largely non-state actors, generally lack industrial infrastructure. What they most often have is funding, either covertly from nations that sponsor them or from criminal and other sources, to acquire weapons, components or fissile material on the world market. However, for terrorists to develop even a crude nuclear device, the greatest difficulty is to obtain weapons-grade fissile material. It is extremely difficult and very expensive to develop and manage the substantial infrastructure that is required to produce enriched uranium or plutonium in sufficient quantity for building a nuclear device. Designing a weapon, while not easy at all, is a less difficult task, since the basic information needed to design a crude nuclear explosive device is publicly available. But beyond a critical mass of fissile material, construction of a nuclear weapon requires other exotic materials; a substantial manufacturing capability; and very substantial technical expertise in building such a weapon, and particularly its igniter: in a uranium-235 fission bomb, two sub-critical masses that are shot towards each other with conventional explosives, whereby neutrons trigger a chain reaction, releasing energy. In a plutonium bomb, a sub-critical mass of plutonium-239 is packed with a mantel of explosives that condense a heavy layer of inert tampering metal which passes the impulse on to the plutonium core which, in turn, becomes supercritical and enters a series of chain reactions, whereby a beryllium layer reflects the neutrons.[60] Terrorists would probably prefer HEU as fissile material, because the assembly design using this material is simpler than the design relying on plutonium. Yet, the possibility of a terrorist plutonium bomb cannot be excluded, given that smaller amounts of such material are needed for it, and that knowledge about implosion designs is now more widely distributed.

The greatest unknown is how sophisticated a facility is required for construction. South Africa, Pakistan, and others have already demonstrated that a Los Alamos type of operation is no longer needed.[61] Another question also remains as to what size device could be constructed by a terrorist group. The first nuclear weapons built were on the order of 10 tons each. During the Cold War both the United States and the USSR developed much smaller nuclear devices, including nuclear artillery shells, atomic demolition munitions,[62] and what have been called "suitcase nuclear weapons."[63] While both were able to shrink the size of these weapons, the technology needed to do so is exceedingly complex. Whether a terrorist group could effectively duplicate this feat in the foreseeable future is a difficult question, about which there continues to be substantial debate. However, even before the U.S. intervention in Afghanistan, U.S. intelligence concluded "fabrication of at least a 'crude' nuclear device was within al Qaeda's capabilities, if it could obtain fissile material."[64]

There is the risk that security weaknesses could allow terrorists to steal enough material or even a nuclear device either from storage or during transportation, or to obtain these with the help of organized crime. Since 1995, the IAEA has maintained an Illicit Trafficking Database, consisting of reports of theft, smuggling, or loss of control of nuclear and radiological material, containing over 827 confirmed incidents—149 alone in 2006— some sixteen of which involved highly enriched uranium or plutonium, including a few cases of kilogram quantities.[65] Thus, the most crucial step in preventing nuclear terrorism is to keep terrorists from acquiring access to such materials or devices—again a step that requires strict implementation of physical protection measures and security routines that the U.S. National Academy of Sciences has described as the stored-weapon standard.[66] Important practical measures must be put in place to limit the available sources, increase physical security, increase safety where transportation is deemed unavoidable,[67] and block terrorist access through better intelligence and security.

Much of the U.S. Cooperative Threat Reduction Program[68] is intended to strengthen the physical security of Russia's nuclear weapon-related facilities and materials and to reduce the risk that nuclear scientists will provide their specialized know-how to terrorists and organized crime. But there remain possibilities of insider conspiracies to steal nuclear weapons or material or to help outsiders to do so. Corruption and insider theft of a wide range of valuables are endemic in all states of the former USSR These problems have penetrated into the military and the security and law enforcement services; theft and sale of arms, fuel, and military property are commonplace.[69] In addition, security systems in these countries remain severely underfunded.[70] The question of the adequacy of upgraded security systems is particularly troubling outside Russia, as these facilities have only been upgraded to meet rather vague IAEA recommendations—a security standard significantly lower than that being implemented in Russia. El Baradei, IAEA director general, recently stated, "in the past five years, the international community has made great progress in securing these materials. But it is a race against time, and it is not yet certain who is winning."[71] Hence, the prospect of a black market in fissile materials and complete nuclear devices cannot be discounted. Thus, export-import controls, border and coast guard, and customs enforcement activities serve vitally important roles in reducing the risk of nuclear terrorism.

Another question is whether terrorists could bring either fissile materials or an entire weapon into a target country. At the present time, both cases are possible. The current generation of detectors will not find packages containing nuclear materials that have even the most minimal amount of lead shielding, particularly in the case of HEU, which is far less radioactive than plutonium. While more effective sensors are under development, the challenge is that the existing nuclear powers need to develop and exercise sufficient control over fissile materials and nuclear weapons to ensure that these do not fall into terrorist hands.[72]

A further danger remains: terrorists could attack nuclear facilities, provoking a nuclear incident, or use hazardous radioactive materials, spent nuclear fuel, or attack nuclear materials in transit, again calling for high standards of physical protection. There can be no guarantee that intelligence services can provide foolproof warning of an impending terrorist attack.

3
Chemical, Biological, and Toxin Weapons

The development of chemical science and industry and the rapid expansion in biotechnology and life sciences has created opportunities for important peaceful uses but also for the production of chemical weapons and uses of viruses, bacteria, and toxins as weapons. While chemical, toxin, and biological weapons proliferation requires less expertise and technical capability than nuclear proliferation, these weapons tend to be less accurate than nuclear weapons and their engagement less controllable. However, it is the random terror that chemical, toxin, and biological weapons portend that makes them appealing to nations, non-state actors, and particularly to terrorists.

The biochemical threat spectrum ranges from so-called classical (lethal) chemical weapons through poisonous industrial chemicals and mid-range agents such as toxins and bioregulators to traditional biological agents and genetically modified agents.

Chemical, biological, and toxin weapons can produce mass casualties if effectively disseminated, but have varying and different effects. Chemical weapons, predominantly man-made chemicals, require the largest amounts of material to be effective and cause their effects in minutes to hours. Biological weapons made of naturally occurring pathogens require the least material to be effective but generally have an incubation period of several days before symptoms show themselves. Toxin weapons, such as ricin, chemical agents formed by biological processes, are intermediate between the two in both amount and timescale. Treatment protocols for chemical, biological, and toxin weapons vary by agent, ranging from weapons with effective treatment and prophylaxis to weapons that have neither known cures nor protection.

The biochemical threat spectrum range

Classical CW	Industrial Pharmaceutical Chemicals	Bioregulators Peptides	Toxins	Genetically Modified BW	Traditional BW
Cyanide Phosgene Mustard Nerve Agents	Aerosols	Substance P Neurokinin A	Saxitoxin Ricin Botulinum Toxin	Modified/tailored Bacteria Viruses	Bacteria Viruses Rickettsia

Anthrax Plague Tularemia |

◄——————— Biological and Toxin Weapons Convention ———————►
◄——— Chemical Weapons Convention ———►
◄——— Poison ———► ◄—— Infect ——►

Chemical weapons are chemical compounds that have a strong, deleterious effect on the human body, even when encountered in small doses. The different types of chemical weapons include vesicants, which blister and burn on contact; choking agents, which cause lung damage; and nerve agents, which interfere with the nervous system and may lead to death. The effects from chemical weapons may occur very quickly after exposure, on the order of minutes to hours.[1]

Biological weapons are pathogens that cause disease and illness in infected humans. Because the pathogens multiply within the victim, a small initial amount of pathogen is sufficient to cause infection. As a consequence, biological weapons require much less material than chemical weapons to produce equivalent casualties and generally take longer to produce effects. Biological weapons include diseases that are primarily incapacitating, such as Q-fever, as well as those that are lethal, such as smallpox. Some are contagious pathogens, such as smallpox, and have the potential to spread the effects of an attack by traveling from victim to victim. The symptoms from a biological weapon attack would require some time to develop, so a covert biological attack might not be recognized for several days.[2]

Toxin weapons are primarily illness-inducing chemicals formed from living creatures, such as bacteria, fungi, plants, and animals. Toxins range in effect from disabling to acutely toxic. The most poisonous compound currently known to science, botulinum toxin, is a bacterial toxin. It paralyzes muscles, including the diaphragm, without which the lungs cannot function, and victims quickly die. Toxins are more potent than chemical weapons, requiring less material to produce equivalent casualties, but they are not self-reproducing so more material is required than for a biological weapon. Symptoms from toxin exposure typically occur on a timescale intermediate between chemical and biological weapons, generally appearing over the course of several hours.[3]

Comparative effects of chemical and biological agents[4]

Using 1 aircraft dispensing 1,000 kg of Sarin nerve gas or 100 kg of Anthrax spores	Area covered in km²	Deaths assuming 3,000-10,000 people per km²
Clear sunny day: light breeze		
Sarin nerve gas	0.74	300-700
Anthrax spores	46	130,000-460,000
Overcast day/night: moderate wind		
Sarin nerve gas	0.8	400-800
Anthrax spores	140	420,000-1,400,000
Clear calm night:		
Sarin nerve gas	7.8	3,000-8,000
Anthrax spores	300	1-3 million

This table shows that biological attacks hold the potential for far greater lethality than chemical attacks on a target population. The examples used compare 1,000 kg of a chemical agent—sarin—with 100 kg of a bioagent—anthrax spores. Ten times the physical weight of a chemical agent produces only a small fraction of the casualties estimated for one tenth of the weight of the bioagent. At the same time, the bioagent covers a far greater area. Results from both chemical and biological attacks depend on the extant weather conditions—largely wind, rain, snow, humidity, or sun producing ultraviolet rays—to influence the location, and the extent of the damage. The scenarios postulate aircraft delivery of the agent, since it is desirable that the agent not "blow back" on the perpetrator, as was frequently the case in World War I and other cases.

Chemical, biological, and toxin weapons pose additional concerns beyond mass casualties. These weapons may contaminate the area in which they are used, emergency vehicles, and emergency responders. The wide array of potential symptoms from these weapons makes identification of the causal agent difficult and complicates treatment. Additionally, public fears relating to disease and poisoning could increase the effect of a chemical, biological, or toxin attack, as worried, unexposed people request treatment from medical facilities.[5] In the case of widespread dissemination of chemical or biological weapons, the number of people requesting treatment and the difficulties involved in separating these with actual illness from those with panic-induced symptoms could greatly complicate effective healthcare and possibly lead to greater public hysteria.

Chemical, biological, and toxin weapons also differ in their medical treatment and the availability of effective prophylaxis.[6] Chemical weapons with their quick-acting effects must be treated as promptly as possible. Because of the large range of potential effects, there is no universal treatment for chemical weapon exposure. Exposure to nerve agents can be directly treated with medication to prevent or reduce symptoms.[7] While exposure to vesicants such as mustard gas is generally untreatable, some of the effects, primarily blisters and lesions, can be treated. Injury from exposure to choking agents, such as chlorine, can be ameliorated by prompt medical treatment to limit permanent lung damage.

Many biological agents either respond to medical treatment or have effective prophylaxis. Single or combination antibiotic regimens, if employed early in the course of the disease, are effective against many bacteria that might be used as biological weapons. Such timely treatment may be difficult if recognition of a bioattack is delayed. Some viruses have effective prophylaxis in the form of vaccines, while others may respond to antiviral drugs. However, some biological weapons lack prophylaxis, treatment, or cure. Additionally, agents can be engineered, with some effort, to be resistant to specific countermeasures.

Treatment of injuries sustained from toxin weapons may be more complicated. Anti-toxins and toxoid vaccines can be developed against toxin weapons, but the process for doing so is intensive and time-consuming. Consequently, stores of these medicines are limited in scope, and a large number of toxin weapon casualties could exhaust local supplies. Some toxins can be treated with supportive care, through artificial ventilation and other means, until the patients recover.

4

Chemical Weapons

Chemical warfare agents are toxic chemicals controlled by the CWC. It has been estimated that more than 10,000 compounds are controlled under the CWC, though the actual number of chemical warfare agents, precursors, and degradation products that are in the OPCW database is in the hundreds. Military forces have employed chemical weapons for over a century[1] with mixed results. They lack the lethality of biological weapons and pose a host of logistic problems. Chemical warfare offers tactical and operational effects and, in theory, may have strategic effect if used against certain centers of gravity. Effects take seconds to days to manifest themselves, and remain located at the point of attack. As their use in World War I and afterwards show, various weather and atmospheric effects have often caused them to blow back on the user, sometimes with disastrous results.

Chemical weapons kill by attacking the nervous system and lungs or by interfering with a body's ability to absorb oxygen. Some are designed to incapacitate by producing severe burns and blisters, choking, and vomiting. Chemical warfare agents have varying degrees of volatility and pose both a vapor as well as a liquid contact hazard. Symptoms can appear immediately or be delayed for up to twelve hours after an attack. Persistent agents can remain in the target environment for as long as a week. But chemical weapons do not self-replicate, are less toxic than biological weapons, and cannot affect more than a few thousand people in the extreme with one weapon. Weapon development and delivery is more expensive and difficult. Fewer than thirty chemical weapons have so far been used or developed. These can be classified in three groups:

- Lethal agents, as toxins and chemical compounds obtained from biological sources, are designed to kill, but non-lethal doses may cause incapacitation.

- Damaging agents produce persistent contact hazard and local downwind vapor hazard causes inflammation and, after several hours, blistering of the skin, eyes, and breathing passages. Designed to cause either short- or long-term damage to humans, they also may cause death.
- Incapacitating agents are primarily designed to cause mental or physical incapacitation that may last for hours or days.

Categorized according to physiological effects, there are four types of chemical agents:

- Nerve agents, which are highly lethal, kill in very small dosages, interfere with the nervous system, disrupt breathing or muscular coordination, and first affect the eyes (myosis). Among these are sarin, soman, and VX.
- Blood agents, which may be lethal, prevent body tissues from using the oxygen in the blood and cause burns and blisters on the body. While very volatile, high concentration can cause rapid death. Among them are mustard sulphurous gas and lewisite.
- Choking agents, also known as asphyxiating agents, which are lethal, attack breathing passages and the lungs and are normally delivered in non-persistent form. Among them are phosgene and mustard gas.
- Toxins are chemical compounds obtained from biological sources that may be lethal or incapacitating.

Possible new agents could result from research on new ways of affecting the human brain to cause aggressiveness, sleepiness, fear, or other emotions. Some of these are known as bio-regulators. Moreover, there are three groups of psychochemicals used as discipline breakers: psychogenic, psychotropic, and psychomimetic.[2] These produce an almost instantaneous effect on troops by means of irritation or nausea or by causing a hallucinatory effect similar in kind to that of LSD, hence preventing them from putting on their respirators, making them vulnerable to concurrent or subsequent attack from other agents.

Chemical warfare agents have often been referred to as warfare gases but, in fact, many agents exist as liquids in ambient temperatures and are delivered as mostly colorless, odorless, and tasteless vapors, aerosols, particles or liquids. In the form of non-persistent agents, designed to contaminate the air and to disperse fairly rapidly, they enter the body through inhalation or direct contact with the eye. In the form of persistent agents, designed to contaminate surfaces or to give off toxic vapor, effective for hours or days, they enter the body through the nose, mouth, eyes, or skin. In addition to the contact hazard, there will usually be both a local and downwind vapor hazard from the point of delivery. The principal classical chemical warfare agents are:

AGENT	CODE	NAME	NORMAL STATE	DISSEMINATED FORM	TIME TO FIRST SYMPTOMS
Lethal	CG	Phosgene	gas	gas	hours
	AC	Prussic acid (HCN)	liquid	vapor	immediate
	HD	Distilled mustard	oily liquid	vapor, liquid	1-48 h
	Q	Sesqui-mustard	solid	aerosol	delayed
	HN3	Nitrogene mustard	oily liquid	vapor, liquid, aerosol	delayed
	GA	Tabun	liquid	vapor, liquid, aerosol	up to 10'
	GB	Sarin	liquid	vapor, liquid	up to 10'
	GD	Soman	liquid	vapor, liquid aerosol	up to 10'
	GF	CMPF	liquid	vapor, liquid aerosol	up to 10'
	VX	—	liquid	liquid, aerosol	up to 10'
Incapacitant	CA	BBC Camite	oily liquid	vapor aerosol	immediate
	CN	CAP	crystals	aerosol	immediate
	DM	Adamsite	crystals	aerosol	up to 3'
	CS	OC BM	crystals	aerosol	immediate
	BZ	—	solid	aerosol	immediate

The most important among the non-persistent agents are HCN, phosgene, tabun, and sarin. Sarin is an extremely potent, quick-acting nerve and paralyzing liquid with a barely perceptible odor. It is fifty times more lethal than HCN and thirty-two times more lethal than pneumonia caused by phosgene. Fatal at about 0.01 milligrams per kg of human weight, death occurs within about ten minutes. The most important among the persistent agents are vesicants, V-agents, and thickened soman, which retain their casualty effectiveness for several hours or days. Soman and VX are the most effective among the semi-persistent agents. Soman is an agent with neuroparalytic action. It is two to three times stronger than sarin in toxicity and achieves, to a considerable greater degree than sarin, an effect through the skin by it vapors.

Traditional chemical warfare delivery means are: bombers, fighter bombers, helicopters,[3] missiles,[4] multiple rocket launchers,[5] and diverse artillery. Chemical weapons can also be disseminated by UAVs, sprayer aircraft, or helicopters over towns or against crops; by vehicles containing electric motor crop dusters or smoke generators; by improvised explosive devices; against buildings through injection into intake vents of ventilation, heating, and air conditioning systems; by using underground sewers or utility and subway tunnels as conduits; by using various stages of food production, processing, and distribution as avenues of attack; by dissemination through pharmaceutical products; via the postal system; through release from industrial facilities or pipelines, using explosive charges or by cutting pipes or opening valves; through sabotage of the transportation system; and by attacking trucks, tankers, railroad tank cars, ships, and barges, which allow rapid transport.

The Threats from Chemical Weapons

The states that in the recent past produced the most chemical weapons were the Soviet Union—over 40,000 tons—and the United States—over 30,000 tons. Four other states have declared stocks of chemical weapons: Albania, India, Libya, and "another state party," not identified at its request but widely understood to be South Korea. Three countries have declared that abandoned chemical weapons were present on their territories, and eleven countries have declared that they possessed old chemical weapons.[6] A final report of weapons possibly remaining in Iraq has yet to be published.[7] Moreover, there are reports that claim that a number of states, including some that are parties to the CWC, have clandestine chemical weapon programs.[8] At the end of 2006, of 71,330 agent tons of declared chemical weapons, 22 percent have been verifiably destroyed; of approximately 8.6 million declared items, about 30 percent munitions and containers had been destroyed.[9] As of the same date, all of chemical weapon production facilities declared by the twelve states[10] have been certified by the OPCW as being inactivated, eighteen of these as being converted for purposes not prohibited under the CWC.

As the slow process of verified destruction of chemical weapons continues under the CWC, the threats from remaining stockpiles are gradually receding. In 2005, Russia issued a revised chemical weapons destruction plan that places the total cost of the destruction program at $5.6 billion. Destruction operations were carried out at Gorny, Saratov Oblast, and now at new facilities at Kambarka, Udmurt Republic, and Maradykovskiy Settlement, Kirov Oblast. Starting in 2008, destruction will be enlarged with new sites at Leonidovka Settlement, Penza Oblast; in Pochep, Bryansk Oblast; and in Shchuchye, Kurgan Oblast. And starting in 2009, destruction will also take place in Kizner, Udmurt Republic. All remaining stockpiles of category 1 CW are to be totally destroyed before April 29, 2012. The U.S. stockpile of chemical weapons is stored at eight locations.[11] Destruction operations are carried out at the Anniston, Edgewood, Pine Bluff, Tooele, and Umatilla facilities. In addition to the destruction programs in Russia and the United States, programs to destroy chemical weapons stockpiles are also being carried out in Albania, India, Libya, and South Korea, and efforts are ongoing to destroy the chemical weapons that Japan left in China after World War II.

The continuing difficulties with chemical weapon destruction mean that it is becoming increasingly unlikely that all states will meet the destruction deadline of April 29, 2012, mandated under the CWC. Since only roughly just over a quarter of declared items has been destroyed so far, numerous stocks of chemical weapons still exist and thus remain as a threat.

The Threats from Chemical Proliferation

While many states have the capability to make chemical weapons, few have the motivation to do so. Such weapons remain repugnant to the overwhelming majority of states and have demonstrated their dubious utility as weapons of war. Nevertheless, there is little to suggest that chemical weapons will not be sought and used again—as seen in the case of the Tokyo subway attack by the religious sect Aum Shinrikyo.

Factors that are conducive to proliferation of chemical weapons are:

1. The relative simplicity of technologies for producing poisons at the present level of development of the chemical industry
2. The ease with which dual-use technologies, equipment, and materials suitable for producing chemical weapons can be acquired
3. The economic profitability and relative ease of carrying out chemical weapon development
4. The difficulty of detecting such programs

The dual-use nature of the commodities and technology that go into the manufacture of chemical weapons remains a persisting concern and a source of uncertainty in any estimates of either arsenal size or latent capabilities to manufacture such weapons.

New risks of proliferation arise with the research and development of so-called non-lethal or less lethal weapons, using the latest advances of the pharmaceutical industry. Though international treaties place clear restrictions on their use, for years the Pentagon has spent millions of dollars to develop a new generation of non-lethal weapons to reduce casualties in war. However, experience shows that in battle, non-lethal weapons are often used as precursors to deadly force. The CWC, for example, bans the use of tear gas and similar things in armed conflict because of the experience in Vietnam had been that U.S. forces drove Vietcong and Vietnamese civilians out of their tunnels with tear gas, and then just mowed them down with machine guns. Using the sedative Valium as an aerial dispersant—another idea once considered by Pentagon researchers—is illegal for just this reason. But currently, research on and tests of non-lethal chemical agents are under way in several countries to determine the effective radius of action of such agents and the best means of delivery.

The Threats from Terrorism with Chemical Weapons

Toxic chemical agents might be acquired by terrorists either through theft or attacks on industries, stocks, or shipments.[12] Terrorist groups may also produce such agents themselves. However, delivering toxic materials effectively enough to kill large numbers of people is more difficult than simply acquiring or making the weapon agents. There are multiple ways to disseminate chemical agents, probably the optimal being by aircraft. Clearly terrorists are likely to have access to sprayer aircraft or various small aircraft that can carry 100 kg of anything as well as 1,000 kg of sarin.[13]

The most plausible use of chemicals as weapons is in attacking aggregations of people in enclosed spaces like subways, airports, financial centers, universities, stadiums, theaters, and cinemas. This would cause disruption to crucial infrastructure services or render them unusable, and potentially cause widespread loss of confidence in the ability of the government to protect its citizens. Small quantities of chemicals would usually be all that would be needed—for nerve agents a few hundred grams. Important conferences, major public sport events, or games could be prime targets.

A deadly means of spreading a volatile chemical agent is to inject it in or to break glass jars of the substance on the intake vents of ventilation, heating, and air conditioning systems of a high-rise office or other building. The intake fans would vaporize the agent and distribute it to the floors supplied by the vents, essentially to a captive group of victims. Air turnover in office buildings is deliberately controlled to reduce energy loss, thus making large complexes inviting targets. Stock markets, internationally important financial centers, highly symbolic government agencies and buildings, and some corporate headquarters could be preferred targets.

Underground sewers or utility tunnels could be used as conduits for releasing gases and volatile liquids of chemical and toxic agents, which could disperse through these systems and eventually emerge from manholes, drains, and other openings. Dissemination might also work in subway tunnels, where the agents would be "pumped" through the city by the trains.

Other ways to use chemicals as weapons include attacking people indirectly by contaminating facilities frequented by large numbers of the public, such as subway and railway stations, stadiums, theaters, cinemas, and department stores. Since nonvolatile chemicals can be very persistent, thus able to taint their targets and interfere with critical services for longer periods of time, other prime targets could be important financial, banking, and insurance centers in order to disrupt their services or to render them unusable.

The various stages of food production, processing, and distribution offer many potential avenues for attack and good prospects for toxic contamination, particularly for foods consumed quickly, such as milk, fresh meats, and vegetables. Three characteristics of this industry create the main vulnerabilities:

1. The concentration of primary production in large, monoculture farms
2. The concentration of commodity food-processing in large centralized facilities
3. A tendency to adhere to rigidly defined patterns of quality control that may not detect unanticipated contaminants

Pharmaceutical products can be used for deliberate contamination of larger segments of the population, particularly via the vast array of vitamins, health supplements, and "natural" remedies, which do not need approval by governmental agencies. Producers of excipients, in particular, offer good possibilities for attack. Widely used, of which several are often common to more than a hundred approved drug formulations, excipients often account for a relatively high fraction of the final dosage form, thus allowing for lethal contamination at low concentrations. While there are multiple suppliers of excipients, previous contamination of a single source could have a widespread impact, including an erosion of public confidence in the safety of medicines generally.

The water supply system could also be used, but might not be the most likely target for producing mass casualties by chemical warfare or toxic agents. Many of these agents hydrolyze in water, react with a disinfectant residual, or are rendered harmless, especially under alkaline conditions. However, some insecticides that are chlorine esterase inhibitors, similar in action to nerve agents, do persist in water, and could—like forced entry of some other highly toxic agents into the supply system after water treatment—have serious consequences.

Harmful agents could also be delivered through existing systems already designed for rapid and widespread distribution, such as the postal system. A concerted attack from multiple locations could result in widespread contamination of many of the automated centers where mail is sorted and distributed, resulting in large numbers of infected mail workers and recipients, possibly shutting down the postal service. Other mass distribution systems like currency, newspapers, or junk mail might also be used to expose large numbers of people to the effects of toxic substances or to interfere with the functioning of society.

Mass transit rail and subway systems in major cities remain vulnerable to Madrid-style attacks with chemical weapons. Improvised explosive devices (IEDs) containing a chemical agent can be detonated, dispersing toxic chemicals causing mass casualties. Such devices with chlorine gas have been used by insurgents in Iraq. Chlorine gas has been used by the Liberation Tigers of Tamil Eelam in 1990.

The Aum Shinrikyo cult filled eleven vinyl bags with sarin and punctured them after having planted them in five different Tokyo subway trains in 1995, killing twelve people. In ten of the seventeen CBW attacks they used chemical agents—four with sarin, four with VX, one with phosgene, and one with sodium cyanide. In June 1994, the cult used a van equipped with a sarin dispenser in an attempt to kill three judges hearing a case against the group.[14] It also reportedly killed several dissident members using VX nerve agent. Poisoning attempts with toxins are also known to have happened in the United States: in 1982, when cyanide-laced Tylenol was placed in retail stores in the Chicago area; in 1984, when fourteen white supremacists plotted in Mountain Home, Arizona, and stockpiled thirty gallons of cyanide to poison the water supplies of Chicago and Washington; and in 1998, the chance prevention of a mailing in which sodium cyanide was sent packaged as a free sample of a nutritional supplement. Years prior to that, Abdel Basit said that he had considered a cyanide gas plot targeting the World Trade Center towers before settling instead on a truck bomb as the vehicle for his 1993 attack. In February 2002, Italian authorities arrested several Moroccan men who allegedly planned to attack the U.S. Embassy in Rome. The men were found with about nine pounds of potassium ferrocyanide. However, a threat assessment based solely on the extrapolation from these past, rather unsuccessful, experiences can be misleading. More effective chemical weapons may become part of terrorist arsenals. And the concept of manufacturing binary chemical weapons also has been around for decades.

Rather than seeking to attack large numbers of civilians directly, terrorist groups could choose to attack targets that would release dangerous chemical agents, like plants, tankers, and transport vessels containing hazardous chemicals, or cause leakages or large releases of toxic industrial chemicals. An IED could be detonated in close proximity to, or within, a chemical storage facility. Or chlorine and ammonia storage facilities could become targets. Chlorine stores at water treatment plants are a top concern because they tend to be close to cities and some locations have large stockpiles of liquid chlorine—the most viable form for a large-scale terrorist attack. Also industrial solvents and fertilizers can be extremely dangerous if disbursed in large quantities that can produce deadly concentrations. Civilian industries that use or produce highly toxic materials are sitting targets.

The potential effects of an attack on a chemical plant—or trains of tank cars, trucks, barges or ships—are illustrated by some large industrial accidents such as that in Bhophal, India, when more than 3,000 people died after an accidental release of methylisocyanate from a pesticide plant in 1984. The accidents in the same year at a liquefied gas storage facility in Mexico City where explosions killed more than 500 and injured about 7,200 people, and the massive explosions at a fertilizer plant in Toulouse in 2001 are other examples. Such chemical industries exist in the vicinity of many cities and some are even located in cities. The regular transport of dangerous chemicals to and from such facilities also raises security risks. In the United States alone, more than 800,000 shipments of hazardous materials are moved along highways, railways, and pipelines each day. Moreover, there are thousands of such sensitive facilities that would need improved protection, while in comparison there are rather few nuclear facilities.[15] Furthermore, there are very few industrial or manufacturing facilities of any kind with security levels sufficient to withstand a determined attack by a committed terrorist group.

While chemical weapons are not optimal for terrorist use, this is not to say that some terrorists will not use them—only that biological and nuclear weapons seem to hold greater promise for them. While definitely a threat, chemical weapons will not necessarily kill more people than conventional bombings. Chemical weapons pose the most likely risk of being used in a number of small-scale attacks, perpetrated either with weaponized agents or industrial chemicals, or by causing chemical accidents through sabotage. Attacks could be conducted either simultaneously or sequentially as part of an extended terror campaign that is directed as much at causing panic as at killing.

Terrorist attacks with chemical weapons would yield almost immediate casualties and would not necessarily involve persistent agents. Although only persistent chemical agents result in contamination by military definitions, even minute residual amounts of a non-vaporized nerve agent are outside acceptable bounds for civilians. The appearance of casualties would be something of an immediate "spike," leaving medical personnel with a tremendous overload but without the specter of additional casualties. Medical requirements would be immediate and massive in nature for casualty management consisting of the administration of atropine and pralidoxime chloride. If neurological involvement is severe, diazepam may be necessary to reduce convulsions and brain damage. Ventilation and suction of airways may also be required. Liquid contamination, a less probable occurrence than vapor but still possible, requires immediate removal of the agent from the victim's skin, and then chemical decontamination if possible.

If a terrorist attack with chemical weapons happens, identification of the agent employed is time-critical. Fortunately, the physical characteristics of chemical weapons have made the analysis of agents amenable to the analytical techniques commonly employed for most environmental analyses, namely gas and liquid chromatography, with a variety of detectors including mass spectrometry. Synthetic or relatively pure samples not requiring chromatographic separation are frequently characterized by nuclear magnetic resonance or Fourier transform infrared spectroscopy.[16]

5

Biological and Toxin Weapons

Germs and warfare are old allies. While the military use of pathogens and toxins dates back several centuries,[1] states have used disease sparingly in modern warfare. British soldiers during the French and Indian War gave unfriendly tribes blankets sown with smallpox. The Germans in World War I spread glanders, a disease of horses, among the mounts of rival cavalries. The most egregious case dates back to World War II when the Japanese Imperial Army unleashed plague, cholera, typhoid, and other diseases against Chinese civilians, killing an estimated 300,000.[2] More recent evidence points to the employment of biological weapons in the Iran–Iraq War, in southern Africa, and elsewhere in the developing world. Despite occasional grim successes, germ weapons have never played decisive roles in warfare. In contrast, certain natural occurring agents and several pandemics have probably caused more deaths over time than weapons of all types combined.[3]

Weaponization of biological toxins and agents has been undertaken for decades and their potential lethality has been well identified.[4] The NATO handbook dealing with biological warfare defense lists thirty-nine agents that could be used as biological weapons.[5] The Soviets organized biological warfare programs around three types of action: anti-personnel, anti-livestock, and anti-crop; and three modes of action: inhalation, oral, and cutaneous. Bioagents can be manufactured or obtained with far less difficulty than nuclear weapons. Rapid changes in the life sciences influence the availability of the information and expertise required to make toxins and genetically modified viruses and other pathogens.

Biological and toxin weapons kill by using pathogens to attack cells and organs in human bodies. They can also be used to target crops and livestock on a massive scale. Biological weapons are more dangerous than chemical weapons because they are easier to conceal, can cause a larger number of casualties, and do not require rare materials, finances, knowledge, or infrastructure to produce. Its underlying sciences and technologies are not secret, and mostly dual-use.

For a microorganism causing disease in man, plants or animals, or deterioration of material to be selected for use as biological agent, it must be such that only a few organisms are needed to initiate the disease, have a relatively short incubation period, high infectivity, high potency, and be unlikely to meet with widespread immunity among the target population. Ease of production and its ability to deliver are important additional considerations.

There are a number of organisms that have the necessary characteristics for selection as biological agents. Bioagents can be lethal or non-lethal, transmissible or non-transmissible, and may enter the body by being inhaled, swallowed, or absorbed across the mucous membrane. The delivery of an aerosolized biological agent in ultra-fine particles that can be inhaled into the lungs poses the highest risk of mass casualties. Such agents may exhibit themselves in minutes or seconds in the case of toxins, or days, if not weeks, to fully manifest themselves in the case of contagious diseases. Biological agents can be grouped in four categories: viruses; bacteria; rickettsiae and chlamydiae; and fungi.

- Viruses are sub-microscopic packages of protein-coated nucleic acids, which require living cells on which to multiply, and are dependent on cells of the host which they infect. They often do not respond to antibiotic treatment. Compared with bacteria, they are less complex and often more deadly. Among these viruses are: chikungunya, Congo-Crimean hemorrhagic fever, dengue fever, hantaan, junin, influenza, ebola fever, machupo, Marburg fever, lassa fever, smallpox, Rift Valley fever, Venezuelan equine encephalitis, and various potential Arboviruses.
- Bacteria are small free-living organisms, most of which can be grown easily in laboratories, which have a cell structure and reproduce by simple division. The diseases they produce often respond to treatments using antibiotics. Among these bacteria are: Anthrax, Brucellosis (abortus, melitensis, suis), Bukholderia (mallei, pseudomallei), Clostridium botulinum, Cholera, Francisella tularensis, Melioidosis, Plague (pneumonic, pubonic), Shigella dysenteriae, Tularemia, Typhoid fever, and Yersina pestis.

- Rickettsiae and chlamydiae have characteristics common to viruses and bacteria, grow only within living cells, yet have a cell structure, and are susceptible to antibiotic treatment. Among the rickettsiae are: Q-fever, Rocky Mountain spotted fever, epidemic typhus, coxiella burnetii, and bartonella quintana, while psittacosis is among the chlamydia.

- Fungi may be regarded as primitive plants which do not use photosynthesis, drawing nutrition from decaying vegetable matter, and do not require oxygen for growth. Most fungi can exist either in a yeast-like state or as resistant spores. Coccidioidomycosis, histoplasmosis, and nocardiosis fall in this group.

In addition, there are some genetically modified microorganisms—natural and synthesized proteins affecting body metabolic and other functions.[6] Among the *human toxins* are: botulinum, clostridium perfringens, conotoxin, ricin, saxitoxin, shiga toxin, staphylococcus aureus, tetrodotoxin, verotoxin, micocystin (cyanoginosin), and aflatoxins. On the *toxins warning list* are: abrin, cholera, tetanus, trichothecene mycotoxin, modeccin, volkensin, and viscum album lectin. Among the *animal pathogens viruses* are: African swine fever, avian influenza, bluetongue, foot and mouth disease, goat pox, herpes, hog cholera, lyssa, newcastle disease, peste des petits ruminants, porcine enterovirus, rinderpest, sheep pox, and teschen disease.

The table illustrates the impact and lethality of a biological attack utilizing three alternative bioagents. In each case the actual amount involved is 100 kg or less, an amount easily carried in a trunk of a car, and the estimated number of deaths exceeds that experienced in the 9/11 attacks by an order of magnitude.

When concerns about possible biological weapon attacks grew in the 1990s, the U.S. Centers for Disease Control and Prevention (CDC) were asked to review what the most dangerous threats to the civilian population were. They made their judgments using four criteria:[8]

1. Public health impact based on illness and death
2. Delivery potential to large populations based on stability of the agent, ability to mass produce and distribute a virulent agent, and potential for person-to-person transmission of the agent
3. Public perception as related to public fear and potential civil disruption
4. Special public health preparedness needs based on stockpile requirements (e.g., vaccines), enhanced disease surveillance, or diagnosis needs

Comparative effects of biological agents[7]

Biological Agent	Amount released	Estimated damage/lethality
Anthrax	100 kg spores released over a city the size of Washington	130,000-3 million deaths
Plague	50 kg Yersinia pestis released over a city of 5 million people	150,000 infected 36,000 deaths
Tularemia	50 kg Francisella tularensis released over a city of 5 million people	250,000 incapacitated 19,000 deaths

Using these criteria, a list of agents posing the greatest threat to civilian populations was drawn up. The most dangerous were designated Category A agents, leading to the following diseases: *variola major* to smallpox; *bacillus anthracis* to anthrax; *yersinia pestis* to plague; *chlostridium botulinum* to botulism; *francisella tularensis* to tularemia; and *filoviruses* and *arenaviruses*[9] to viral haemorrhagic fevers. The CDC also produced a list of Category B and C agents, which, though not as dangerous as those in Category A, nevertheless present a considerable risk.

However, when the U.S. National Institute of Allergy and Infectious Diseases (NIAID) began its program to develop countermeasures, it used a more developed listing for its research agenda in which the individual agents were organized into various groupings of Category B and C agents which are easier to understand than if the agents had just been presented in a very long list that is laid out on page 46.

All these pathogens offer multiple weapons, all with specific and unique modes of action and characteristics.[11] Dissemination may be in the form of liquid droplets, aerosols, smoke or dry powder, as an addition to food and water supplies, or carried by insect vectors.[12] Deployment against civilians does not require missiles or artillery and can be successfully achieved often with cheap, off-the-shelf systems. Aerosol deployment can be done with crop dusters, robotic aircraft or drones, balloons, or even model airplanes. People or livestock can be exposed to bioagents from inhalation; through cuts or abrasions on the skin; or by ingestion of contaminated food, feed, or water. Pharmaceutical products delivery,[13] food processing and packing facilities, or mail delivery can be used for dissemination as well as pyrotechnics and fireworks; or filled glass light bulbs and larger glass-like containers exploding on electrical ignition. Subway and commuter tunnels, openings for elevators, air-intakes, ventilation, and heating and air conditioning systems can be used as well as backpack sprayers in vital nodes such as airports and stations.

Microbial pathogens can cause enormous problems in agriculture. Animal husbandry is particularly vulnerable because it is often very intensive with thousands of animals kept in confined areas. It is also vulnerable because the animals reared are often from very limited genetic stock so that a large percentage of them could succumb to a single strain of pathogen. Finally, as is well known from disease outbreaks such as the Foot-and-Mouth disease in the United Kingdom[14] and the Newcastle disease,[15] the viral agents that cause disease in animal stocks are usually very virulent. As far as plant pathogens are concerned, we just have to be reminded of the nineteenth century Irish potato famine to realize how devastating fungal diseases can be to staple crops. In fact, all staple and economically important crops have to be constantly guarded against the ravages of pests and diseases, and even then there can be huge production losses. It is hardly surprising, therefore, that virtually all state-level offensive biological weapons programs, of which we have knowledge today, carefully investigated anti-plant attacks.

In 1997, during the negotiations in Geneva aimed at strengthening the BTWC, ten plant pathogens were identified as potential anti-plant biological weapons agents producing the following diseases:

1. *colletotrichium coffeanum*—the coffee berry disease
2. *dothistroma pini*—the blight of pines
3. *erwinia amyovora*—the fire blight of apple, pear, and related species
4. *pseudomona solanaceorum*—the potato and tomato wilt, and Moko disease of banana, etc.
5. *pyricularia oryzae*—the blast disease of rice
6. *ustilago maydis*—the maize smut
7. *xanthomonas albilineans*—the leaf scald of sugarcane
8. *xanthomonas campestris*—the bacterial blight of rice
9. equally *tilletia tritici*—the cover smut, stinking smut, and common bunt of wheat
10. *sclerotinia sclerotorium*—the cottony soft rot, white mould, and watery soft rot on vegetables, beans, soya, etc.

Category B and C priority pathogens

Group	Examples of biological agent	Common name of disease
INHALATION BACTERIA	*Brucella* species	Brucellosis
	Bukholderia pseudomallei	Melioidosis
	Burkholderia mallei	Glanders
	Coxiella burnettii	Q-fever
	Rickettsia prowazekii	Typhus
	Rickettsia rickettsii	Rocky Mountain spotted fever
ARTHROPOD-BORNE VIRUS		
Alphaviruses	Venezuelan equine encephalitis	VEE
Flaviviruses	West Nile & Yellow fever virus	WNV & YF
Bunyaviruses	California encephalitis virus	CE
TOXINS	*Ricinus communis*	
	Chlostridium perfringens	
	Staphylococcal enterotoxin B	
FOOD & WATERBORNE PATHOGENS		
Bacteria	*Salmonella typhi*	Typhoid fever
Viruses	Caliciviruses	e.g. Norwalk
Protozoa	*Toxoplasma gondii*	Toxoplasmosis
EMERGING INFECTIOUS DISEASES	Multi-drug-resistant tuberculosis	MDR-TB

Attacks with such agents can be extremely destructive, in particular those on wheat and rice staple crops. At the least, such attacks can cause economic damage. The danger of attacks has increased in recent years because of great advances in the understanding of biocontrol of plant pests and plant inoculants. Efforts to develop fungal agents to attack drug crops such as poppies could be dangerous, at the very least in developing techniques that could be used in biological warfare. As with animal husbandry, the plant species used in agriculture are often of an extremely limited variety. Such monocultures are particularly open to attack with biological agents.

An attacker who has obtained a pathogen with the required characteristics still faces considerable difficulties—for example, in mass producing the agent and effectively disseminating it. Mass production is difficult enough in itself, particularly of extremely virulent agents. If a massive aerosolized attack is planned, effective dissemination in order to cause mass casualties is extremely difficult. The technical hurdles are:

1. The munitions or delivery system must generate a cloud of aerosol particles with dimensions that allow them to be inhaled deep into the lungs of the target personnel.
2. The agent must be physically stabilized so that it can survive the process of dissemination long enough to infect the target population.
3. The agent must disseminate slowly, meanwhile avoiding loss of viability or toxicity.
4. The overall size and shape of the aerosol cloud, and the concentration of agent within it, must be reasonably predictable, so that the dispersion pattern can be matched to the target.

The susceptibility of biological agents to meteorological conditions—particularly ultraviolet rays that can quickly kill the agent—complicates the ability to execute an effective biological weapons attack. Agents can be hardened against some meteorological stresses but a change in wind direction can still blow the agent off target. Biological agents can be dispersed in wet slurry, which is more vulnerable to environmental stresses, or in dry form, where the agent is dried and microencapsulated with a coating that helps stabilize and preserve the agent, and also facilitates its spread from the original release point.[16]

More than eighty naturally occurring pathogens and toxins might be used for attacks. Without real-time detection or declaration of an attack, they will infect and affect until recognized, identified, and mitigated. Definitively determining whether an outbreak is an attack or a naturally occurring disease can be a tough challenge. Even if an incident is known to be an attack, it would be extremely difficult to demonstrate who initiated it because distinctions between state and non-state actors are often insidious, and distinctions between home and abroad no longer operable. More sophisticated biological warfare of today is firmly grounded in applied microbiology and molecular biology. The modern form of biotechnology has evolved to include biology, agriculture, microbiology, biochemistry, pharmacology, cell biology, proteinomics, bioinformatics, and genetic engineering—which portend great, though not unlimited, expansion of weapons.

The Threats from Biological Weapons

No state would acknowledge possession of biological weapons—or that it has programs to develop them—since this would enhance neither its status nor its prestige and reputation. This provides quiet testimony to the strength of both the international stigma attached to biological weapons and to the fact that they are outlawed by the Biological and Toxic Weapons Convention (BTWC)—which is signed by 155 parties, fewer than either the NPT or the CWC. A further sixteen states have signed but not ratified it,[17] while more than twenty states have neither signed nor ratified the convention.[18] An additional problem is that many governments have not adopted or fully implemented national legislation and other instruments to ensure fulfillment of their obligations. The vast majority of state parties is complying with their obligations under the BTWC, and contributes in an important way to stability and confidence. Nevertheless, the many years of undiscovered non-compliance with the convention by the USSR,[19] and later Iraq, took a toll on that treaty. Moreover, the BTWC has no provision for the formal monitoring or verification of compliance or implementation and, unlike the CWC, there is no central institution or verification regime for it.

It is clear that it would be far easier for any state to obtain or manufacture significant quantities of bioagents than is the case with nuclear weapons. This is partly due to a special problem that arises from the right affirmed in the BTWC for states to retain biological agents and toxins for prophylactic, protective, or other peaceful purposes. In the absence of any verification system, this provision, which some have called a loophole in the treaty, makes it difficult for the international community to determine conclusively if a country's declared defensive programs do not have an offensive military purpose.

Russia and the United States[20]—the countries that in the recent past possessed the largest biowarfare programs—are often cited as retaining various weapon-related capabilities, along with a few other states in the Middle East and East Asia. However, the potential global threat posed by biological weapons is not limited to those states that once had sophisticated programs to develop such weapons.[21] This threat stems from the problematic fact that facilities designated to undertake research on or to produce biological agents are more difficult to detect and easier to hide than facilities to produce fissile material for nuclear weapons. The difficulty of detecting these facilities enhances the risk of surprise appearance of a new biological weapon capability.

Concerns about possible future weapons are greater than the concerns about today's biological weapons. New biowarfare agents can be developed through genetic engineering and ways can be explored to weaponize biochemical compounds called bioregulators, which control basic human functions like thought and action.

The Threats from Biological Proliferation

The BTWC requires parties to not "in any way to assist, encourage, or induce any state, group of states or international organizations"[22] to manufacture biological agents for use as weapons. Unlike nuclear weapons, biological weapons do not require unique ingredients that are ready objects of arms control. Hence, regrettably, export-import controls are not enough to prevent the proliferation of these weapons. The large biological weapon program discovered in Iraq, a party to the BTWC, after the 1991 Gulf War relied on imported agents and growth material to a large extent, some sent by mail from U.S. and European laboratories.[23] In addition, not only do dangerous biological agents travel internationally unaided by man, they exist in nature inside countries all over the world.

The rapid advances or innovations in the life sciences influence the availability of the information and expertise required to make toxins and genetically modified viruses and other pathogens. As the scientific, engineering, and industrial uses of biological organisms grow throughout the world, states and non-state actors will be able to produce large volumes of lethal biological agents, engineer new pathogens, and develop effective delivery systems. The interest in acquiring biological weapons may be based on the following reasons:

1. To offset an opponent's conventional or nuclear military advantage[24]
2. High economic profitability, and relative technical ease of carrying out biological warfare programs
3. Dual-use of technologies, equipment, and materials suitable for creating

biological weapons—for example, the capability of using them both for peaceful and for military purposes
4. The possibility of covert existence of military biological warfare programs connected with the lack of clear distinctions between offensive and defensive operations
5. The difficulties of detecting relevant infrastructure

U.S. intelligence assessments have highlighted biological weapons proliferation concerns about such nations as North Korea and Syria.[25] However, Iraq is the only other country confirmed in recent years to have had an offensive biological weapons program. United Nations Special Commission Inspectors uncovered sufficient evidence of a covert bioweapons program to compel Iraq, a signatory of the BTWC, to admit that it had produced and weaponized biological agents—anthrax, aflatoxin, and botulinum toxin.[26] The Iraqi and Soviet programs went undetected for years, underscoring the problem of relying solely on national technical means to monitor compliance with the BTWC. A related concern is that a state might decide to share its biological weapon capabilities with non-state actors.

Concern also arises from the possible misuse or negative impact of biodefense programs, such as their potential to provide cover for the illegal development or maintenance of biological weapons-related expertise. Yet another risk of proliferation of biological weapons is occasioned by the prevalence, in some cases, of lack of control over the circulation, trade, and transfer of components for acquiring these weapons—strains of causative agents of dangerous infectious diseases, dual-use equipment, nutritive media, and technological information.

What makes the prevention of biological weapons proliferation a particularly formidable task is that the biotechnical revolution[27] is using the blueprints of all life—DNA—to create new forms of life and modify existing ones. There are three trends in the biotechnology revolution:

1. It offers tools to unravel the complex genetic codes and functions of organic molecules on which all life depends: the science of genomics—a powerful weapon for understanding how diseases affect the body in order to develop new countermeasures. At the same time it can also aid in developing more precisely targeted and therefore more effective weapons. New sequencing technologies coupled with bioinformatics

are exponentially increasing the speed and accuracy of genomics. Entire "genomic encyclopedias" for various bacteria, viruses, fungi, and higher animals, including man, will soon be available. Numerous viruses, bacteria, and higher order of forms have already been genotyped.

2. New tools for precisely targeting and manipulating organic molecules, commonly referred to as genetic engineering or recombinant DNA technology, allow gene transfer and subsequent cloning to produce new "species" with multiple pathogenicities—like plague with myelin toxin or endemic, non-pathogenic bacteria with regulatory peptides. Already the Soviets have successfully transferred the myelin toxin, which degrades the central nervous system, into the plague bacteria *yersinia pseudo-tuberculosis*, managed to engineer *tetracycline resistant anthrax*, and extensively studied *regulatory peptides*.[28]

3. The third trend operationalizes the first two. Production technology is rapidly advancing, enabling more efficient and compact means for manufacturing and distributing biological material. Genetic decoding, molecular manipulation, and efficient mass production will enable designer vaccines, antidotes, and other therapies. As bioscience becomes more computational and less about wet labs, and as all the genomic data becomes easily available on the Internet, at some point, it will be possible to design vaccines on the laptop. Conversely, the same trends could combine to enable designer biological weapons for those that have the will, knowledge and resources to apply the technologies, creating *binary weapons, novel designer genes* and life forms, *stealth viruses,* and *host-swapping viruses.* The other side of the coin is, fortunately, that the same technologies may also produce novel antibiotics as well as *broad-spectrum immune enhancers,* rapid and precise detection, *new antivirals,* and *metabolic-based defenses.*

Potential problems may emanate from the rapid developments in the life sciences, including new understandings of genes and proteins that could eventually outpace national and international efforts to prevent, control, or manage hostile uses of biology. In recent years, materials and technologies have become accessible to many more researchers and technicians through the pharmaceutical and biotechnology industries. Inevitably, scientific advancements in biotechnology and the increase of facilities capable of producing biological agents make it more difficult to prevent the development of biological weapons, complicate efforts to ensure their non-production and the elimination of stocks, and make it exceedingly difficult to pinpoint potential biological threats.

In the twenty-first century, the ever-expanding global transport of goods and livestock and the growth in international travel mean that an outbreak of a highly contagious disease in one place could quickly spread around the world.

The Threats from Bioterrorism

The biological terrorist threat probably is the most pressing today. Biological weapons (BW) are strategic in that they have the greatest potential for lethality of any weapon. Radiological devices, nuclear weapons, and chemical weapons, respectively, tend to be rank-ordered as lesser terrorist threats. The insidious nature of BW, coupled with its ease of concealment and potential for mass casualties, increases its attractiveness to terrorist groups. Biological weapons have utility across the spectrum of conflict that allows them to be employed for a variety of attacks, large or small, against a wide range of targets and with an equally wide range of effects. The diversity of the biothreat inventory and the ubiquity of targets make it impossible to provide a uniform picture of the threat problem. Choices in agents and tactics are perhaps the most difficult aspect of the terrorism problem to assess or predict. Studies at the Monterey Institute of International Studies showed that there had been 285 incidents throughout the world since 1976 in which terrorists had used chemical or biological weapons. In 44 percent of those cases, no one had been killed or seriously injured; in 76 percent of them, five or fewer people had been hurt. The small data set relating to terrorist attacks using biological weapons to date only increases the difficulty for assessing the BW risks. But some agents could have massive, unpredictable, and potentially uncontrollable consequences, and could also profoundly affect the health of future generations.

Non-state actors in the United States have used biological agents already in 1972, when the "Order of the Rising Sun," a neo-Nazi group, produced eighty pounds of typhoid bacillus. In 1984, followers of the Bhagwhan Shree Rajneesh poisoned with salmonella the salad bars of a small Oregon town. In 2001, 2003, and 2004, biological agents have been used in local incidents, including some that produced fatalities. Anthrax infected individuals in Connecticut, New York, Washington, D.C.,[29] and Florida. Ricin was mailed to the White House in 2003 and Congress in 2004. Other states also have had to cope with bioterrorist threats. In 1979, a Palestinian terrorist poisoned

Israeli orphanages. In 1984, Paris police raided an apartment rented by the Baader-Meinhof gang and found flasks of clostridium botulinum culture. In 2003, British law enforcement officials arrested several people accused of manufacturing ricin in a London apartment.[30] While none of these incidents resulted in many casualties, the risk will remain in the years ahead that biological or toxin weapons could be used by terrorists. The list of agents that could pose the greatest public health risk in the event of a bioterrorist attack is short. But it includes agents that, if acquired and properly disseminated, could cause a difficult public health challenge in terms of a country's ability to limit the numbers of casualties and control the damage to cities and the nation. Probably one of the greatest dangers is that the smallpox virus could be used by terrorists. Cessation of the practice of vaccination in almost all countries may have catastrophic consequences.

There is evidence that al Qaeda is looking at possibilities of acquiring pertinent materials. But expressions of interest by non-state actors in acquiring biological weapons do not prove the existence of a weapon program, nor do they constitute evidence of a credible capability to deploy such weapons on a large scale. Despite a diverse and highly trained scientific workforce, modern technical equipment, financial resources reportedly of a value of over $1 billion, and little scrutiny either from law enforcement or intelligence agencies for a number of years, the Japanese Aum Shinrikyo cult failed in its attempts to use chemical and biological weapons with large-scale effects in seventeen known CBW attacks or attempted attacks[31] between 1990 and 1995: seven using biological agents, four with anthrax, and three with botulinum toxin.[32] However, past failures by terrorists offer a fragile basis for confident predictions that bioterrorist events will not occur in the future.[33]

Bioterrorism is a real threat, though cataclysmic incidents are probably less likely than smaller-scale attacks. The historical record of individual killings is long. A large number of toxins are suitable for terrorist use as sabotage-infectants or to bring about the death or temporary incapacitation of individuals or groups of persons. Complicating the terrorist quest for producing biological agents of mass destruction is the substantial technical proficiency required to produce highly virulent agents. In addition, the difficulties involved with proper aerosolization and the creation of a milled, powdered agent—rather than the less effective slurry—further hamper a terrorist group's ability to cause mass casualties.

However, vulnerability and capability, the two prerequisites of bio-terrorism, are in place. In fact, there is a heightened fear of the impact of terrorist actions, coupled with profound concerns that modern economies may be particularly vulnerable to disruption from the deliberate spread of disease. The variety of biological attack methods is nearly inexhaustible. So many high-value targets are at risk and so many vulnerabilities exist that biodefense will remain problematic for the foreseeable future. In addition to potentially substantial economic costs associated with such an attack, the psychological impact an attack will have on the population could also prove attractive to some terrorists. Humans, obviously, are highly susceptible, but also at risk are agricultural assets—livestock, crops, and even soil.

Plant and animal pathogens may be acquired more easily than human pathogens—isolating pathogens from the environment or obtaining them from state sponsors are the most likely sources. Unlike human pathogens, these avenues for acquisition require less specialized equipment and expertise. Terrorists can choose among several plant or animal pathogens that need to come in contact with only the surface of the target host to cause infection. Moreover, for many diseases, once the initial infection has been established, they can be spread effectively through the wind. Because agroterrorism involving biological agents has largely been overlooked until recently, agriculture is nearly unprotected against serious attack in spite of the potentially huge economic impact of a successful attack. Such an attack would not be devastating in terms of numbers of casualties, but rather in terms of economic dislocation and shortages. Such attacks could come from: contamination of crops using organic pesticides or herbicides; contamination of livestock, food and animal feed; engagement of adulterated seeds; to the more complex and difficult contamination of water supplies; aerosol clouds from sprayers, ground or aerial—which would need to be modified to achieve the correct particle size for dissemination—automobiles, and boats; or missiles. Bombs are less useful since they tend to destroy the agent. To make matters worse, attacks could involve a mix of different biological agents that could confuse and disrupt identification of, and thus response to, an attack.

There are few barriers to developing such weapons with a modest level of effort. Tricothecene mycotoxins, known as "yellow rain," can be produced by simply using a corn meal slurry and the appropriate strains of fungus. The specific laboratory technologies needed are common to the pharmaceutical, dairy, and beer industry; not subject to international controls; and are readily available on the world market. Common laboratory supplies can be easily obtained from commercial suppliers or through the

Internet, and are largely uncontrolled, unregulated, and unknown. Thus, a terrorist group could construct a substantial laboratory with equipment and supplies purchased anonymously. It would be difficult to locate and detect a covert laboratory. If the equipment and supplies were purchased anonymously and operational security maintained, there would be few, if any, "signatures" that could be detected by external means.

There is also the possibility that terrorists could recruit highly skilled scientists. Any group able to recruit skilled professionals will increase its chances of obtaining or successfully developing biological agents, need less time to construct a BW capability, and increase its chances of conducting an effective attack. However, while it could be within the reach of a group of skilled biologists to concoct a lethal biological agent, it requires a different set of skills, expertise, and equipment to weaponize it to target and deliver it over a large population. It is less clear whether terrorists would soon be capable of doing this.

Should a bioterrorist attack occur, however, it may go undetected for some time, particularly if it were a naturally-occurring pathogen and the vector was food-borne or introduced via water contamination rather than aerosol dissemination. Both naturally occurring and human-created diseases pose serious challenges to national security. It must be recognized that, since biological weapons can be disseminated by means of air, food, or water, and it is not possible to predict where, when, and with what a bioterrorist might strike, full protection is not possible to achieve. The point is to be as well prepared as possible. This calls for cooperation between civilian health and security-oriented authorities, nationally, regionally, and worldwide. Responses to bioterrorism will differ greatly from responses to nuclear and chemical terrorism, probably much more closely resembling responses to "emerging infectious diseases." The bioterrorist threat merits revitalized national and international efforts to prevent such attacks and to substantially improve measures to protect the public against these deadly and indiscriminate weapons.

Enhancing emergency preparedness and supporting advanced pharmaceutical research for multivalent drugs, among other measures, will help to deter and defeat deliberate and naturally occurring pathogen releases, and will increase the general health and well-being of the population. The intention of potential attackers is difficult to manage. Therefore, limiting the vulnerabilities is the most promising way to prevent or mitigate biological attacks.

A pervasive sense of vulnerability to unseen microbes is more disturbing to the public psyche than many other potential threats. The five deaths and eighteen infections caused by the anthrax-by-mail incidents in the United States were a fraction of one day's carnage from American traffic accidents, but round-the-clock media coverage fuelled public fear and an overreaction by legislators. The incidents also revealed the inadequacy of current defense measures in responding to even a minor incident.

Nuclear, chemical, and biological threats are each uniquely complex but the detection and control of biothreats is by far the most complex. These difficulties reflect several unique aspects of the biothreat. In assaults with nuclear and chemical weapons, the scale of damage is evident immediately. In contrast, the effects of a bioattack are unlikely to be recognized quickly. Depending on the method by which a pathogen is released and dispersed, initial infection of victims can, for large airborne releases, occur within a few hours or, for release by contagious carriers, extend over weeks or months. The initial symptoms of many bioagents often are indistinguishable from common infections such as colds and flus.

Biological agents used offensively can be genetically engineered to resist current therapies and evade vaccine-induced immunity. Though it is vital that the molecular mechanisms by which classes of organisms cause disease be elucidated in order to understand and counter their effects, this is no simple matter. The large number of potential agents complicates the preparing for a biological attack against people, crops, or livestock. The long incubation periods of some agents, and their potential for secondary transmission.

Prevention of bioattacks before they occur is obviously the most desirable situation. Substantial research and development (R&D) investment has been made by the United States since the Gulf War to develop sensors to detect biothreat agents in the environment. However, this is a difficult technical challenge and progress has been slow. The use of environmental sensors to detect illicit production of bioagents is unlikely in the near future. Hence, biodefense must rely mainly on faster medical diagnosis and containment of an incident once it has begun.

The fragility of current public health capabilities in most countries means that the first indication that a bioattack has occurred will come only after doctors report abnormal numbers of ill people who share symptoms. The most realistic object for diagnosis is an infected person or group of people. Speed and precision of establishing a diagnosis of the disease are critical and require both the presence of reliable methods and test systems and highly trained infectious disease specialists. But the diagnostic laboratory tests for many of the anticipated biothreats are either not yet developed or available only in a few specialist laboratories. This makes it difficult to ascertain the full scope of an attack and to guide treatment strategies. Moreover, genetically engineered microorganisms "raise the technology hurdle" that must be overcome to provide for effective detection, identification, and early warning of biological attacks.

A mere few hundred casualties requiring intensive care would overwhelm the hospital network in most cities. Health facilities would not only have to diagnose and treat victims of the attack while still providing care for those ill from natural disease, but they would also be confronted with a tidal wave of "the worried well" who believe they are victims. If the agent is contagious in human-to-human transmission, the first people to die would be the medical caregivers, and the emergency responders. Then, doctors, nurses, ambulance crews, firemen, and police could also die soon after. A low number of deaths from a biological attack could leave a city without any medical-care system, except for what could be taken care of by the military.

Management of a bioincident would be complicated by a lack of drugs and vaccines. Current stockpiles of the few drugs and vaccines that are currently approved for use against biothreats are insufficient if a bioincident required treatment of many thousands of people. And little investment has been made to develop new drugs and vaccines against the biothreat agents for which no meaningful medical interventions exist.

Actions to limit the consequences of a bioattack require swift response by public health, military, and law enforcement authorities in concert with multiple private sector entities. These groups may have little or no prior experience of working together. Decision makers would be confronted with unfamiliar and complex technical issues that have the potential for catastrophic outcomes if the wrong judgments were made. National leaders would have to decide whether to impose martial law and quarantine, ban trade and travel, and authorize emergency seizure and diversion of private assets.

Those involved in the containment of infection would also be forced to make hard decisions regarding rationing of drugs and vaccines, the mandatory testing and treatment of people without their consent, imposition of quarantine, and other constraints on freedom. They would also be required to maintain essential services, and to address the problem of mass disposal of corpses.

Mass psychological trauma would be aggravated by any perception, real or imagined, that a bioincident was being mismanaged or was out of control. The near certainty of irresponsible actions by the media would augment public panic and civil disorder.

6
Radiological Weapons

A radiological weapon is any device that is designed to spread harmful radioactive materials into the environment, either to kill or to deny use of an area. Americans use the term RDD because radioactive materials can be spread in many ways in addition to conventional explosives with what is generally called a "dirty bomb." For example, radioactive powders scattered by the wind could theoretically have as severe an effect and would not be considered a bomb. Thus, dirty bombs are simply one type of RDD. Depending on the motives of those involved in planning the incident, such a device could be a low-key weapon that surreptitiously releases aerosolized radioactive material, dumps out a finely powdered radioactive material, or dissolves the radioactive material into water. It would be intended to slowly expose as many people as possible to the radiation. A dirty bomb, in contrast, is an RDD made of a traditional IED with a radiological substance added. Radioactive material not only is dispersed, but the dispersal is accomplished in a planned manner, and the explosion immediately alerts the victims and authorities that an attack has taken place.

The detonation of an explosive device to which radioactive substances have been added produces both local and extensive contamination. The local contamination is caused by ejected radioactive material. The larger area of contamination results from the propagation and deposition of aerosols produced by the explosion. An effective RDD must convert the radioactive material into a fine powder or aerosol to disperse it. The heat and blast effect of a conventional explosive can help accomplish both goals. But a flare-like pyrotechnic or just scattering a fine powder from a tall building will also get the material dispersed into the air.

Although radioactive material is utilized in constructing RDDs and dirty bombs, they are not nuclear weapons. Nuclear weapons induce nuclear chain reactions in bomb materials—materials less radioactive than the products of the reactions. This produces large energy releases and radioactive products more radioactive than the original material. In contrast, radiological weapons disperse material that is already radioactive. In such weapons, there is no energy release and no increase in radioactivity; hence they cannot be equated to the catastrophic effects of nuclear weapons. Even if uranium or plutonium is spread by a radiological bomb, the blast effect is due only to the high explosive and is therefore the same as that of a conventional bomb. In most cases, any immediate deaths or serious injuries would likely result from the explosion itself, rather than from radiation exposure.[1] Typically, radioactive contamination in an affected area decreases with the distance from ground zero. Contamination also decreases with time. First, weather conditions continuously remove radioactivity from the contaminated area, and second, there is also the natural decay of the radionuclide.

Because it is used in nuclear reactors and nuclear weapons, uranium is often thought to be highly radioactive and thus a potential RDD material. Though uranium is chemically toxic, it is slightly radioactive. Whether or not an element or the isotope of an element is highly radioactive depends on the rate at which the atomic nuclei disintegrate, or decay. The rate is measured by the isotope's half-life, the length of time it takes half of the material to decay. More than 99 percent of natural uranium consists of the isotope uranium-238 with a half-life of 700 million years, indicating it is quite stable and not an effective RDD material. Plutonium is about ten times more toxic than nerve gas and a highly carcinogenic alpha ray emitter with a shorter half-life: 24,000 years for Pu-239, and eighty-eight years for Pu-238. Inhaled, plutonium can cause lung, bone, and liver cancer. In contrast, the half-life of cobalt-60 is only 5.7 years, hence a material more suitable for an RDD.

A radiological weapon uses the radiation of the nuclei of a radioactivity element's atoms. Just a few elements have the right combination of radiation emission and half-life to be useful in RDDs. Radioactivity is measured in units of curies. A 1 curie radiation source is dangerously radioactive, requires special handling, and can be produced by small amounts of material. For example, a curie of cesium-137, an isotope or form of the element cesium, is just one hundredth (0.01) of a gram of material. To contaminate a city center would require hundreds of thousands of curies or just a few grams or tablespoons of cesium-137.[2] The Chernobyl nuclear accident released only about 5 percent of the radioactive inventory into the atmosphere: about

12,000,000 curies in the initial explosion, and another 40,000,000 curies by the fire during the next nine days.[3] In contrast, a nuclear explosion with a yield of 20 kilotons[4] results in radioactive daughter products with radioactivity of 600,000,000 curies one minute after detonation, and 5,000,000 curies one hour after detonation.

The *dose* is the term used to describe the amount of radiation a person receives. The dose rate is measured in units of thousands of a Sievert (Sv), called the milliSievert (mSv).[5] Basically, one can distinguish between acute effects with the symptoms of radiation sickness and possible death shortly after the irradiation, and long-term radiation effects with an increased probability of cancer mortality many years after the irradiation. The threshold value for the appearance of acute radiation damage is around a whole-body dose of 1,000 mSv. For a population of all ages, the number of cancer deaths resulting from a chronic irradiation is estimated at 5 to 6 percent per Sv.[6]

There can be a wide range of effects produced by either an RDD or a dirty bomb, depending on:

1. The size of the IED
2. The amounts and types of radioactive material dispersed
3. Environmental conditions such as terrain, season, temperature inversions, humidity, and prevailing winds
4. The size and population density of the affected area

The health hazard from an RDD depends on the type of radioactive material, its form, and the surroundings where it is released. There are three types of radioactive emissions: alpha, beta, and gamma rays. Both alpha and beta rays are particles that are ejected from atomic nuclei at tremendous speeds but are stopped after traveling very short distances. For example, an alpha particle from the isotope polonium-210 will travel 3.8 centimeters in the air before being stopped, primarily due to its interaction with electrons in gases in the air. Beta particles can travel somewhat farther and can penetrate matter more deeply. For example, an alpha particle can penetrate aluminum metal only for a few thousandths of a centimeter, whereas a beta particle can penetrate into aluminum a few tenths of a centimeter.[7]

The walls of a building will easily stop alpha and beta radiation. Alpha and beta emitters are most dangerous, therefore, when they are inhaled or swallowed, or come into contact with the skin. They can then cause radiation sickness and, over longer periods, induce cancers. Gamma rays are high-energy electromagnetic radiation, like light, and can penetrate much farther than alpha and beta particles. Some gamma rays will even get through walls. Thus, sources of gamma rays are dangerous if they are simply in the environment. They do not have to be ingested. The physical form of all radiation emitters is important; the finer the powder they are in, the deeper they can be carried into the lungs, and the more difficulty the body has in getting rid of them.

While RDDs would cause few immediate casualties from radiation, they would leave behind radioactively contaminated areas and buildings, up to several city blocks. Little is known about the techniques for, or costs of, large-scale decontamination of buildings. The difficulty of decontamination depends on the type of isotope used in the RDD because each element has a different chemical reactivity. Decontaminating streets, squares, and buildings is complicated; they must be sprayed with plenty of water and scrubbed, sometimes even vacuumed. Depending on the type of contamination and the surface, this may eliminate 10 to 90 percent of the radioactivity. Certain radioactive substances may combine with asphalt or concrete, rendering even repeated decontamination operations ineffective. The choices for recovery are limited to decontamination, demolition, and abandonment. No one knows how much it would cost to clean up, abandon, or demolish these buildings. Other economic costs would include jobs and services lost while the buildings remain contaminated. The affected town or region would lose much of its attraction for inhabitants, investors, companies, and tourists. Because they temporarily render the contaminated areas uninhabitable, RDDs have been referred to as weapons of mass disruption or mass dislocation rather than WMD. The vast expense of decontaminating a large, densely populated area would also make a dirty bomb a type of economic weapon.[8]

Even a large RDD attack will, with proper warning, allow time for people in the affected area to evacuate, thus limiting their exposure to radiation and resulting in few if any immediate casualties from radiation. The detectability of radiation is a major asset in reducing health and safety impacts and in evaluating a radiological incident. Warning from a radiological attack could come from radiation detectors. In the United States, such detectors are now being used at some critical sites like bridges and tunnels leading to large cities. Precautions as simple as removing contaminated clothing and taking a shower can significantly reduce total radiation exposure. A few isotopes can be countered with chemical treatment. For example, taking excess doses of normal iodine helps the body flush radioactive iodine. However, the trust of the population that the authorities are doing the right things could easily be undermined by contradictory recommendations and instructions on radiation protection.[9]

The Threats from Radiological Weapons

Radiological weapons—with the controversial exception of depleted uranium munitions[10] used by the United States in the 1991 Gulf War, in the 1999 Balkans wars, in Afghanistan 2002–03, and in Iraq 2003—have not been deployed or used in conflict for both practical and ethical reasons.

Neither have radiological weapons yet been used deliberately to cause harm by irradiating a population or an environment. So far, Chechen militants are the only known group that has attempted to use RDDs.[11] A few countries have pursued the development of radiological military weapons, only to abandon these efforts in favor of more practical and effective weapons.

The history of radioactive weaponry may be traced to a 1943 memo to Brigadier General Leslie Groves of the Manhattan Project:

> As a gas warfare instrument the material would . . . be inhaled by personnel. The amount necessary to cause death to a person inhaling the material is extremely small. It has been estimated that one millionth of a gram accumulating in a person's body would be fatal. There are no known methods of treatment for such a casualty. . . . It cannot be detected by the senses; It can be distributed in a dust or smoke form so finely powdered that it will permeate a standard gas mask filter in quantities large enough to be extremely damaging. . . .
>
> Radioactive warfare can be used . . . to make evacuated areas un-inhabitable; to contaminate small critical areas such as rail-road yards and airports; as a radioactive poison gas to create casualties among troops; against large cities, to promote panic, and create casualties among civilian populations.
>
> Areas so contaminated by radioactive dusts and smokes would be dangerous as long as a high enough concentration of material could be maintained. . . . They can be stirred up as a fine dust from the terrain by winds, movement of vehicles or troops, etc., and would remain a potential hazard for a long time.

These materials may also be so disposed as to be taken into the body by ingestion instead of inhalation. Reservoirs or wells would be contaminated or food poisoned with an effect similar to that resulting from inhalation of dust or smoke. Four days production could contaminate a million gallons of water to an extent that a quart drunk in one day would probably result in complete incapacitation or death in about a month's time.[12]

In 1950 the United States considered using radiological weapons in Saudi Arabia as a way to prevent a Soviet invasion force from using the Saudi oil or destroying the oil fields. The CIA ultimately recommended against the use of radiological weapons.[13] By 1953 the USSR developed a radiological warhead for the R-2 ballistic missile, which was retired as nuclear warheads became available.[14]

In 1987 Iraq pursued development of a radiological weapon.[15] The purpose was to combine the effectiveness of conventional aerial munitions with the spreading of radioactive materials as a means of "area denial" to be used in the final stages of the Iran-Iraq War. Three prototypes were made based on modified "Nasser 28" aerial bombs, each having 1,400 kilogram and a radioactive content of some two curies, derived mainly from the hafnium impurity present in the zirconium oxide that had been irradiated in the research reactor at Tuwaitha. One bomb had been detonated as a ground-level static test, while the other two had been fitted with impact fuses and were dropped from an aircraft. The results of these tests were disappointing in that the majority of the radioactive material concentrated on the crater with a sharp decline in the radiation level at a relatively short distance away. Moreover, the weapon was found to be impractical because the radioactive isotopes in the weapon would decay quickly, rendering it useless within a week after manufacture. Furthermore, it was discovered that for the radioactive material to spread, weather conditions had to be ideal. All forms of airborne radiological warfare share these general problems. The development was discontinued as Iraq concentrated on chemical, nuclear, and biological weapons programs.

Radiological weapons are widely considered to be militarily useless. Such a weapon is of no use to an occupying force as the target area becomes uninhabitable. Moreover, area-denial weapons are generally of limited use to an attacker as it slows its rate of advance. Finally, like biological weapons, radiological weapons can take days to act on the opposing force. They therefore not only fail in neutralizing the opponent but they also allow time for massive retaliation.

The Threats from Proliferation of Radiological Weapons

The existence of an illicit private global market where WMD expertise, technology, material, and designs for weapons could be acquired is a special threat at the time of growing organized crime and worldwide terrorism. Illicit trafficking in nuclear material is a matter of great concern. In the hands of terrorists or other criminals, nuclear material may contribute to the construction of an IED and RDDs, which could be used for terrorist purposes.[16] The global illicit trade has embarked on a great mutation—the same as that of international terrorist organizations like al Qaeda or Islamic Jihad. All have moved away from fixed hierarchies toward decentralized networks of loosely linked, dispersed agents and stealthy cells; away from rigid lines of control to exchange and toward constantly shifting transactions as opportunities dictate.

Networks of stateless traders in illicit goods are changing the world as much as terrorists are.[17] Links between proliferators, illicit traders, and terrorists are not random even though the connections between this unholy trinity of non-state actors are not readily apparent. All three groups are specialists in subterfuge. They manage to mask their interactions, which occur in prisons, uncontrolled territories,[18] or diasporas communities, where they are not observable to outsiders. Organized crime, proliferants, and transnational terrorists are becoming part of an integrated network that includes professionals whose well-established smuggling networks, facilitated by corruption, have the capacity to move significant quantities of nuclear materials and transport it to terrorist purchasers.[19] The newer crime groups may not share the ideological motivations of the terrorists but they too do not want a secure state. In fact, they may promote grievances because it is through the prolongation of conflict that they enhance their profits. The milieu in which proliferators, transnational crime, terrorists, and corruption merge threatens the international order. Left unchecked, illicit trade can pursue its already well-advanced mutation. There is ample evidence that it offers proliferators, terrorists, and criminal miscreants means of survival and methods of financial transfer and exchange.

Today, the reality is that no government or organization around the world has a complete picture of all the factors involved in prioritizing where the most urgent threats of nuclear theft lie.[20] The United States attacked Iraq because it feared that Saddam Hussein had acquired WMD. But for years up to then, a stealthy network led by A.Q. Khan, the "father" of Pakistan's nuclear weapons, was profiting selling nuclear bomb-making technology to whoever could pay for it. For the task of strengthening security, and accounting measures for nuclear warheads and fissile materials, the United States alone invested over $2 billion in the decade leading up to the announcement of the "Global Partnership Against the Spread of Weapons and Materials of Mass Destruction" launched at the 2002 G8 summit—over $200 million per year on average. Since then, U.S. budgets for that task have been running at over $400 million per year.[21] Together with its partners, the United States still is engaged in programs to secure nuclear weapons and fissile material in the former USSR, and is aware of the progress made. Russia has continued to take steps to strengthen nuclear security on its own—though these appear to be limited initial steps toward putting in place the security measures that are needed to meet today's threats.

Despite general improvements, the corruption case against former Minister of Atomic Energy (MinAtom) Yevgeny Adamov[22] is only one of the indicators suggesting that corruption and insider theft have penetrated Russia's nuclear establishment as well as those of other states of the former USSR. His predecessor, Viktor Mikhailov, was ousted, possibly in connection with technology transfers to Iran and Iraq.[a] In April 2006, Russian police arrested a group of conspirators that included a foreman at the Elektrostal nuclear fuel fabrication facility for stealing 22 kilograms of low enriched uranium. Several of the mayors of Russia's ten closed nuclear cities have been arrested or forced out of office either for corruption or for helping to set up fraudulent tax schemes. An investigation by a team of American and Russian researchers uncovered extensive corruption, drug use, organized crime activity, and theft of metals and other valuable items at the Mayak plutonium and HEU processing facility in the closed city of Ozersk.[24] The United States funded radiation detectors installed at eight border crossing points have until the beginning of 2003 identified more than 275 consignments involving materials that might have been used in RDDs.[25] Thus, the threat of corruption and insider theft remains real, and bigger than plausible security systems will be able to handle. Hence, improved security and accounting measures can only reduce, never eliminate, the risk that a particular cache of nuclear materials will be stolen.

However, even if all nuclear materials in Russia and the former USSR were secured against all plausible threats, an unacceptably high risk of proliferation of nuclear materials and radiological terrorism would remain because of the insecurity of such materials in other countries around the world. Civilian facilities pose a major concern as many have only minimal security in place. There are no binding global standards for nuclear security and, in practice, the security at sites where the essential ingredients of nuclear weapons and radioactive materials are located ranges from excellent to appalling.

While nuclear wastes are less likely proliferation options for weapon source material, potential radiological weapons materials exist in hundreds of thousands of locations worldwide. There are an estimated ten million radioactive sources in existence around the world. But even in the United States there is no effective mechanism at the federal or the state level for tracking throughout their lifecycle the numbers and location of the estimated two million radioactive sources.[26] Hundreds of plutonium, americium, and other radioactive sources are stored in dangerously large quantities in university laboratories and other facilities. In all too many cases they are not used frequently, resulting in the risk that attention to their security will diminish over time. At the same time, it is difficult for the custodians of these materials to dispose of them since in many cases only the Department of Energy (DOE) is authorized to recover and transport them to permanent disposal sites.

In the United States, the Nuclear Regulatory Commission (NRC) has regulatory authority over radiological sources. At the request of thirty-three states it has delegated that authority to them, and retains it in the remaining seventeen states. Unfortunately, the NRC stopped tracking sources by serial number more than twenty years ago and has had a difficult time locating the majority of those licensed to use radiological sources, known as "general licensees." A Government Accountability Office (GAO) study found serious gaps in agreement states' regulatory practices—almost half were unable to identify the number of radioactive sources in their jurisdictions.[27] Not surprisingly, lost, abandoned, or stolen radioactive sources pose a major problem. As many as one radioactive source is "orphaned" in the United States every day because legitimate disposal options are limited and physical security is uneven. Following the 9/11 attacks, the NRC and the states advised their licensees to increase the security of nuclear material, be alert for, and immediately report any unusual activities that might indicate a threat.

Because such threats equally exist abroad, the United States has pursued nuclear security cooperation for countries outside the former USSR. For the most part, however, progress has been slow. In China, security at one facility with HEU had been upgraded by the end of 2005 but no agreement is yet in place for the remaining facilities. While there is a United States–India nuclear agreement, no cooperative security upgrades exist with India. There is neither official confirmation on security cooperation that is rumored to exist with Pakistan, nor is there publicly known cooperation on nuclear security with Israel. For non-nuclear weapon states beyond the former USSR, by the end of 2005, U.S.-sponsored upgrades—often implemented in coordination with the International Atomic Energy Agency (IAEA) Office of Nuclear Security (NSNS)—had been completed for only seven facilities with six more then in progress.[28]

Significant amounts of radioactive materials are stored in laboratories, food irradiation plants, oil drilling facilities, medical centers, and many other sites worldwide. Among those, there are at least eight powerful radioactive elements that pose a serious threat, if sufficient quantities were used for RDDs:

1. Americium-241—an alpha and gamma ray emitter with a half-life of 432.7 years, used in smoke detectors and in devices that find oil sources, to detect petroleum deposits, to calibrate instruments, in industrial gauges, distance-sensing devices, and medical diagnostics
2. Californium-252—an alpha and strong neutron emitter with a half-life of 2.65 years, used to detect oil deposits
3. Cesium-137—a gamma ray emitter with a half-life of thirty years, used in moisture-density, leveling, thickness gauges, and well-logging in the drilling industry. It is also used to treat diseases, sterilize food and medical equipment, and detect oil deposits
4. Cobalt-60—a beta and strong gamma ray emitter with a half-life of 5.27 years, used in industrial gauges and radiography, to treat diseases and cancer, to sterilize spices, food, and medical equipment, and to detect hidden flaws in structures
5. Iridium-192—a beta and gamma ray emitter with a half-life of 73.8 days, used to detect hidden flaws in structures, metal parts, pipes and welds, and for treatment of diseases
6. Plutonium-238—an alpha ray emitter with a half-life of eighty-eight years, used to generate low-levels of power for devices that must function without direct maintenance for timescales approximating a human

lifetime in spacecraft and interplanetary probes, and to power artificial heart pacemakers

7. Strontium-90—a beta ray emitter with a half-life of twenty-nine years, used to generate low-levels of nuclear power supplies for use in remote locations, weather stations, and space vehicles, navigational beacons, electron TV-tubes, in industrial thickness gauges, and for treatment of eye disease

8. Radium-226—an alpha and gamma ray emitter with a half-life of 1,600 years, used in industrial gauges, luminescent paints and dials, tips of lightning rods, radiography devices, and to produce radon for cancer treatment

What makes these elements especially proliferation-prone is their combination of radioactivity levels and relative prevalence.[29] Because of their level of radioactivity, and relative facility in handling and manipulating, the weapons of choice may be Strontium-90, Cobalt-60, and Cesium-137.

The Threats from Radiological Terrorism

Radiological terrorism is a more attractive option than nuclear terrorism because of the relative ease with which either a radiological weapon can be made and used or an already existing nuclear facility can be attacked. Of the two types of radiological terrorism, use of an RDD or a dirty bomb can be considered easier than attacking a nuclear facility. Successfully causing a large release of radiation through a terrorist attack on a nuclear power plant requires knowledge of the plant's physical design and layout, security measures, and weaknesses. It also demands either accurately attacking and damaging the core of the nuclear reactor or causing a sustained loss of coolant to the core, which is usually heavily shielded and protected by automatic shutdown functions and emergency cooling systems. The containment structures and the reactor design for modern commercial nuclear power plants make a deadly radiation release through sabotage or attack exceedingly difficult to produce. Thus, terrorists may find it easier to gain access to radioactive materials in order to build a dirty bomb.

Due to their inherent features and demonstration effects, dirty bombs may prove to be a more reliable, tempting, and prestigious option than chemical and crude biological weapons. The first terrorist use of a radio-logical device might set a dangerous precedent, particularly because they would be able to capitalize on the psychological impact stemming from the fear of radiation among the general population. A radiological attack would likely result in mass panic, perhaps some human deaths and injuries, extensive physical and economic damage, and a great deal of attention for the terrorists themselves. Theoretically, this outcome might be considered ideal for groups that seek publicity for their name and cause without causing widespread devastation. Evidence uncovered in Afghanistan in January 2003 has led the British authorities to believe that al Qaeda already possesses a dirty bomb, although the weapon has not yet been used.[30] On September 28, 2006, an audio statement was released by al Qaeda leader in Iraq, Abu Hamza al-Muhajer, who called for scientists to join his group's efforts against United States and coalition forces in Iraq, advising them that the large U.S. bases there are good places to "test your unconventional weapons, whether chemical or 'dirty' as they call them."[31]

Not all nuclear materials are equally useable. Highly enriched uranium and plutonium may be suitable for direct use in an improvised nuclear explosive device with little or no additional processing. Nuclear material in the form of low enriched uranium, depleted uranium, natural uranium, and thorium requires extensive, technically complex processing to be used in a device that would be intended to slowly expose as many people as possible to the radiation. By its very nature, this kind of RDD will not generate immediate terror, panic, or the type of media coverage coveted by most terrorists. Therefore, terrorists more likely may opt for a dirty bomb. The opposite of a surreptitious device, a dirty bomb is intended to immediately cause panic and mass hysteria.

Generally, a dirty bomb that uses a large quantity of highly dangerous radioactive material such as Plutonium-238 or Cesium-137 will produce more contamination than a device that uses less material or material that is less radioactive. However, the most highly radioactive materials are the hardest to obtain, the most difficult to work with, and so dangerous that even suicide bombers would die before they could use one if they were not properly shielded.[32] There are many more common, less dangerous materials that would be easier to obtain and work with. Radioactive sources are used in medical, industrial, agricultural, petroleum survey, and research applications. They can be found in hospitals, medical, industrial facilities, food irradiation facilities, universities, and even homes. However, not all of these sources would be suitable for use in a RDD. Many are far too weak to cause extensive damage. Furthermore, many radioactive sources are in metallic form, thus would not be dispersed very effectively by high explosives.

Nonetheless, the ubiquity of radiological materials and the crude requirements for detonating such a device suggest a high likelihood of use, even if the technical feasibility is not trivial. It requires advanced knowledge and planning, a very targeted approach, and some expenditure. The impact would be great if the radiological device in question released the enormous amounts of radioactive material found in a single nuclear reactor fuel rod. But it would be quite difficult and dangerous for anyone to attempt to obtain and ship such a rod without death or detection. It is the portability of certain types of radioactive sources that enhances the attractiveness of radiological terrorism. Radioactive sources differ greatly in size and level of radiation. Some sources may be relatively big and bulky because of the layers of shielding surrounding the radioactive material. The difficulty in moving these around may make them less attractive to terrorists. Other sources, however, are small enough to be even carried by hand. Radioactive Cobalt "pencils" from a food irradiation plant are about 25 millimeters in diameter and 25 millimeters long with hundreds of such pieces often being found in the same facility. Some Cobalt rods may contain 10,000 curies.

Different scenarios for employments are possible. Terrorists could engage RDDs as an enclosed radiation source, to contaminate food, to irradiate drinking water, as a dirty bomb, or as aerosols. Thus, a strong gamma-emitting source could be hidden in high-profile areas, such as densely populated urban sites or government facilities, which could expose a large number of people to intense radioactivity over a shorter or longer period of time. For the short time case, it is unlikely that people would suffer an acute radiation syndrome. However, on discovery, panic reactions may be expected among all persons who have spent time close to the radiation. In the longer time case, persons could suffer from acute radiation syndrome and could even die as a consequence of the irradiation, but the number of victims of such an attack would be limited.[33]

Food or beverages could be contaminated by adding radioactive substances—for example in production plants—at distribution centers, during transport, or at the retail shop. The main danger in this case is internal contamination of the consumer. Even a selective and weak contamination of only a small number of items would have a considerable effect on the public, cause panic, and greater economic damage. An alternative option would be the contamination of drinking water by addition of soluble radioactive substances in the water supply and distribution system of larger cities, which would also have a considerable effect on the public. However, because of the high dilution of soluble radioactive substances in large amounts of water, this may not result in highly dangerous contamination for the consumer. Nonetheless, the low tolerance values for drinking water may well be exceeded and require costly mitigation and cleaning measures.

The detonation of a dirty bomb in a densely populated or industrial area would produce both local and extensive contamination. Terrorists can place explosive RDDs in parcels and luggage of various types, which can be triggered either with an internal mechanism such as a timer or remotely through a cell phone connection or similar technique. Such devices can vary greatly in size, ranging from birdcages to much larger luggage left on subways, or vehicles, such as cars, taxis, or trucks at places where people congregate. The degree of sophistication depends on the ingenuity of the designer, the tools, and the materials available. Since a dirty bomb is intended to cause a panic, the explosion of such a device in a heavily populated urban area could very well result in a panic that could kill more people than the IED or the radiation it disperses. Moreover, the radiological effects of a dirty bomb will be larger than the killing radius of the IED itself and will persist for far longer. While the radiation level may not be strong enough to affect people who are exposed briefly in the initial explosion, the radiation will persist in the contaminated area and the cumulative effects of such radiation could prove very hazardous. Due to this contamination, it will be necessary to evacuate people from the contaminated area in many, if not most, cases involving a dirty bomb. People will need to stay out of the area until it can be decontaminated, a process that can be lengthy and very expensive.

With suitable technical equipment, an easily respirable aerosol can be produced. The introduction of aerosol into air intakes or air conditioning systems, or its dissemination with crop dusters or sprayers from the top of elevated buildings, or even the spraying of a solution of radionuclide in a major building, would result in breathing contaminated air by the people. In addition, the deposition of aerosols would cause a contamination both of the people and of the ground surface or the floor of a building. Such an attack may give rise to fears of cancer for the people involved and lead to closure of the area for the time required for decontamination, causing subsequent economic loss and high decontamination costs.

Part II: Reforming the Security Sector

7

Preparing the Security Sector for the Preeminent Threats

WMD and their proliferation, terrorism, and transnational organized crime are the preeminent security challenges confronting the world—the fulcrum of evil. A handful of states are continuing to develop WMD in defiance of international rules and norms. Proliferation activities have become more sophisticated, assisted by opportunities created by globalization, increased availability of WMD-related materials, and know-how. As technology is more accessible, society has become more vulnerable. And more elaborate international networks have developed among organized crime, drug traffickers, arms dealers, and money launderers: the necessary infrastructure for catastrophic terrorism. Several terrorist groups have made no secret of their ambitions to acquire WMD. Practically unchallengeable Western military superiority on the conventional battlefield pushes the new adversaries toward unconventional, mostly asymmetric, alternatives. Meeting these preeminent challenges of today's threats means getting serious about prevention of proliferation, terrorism, and organized crime. The consequences of allowing these latent threats to become manifest, or of allowing the existing threats to spread, are simply too severe.

Preventing the spread and use of nuclear, chemical, biological, and radiological weapons is essential for creating a more secure world. This requires doing better at reducing demand for these weapons, their means of delivery, and curbing the supply of weapons materials and know-how. For states, it means living up to the treaty commitments existing, including for negotiations towards disarmament. It also means enforcing international agreements.

Terrorism is a threat to all states. New aspects of the threat—including the rise of global terrorist networks that recognize no restraints, and the potential for terrorist use of nuclear, chemical, biological, and radiological weapons—require new responses. As of yet, not all has been done that can be done. Foremost, an internationally agreed upon strategy of counterterrorism is needed that is respectful of human rights and the rule of law and can reverse the trend to radicalization. Such a strategy must encompass coercive measures when necessary, and create new tools to help states combat the threat domestically.

The spread of transnational organized crime increases the risks of proliferation and catastrophic terrorism. Terrorists use internationally organized criminal groups to move money, men, and materials around the globe. The corruption practiced by organized crime weakens the states' capacity to establish the rule of law. Combating organized crime is thus essential for helping states to build the capacity to exercise their sovereign responsibilities in countering proliferation and terrorism.

The UN Charter provides a clear framework for the use of force. States have an inherent right to self-defense, enshrined in Article 51. Long-established customary international law makes it clear that states can take military action as long as the threatened attack is imminent, no other means would deflect it, and the action is proportionate. The UNSC has the authority to act preventively, but has rarely done so. It may well need to be prepared to be more proactive in the future, taking decisive action earlier.

The United Nations, the United States, the EU, NATO, and the Group of Eight (G8) all have developed systems to prevent the proliferation of WMD and for fighting transnational terrorism. But in the end it is the nation-state that has primary competence for contributing to nonproliferation and countering terrorism. Each state has developed its own legal framework and internal organization to comply with its international obligations. As a result, numerous differences in the national efforts exist that weaken the overall international ability to prevent proliferation of WMD and to fight transnational terrorism more efficiently. To eliminate these differences and bring individual states better in line with the aims set by the international community, governments have to review and reorganize their national efforts to prevent proliferation and counter terrorism in the most comprehensive way.

National security measures play a vital role in a nation's response to the threat posed by the proliferation of WMD and the risk they may be acquired by terrorists. Responding to the risk of illegal or unauthorized access and use of sensitive materials requires an inventive, flexible, and sustainable long-term approach. In all these issues, there is a delicate balancing act between sufficient security and the commitment to civil liberties and human rights; between legitimacy, proportionality, and effectiveness; and between the interests of legitimate users of sensitive goods, and the risk that these goods may be diverted to illicit uses.

In order to be optimally prepared and organized to counter the preeminent threats posed by the unholy trinity of proliferation of WMD, terrorism, and organized crime, a state must have:

- A centralized national security decision making structure able to consolidate and coordinate the various aspects of decision-making, and to master crisis management
- The most effective intelligence services as the first line of defense
- Updated national legislation that fulfils the obligations contained in the international conventions to counter proliferation and terrorism ratified by the state, details offenses in effectively enforceable penal law, and establishes appropriate penalties for all activities banned by the conventions
- Clearly defined National Interests, an adequate National Security Policy, and a sound National Security Strategy that find acceptance and support of the majority of the population and by the international community
- A comprehensively reformed, fully accountable, well coordinated and led, inter-operable, modern security sector that is well prepared and ready to cope with all major contingencies
- A layered, in-depth homeland defense providing adequate protection of the critical national infrastructure and the population with a sufficient emergency preparedness and response potential that can also cope with all health aspects that may result from the preeminent threats
- Enhanced foreign, intergovernmental, and interagency collaboration with a vastly improved information exchange

Most important of all, the national contribution to building a more secure world requires strong national leadership; national resources that are equal to the scale of the strategic challenges ahead; a sophisticated public information policy that does not feed the population's insecurities; full cooperation and coordinated input from all ministries, government agencies, regional and local authorities and their agencies, as well as from the private sector, where these are essential and relevant for countering the preeminent threats.

What follows is an exploration of these aspects and the role they play in preparing and organizing a state to counter the preeminent threats.

8
Centralizing National Security Decision Making

Today, the old strategic approach of risk avoidance, which, until the end of the last century, served states fairly well to ensure national security against predictable state adversaries, is not only no longer financially affordable but it is also no longer adequate against the threats posed by a growing number of less predictable non-state actors. Budgetary constraints and new threats forced states to move from prevention of the known to management of the unknown—from *risk avoidance* to *risk management.* Hence, old concepts of threat analysis have been supplemented by *risk analysis* and *vulnerability analysis,* which means that resources for ensuring national security are now allocated on the basis of the threats and national vulnerabilities—alternatively viewed as likelihood and consequences.[1]

States' vulnerabilities are infinite and states cannot protect every place all the time. As such, decision makers need to prioritize their policy goals and allocate the finite resources efficiently. Before this can happen, the critical step of determining the risks arising from threats and vulnerabilities must be taken. The determined risks will then form the basis for subsequent decision making.

A risk-based approach can enhance strategic early warning. Risk-based techniques like "event trees" and "fault trees" can be used to identify the possible and plausible scenarios based on threats, vulnerabilities, and possible consequences. Subsequently, risks associated with the scenarios can be determined. With these as filters, probabilistic models will help to extract relevant data from large databases. Bayesian network models then can postulate the different conditional probabilities of different scenarios while simulation tools enable analysis of "what if" scenarios. These analyses can be made more rigorous with qualitative techniques like wargaming and "red teaming." Consequently, an effective intelligence cycle can be formed because once the possible scenarios are identified, resources can be allocated efficiently and effectively for intelligence collection, analysis, and anticipation. This forms the basis for dynamic and robust strategic early warning.

Strategic risk assessment and operational risk assessment must be differentiated. Strategic risk assessment seeks to identify the possible and plausible scenarios for risk monitoring. Operational risk assessment seeks to identify the risks associated with specific threats and vulnerabilities. The former provides the greater context for operational risk assessment to assess and act.

Prerequisite for a risk-and-vulnerability oriented approach in national security decision making is a systematic evaluation and assessment of all possible threats, incidents, and developments—including natural disasters, technological mishaps, ecological destabilization; cut-offs in the supply of energy, food, and strategic goods; economic meltdown, health system degradation, epidemics or pandemics, migration, political and social crisis, and the threats to internal security—that could seriously endanger the nation, the critical national infrastructures, and the livelihood of the population. All of them may be interlinked and thus call for a comprehensive approach to preparedness and response by the entire national security structure.

Achieving a Maximum of Synergies in the Provision of Security

Today, states must be able to act in a much more coherent and unified manner through a more comprehensive, better coordinated and synchronized engagement of all instruments of national security policy: foreign policy, economic policy and aid, the armed forces, law enforcement and internal security forces, the forces for homeland defense and critical national infrastructure protection, border guard and coast guard, custom authorities, visa and immigration services, the aviation, transportation, and health agencies, the institutions supervising financial transfers, and the emergency responders.

National security decision making has to be comprehensive because it requires participation and cooperation of several ministries, a wide range of institutions, organizations, and agencies at different levels—national, province or district, municipal, and private sector organizations—in essence for three major tasks:

1. Crisis management
2. The prevention of and defense against force of strategic magnitude
3. To overcome emergencies

In addition, it must be flexible because only the most appropriate combination of measures and resources should be employed based on real needs. Thus, the management of national security is the art and technique of integrating all actors and components of security and making them function in a coordinated, effective, and harmonious manner in times of normalcy and, in particular, in times of crisis and conflict. The objective of national security management is to achieve a maximum of synergies in the provision of security and to ensure the availability of options to expand capacities and assets should this be required. At the same time, it should allow avoidance of a costly permanent orientation towards the worst case.

The challenge is to ensure that the collective decision making of the government is based on the best-informed articulation of the threats faced and a strategic assessment of the relative merits of different approaches to how they might be addressed. Any attempt to deal with any type of security threat, challenge, or risk will use resources including intangible ones such as the support or acquiescence of the population—and the only fully rational resource strategy is one that identifies all the areas of related spending before setting priorities and, ideally, seeking synergies among them. For this, a comprehensive whole-of-government approach is required,[2] and a centralized structure is needed that can consolidate and coordinate various aspects of national security decision making. Well-run interdepartmental committees are very effective in coordination—including crisis management—and in producing policy options. Dedicated task forces under strong leadership and working directly for the president, prime minister, a senior minister, or a committee of cabinet members can produce high-quality outcomes. Such a centralized structure may be called on to implement policy, coordinate policy, or simply to assess and advise. Its role is always to bring the disparate parts of the security agenda together. Concomitantly, this structure can function as a crucial component of security sector transformation, both as a target and driver of change. Given the interdependence of security and economic factors, the way in which a country structures its national decision making can have a direct impact not only on what are traditionally seen as security concerns, but also on the broader, but not less crucial, socioeconomic development of a country.

In general, centralized national security decision making structures perform the following roles:

1. Ensuring joint assessments on which decision- and policymaking are based
2. Resource allocation for countering national security threats
3. Oversight of security sector institutions and organizations, procedures applied, and mechanisms used in the provision of national security
4. Setting priorities for national security planning, measures to be taken, and operations
5. Integration and coordination of the organs responsible for responding to emergencies, natural or otherwise

The post–Cold War evolution of the concept of national security management has identified other subcomponents that need equal attention for preserving national security and well being. These are disruption control management, disaster mitigation and management, and consequence and national resilience management—particularly since new measures taken to ensure national security now include implementing civil defense and emergency preparedness.

The Focal Point for National Security Issues

Many governments have established institutions that serve as a central point for national security issues, such as the NSC in the United States, India, Pakistan, South Africa, Israel, the Republic of Korea, and other countries; the Cabinet Office in the United Kingdom; and the Advisory Council on National Security in Canada. These serve a variety of specific functions while sharing a general effort to centralize senior-level government thinking about national security issues. The advisory, coordination, decision making, and implementation functions of an NSC-type structure are found in various combinations in different countries.

The United States NSC is arguably among the most powerful models for a NSC.[3] It is a statutory body in U.S. legislation and sanctioned by an act of Congress, which has oversight over national security issues. The NSC exists to advise the president on the integration of domestic, foreign, and military policies relating to national security; to manage and coordinate foreign and defense policies; and to reconcile diplomatic and military commitments and requirements. The NSC, located in the Office of the President, is chaired by the president. Its members include the secretaries of state, defense, and the treasury, the vice-president, the assistant to the president for national security affairs—the national security adviser—the chairman of the joint chiefs of staff as military adviser, and the director of national intelligence as intelligence adviser. Other individuals—such as the president's chief of staff—participate on an ad hoc basis. The NSC is a forum in which new policies can be initiated and shaped and the president, advisers and cabinet officials discuss domestic, foreign, and defense policies relating to national security.

The national security adviser plays two roles in the decision making process: as the president's adviser on national security matters and as the senior government official responsible for managing senior-level discussions of national security issues. The deputy national security adviser is responsible for crisis management on the part of the NSC. In these tasks, the adviser and his deputy are supported by the NSC staff that is comprised of political appointees, civil servants lent out by other agencies, and other personnel.

The NSC staff coordinates policy development and implementation in the executive departments and agencies but it does not engage in implementation; this is the role of the organizations whose leaders sit on the Council. The NSC staff provides advice to the president on national security issues, ensures that he has adequate information on which to make his decisions, and that policies, once decided upon, are implemented. The NSC structure ensures that most issues are regulated at lower levels of the bureaucracy, and that only those issues that require presidential attention on decision making reach the president.

There are three levels at which national policy is considered within the NSC:

1. That of the Principals Committee, the most senior interagency forum
2. The Deputies Committee, which is a senior sub-cabinet interagency forum that prescribes and reviews the work of interagency groups while ensuring that NSC issues have been properly analyzed and prepared for discussions
3. Policy coordination committees that represent a day-to-day forum for interagency coordination of national security policy while providing policy analysis for the senior committees

Strategic Decision Making

In essence, decision making on national security is strategic decision making. Strategic decisions are far-reaching and consequential for the state and involve the commitment of vast resources. They play out over longer time frames and may have significant opportunity costs. This is why strategic decisions should be made within the context of a long-term view—or vision—of both the desired end-states and potentially undesired end-states brought about by the contemplated courses of action. These can be differentiated by the intended and unintended second- and third-order effects of a strategic decision.

Strategic decisions often must be made under conditions of substantial uncertainty, particularly when complex national security objectives must be reformulated in the face of a dynamic, sometimes volatile, strategic environment. Initial assumptions about the environment and other players may be incorrect or incomplete. The range of factors relevant to complex decisions is seldom fully known to any one player in the decision process. The total range of possible effects—direct, second-, third- or even fourth-order—of a given national security decision may be so complex that even the most exacting search misses something. Nonetheless, effective strategic decision making also requires planned responses to second- and third-order effects.

The strategic decision making process must deal with four barriers:

1. Volatility due to the accelerating rate of change in the strategic environment
2. Uncertainty due to the unpredictability of the changes
3. Complexity because of the intricacy of key decision factors
4. Ambiguity due to the vagueness of the current situation and potential outcomes

Added to these problems is the difficulty of determining the validity of inputs to the decision making process. Many key events are ambiguous, especially when dealing cross-culturally, leading to differences in interpretation and contextual meaning. Such conditions foster biases, special interests, and tensions between institutional and organizational subcultures. There also is the dilemma of assumptions. Some assumptions taken as incontrovertible may turn out to be questionable. Thus, strategic leaders must know how to identify sound inputs embedded in a swamp of biased arguments. This task is made more difficult when inputs come from a wide variety of disciplines beyond the scope of any single executive. Moreover, many strategic decisions must be made in crisis situations or under other stressful conditions.

Strategic decisions often emerge from arenas of strong partisan competition for resources. The national political arena is intended to foster debate about the allocation of resources for the national good. Partisan competition for resources reflects the advocacy positions of the major parties as they represent their constituencies; their positions are represented in an adversarial manner. The bargaining often takes the form of positional negotiating rather than in a process of searching for common goals and pathways acceptable to all constituencies. This is why the decision making process must ensure that all competing views are heard and that priorities among them are sorted out. More importantly, the process must ensure some reasonable level of agreement or consensus about the intended end-state and a commitment to the course of action. Without agreement on goals, the collective effort will always suffer.

The decision making process at the national level is similar to that at lower levels, but there are important differences:

1. Most decisions are shaped and made by small groups involving diverse personalities, ideologies, and organizations.
2. Negotiation and compromise are the norm because of the small-group process.
3. Decisions are rarely final; rather, the dynamic environment requires continuous reassessment and re-adaptation.
4. The large amount of relevant data from diverse disciplines at the national level necessitates the use of sophisticated techniques to integrate quantitative and qualitative factors in a manner not found in lower levels of decision making.

Some of the skills effective for decision making at the operational level are also needed for national security decision making. Sound judgment, analytical abilities, and a systematic approach to problem solving are among the critical prerequisites.

The challenge to strategic leadership is twofold: a frame of reference, or perspective, that is dynamic enough for the decision maker to recognize, understand, and explain to others; and a leader's mastery of decision tools and processes that enable him to bring a broader set of perspectives than just his own into the decision making process.

The Strata of Leadership to National Decision-Making

There are three broadly defined strata of leadership to decision making at the national level:

1. The level of the top leadership, which is strategic
2. The mid-levels, which are organizational
3. The lower levels, which are production or action oriented

Relatively inexperienced leaders at the lower levels are responsible for getting things done. They generally have little latitude in the decisions they make, procedures they use, and the degree of innovation they can employ. They may improvise, but rarely can they innovate because consistency of national action is important at that level.

The mid-levels are responsible for setting mid-term goals and directions, and developing the plans, procedures, and processes used by the lower levels. Plans, procedures, and specified processes are major tools for the *coordination* of the efforts, particularly in larger institutions and organizations with many independent parts that must act in a coordinated way. They are also responsible for prioritizing missions and allocating resources to tailor capability at the lower levels. This includes supervising resource allocation plans that implement concepts developed at higher levels.

Top-level leaders are responsible for the strategic direction of the national security effort within the broad context of an increasingly global strategic environment. This implies broad scale and scope and a mode of forward vision extending over a longer time span. Thus, strategic leadership and decision making is a process by which those responsible for national security set long-term directions and obtain, through consensus building, the support of constituencies necessary for the commitment of resources to national security.

Lucid analysis of threats, dangers, risks, vulnerabilities, opportunities, and chances is the starting point of effective national security decision making, implementation, and coordination of the national effort. More importantly, it is the prerequisite for successful crisis management.

Crisis Management

The classical mechanisms of response to a crisis focused on clearly separated roles of the individual elements of the national security apparatus. Thus, international crises were usually met by the combined use of military and diplomatic means, assisted by intelligence services, while internal crises were managed by domestic law enforcement agencies and the civil emergency system, involving the local and, if required, national civil administration.

This separation of roles is no longer tenable. The new threats bring about the prospects of a crisis to which the response, if it is to be effective, must be organized on a much wider front, drawing on many or all available institutions and forces. All must contribute in a comprehensively concerted effort, bearing directly or indirectly on the final result or end-state to be achieved.

Crisis prevention is cost prevention. This is particularly pertinent when it comes to fending off the preeminent threats. A culture of prevention, which deserves its name, is about warning and response. Crises demand fast and effective responses, particularly if terrorists and WMD are involved. Recent history offers no single tried and tested model for this. It is important to establish political will and authority early to drive this response. Clear understanding of the role and responsibility of all of those involved in the response is also critical. According to the classical norms of any strategy based on multi-factor, multi-agency, multi-force, across-the-board activity, such an approach presupposes common legal frameworks, availability of the full range of information about the threats and risks, broad dissemination of information in time-urgent fashion, uniform understanding of the intentions of the commanding authorities, readiness of various assets, and standardized training for various contingencies.

Joint management must ensure coordinated planning and preparation and operational command in case of use or deployment of the instruments of security policy. These instruments are closely interlinked and if even one of them is weak, national security as a whole will be correspondingly weakened. The resources of the organization of strategic decision making and leadership must have a modular structure with everyday incidents forming the basis. Resources must be coordinated and reinforced according to the type and severity of the threat or incident. Thus, roles, missions, responsibilities, and accountabilities have to be clearly defined. This can only be done properly if the processes needed for strategic decision making and leadership are determined and clearly defined. Only when these processes are determined and established can the decision be taken on the organization of decision making and leadership as well as the necessary supporting organs.

With the multiplication of new threats, crisis management must be prepared to deal with all possible contingencies and targeted against a vast range of possible perpetrators. Crisis management must be able to generate a massive surge in "response capabilities," must prepare all elements of the system for quick or instantaneous reaction, and must have the ability to respond in a measure commensurate to the threats and vulnerabilities. On top of this, it must respond with all organic and supportive elements commanded, controlled, and coordinated in a comprehensive and timely manner, ensuring both unity of command and unity of effort in usually messy and dramatic circumstances.

The key elements of importance in crisis management are the reality of the threat, the amount of time available, and the degree of surprise in a given situation. Decision making in a crisis situation depends substantially on the specific perception of the situation by the actors involved in the decision making process. If the actors are well prepared, the threat is well anticipated, and the bureaucratic, legal, and technical frameworks are ready for a wide spectrum of contingencies, the typical crisis situation is transformed into a more reflexive situation. In this case, reflexive decisions can be made based on expected circumstances.[4] In spite of time pressures and a lack of chances to consider major alternatives to an action, the flexibility exists for a proper adaptation of reaction and the decision can be made more rapidly.

As a host of different institutions and agencies must participate in crisis management, separated in their professional functions for decades, the comprehensive integration of effort and response is a very tall order. It requires time, concerted effort, and tangible resources to execute. The role of crisis management can no longer be confined to functions such as search and rescue, fire protection, sheltering, and supporting a local population. For a crisis and emergency management system to be at the forefront of any state's national security protection mechanism, the technical, organizational, and resource capacities of the existing systems need to be seriously augmented to be able to meet the new challenges. Moreover, politicians can no longer treat the task of crisis management as a secondary one from the point of view of state security, heretofore understood mainly as a matter of defense or law enforcement.

9
Transforming the Intelligence Services

Intelligence provided by the nation's intelligence community is of fundamental importance to a government's understanding of WMD programs, proliferation, and procurement activities, as well as of intentions, plans, and activities of terrorist networks and the support these may receive from organized crime groups. A strong intelligence capability is essential for the development of whole-of-government policies and strategies for countering the proliferation of WMD, terrorism, and organized crime, and to understand and respond to the evolving threats.

The track record of the capabilities of intelligence services to detect, locate, identify, evaluate, and counter the proliferation activities of WMD is not an impressive one.[1] The U.S. experience in combating proliferation in the 1990s and beyond highlights the challenges inherent in efforts to accurately assess proliferation. The flawed assessments of Iraq's weapons systems by the U.S., UK, and Australian intelligence communities—and the Bush administration's decision to go to war in part based on those assessments—illustrate the political and policy challenges of combating the proliferation of WMD. However, cogent and insightful assessments of state and non-state actor WMD capabilities are a daunting task for intelligence services. Credibly assessing the dynamic and evolutionary WMD problem is further compounded by active deception and denial measures, the spread of dual-use technologies, growing indigenization of production for many proliferators, the introduction of new technologies, more secure communication modes—fiber optics, Internet, and laser—that further complicate the collection process, and the analytic challenges inherent in discovering alternative weapon system acquisition pathways or production processes. Together, these developments reduce the intelligence collection window, and increase the margin of error for WMD-related threat assessments.

The proliferation enterprise is neither static nor straightforward but dynamic and all too often ambiguous. Predicated on disparate facts that require key analytic judgments relating to the intentions and capabilities of proliferants, it is a complex and difficult intelligence challenge. Accurately interpreting the range of political, technological, and other developments that affect the evolving WMD threat requires both a range of new collection techniques and multiple analytic methodologies. These, in turn, presuppose sufficient resources allocated for the task, an appropriately trained workforce, and an attentive consumer community.

Thus, the government has to expand the nation's intelligence capabilities to enhance the provision of specialist and technical advice on WMD, global proliferation developments, terrorism, and illicit activities of organized crime groups. Among other outcomes: an expanded intelligence capability will improve warning, the implementation and enforcement of the nation's export licensing and control system, precautionary measures to ensure security and safety of sensitive sites, and interdiction and interruption of illicit activities.

With new dynamics and vulnerabilities at play, state leadership has become more complicated. Governments must understand these better in order to respond to them. Often options available will depend upon how early problems are identified. Choosing the right option, in turn, will depend on knowing what the consequences are apt to be. Once a course of action is chosen, it becomes imperative to know what the effects of the decision have been, so that any necessary adjustments can be made. In every instance making the right choice will hinge on the quality and timeliness of the intelligence available. Hence, informed decision and policy making require good intelligence, assessments, and warning. Good intelligence does not guarantee good policy, but poor intelligence likely leads to bad policy.

But What is Intelligence?

Definitions abound[2] but are more often obfuscating rather than clarifying. In general usage, intelligence denotes five things:

- A particular knowledge—the knowledge of the hidden and foreknowledge of the unpredictable, and the knowledge that meets the stated or understood needs of decision and policy makers relevant to a government's formulating and implementing policy to further its national interests as well as deal with dangers and threats from actual or potential adversaries.

- The type of organization producing that knowledge—the functional structures that exist to undertake intelligence activities and the production of intelligence and knowledge. There are four different but frequently overlapping types of intelligence—foreign or external, domestic or internal, defense or military, and, in some countries, criminal intelligence.
- The activities pursued by such organizations—generally, the activities of all intelligence services fall into three categories of basic functions: collection, analysis, and counterintelligence. In addition, some states may have a need for covert action, which is a more occasional fourth function, usually performed by foreign or external intelligence services.
- The process guiding these activities—the process by which government and the military leadership request intelligence needed and by which intelligence services respond to these needs in a sequence of six steps: planning and direction, collection, processing, analysis and production, dissemination of intelligence products, and feedback.
- The product resulting from these activities and processes—ranging from warning and situation reports, briefings, assessments, and estimates to analyses in the most usable form: a tailored output that meets the specific user needs and persuades through analytic tradecraft of a trail of evidences, assumptions, conclusions and, where needed, implications for the state.

What is the Purpose of Intelligence Services?

The purpose of intelligence is to inform government—telling truth unto power. Intelligence produces the particular knowledge that a state must possess regarding the strategic environment, other states, and hostile non-state actors to assure itself that its cause will not suffer nor its undertakings fail because its statesmen, agencies, and soldiers plan, decide, and act in ignorance. Intelligence is production of unbiased information about risks, dangers, and threats to the national vision. The more accurate and timely the intelligence, the more it will allow for limited resources to be applied efficiently towards national security goals.

The fact that states and hostile non-state actors seek to hide intentions, capabilities, plans, and other information from other states and actors and engage in disinformation, denial, deception, subversion, and other clandestine activities creates a need for a national organization with secret or covert capacities, capable to be tasked to discover what is kept secret or hidden, and to collect information which cannot be acquired better, more safely, or more cheaply by any other organization or means.

In addition to intelligence collection, intelligence services exist to:

- Ensure early warning—intelligence must at all times help prevent the government, the nation, and its armed forces from falling victim to strategic surprise by being able to warn of impending crises and by detecting possible surprises, risks, dangers, threats, or attacks in advance.
- Provide long-term expertise—transcending the exclusive competence of other governmental entities in areas relevant for national security by providing the knowledge about probable developments in the strategic environment and foreign capabilities in order to periodically review and adapt the definition of national interests, the national security policy, national security strategy, and the national defense strategy.
- Support the national decision and policy making process—for a government, intelligence is critical for deciding what has to be done and determining which of several options, steps, and measures may be most effective in achieving national security and foreign policy objectives in order to ensure the security of the society and the freedom of its citizens.
- Support national and international crisis management—where intelligence's most important contributions are determining the intentions of actual or potential opponents, and determining the risks for violent change, threats of it, and instabilities, as well as situations in which these figure, along with all means and methods of conflict, the capabilities they provide, and their scope for development.
- Support national defense and, in case of conflict or war, military operations—intelligence is the prerequisite for comprehensive defense planning and organization, and as a guide for defense research and development (R&D), and the procurement of weapons and equipment. Superior intelligence support is the *conditio sine qua non*—without it there can be nothing—and particularly critical for achieving decision dominance and success in conflict and war.
- Assist good governance—by providing honest, critical intelligence that highlights national vulnerabilities as well as the weaknesses and

errors of government. Objective analysis has the potential to debunk a policy maker's preconceptions and reveal how his preferred policy fails. Intelligence services should tell government what they ought to know and certainly not only what they want to know.

- Maintain and protect secrets—the lifeblood of intelligence. The basic conundrum for intelligence lies in its requirement for secrecy to be effective. Intelligence services cannot disclose their sources, methods, means, intentions, knowledge, plans, budgets, or the identity of the collaborators of the service and their activities to the public without disclosing them to their targets at the same time.

What are the Activities of Intelligence Services?

All intelligence services normally have three basic functions: collection, analysis, and counterintelligence. Covert action, the occasional fourth function, may be performed by external intelligence services.

Collection is the bedrock of intelligence: the acquisition of data and information that forms the basis for refined intelligence and knowledge creation. Without collection, intelligence is little more than guesswork. The collection process involves open sources as well as clandestine and secret sources such as spies, agents, and defectors who provide information that is obtainable in no other way; It also involves a number of secret technical collection disciplines using a variety of collection methods and means.

Analysis is the collation, evaluation, and analysis of data and all-source information and their transformation into intelligence products. If collection is dominated by smart technology, analyses and assessments still reflect the perspicacity of human minds. No amount of data can substitute for an insightful analyst able to discern the critical policy or operational significance of an event, action, or trend that may be hidden within a mass of confusing and contradictory information. While analysts must prove their capability to connect the dots, the overarching goal of analysis is to minimize the uncertainty with which policy makers must grapple in making decisions about national security and foreign policy. Furthermore, analysis must help to make sense of complex issues and to call attention to emerging problems or threats to national interests. The importance thereby is not only to determine what is accurate but also what is most relevant to the policy maker's needs.

Counterintelligence is the national effort to prevent foreign intelligence services and foreign-controlled political movements or groups from infiltrating the state's institutions at home and abroad in order to engage in espionage, subversion, and sabotage. Straddling the foreign and domestic boundaries, counterintelligence consists of offensive and defensive measures of protection. Defensive measures are taken through inquiries and vetting of civil servants and employees through investigations, monitoring of known or suspected agents, and surveillance activities to detect and neutralize the presence of foreign intelligence services. Offensive measures are taken through the collation of information about foreign intelligence services and their modus operandi, recruiting agents, and initiating operations to penetrate, disrupt, deceive, and manipulate these services and related organizations to one's own advantages. Counterintelligence is, moreover, an integral part of the entire intelligence process. It has to ensure that what is collected is genuine through continuous evaluation of sources and information. It differs from intelligence collection in that it exists to counter a threat and is reactive. Results are not generally produced in the short term and counterintelligence investigations cannot be limited to arbitrary time periods.

Covert action are activities to influence political, military, or economic conditions, situations, and developments abroad where it is intended that the role of the government will not be apparent or acknowledged publicly. These may consist of propaganda measures, support to political or military factions within a specific country, technical and logistical assistance to foreign governments to deal with problems within their countries, or actions to disrupt illicit activities that threaten the own national interests or security such as terrorism, organized crime, and narcotics trafficking. Covert action is an option short of military action to achieve objectives that diplomacy and other means of security policy alone cannot.

How is Intelligence Produced?

Intelligence is produced in a process by which government, the military leadership, and other agencies or customers request the intelligence needed. Intelligence services respond to these needs in the six steps of activities of the intelligence cycle: planning and direction, collection, processing, analysis and production, dissemination of finished intelligence products, and evaluation and feedback.

Planning and direction involves the management of the entire intelligence production effort including: the requests or requirements   for intelligence on subjects based on the needs of decision and policy makers; the identification of the need for data that is derived from the threat assessment or the priority listing of unsolved strategy and policy issues; deciding which states or non-state actors warrant intelligence surveillance and collection and in which priority; and the delivery of an intelligence product to the customer.

Collection is the procurement of data and information pertinent to decision and policy makers, the military leadership, and other agencies or intelligence customers. Collection management systems of a variety of methods and means are used in the following intelligence collection disciplines:

- Open source intelligence (OSINT)—the assembling of all openly available data and information from the Web, Internet search and conversations, radio, television, and printed news sources, magazines, periodicals, grey literature, studies, books, unclassified diplomatic and attaché reporting, as well as forecasts from businessmen, think tanks, universities, travelers, etc.

- Human intelligence (HUMINT)—information collected by humans: from spies, agents, insiders or informers; or gleaned from defectors, turncoats, "walk-ins," diplomats, businessmen, and travelers; or gained by debriefings, interrogation, and from discussions with foreign personnel; or from reports of counterintelligence operations, etc.

- Signals intelligence (SIGINT)—data and information collected through intercepts, monitoring, and localizing of radio, microwave, radar, and other electromagnetic emission, gathered by ground sites, ships, submarines, aircraft, RPVs and UAVs, or satellites, all generally recording and telling what has happened. SIGINT can provide data on intentions, plans, organization, activities or events related to the preeminent threats as well as on the characteristics of materials and weapon systems. SIGINT has five subsets of collection disciplines:

  1. Communications intelligence (COMINT)—data and information collected through communications intercepts, direction finding, traffic analysis, and monitoring of the changes in volume, pattern and other characteristics of communications like burst, frequency hopping, spread spectrum, etc.

2. Electronic intelligence (ELINT)—electromagnetic pickup and signals monitoring of electronic emissions of events, activities, relationships, frequency of occurrence, modes, sequences, patterns, signatures and content; or intercepts of emissions from tracking, radar, and weapons systems for gauging their capabilities, such as range and frequencies on which they operate.

3. Foreign instrumentation signals intelligence (FISINT)—the pickup and monitoring of data relayed by weapons, beacons, video links, etc. Non-imaging radar can detect and track missile launches and gather data on missile characteristics. One category is telemetry intelligence (TELINT)—data obtained from intercepting the signals transmitted during missile tests. Interception of those signals makes it possible for analysts to determine many of the capabilities of foreign missile systems, including the number of warheads carried, payload and range, warhead accuracy, and warhead size, which often is needed to estimate yield.

4. Cryptology intelligence (CRYPINT)—code-breaking and decryption of ciphered messages, which requires supercomputers and mathematicians.

5. Computer network exploitation (CNE)—data and information collected from network and traffic analysis by monitoring mail and intercepting messages, computer intrusion, and penetration of databanks.

■ Imagery intelligence (IMINT)—data and information collected via photography (PHOTINT), film, video, high-definition TV, and radar by satellites, aircraft, RPVs and UAVs, ships, terrestrial imagery, satellite signals, and data streams received and reconstructed as images from reflections of several bands, including infrared, ultraviolet, electronic, and other image-capturing technologies,[3] all more often recording and telling what may happen. IMINT is used to find NBC facilities, terrorist training camps, transports and other movement, missile sites, weapon arsenals, military deployments, etc.

■ Measurement and signatures intelligence[4] (MASINT)—is straddling both IMINT and SIGINT, using visible light, infrared, ultraviolet, multi- and hyperspectral data derived from spectral analysis of reflections from several bands across the spectrum of light as well as exploitation of physical or magnetic properties, emitted and reflected energy of radio frequencies, lasers, shockwaves, acoustics of mechanical sound, vibration, or motion, and materials sampling of soil, water, and air. MASINT offers not only means to detect capabilities and performance characteristics of missiles, space, aerial, and other military systems, but also for the detection of the presence of materials associated with WMD, related research, development, storage, or production.[5] Sensor systems range from multispectral (2–100 bands) to hyperspectral (100–1,000 bands) to ultraspectral (1,000 + bands), including visible light, infrared, ultraviolet, and radio wave segments of the electromagnetic spectrum, which allow detecting shape, material composition, density, temperature, brightness, movement, and chemical composition of objects.

Processing is the conversion of data and information collected into a more suitable form for analysis and production of intelligence, such as language translation, decryption, and rendering texts readable. Data and information not directly analyzed is tagged, sorted, and made available for rapid computer retrieval. Thus, processing also refers to sorting by subject matter as well as data reduction—interpretation of the information stored on film or tape through the use of highly refined photographic and electronic processes.

Analysis and production is the conversion of data and information into finished intelligence products. It includes the collation, correlation, integration, evaluation, and analysis of all available data and information, and its transformation into a variety of intelligence products. The data and information collected is frequently fragmentary and at times contradictory, requiring the human mind and specialists to give it meaning and significance. Thus, good analysis depends on assembling the best brains possible to evaluate events and conditions, drawing upon a blend of public knowledge and secrets purloined from adversaries. The subjects involved may concern intentions, current events and activities, capabilities and vulnerabilities, probable future developments, different regions and problems, and personalities in various contexts—political, geographic, economic, scientific, military, or biographic. Exercising collection management, analysis can draw on the collection disciplines to provide data and information for evaluation, and the tailoring of the products precisely for the users' needs.

Dissemination involves the handling and distribution of the finished intelligence product to the customer—the same decision or policy makers whose needs triggered the intelligence cycle. The product must have five essential characteristics for it to be useful: relevance, timeliness, accuracy, breadth, and purity—meaning that it is free of political spin, misinformation, disinformation, propaganda, deception, etc. The products should contain what is known—the facts; how it is known—the sources where possible; what drives the judgments—linchpin assumptions; the impact if the drivers change—alternative outcomes; and what remains unknown. The key issue for intelligence services is how to present the collected, processed, and analyzed information in a manner that meets the requirements of the customer—both in content and presentation—while ensuring that it highlights sufficiently the limitations of the intelligence to answer the questions.

Feedback expressing satisfaction or discontent and conveying new requirements for answers to new questions is what the customers must provide. The user of intelligence then ideally provides additional direction to the collectors and intelligence producers, who should, in turn, provide more and better intelligence. Feedback may also be used to guide new areas of inquiry, to identify gaps in information, and to adjust priorities or emphasis.

The Intelligence Process

The role of intelligence services in the making of national foreign and security policy is relatively straightforward: intelligence is designed to support national decision making by policy makers and operations at the operational and tactical level by the military and other organizations of the security sector. While an ideal type, the so-called intelligence cycle is at the core of this relationship. In this construct, policy makers first specify the range, importance, priority, and their issues of concern to the intelligence community. The intelligence services then collect the relevant data with their means of collection. The collection intake is then processed, exploited, and analyzed, and then assessments are produced and disseminated to the appropriate policy or operational consumers. Finally, analyses and assessments are reviewed by consumers who then provide feedback to the intelligence producers that lead to re-tasking of collection, new analyses, and estimates.

There are times when this "normal" intelligence process develops and works as here described. However, often it does not, though performance likely varies across the subject matter in question or the country covered, through different means of exploitation, and over time. In practice, requirements are often vague, ill-specified or poorly defined; collection proves infeasible or is unduly delayed; analyses are overtaken by events or perceived by consumers as unhelpful, inaccurate, or irrelevant; intelligence products disseminated compete for limited consumer attention; and feedback is inconsistent, infrequent, or nonexistent. Consumers view intelligence products as one of a number of sources of information to consider. They are often dissatisfied with what they perceive as inadequate or counterproductive analyses, sometimes confused or disturbed by the many different views presented by the different intelligence services on specific issues, and often disappointed by the net performance of intelligence.

On the other hand, intelligence producers are often dissatisfied with what they perceive as sparse, unclear, or contradictory guidance and feedback; unrealistic expectations and unwarranted criticism; the politicization or perceived misuse of intelligence; and the inattentiveness of, or cold-shoulder treatment by, policy makers, which marginalizes or excludes intelligence output from policy judgments. Intelligence producers either try to maintain a distant relationship with consumers in order to help prevent the corruption of intelligence, or they pursue a closer relationship in order to maximize the utility of intelligence. But striking an appropriate balance that both enhances the utility of intelligence products and maintains their integrity continues to be a difficult challenge. This is particularly true for the preeminent threats.

Intelligence is a valuable instrument and it can make an immense contribution to the success or failure of any political or military move. For that very reason, it is imperative for decision makers to be highly knowledgeable on the subject of intelligence. The relationship between those who collect and evaluate intelligence and those who use it in the preparation of state policy—the providers and the consumers—is of ever greater importance. Different countries with different needs inevitably conduct the relationship between their intelligence services and their governments differently. The prerequisite for effectiveness is that there is political guidance and policy maker direction of intelligence. The need for competent political guidance of intelligence services from the people they serve is the most important aspect of executive control of intelligence agencies.

Policy maker direction must be both the foundation and the catalyst for the work of intelligence. If intelligence services do not receive direction, the chances increase of resources being misdirected and wasted. Intelligence agencies need to know what information to collect and when it is needed. They need to know if their products are useful and how they might be improved to better serve decision and policy makers. Guidance must come from the very top. Hence, policy makers need to appreciate what intelligence can offer them to a much greater extent, and they need to become more directly involved in the ways in which intelligence capabilities are used. Top executive decision and policy makers only can provide the necessary guidance to intelligence services and make sound judgments on policy if they are well informed. Examples clearly show that political leaders whose understanding of intelligence predates their arrival in office are more likely to handle intelligence better than those who are introduced to it on their advancement.

As an arm of the government, all intelligence agencies must act according to the policies of the government of the day and in pursuit of objectives relevant to these policies. However, if policy and intelligence are too closely linked—such as when intelligence becomes policy-driven or when there is political interference in operational activities—intelligence services may become susceptible to being used by political actors as a tool to retain power or to discredit and undermine opponents. Thus, the misuse of intelligence services with their extraordinary powers by an elected government for its own political ends must be excluded. To this end, intelligence services should be at arms length from policy makers, should not be affiliated with any party, and must be neutral or depoliticized.

Management of Intelligence

Good intelligence management is dependent on the optimal mastering of the intelligence cycle. The ability to transform the services and improve the intelligence cycle through better integration and innovation is what will distinguish successful intelligence management in the future. This, with the aim to fuse and integrate all elements of the intelligence process, provides seamless support for decision and policy makers, military operations, and others with accurate, timely, and more actionable products that are tailored to fulfill their needs. Achieving this is ever more demanding in view of the following challenges:

- The tasks assigned to intelligence services have become more complex, more volatile, and more numerous.
- The need to serve a much broader range of government and other clients with a growing variety of requirements has expanded.
- The requirements for intelligence contributions to regional and inter-

national security; and for international, regional, interdepartmental, and local collaboration have greatly expanded.

- Expanding missions, requirements, and customers require improved coordination of the collection, analysis, production, and collaboration of the services and the dissemination of their contributions.

Adapting to the Changes that have Taken Place in the Subject Matter Intelligence Must Cover

The growth of transnational threats is new: the dark side of globalization having become one of the basic features of international relations. The main transnational forces shaping the world are:

1. Economic integration, financial, and trade liberalization and expansion, and interdependence of national economies
2. The growing speed and volume of information flows around the world
3. The rise of transnational organizations: international organizations, NGOs, multinational corporations, and media which are shaping the way people view the world.

Transnational threats largely result from the impact of these forces.

Globalization increases the interdependence of states and societies, resulting in new global divisions of labor, enhanced opportunities and demands for cooperation. This leads to higher overall efficiency and earnings. At the same time, globalization reduces the abilities of states and international organizations to act while enhancing the power of transnational actors such as business groups, NGOs, proliferators, and criminal or terrorist networks. Particularly the networks of the latter frequently have no public face and are far more difficult to address than nation-states.

Global competition creates winners and losers, leading to sharp asymmetries between different regions, countries, and social groups in economic, social, military, and ideological terms. Asymmetric interdependence provides the background for transnational threats, dangers, and risks. Often originating from outside a specific region and affecting the security and stability of states and population groups within other regions and countries, they have become a global phenomenon. Bred by conflicts, violence, impoverishment, radicalization, and other features of the globalization process, these threats are more complex, multidimensional, multifold interlinked, and long-term in nature, representing a category of problems that can be neither simply solved nor easily contained. States and international organization have yet to find viable answers to counter these dangers. Long-term strategies to address the root causes of these threats are mostly inexistent and very difficult to develop.

While importance and urgency of the threats of the traditional type pale compared to the new transnational threats, other topics that intelligence services have to cover have become quite different from those that concerned governments previously, such as destabilization, diminishing availability of resources, environmental degradation, economic, financial, demographic, migrational, and pandemic forces. The number and diversity of risks, dangers, and threats has dramatically changed for intelligence. All these topics may be successfully covered by traditional intelligence organizations.

Still remaining are some military threats and a few states with rogue governments, which promote destabilization in their strategic environment, produce WMD, provide safe havens for terrorists, and sponsor the assassination of their political opponents abroad. Moreover, there are the failing states provoking endemic conflict and mass migration, and likely to turn into prime breeding grounds for terrorism and organized crime. In addition, there are some multinational corporations, NGOs, violent groups opposed to international developments and events, new intelligence services, and—since nowadays it is fashionable to reject the bureaucratic state and to transfer its task to the private sector for the sake of efficiency and cost reductions—private military, security, and intelligence entities that might require monitoring. Most of these topics render the warning function more difficult for traditional intelligence services.

There are growing numbers of non-state entities and actors: international terrorist organizations; ideological, ethnic or religious extremists; mafias; and large criminal organizations that present serious threats to all societies. Extremists, proliferators, weapons and drug dealers, traffickers in human beings and organs, specialists in the laundering and recycling of dirty money, or in the clandestine disposal of noxious waste or polluting materials prosper by taking advantage of globalization, technological innovations, and the opening of borders, and skillfully exploiting the discrepancies between various national laws and judicial procedures. All these actors have made the problem of predicting what their next moves and targets are going to be many times more complicated. Hence, the missions of intelligence have greatly expanded, and at the same time the sets of tasks assigned to intelligence services have become more complex, volatile, and numerous.

Among all these threats, transnational terrorism, proliferation of WMD, and organized crime have become the preeminent security challenges confronting the world—the fulcrum of evil—and the new intelligence priorities. In essence, four characteristics distinguish these preeminent threats from the old conventional threats:

1. Clandestinity
2. Privatization of violence
3. Exploitation of asymmetry
4. Their transnational reach and impact

In particular, it is the conspiratorial clandestinity of unknown groups of non-state actors that make up the intelligence services to the central instrument of security of a state, because more than ever intelligence is the prerequisite for the prevention of and timely counteraction against these new threats. These threats emerge from ecologies of malevolence that stoke privatization of violence. And Western military superiority on the conventional battlefield pushes these new adversaries toward unconventional and asymmetric alternatives, which are emergent in form, networked and distributed, and adapt and evolve as states do by developing strategies to combat them. Unlike traditional threats to national security from rival nation-states, transnational threats are more difficult to anticipate, assess, and combat. Transnational reach, impact, and implications of clandestinely operating groups are making enhanced international cooperation and intelligence sharing mandatory for all intelligence services. Moreover, models of deterrence fail. The implication of transnational threats is that intelligence needs to combine specific geographic expertise with a global vision. Because of the geographic diversity of transnational threats, teams that combine functional expertise on particular threats with combinations of country and regional expertise will prove to be particularly valuable.

Growing Complexity of the Intelligence Environment

For the preeminent threats, the unstripping of secrets remains the primary function of intelligence. However, implicit in globalization is the growing complexity of the intelligence environment, which brought about two major changes for intelligence: There are more mysteries than puzzles to solve, and there is a growing divergence between the object and the subject of intelligence the services must cover in collection and analysis.

During the Cold War, intelligence services were mainly involved in puzzle solving—seeking answers to questions that had answers, even if these answers were unknown. There were few mysteries. Basically, puzzle solving is frustrated by a lack of information. Given the need to find out how many missiles the Soviet Union had, where they were located, their range and accuracy, and how many warheads they carried, the United States spent billions of dollars on satellites and other technical collection systems. But it made sense to approach the military strength of the USSR as a puzzle—the sum of its potential and quality. This also because puzzles are relatively stable: If a critical piece of information is missing one day, it usually remains valuable in the next weeks, months or even years. Collecting secrets was and still is crucial to solving puzzles in today's chaotic world.

The collapse of the Soviet Union and the rise of the preeminent threats changed that all. It upended intelligence services to the point that their major challenges now are more mysteries, which often grow out of too much information with clues buried in too much "noise" and too many scenarios. Treverton wittily describes the differences between puzzles and mysteries in the following way: Mysteries pose questions that have no definite answers because the answers are contingent, depending on a future interaction of many factors, known and unknown. A mystery cannot be answered; it can only be framed by identifying the critical factors and applying some sense of how they have interacted in the past and might interact in the future. Mystery solving is an attempt to define ambiguities. Their importance, though, warrants grappling with possible outcomes regardless. Mysteries differ from puzzles in that puzzles have already happened. The result has occurred, though it may not yet be known. Any opportunity for government to influence the outcome has been lost. By contrast, many of the most interesting mysteries are not only currently unknowable, but their eventual answer is intertwined with what the government does, or can do. Nowadays, governments often care most about events they hope to influence, or they hope to influence certain events because they care about them. For solving mysteries, information collected secretly may be helpful, but it is less critical as it was to solving puzzles during the Cold War when information was scarce. Now it is overwhelming. Solving puzzles is useful for detection while framing mysteries is necessary for prevention and counteraction.[6]

The nature of the preeminent threats of terrorism, proliferation, and organized crime are predominantly mysteries, not puzzles. These threats shape themselves to our vulnerabilities—the seams in our defenses. The threats they pose ultimately depend on us. Treating them as puzzles is like trying to solve the unsolvable—an impossible challenge. True, Iraq practiced denial and deception about its WMD, denied access to its WMD programs, and had "dual-use" factories built in that provided plausible cover stories, all of which caused tremendous problems to intelligence. But whether Iraq had nuclear or chemical weapons—stockpiled since 1991 and believed ready for dispersal to terrorists by Saddam Hussein at some point if the UN embargo of Iraq was not lifted—seemed a quintessential puzzle that U.S. intelligence treated that way, and got the answer wrong. Had it been treated as a mystery, it might have turned the exercise away from technical details, and toward Saddam's thinking, and questions like whether he was more afraid of his local enemies than of the United States, and whether this could lead him to boast that he had weapons he really did not have.[7]

The growing complexity of the intelligence environment also brought about a change in the quality of the object of intelligence collection and analysis. There were few qualitative differences between the subject and the object of intelligence collection and analysis during the Cold War. Nations and alliances spied against each other with comparable intelligence cultures. Non-state actors were at most niche faculties. Today, however, with ever more non-state actors engaged in potentially increasing symbiotic activities, there is growing divergence between the object and the subject of intelligence. Strategic motivation of terrorism is combining with tactical professionalism of organized crime, which, together with enhanced possibilities for proliferation, is opening qualitatively completely new threat dimensions. If states do not succeed in finding effective countermeasures, this unholy trinity of non-traditional threats could become the biggest threat since the Cold War with ever more divergent costs for attacker and defender. 9/11 cost the attackers 500,000 dollars. It created damage of hundreds of billions of dollars for the United States. If terrorists succeed in placing a nuclear weapon in a U.S. or European city, the damage could be apocalyptic.

Though the safeguards against nonproliferation are weaker today than fifteen years ago, intelligence coverage of proliferation is still somewhat easier than that of organized crime and transnational terrorism. Dominant is proliferation from state to state and from state to non-state actor. This is demonstrated in the case of Libya acquiring Semtex and passing it to the IRA, as well as in the case of Iran and Syria providing Hezbullah with the rockets it fired against Israel in the recent Lebanon conflict. Apart from the Abdul Qadeer Khan mafia network, there are very few confirmed cases of proliferation from non-state actor to state,[8] or from non-state actor to non-state actor. Hence, intelligence collection on proliferation may require less transformation of intelligence services as is the case with organized crime and terrorism. However, efforts are needed to more comprehensively integrate the disparate intelligence disciplines of analysis of weapons and proliferation and the monitoring of treaties, international organizations, and agencies engaged in proliferation issues while concomitantly striving to cooperate much more intimately with those engaged in the fight against terrorism and organized crime.

Organized crime has now reached a stage that is characterized by extreme adaptability to profit maximization, optimization of internal and external control, and optimal security. Organized crime is structurally moving ever further away from hierarchic-bureaucratic organizations to more decentralized forms. This fluid and fleeting characteristic handicaps intelligence bureaucracies in their efforts to get clear insights into activities and organization of organized crime. The quicker the subject of intelligence is changing the harder it is for conventional intelligence apparatuses to follow and adapt with the conventional priority setting system existing for collection.

Covering terrorism is even more difficult. The most important limits to collecting information about terrorism are inherent to the subject and the way terrorists operate. Those limits are permanent and ineradicable. Only very few of the conspirators know the intentions. Though they might get help from others, nothing is known about their plot by anyone they cannot absolutely trust. Plans are no longer communicated in a form that can be easily intercepted and interpreted. Terrorists do not expose to others any materials that would betray their intentions. They do not purchase, procure, or build anything that, on the face of it, is suspicious. They live and move inconspicuously, and any preparations that cannot be done behind closed doors they do as part of those movements. Moreover, the bull's eye of this intelligence target—an individual terrorist plot—lacks the size and signatures of most other targets. Compounding the problem is the fact that the conspirators may not have had any prior involvement in terrorism or be members of a previously known terrorist group. Thus, the target for intelligence is anyone who might commit terrorism in the future. Hence, terrorism is a fundamentally different and more difficult object than the great majority of other topics the intelligence community is asked to cover.

Intelligence collection in the past has been designed to confront other intelligence organizations, or to collect intelligence against organizations with similar hierarchical structures. Contemporary terrorist groups do not have such structures. For the new terrorists, it remains important to evade detection before committing atrocities that attack the critical national infrastructure and the labile psychological state of mind of post–modern Western societies. To this end, the structure of terrorist organizations in small groups of de-territorialized networks is the optimally adapted form, transforming terrorism into the more diffuse and amorphous phenomenon that it has now become. If hit, this adversary will adapt, regroup, generate new leadership, shift geographic locus, adjust tactics, and evolve into a new collection of cells and networks capable of self-healing, dispersal, reassembly, and innovation. Therefore, intelligence collection efforts have to be recast in order to more closely mirror the groups they are working against. Networks can only be fought effectively and flexibly with networks.[9]

The issue is not only networks. There are several aspects of organizing for transnational threats. Central intelligence bureaucracies impede operational effectiveness, especially in the areas of timeliness and their ability to discern the relative importance of the "fine grains" of intelligence data. In terms of organizational structure, it is necessary to mimic the threat: For fighting the unholy trinity, intelligence services need to move from center to cluster or "edge organizations," place less emphasis on directors and more on connectors and coaches, develop transnational partnerships, emphasize sharing rather than secrecy, develop more effective "red team" analysis through rule-free thinking and simulations, and become more adept at early warning based on environmental scanning and improved situational awareness.[10] Foremost, they need a deeper, more profound understanding of the threat and of the enemy. Furthermore, intelligence organizations need to develop more effective methods of organizational learning.

To create edge organizations that are responsive to the dimensions of complexity and the nuances of the targets requires moving power to the edge, that is: Changing the way individuals, organizations, and systems relate to and work with each other. It involves the empowerment of individuals where the organization interacts with its operating environment to have an impact or effect on that environment. Empowerment means expanding access to information and the elimination of unnecessary constraints. Edge organizations must have greatly enhanced peer-to-peer interactions and diminished significance of those whose role is to manage constraints and control measures. By removing barriers to information sharing, edge organizations can become highly inclusive, agile organizations. Agility requires that: available information be combined in new ways, a variety of perspectives are brought to bear, and the assets can be employed differently to meet the needs of a variety of situations. Integration of intelligence and operational information must occur as soon as possible at the lowest levels, which are closest to the "front lines." Front line intelligence operatives and investigators, together with mid-level front line managers, are in a better position to assess the potential impact, validity, and required responses than large central intelligence bureaucracies. Analysts have to be moved as close as possible to operational facilities for the creation of actionable intelligence and feedback to operations.

Such front line communities cannot be composed of traditional centralized, hierarchical institutions. Developing new institutions that can collaborate effectively and generate high-quality intelligence on the preeminent threats cannot be done with more of the same. Not only do such institutions require innovative thinking, they also require adoption of some of the enemy's methods of operating and ways of thinking. Intelligence gathering for the countering of terrorism, proliferation, and organized crime will have to follow a new paradigm. Trying to continue to handle these with large intelligence bureaucracies is a frivolous luxury. The future here is less about classic espionage than persistent tracking of terrorists, proliferators, and organized crime groups by good detective work, infiltration with engagement of all sorts of modern miniature sensors and robotics, and perceptive mining of reams of open sources. It is no longer back-alley skulking, but more down-and-dirty police investigative work, tracing radicals and their weapons materials, and recruiting informants to watch meeting sites of radicals, proliferators, and criminals. In terrorism, the tactical and strategic blur—operational success on the tactical level yields strategic results, new leads, more data, and better analysis. With the growing complexity of the intelligence environment, the waste and inefficiency of central planning in huge intelligence bureaucracies is no longer affordable and can no longer adequately anticipate missions and intelligence requirements, let alone identify and assess all of the alternatives for meeting them. Cost-effective intelligence requires the resiliency and discipline of the marketplace and new rules of engagement.

The differences between new flexible alternative intelligence services and the current intelligence bureaucracies are somewhat comparable to that between a symphony orchestra and a jazz band. The conventional symphony orchestra is playing according to a given full score, and it is the conductor alone that is imposing the obliging interpretation, though individual musicians may propose limited changes. Quite different the jazz band. There, hierarchically unregimented musicians are interpreting the theme individually, and with their contribution promote group creativity. The new unconventional threats, terrorism in particular, are better fought in this way.

Growing Complexity of Intelligence Collection

Methods of collection have changed dramatically during the latter part of the twentieth century. Satellite imaging and electronic interception are the most obvious evidence of this, having become the tools of choice. However, many of the new non-state actors lack large, fixed facilities and means that technical collection capabilities can most easily target. Furthermore, there are other changes negatively affecting intelligence collection on the subject matter that the intelligence services must cover:

- There have been technological advances that help intelligence targets to better protect their secrets and better hide their activities. This is due to the growing availability in the open market for anyone with money of sophisticated concealment, deception, and evasion technologies.
- Intelligence efforts must be spread more equally across a much larger number of targets. This is rendering planning, management, collection, and analysis much harder and requires much greater flexibility for intelligence collection.
- Surprise comes more often from unanticipated combinations of non-conventional threats. To avoid it, intelligence has to cast a wider net of constant monitoring of all relevant countries and topics—not necessarily in collection, but in terms of "pulsing" and "change detection."
- Important intelligence is ever more often to be found in an increasing number of foreign languages. These require a much greater capability to rapidly scan foreign materials, route them to the right person, and get back accurate translation ever more quickly.
- Building the best possible collection systems can no longer be sustained. Not only have costs escalated, but the vulnerability and inflexibility caused by the resulting decrease in the number of affordable systems is limiting sophisticated technical collection ever more.

- Massive increases in the volume of communication are complicating targeting. While reliance on microwave transmissions has diminished, new methods of communications, such as fiber optic cable, laser, cellular phones, and e-mails are harder to intercept.
- Widening access to the Internet facilitates intelligence collection, acquisition of knowledge and technology, transfer of funds for adversaries, and equally the use of clandestine communications by burying messages in websites and pictures.[11]
- The loss of the monopoly of, and state control over, cryptology, and the open availability and rapid proliferation of means for relatively high-grade encryption of private communications are diminishing the possibilities to gain important SIGINT and COMINT intakes.
- The growth of commercially available satellite photography, capable of resolutions of less than 1 meter, and 2 meter multispectral images, further narrowing the gap with U.S. satellites, represents a new open source that not only the services, but also all opponents can use.

Today, 85 to 95 percent of intelligence reporting on the preeminent threats posed by the unholy trinity comes from OSINT. A diminishing part comes from intelligence exchange with foreign partners, and from HUMINT, SIGINT, and IMINT. Hence, there is a growing disparity between the growth of the preeminent threats and the intelligence means at disposition. As far as OSINT is concerned, hard facts on terrorism, proliferation, and organized crime can often only be gained *post festum*—after the event. The same applies to the mosaic pieces contained in the intelligence exchange, which—as far as quantity, quality, and actionability for prevention is concerned—tends to shift increasingly below the indispensable minimum of "critical mass." To establish the final picture of the threat puzzle from the mosaic pieces exchanged is more often impossible. Each of these collection disciplines require additional resources if the challenges are to be met effectively. While SIGINT and IMINT will continue to play their part in dealing with these priorities, all clearly demand more HUMINT as a means of detection.

Counterterrorism is highly dependent upon HUMINT, the use of agents to acquire information, and, in certain circumstances, upon successful covert actions. Though it is one of the least expensive intelligence disciplines, HUMINT can be most difficult, and is undoubtedly the most dangerous for practitioners. Mistakes can be fatal, embarrass the government and the country, and undermine important policy goals. Moreover, it requires in-depth knowledge of local dialects, customs, and culture. Much time and patience will be needed to train collectors in difficult skills and languages. Furthermore, there is a long list of groups around the world that might at some point in the future be involved in terrorist activities. Determining where to seek agents whose reporting will only be important under future eventualities is another difficult challenge, with the risk of needlessly involving the state with corrupt and ruthless individuals.

A reorientation of HUMINT collection requires some hard policy decisions. One is a move towards greater reliance on non-official cover—to agents working as employees or owners of a local business, which are removed from the support and protection of embassies that would be available if the agent had cover as a government official. Recruitment is more difficult since families will be divided—such tours in areas of prime concern are not safe for spouses and children. If the agent must be seen as engaged in business, considerable time must be devoted to the cover occupation. Providing support, travel, pay, health care, and administrative services is much more difficult. The agent will not have diplomatic immunity and cannot be readily returned to his home state if apprehended in the host country. He may be subject to arrest, imprisonment, or execution. Moreover, there is a potential for agents working in businesses to become entangled in unethical or illegal activities—going into business for themselves—that could, if revealed, be highly controversial, embarrass the government and detract from the official mission.[12] And there are the monumental problems of the tradecraft of HUMINT.

Penetration of terrorist organizations is an extremely difficult task. It is much easier to penetrate the sensitive establishments of an adversary state than a terrorist organization. One way of penetration is by winning over and recruiting terrorists. Another is by corrupting or blackmailing those who are already accepted members of the terrorist organization. Both are extremely difficult operations with little likelihood of success.

The alternative to recruiting an insider is insinuating an agent into the group. However, the deep mistrust of outsiders makes such an infiltration improbable. Moreover, it poses ethical problems that are not appreciated by public opinion. If an intelligence service plants a mole in a terrorist organization, its leadership would first ask him to carry out a killing or some other similar act to test the sincerity of his adherence to its cause and his motivation. If the agent comes back and asks his handling officer whether he should kill in order to establish his credibility in the eyes of the terrorist leaders, the handling officer would be faced with a dilemma. He cannot tell his agent to kill so that we can prevent other killings in future. Setting a thief to catch a thief may be permissible for security agencies under certain circumstances, but committing a murder to catch a murderer is not.

Other factors conspire to immunize radical Islamists against Western HUMINT. Fundamentalist strains associated with terrorism preach self-denial. Offers of money or sex, the time-honored lures in espionage, would probably do more harm than good. Also, fanatical devotion to their cause makes it hard to turn members of terrorist groups and to get useful information out of apprehended terrorists. These do not care if they are jailed, and they are not afraid to die.

This is why a larger and better-trained generation of spies must be afforded improved methods of collecting information. Implicit in the intelligence mission objectives is the development of innovative ways to penetrate and analyze these most difficult targets that are also becoming better at hiding their intentions and capabilities. The challenge for intelligence is to move away from traditional surveillance techniques and toward more directed collection. Collection will have to become much more targeted and more innovative. It needs to become sharp and focused on what counts. Improving the analytic component of counterterrorism may be one of the most promising ways to ensure that collection is well focused. The issue is not exclusively tactical intelligence; it is also enabling the counterterrorist community to tailor long-term development of collection systems to the target.

Collection performance has to be enhanced in terms of precision and speed. HUMINT will have to focus less on collecting information and more on facilitating its collection by technical means. Clandestine collection will gather less through what its own spies hear and more through a great variety of sensors they can put in place—hence by using already existing acoustic, seismic, magnetic and optical sensors—and by full exploitation of the rapid progress that is occurring in the development of robotic technologies, tags, RFID, and in products born of the revolution in nanotechnology such as wireless micro-electromechanical and other sensors as small as a grain of sand in size. Scattering such "smart dust" sensors that can detect, compute and communicate by means of two-way-band radio terrorism-related activities, and changes in the level of such activities, can vastly improve the gathering of counterterrorism intelligence.[13] Smart dust can make it possible to track individual terrorists over great distances without detection.

Thus, more probative intelligence about less detectable terrorist activity will require improved HUMINT, upgraded by the most modern collection technologies.

There is another HUMINT dimension to modern collection technologies. Intelligence can probably break codes faster by stealing code books and new encryption software than by breaking the codes with supercomputers and mathematicians. There is more need for clandestine or unconventional SIGINT collection resources because these can get better intelligence by getting closer to the targets than most other sources. Better cooperation between HUMINT and technical intelligence makes both stronger. HUMINT can provide access to valuable SIGINT, which can validate information provided by HUMINT. With hundreds of communications bundled into fiber optic lines, there is less for satellites to intercept. If SIGINT is to intercept those signals, it will have to tap into particular lines in specific places. SIGINT also will have to collect keystrokes straight from the personal computer before software encrypts the message.[14] Equally, HUMINT can also help to improve IMINT. What is required for IMINT to become more effective are innovative adapting means such as exploiting new parts of the spectrum to identify, for example, effluents from buildings, as well as better use of a range of MASINT technologies that HUMINT can put in place, or by materials sampling it can do.

The characteristics required for HUMINT agents are: imagination, intuition, creativity, non-conformism, comprehension for cultural relativity, capable of scientific thinking combined with an interdisciplinary approach, social and individual-psychological empathy, and the capability to instantly adapt to an unknown or quickly changing situation. This is not to say that people with these characteristics do not already exist in intelligence services, only that in the work processes of huge bureaucracies, such types normally cause more problems than they solve. Increasingly, operatives will bring back key intelligence only by acting with the flexibility, the skills, and the cover it takes to run operations unlinked with an official installation. Consequently, the problems operatives face will be more dangerous. Furthermore, the counterintelligence function with much more sophisticated surveillance and counter-surveillance techniques will gain enhanced importance.

Reforming Intelligence

Most intelligence services have been reorganized or are in the process of reorganizing. Reorganization alone does not ensure improvement, but it can make it possible. However, despite many changes, there is ample reason to believe that the reforms implemented so far in almost all Western intelligence services do not go far enough. Many changes have been ones of emphasis rather than substance. Much of the interdependent global community now faces nontraditional challenges for which the state-centric paradigm that served reasonably well during the twentieth century no longer provides sufficient guidance for intelligence services. What is needed is a more dynamic intelligence organization that is better able to deal with the challenges of the preeminent threats and of the future. True reform must produce leaner, more effective, efficient, and far more responsive intelligence services, which will enable policy makers to take the right decision based on the right information.

Generally, there are two groups among the reformers. One is following a "system-immanent" approach, believing that intelligence bureaucracies can be reformed as they exist. What is needed is more money, better personnel, better information sharing, improved cooperation between ministries, think tanks and academics, and enhanced international cooperation. The other group, maintaining that intelligence agencies will remain bureaucracies like other big state agencies, believes that such organizations have reached clear limits for improvement. Totally new systems of intelligence collection, intelligence work, and intelligence marketing are necessary to counter the new quality and magnitude of threats. What is needed are organizations that better fit into, and can better exploit the knowledge-strategies of the information society. Restructuring bureaucracies in the context of the lean state, flatter hierarchies, more controlling, and more outsourcing, is leading nowhere. Intelligence bureaucracies are doomed.

This leads to the question of how to turn intelligence services into learning organizations. "Intelligence is not a science, certainly not a natural science. It is an art or a craft, and as such it cannot be governed by the basic tenets of logic. Intelligence officers must be unconventional thinkers and doers, gifted with imagination and creativity, to peer behind the curtain of apparent reality."[15]

However, it is exactly those characteristics which hierarchically struc-tured bureaucracies find counterproductive or even destructive. Over-conformity, goal displacement, and mission creep are the typical trends also in intelligence bureaucracies that are making procedures to aims, and means to purposes. Making a career depends on the reality as it is seen and assessed to be by the superiors. This makes conformity a constituting element in intelligence bureaucracies, which abhor ambiguity, and disloyalty in the relationship between superiors and subordinates. Those who do not conform have little chance to make a career.

REFORM AS CONTINUOUS TRANSFORMATION

What is needed for intelligence enterprise rebalancing is continuous transformation. The future requires continuous change and the greater risk would be in not changing. The defining characteristic of the best organizations will be the capacity to transform themselves faster than their competition so that they may take advantage of the unrelenting acceleration of technological progress.

Continuous transformation of the intelligence services must become a process for developing them into a preeminent learning organization that puts great value in the pursuit and application of knowledge across all disciplines. Professional education is the best means to effect a cultural change. Transformation is first and foremost an intellectual exercise, requiring the brightest minds actively engaged in taking intelligence services to higher levels of effectiveness.

More elemental than implementing a continuous quality process for transformation is the cultural conversion that must accompany this change process for it to become genuinely valued by the profession. This cultural conversion is best exemplified by the concept of the learning organization: an organization skilled at creating, acquiring, interpreting, transferring, and retaining knowledge, and at purposefully modifying its behavior to reflect new knowledge and insights.

The challenge of intelligence transformation is to respond to change in such a way as to enhance the overall effectiveness of intelligence to perform all assigned missions. This does not imply that the performance of technological innovations will be maximized. It means that overall effectiveness will be improved by the successful integration of the innovations with all aspects of intelligence effectiveness: technology, doctrine, organization, leadership, and training.

Management at every level of complex organizations is increasingly accomplished by self-organizing systems that both defy centralized management, and change the meaning of individual accountability. Innovation in complex organizations derives from the ability to routinely produce new and enhanced processes and products by combining technology and knowledge in ways that deliver synergies.

Only networks can provide access to the wide-ranging knowledge domains required, and only self-organizing networks that work horizontally can provide the intimate interactions among the participants that permit the synthesis of this knowledge. Thinking horizontally now applies to everything from business to education to military planning. It takes an adjustment to move from vertical to horizontal thinking. Vertical thinking always starts by asking who controls what system while horizontal thinking starts by asking what is the outcome or effect to be created. This can no longer be done with the hierarchical, traditional structure existing in intelligence bureaucracies. Dynamic, self-organizing networks not accounted for on organizational diagrams must be cultivated and nurtured if intelligence innovation is to flourish.

NETWORKING

One of intelligence's central tasks is to improve the formation of its own networks so as to be able to counter the networks of the preeminent threats. There is no viable alternative for intelligence for two reasons: Only networking can make the existing "in-house knowledge" of the intelligence community more readily accessible and available in a timely fashion; and networks, unlike hierarchies, have built-in redundancies. If part of a network is hit or becomes dysfunctional, other parts of the network can take over. This makes well-managed networks the most efficient organizational structure for the fight against the preeminent threats and in times of crises.

For intelligence, such a network should look like a system of concentric circles with each circle describing one network and all these circles communicating with each other on the pattern of a network. The innermost circle is the intelligence service where the network potential has always been underexploited. What is required is enhancing lines of intraservice communications, questioning the vertical and horizontal firewalls that hedge bureaucratic competences rather that secrets, and task force building. The tools to get better results are: tighter networking of analysts with all those engaged in collection; practicing the "desk model" for reuniting subject-specific collection and analysis in close units; regular meetings of regional experts from the various areas; and collective tasks for multi-experts resulting in interdisciplinary and supra-regional analysis.

This inner circle of the intelligence service then needs to network with the entities in the next circle—the national arena: service-government relations, interagency relations, relations with lower layers of administration, and regional and local agencies. There is much to do in terms of better networking within government. There are the communication gaps between the services and government, and the rivalries between the services domestically. The answer must be to move away from this type of inter-blocking institutions and create interlocking institutions instead. Moreover, intelligence services need to reach out to the many national competence hubs that have the expertise intelligence is lacking: think tanks, academic institutions, NGOs, risk assessment, and many other specialist entities in the private sector. To this end, intelligence has to critically review its self-created firewalls and the needs of its partners in civil society whose professional purpose and integrity must not be compromised.

The "open source" revolution has led to a previously unthinkable privatization of assessment with a plethora of private sector companies offering expertise in global, regional, country risk analysis, and on many other themes and subjects. Already in existence are a significant number of reputable private firms capable of providing timely, high-quality political, economic, strategic, and technical analyses on a subscription basis. Intelligence must learn to understand how best to leverage the capabilities of the private sector. Creative alliances with think tanks, academic institutions, other centers of expertise, and hubs of specialized competence are force multipliers.

The outer concentric circle in this system of network-centric intelligence contains the network at the international level. As far as outreach to other entities such as international and regional competence hubs, think tanks, academic institutions, and NGOs is concerned, the rules of the national arena should apply *mutatis mutandis*—after the necessary changes have been made—and new approaches should be sought. When it comes to networking of chiefs of intelligence services or intelligence analysts and collectors among themselves, this is a standard practice in long-standing bilateral exchanges with other intelligence services. Today, there is also growing intelligence networking at the multilateral level, and even multilateral intelligence sharing and exchanges. But most of these are still exchanges of finished intelligence, which may no longer be sufficient in the future. Networking must find out how to: look at the world, have insight on key issues of concern, and take advantage of differing strengths of other services and countries. Building partnerships among different services takes long-term commitment, understanding the sensitivities of each of the partners, and the importance of reciprocity and respect.

Decisions regarding countering the preeminent threats to our societies are ever more regularly made at the multilateral level: by the UN, NATO, the EU, and others. But the intelligence assessments that serve as the basis for governments to take their decisions are produced autonomously at the national level. While there is some justification for that due to the very nature of the product and the sovereignty of states, more fissures may be generated in the international community. As long as national threat perceptions are potentially divergent, how can policies at the international level become more convergent? This is why intelligence networking at the international level has to expand further to selective joint multinational assessments.

The EU is already performing such joint multinational assessments. For one thing, a EU counterterrorism czar has been appointed in the aftermath of the Madrid terrorist attacks, and regular meetings of all EU security services are held, doing joint assessments. More important, with its Joint Situation Centre (SITCEN) in its Secretariat General, the EU has made the widest-ranging attempt at the international level so far to lay the groundwork for its Common Foreign and Security Policy (CFSP) by generating integrated situation and threat analyses. Made up of analysts seconded from external and internal intelligence services of EU member states, the SITCEN operates on the basis of the so-called watch list of about twenty-five to thirty crisis regions. Their joint assessments are to facilitate decision making in the EU Council. The merits of this unique networking approach at the multinational level are that they result in four advantages and improvements:

1. The knowledge base is broadened.
2. Different information from different intelligence services with different strengths are pooled.
3 The warning culture is harmonized.
4. Joint assessments and conclusions help to enable unified decisions.

Thus, the clear message emanating from all this is: If a state wants to live up to its responsibility to protect its citizens from the preeminent threats, the state does not really have a choice. There is no more powerful alternative to fighting networks than with this level of multinational networking amongst intelligence services.

Becoming a Learning Organization with Knowledge Leadership

Two serious obstacles must be overcome before intelligence services can become the preeminent institutions at adapting to change. The first hurdle is the capacity to develop the culture of a true learning organization that values intellectual curiosity and innovation at all levels. To surmount the second barrier, intelligence leaders must learn to use new skills and concepts to lead in an increasingly complex world.

To effectively handle network-centric intelligence and exploit networking to its the fullest, knowledge leadership is required. Leaders of intelligence at every level must become knowledge leaders. For this, new skills are needed in order to facilitate greater knowledge sharing and collaboration in the networks, task forces, and teams. No single skill set is sufficient to the task of knowledge leadership. On the contrary, individuals must demonstrate a broad range of qualities if they are to bring out the best in themselves and their people. Apart from vision, courage, integrity, honesty, perseverance, and energy—which all feature high—leadership demands an approach and style that is instantly recognizable as such.

With regard to collaboration, a knowledge leader's authority is determined entirely by personal behavior. Greater knowledge sharing and collaboration will not be possible unless the leader engages in such activities. In the twentieth century workplace, authority was based on what an individual knew—knowledge was power. In the twenty-first century workplace, authority is conferred to those who share what they know and, in doing so, elevate the value of their staff—knowledge sharing is power. Having the courage to do so is essential in the long-term prosperity of knowledge-driven cells and organizations.

This leads to the issue of credibility. A knowledge leader's credibility cannot be driven top down; it has to be conferred bottom up. Thus, knowledge leaders have to lead from the rear as well as from the front. Engaging the ideas and opinions of staff at all levels of the cells and task forces is essential to establishing credibility and building trust.

The knowledge leader has to stimulate sharing and collaboration by demonstrating its value and worth. Successful collaborative projects have to be celebrated and communicated; knowledge sharing has to be incentivized and rewarded—great ideas should never be stolen by management; original thinking has to be encouraged; and, where necessary, long-standing organizational orthodoxies have to be opened to revision.

Moreover, in a rapidly changing business environment like intelligence, knowledge leaders will have to recognize that collaboration must not be a purely internal exercise. Opportunities for collaboration that exist with many outside organizations must be fully used—even with competitors. The future of an intelligence service is determined by its ability to exploit collaborative knowledge on both a local and global scale.

Soft skills also figure high among the requirements for twenty-first century knowledge leaders, who must have the ability to:

- Engage with staff at all levels of the network or task force, and to demonstrate empathy with the challenges they face
- Understand the interests and motivations of staff, and, in doing so, nurture their innovation and sense of inquiry
- Offer feedback and be open to criticism themselves
- Recognize others for their efforts, ideas, and contributions
- Create the right work environment and establish a culture of mutual trust and respect; ensure that no one gets ahead at someone else's expense
- Change the behavior of others by personally demonstrating the qualities they hope to inspire
- Encourage leadership and initiative at all levels of the network or task force, and recognize that by doing so they strengthen their own authority as leaders
- Champion further education, and the personal and professional development of *all* staff

In addition, there is a need for knowledge leaders to synthesize the above skills in order to address specific organizational needs and problems. Recognizing the right people for a particular project, enabling different motivations to fuse into a single goal, and cultivating the exchange of ideas between different teams are essential skills that enable a knowledge leader to synthesize the best thinking from across the network, task forces, or cells.

Finally, while leadership is traditionally seen through the prism of authority and strength, knowledge leadership demands humility and a willingness to have one's own ideas challenged, improved, and, if necessary, discarded. In the knowledge-driven workplace, leaders cannot pretend to know everything, nor can they claim to have a monopoly on good ideas. The education of the knowledge leader begins by acknowledging what others have to teach and how much one has to learn.

KNOWLEDGE STRATEGIES

Knowledge strategies have to build on an intelligence service's short, medium, and long-term goals. To realize these goals, knowledge leaders have to ask a series of questions:

- What skills will staff need to meet the challenges ahead?
- What expertise do we have internally? How can this be improved?
- What expertise exists outside that we can co-opt or collaborate with?
- Who are the people we need to bring together to brainstorm the risks and opportunities we face?
- How will the knowledge we acquire realizing our current goals benefit our other activities?

A careful consideration of these and other questions should enable the knowledge leader to undertake a program of organizational change so that the intelligence service is better prepared to anticipate and respond to future challenges.

The knowledge leader must also be conscious of what is happening in other networks and circles as a whole. Gathering and exploiting competitive intelligence is essential if opportunities are to be properly realized. Studying competitors thoroughly and learning from their experience can help the knowledge leader avoid repeating the same mistakes while leveraging the knowledge gained for competitive advantage. Ultimately, the knowledge leader must cultivate those strategic values—respect, knowledge sharing, trust, innovation, and creativity—that will flow into all other organizational processes.

This new approach, as well as fostering individual initiative, represents a sharp break with the past. Senior leaders were accustomed to being the authors of new initiatives rather than their enablers. Managers and senior analysts climbing the ranks were used to avoiding risks that would take them off the fast track. The tendency to confine taking risks to the top and to constrain individual initiative because it might lead to a mistake is one of the things that must change if the fight against the preeminent threats is to succeed.

Intelligence reform must recognize the dysfunctional nature of traditional barriers that separate organizations and roles. Complexity has generated many new ways to consider how organizations operate and how innovation is developed. The most successful future policies will be those that pursue adaptation and innovation through trial and error.

The objectives can be differentiated as mission objectives and enterprise objectives. Mission objectives relate to the efforts to predict, penetrate, and preempt threats to national security, and to assist all who make and implement national security policy, fight the wars, protect the nation, and enforce the laws in the implementation of national policy goals. Enterprise objectives relate to intelligence capacity to maintain competitive advantages over actors and forces that threaten the security of the nation.

An important goal is to create capabilities to defend and promote national interests in a new environment where threats are both diffuse and uncertain, and conflict is inherent and unpredictable. These new patterns of uncertainty combined with overstretched resources pose difficult challenges to intelligence reform and national security. Further complicating matters are the combined revolutions in technology and global affairs that have shattered traditional boundaries, merging the strategic, operational, and tactical levels into a single, integrated universe in which action at the bottom often has instant and dramatic impact at all levels. In all this, intelligence management has to learn to expect and cope with the unexpected connected with the new risks, dangers, and threats.

Better Exploit and Leverage the Accelerating Scientific and Technological Progress and the Changes that are Underway in Information Technology and how Information is Used

The information revolution is the single most important factor affecting the management and work of intelligence services. The information environment has exploded beyond anything conceived. No aspect of society and the economy is changing as quickly as the world of information, information technology, and communication. More so than any other government entity, intelligence is affected by virtually every one of these changes.

The basic technology trends resulting from the information revolution are: growing capabilities, falling costs, and much greater connectivity. Such progress has led to major changes in how intelligence services work and use information. making decentralization, distributed operations, networking, and tailored systems possible.

However, progress has also enabled the private sector to exploit modern technology and develop products and services, frequently superior to those of government-bound intelligence organizations. In some cases, the commercial sector will also have better information. Thus, intelligence needs to be capable of changing continuously too. This will require changes in the craft and management of intelligence going beyond the redrawing of organizational charts and redesigning chain of command.

With the advance of the Internet alone, there is growing access to an ocean of information. The majority of the information a government needs to establish an autonomous national assessment will come from OSINT. The rest of it must be obtained by technical collection means and clandestine intelligence work.

The major challenges facing the management of intelligence is sifting through and processing unprecedented amounts of data and information to find the relevant knowledge for evaluation and assessment.

SIFTING THROUGH AND PROCESSING UNPRECEDENTED AMOUNTS OF DATA AND INFORMATION

The information revolution, followed by the Internet revolution, changed the way in which data and information could be stored and retrieved, and altered the nature of interactions between individual analysts and analytical groups within intelligence services. The Internet revolution, in particular, opened the prospect of open source information as a vital tool. Fast access to a global stockpile of knowledge, assisted by increasingly sophisticated search engines, has transformed the nature of intelligence assessments and fundamentally altered its traditional reliance on secrets.

Technology has delivered real time intelligence as it has vastly broadened the conceptual lens through which data and information is collected and assessed; and it has facilitated the processing and delivery of knowledge to decision makers. One downside is that technology's contemporary bounty has come to threaten the integrity and quality of the intelligence process itself. For much of their existence, intelligence services trafficked in scarcity. Secrets were hard to acquire and truly valuable secrets were a rare commodity. But at some point during the Cold War, the technological tide turned and the normal conditions of intelligence scarcity were replaced by the opposite problem of an increasing surfeit of intelligence, often generated through high tech collection systems. "Information overload" is now a common problem for all major intelligence systems. The ability to filter through the huge volumes of data and to extract the information from the layers of formatting, multiplexing, compression, and transmission protocols applied to each message is the biggest challenge.

Another downside of the surfeit of information, the information overload, and particularly with OSINT is the difficulty of distinguishing true "signals" from the ambient "noise" in which they are embedded—the central problem explaining intelligence failure at Pearl Harbor in 1941 and many others now truly defines the twenty-first century intelligence challenge. What has changed is the sheer volume of both signals and noise. As the mass of raw data grows, it spawns worrisome problems for intelligence warning, analytical failures, and politicization and manipulation of data and assessments by decision makers.

The problem is how to swim through oceans of data without forgetting to ask the right questions or focusing on recycled intelligence. No single technology or technique will emerge any time soon to help intelligence agencies swim through the expanding oceans of data around them. In Europe, public authorities acknowledge that in addition to traditional HUMINT, their reliance on open source digital information sources of all kinds—voice, data, and visual—is exponentially increasing. Yet the richness of information sources is matched by an equally rich range of problems:

- Today's information technologies are sold on the merit of speed of delivery, which create real-time awareness but weaken authenticity. The new communications technologies have forced media to send out news in fragments or small batches with diminishing attention to fact checking and cross-verification, which, in turn, forces users to conduct their own analysis and verification to get at the real facts.
- This trend is aggravated by the "near-media" phenomenon: bloggers and would-be journalists who offer a plethora of competing alternative views, rumors, cant, and outright propaganda passing as news. Ultimately, these products are sold as timesaving devices, but, in the end, they waste more of intelligence's time.
- Digitization makes information more fungible and manipulable; data reduction to bits and bytes can be more easily acquired, indexed, referenced, and transformed within and among sources.
- There are no EU-wide norms in intelligence training and analysis or standards for interoperability to connect OSINT databases across Europe. A staggering number of data-mining groups in France exist, for instance, each using different software and interfaces. Less than half of them are interoperable with each other. The OSINT community has not even gotten close to standardizing anything because they quickly

run up against the constraints. There is a need to get all parts of the OSINT-user community "in the same room." So far, very few are there yet. Until then it is impossible to put together an end-to-end OSINT value chain.

Finally, there is the sober fact that most of the Internet resides in a digital black hole whose content is either evanescent or immune to conventional search engines and thus, for the time being, lies beyond the reach of analysis. The size of the web that can be searched by Google is an estimated 60 billion pages, but there is 500 times that found in the "deep web" that cannot be accessed. Thus, one cannot rely too much on the Internet. Unless one has the most sophisticated tools and huge teams of highly qualified people, one just cannot get full access or value from it.

Due to the increasing availability and quality of digital mapping technology such as Google Earth, DigitalGlobe, Windows Live Maps, blogs, cable television, and the miniaturization of camera devices, OSINT sources are changing in every way. Detailed images printed from Google Earth were found in the homes of known Iraqi insurgents. Jihadist groups are using mini-cameras to post propaganda films to YouTube, for example. Many new Arabic channels are being created, and they are radically changing the audiovisual situation that needs to be monitored.

Should intelligence nonetheless aim for a global approach to data control to match a medium that has no geographical boundaries? Yes, but ideas are lacking on how this could be done. Officials responsible for coordinating the EU nations' vigilance against terrorism and other threats know what they would like, however. The dream tool: Something that trawls the entire voice-Internet-and-image universe and produces prioritized results, like Google, and which is as easy to use as an iPod. In high demand is a tool that offers rapid verification and reveals redundant sources while mitigating the choice between the need for speed and that for accuracy. There is always this balance that has to be struck. Unfortunately, no such tools exist. For the time being, the challenge boils down to one of achievable effectiveness and cost efficiency.

For these problems, solutions could be found by initiating uploading— harnessing the power of communities, the flattener No. 4 of Friedman's ten flatteners.[16] As described on the example of the "Apache" development process of individuals that was later joined by IBM, solutions for creating a means that trawls the entire voice-Internet-and-image universe, and for a means that can access the "deep web" could be found,[17] this time, however, by combining uploading with "Informing," the flattener No. 9,[18] where Google's phenomenal global popularity has spurred Yahoo! and Microsoft's MSN Search.

Informing may also help to solve another problem for intelligence services: to know the in-house knowledge—or institutional wisdom—of the intelligence service. This refers to the fact that in big organizations the piece of information one is looking for is often hidden somewhere in the system but not available to the person or unit that needs it most. Networking and communications can prevent that. However, a much better approach is to use the power of improved search engines. All major search engines have recently added the capability for users to search not only the Web for information but also their own computer's hard drive for words or data or e-mail they know is in there somewhere but have forgotten where. Taking this a couple steps further will provide intelligence professionals almost instant access to in-house knowledge of the intelligence community.

Another problem to solve is that of intelligence fusion. Mainly hampered by secrecy, stovepipes, and compartmentalization, intelligence fusion requires breaking down bureaucratic cultures and the vertical and horizontal barriers in and between the different organizations, as well as organizational measures that connect the best brains for intelligence analysis and evaluation. The best analysis emerges from a competitive environment where different perspectives and dissenting opinion are welcomed, and alternative hypotheses are encouraged.

Better fusion of intelligence can be achieved by pulling together data and information at centralized databases and collaborative workspaces using the most modern information technology available, enabling knowledge detection, and exploiting new discovery methods. Developing "systems of systems" to provide interoperability, integration, and interdependence between these separate databases may be the key to greater overall intelligence effectiveness. This effectiveness can be greatly expanded again with Friedman's flattener of "Informing," which will enhance the possibilities for intelligence fusion. The products based on fused intelligence can provide a more comprehensive understanding of the situation, sensibilize or alert all that have access to them to new risks and activities, reduce surprise and reaction time, improve and accelerate the tasking of collection, and so enhance efficiency, efficacy, and unity of effort.

The First Line of Defense

Only if top executive decision and policy makers, the National Security Council, the leadership of the armed forces, and their planners and counselors are sufficiently informed about the state of the world—the likely developments, the potential and existing threats, dangers, risks, opportunities, and chances—can they be expected to make sound judgments and policies in the areas of internal security, external security, national defense, and foreign relations. Intelligence knowledge is also the prerequisite for the definition of the national interests; the development of an adequate security policy, a sound national security strategy, and corresponding security sector strategy and military strategy; the determination of the missions of the forces protecting the critical national infrastructure, of the security and the armed forces; and the establishment of doctrine and its translation into operations. Moreover, intelligence knowledge, contingency planning, and timely warning are the prerequisites for efficient and effective crisis management. No other government entity but intelligence services can provide the basis for this knowledge.

To obtain information on intentions, capabilities, means, and methods that actual or potential opponents deny or keep secret, the government must rely on intelligence services that require capabilities and authorities that are unavailable to other government entities. Intelligence is the only domain of government activity where innovative thinking, calculated risk taking, audacious daring, and sacrifice for the national cause should be encouraged. No other domain must rely so heavily on the initiative, dedication, professional motivation, judgment, and candor of its personnel. And no other government organization is so highly dependent upon the cooperation of other agencies, foreign governments and intelligence services, private individuals, and volunteers.

Intelligence is the major contributor to the state's absolute obligation to its people to make sure that intentions are known and threats to security detected in time to be counteracted for harm, death, and destruction to be prevented. Thus, intelligence has become indispensable as the first line of defense, and the most critical resource in the fight against terrorism, proliferation, organized crime, and other threats of the transnational kind. Intelligence as objective judgment and forecasting deserves recognition and a prominent place, not only in any concept of democratic order, but even more so in the multilateral scope of international cooperation—the more so since there is no substitute for effective and efficient intelligence services.

10
Legislation

Agreements play a fundamental role in international relations. *Pacta sunt servanda* is one of the basic principles underlying international agreements. It along with the principles of free consent, good faith, and the obligation to uphold agreements are universally accepted. In order to give effect to agreements, states must bring their domestic laws into conformity with their obligations under international law.[1] Treaty obligations are legal thresholds. The cost for a state to be seen as an unreliable treaty partner can be very high. If a state fails to implement the obligations, it is contrary to the principles of good faith and *pacta sunt servanda*, and risks noncompliance, since it cannot invoke the provisions—or absence thereof—of its internal law as justification to perform a treaty obligation.[2] Thus, the effectiveness of agreements depends on the capacity of each member state to fully enforce the treaty obligations on its national territory.

The Problems

A common problem with the conventions regulating WMD is that many governments have not adopted or fully implemented national legislation to ensure fulfillment of their obligations. National implementation obligations regularly receive less critical attention than the international conventions themselves, and are rarely verified. Some states consider national implementation to be a purely legal or technical matter of less importance than committing to the treaty. In general, they pay less attention to provisions requiring national implementation measures in treaties concerning WMD than to treaties that have an economic impact, such as those regulating trade, transport, migration, or the environment. Moreover, the implementation of nuclear, biological, and chemical arms control and disarmament law is perceived by states as a sensitive issue because its primary focus is on the security of the state rather than the individual. The absence of an international verification organization for certain WMD treaties contributes to this problem, while state parties' reluctance to effectively address these matters in treaty meetings has compounded the problem of ineffective national implementation.[3]

Furthermore, there are differences with regard to the practice between states with a common law tradition and those with a civil law tradition. Common law states require national legislation to transform international obligations into enforceable national law and, specifically, penal legislation that details offenses and establishes appropriate penalties for activities banned. States with a civil law tradition, however, may consider treaties they have joined as "self-executing," whereby the text of the accord is automatically incorporated into national law when the agreement enters into force. The state's constitution will provide guidance on whether or not a treaty is self-executing and whether further implementation measures are required.[4]

Each international organization has a different mandate and set of member states. For this reason, some international organizations may be wary of involvement in the UNSC imposed arms control and disarmament obligations. They may also be unable or reluctant to cooperate with other organizations in a similar field. This lack of coordination internationally is often mirrored by a lack of coordination at the national level where government departments often do not communicate or cooperate with each other.

The maintenance of global norms depends not only on the universality of these treaties but also on the ability to face challenges to these norms. The UN has been involved in playing a leading role in these situations. Under Chapter VII, the UNSC enforces norms of securing the peace. Though the UN Charter permits the use of force, past experience has shown that the use of force alone does not restore compliance. In instances of noncompliance, the international community has recognized the need to use sanctions as an alternative means to the use of force. However, it cannot rely solely on sanctions either. Thus, opportunities for constructive engagements must be encouraged. The UN can do this bilaterally or on a sub-regional basis.

While national compliance is essential for the success of these treaties, the failure to strengthen the treaty verification systems has made it more difficult to assess the status of states' national implementation measures. The burden of proof in demonstrating compliance with international conventions must shift away from those alleging noncompliance to those states or groups whose compliance is in doubt. International norms must be adapted so that such states are obligated to reassure those who are worried, and to take reasonable measures to prove they are not secretly developing WMD. Failure to supply such proof, or prosecute the criminals living within their borders, should entitle worried nations to take all necessary actions for their self-defense.

UN Security Council Resolution 1540

UNSC action since 9/11 is marked by a shift in emphasis from international verification to national compliance, as well as by creating obligations for those states that remain outside the treaty regimes. The UNSC Resolution 1540 of April 2004 amplified these trends. It established a mandatory requirement for all states to refrain from providing any form of support to non-state actors in obtaining WMD, and mandates them to adopt domestic legislation to implement this obligation. More broadly and importantly, it requires states to establish national controls to prevent the proliferation of WMD and their means of delivery. Resolution 1540 does not alter states' existing obligations under the NTP, BWC or CWC. It urges states to "renew and fulfill their commitment to multilateral cooperation," thus helping to solidify the foundation of traditional cooperation while expanding the scope of many WMD-related obligations to non-state actors in those states that remain outside the WMD regimes, and to the several conventions against terrorism.

The resolution contains little guidance on the form of national measures states should adopt to give effect to their obligations. However, states have to report the approaches they have taken to enforce the resolution to the 1540 Committee, which is tasked with monitoring and reporting on states' implementation to the UNSC. Not all states have provided reports, and many of those that have lack substantive detail. But the reports available show that some states consider their existing legislation to be sufficient to implement some or all their obligations, such as those states that have already criminalized WMD in their national criminal codes or equivalent legislation.[5] Some states have adopted a single dedicated legal instrument[6] or have amended existing legislation in order to comply with Resolution 1540. Other states have chosen to implement the prohibitions in general weapons control legislation. Some other states have specific NBC acts or have incorporated WMD regulations in antiterrorism legislation.[7]

If the UNSC provides the necessary resources for monitoring the implementation of the resolution and assists states in complying, it will have a significant potential. Resolution 1540 illustrates the potential of the UNSC to bring about rules that are mandatory for the entire world community. It is the only institution in the world that has the legal authority to examine—and if need be to harmonize, supplement, and enforce—the many efforts made to counter and reduce the threats posed by WMD. However, this responsibility, if the world community of nations will accept it, should not be exercised by a small group dominated by five great powers, but in broad consultation with the whole UN membership.

There is a clear link between maintaining the rule of law and the treaty regimes. The UN plays an important role in these treaties. In the Millennium Declaration of September 2000, heads of states made commitments to ensure the implementation of treaties in arms control and disarmament by state parties. However, each of the major treaties relating to WMD has different requirements for state parties' national implementation.

The Major Treaties

NUCLEAR NON-PROLIFERATION TREATY (NTP)

The 1968 NTP is silent on how to assess compliance, how to resolve compliance disputes, and what procedures to follow in the event of non-compliance. Specifically, there is no verification of the obligations in Article I and II not to transfer or receive nuclear weapons. In terms of Articles IV and VI, the treaty offers no definitions or ways of assessing whether states are living up to their obligations. In addition, the NTP does not contain provisions that explicitly require state parties to adopt national implementation measures to give effect to the treaty. It only requires states to enter into nuclear safeguards agreements with the IAEA, which has promulgated nonbinding guidelines for national measures to protect nuclear materials and equipment from security breaches. The IAEA, whose verification mandate covers only safeguards of NTP compliance, verifies compliance primarily through material accountancy measures. But its agreements with state parties to the NTP provide it with measures to be taken in case of non-compliance. According to Article 19, the IAEA can suspend membership of a noncomplying state.

CONVENTION ON THE PHYSICAL PROTECTION OF NUCLEAR MATERIAL (CPPNM)

The lack of provision for national implementation in the NTP, which governs nonproliferation of nuclear weapons, contrasts directly with the inclusion of provisions in the 1980 CPPNM that specifically requires states to adopt measures to prevent the illicit diversion of nuclear materials in international transport. However, many of the 193 state parties to the NPT have not yet joined the CPPNM. Further efforts are underway to expand the scope of the treaty to require the physical protection of nuclear material in national use, storage, and transport, and to require state parties to take steps to protect nuclear materials and facilities in their territory against sabotage.

INTERNATIONAL CONVENTION FOR THE SUPPRESSION OF ACTS OF NUCLEAR TERRORISM (CSNT)

The UN General Assembly adopted the CSTN in April 2005, which defines nuclear terrorism as a crime and specifies criminal legislation as the appropriate form of national implementation. Hence, it requires domestic criminalization of acts of nuclear terrorism, and commits its parties to international cooperation in the prevention, investigation, and prosecution of acts of nuclear terrorism. Under this treaty, which opened for signature on September 14, 2005, states are required to notify the UN Secretary-General of the jurisdiction they have established under their national law to implement and enforce the treaty. Should any state change these arrangements, it is obliged to notify the UN Secretary-General immediately. While offering no panacea, this convention is a significant and welcome achievement. States should proceed to early ratification and implementation.

THE BIOLOGICAL WEAPONS CONVENTION (BWC)

The 1972 BWC requires state parties to take "any necessary measures"[8] in accordance with their constitutional processes to implement the treaty prohibitions which are specified in Article I, using a "general purpose criterion." Other treaty provisions, however, must also be given effect through national implementation, such as Article III prohibitions on the transfer of BW and the provision of assistance to develop BW. This necessitates state parties' establishment of national export control regimes for potential biowarfare agents, related materiel, and delivery systems. While the BWC leaves the choice of the form of national implementation measures to state parties, the scope of obligations they must cover is clear: Comprehensive measures are necessary to ensure compliance with the general purpose criterion throughout state parties' territories. In addition, the term "measures to prohibit and prevent" requires credible national enforcement processes. State parties have reaffirmed the need to ensure effective national implementation at the treaty review conferences. Indeed, the mandate of the 2003 BWC Experts Meeting and Meeting of States Parties specifically required state parties to consider "penal legislation"—criminal offenses and penalties—for violating treaty obligations.

THE CHEMICAL WEAPONS CONVENTION (CWC)

The 1993 CWC contains the most detailed national implementation provision of all WMD agreements. In contrast to the BWC, the CWC explicitly requires state parties to adopt criminal legislation[9] for activities that violate the treaty and to extend these measures also to offenses committed by their citizens outside of their territory. National laws are also necessary to establish and operate the National Authority required under the CWC. The Organization for the Prohibition of Chemical Weapons (OPCW), an international organization established by the CWC, is responsible for all aspects of compliance with, and implementation of, the CWC. The OPCW on-site inspection procedures monitor the elimination of all inventories of CW and former CW production facilities. They also perform routine inspections of a large number of commercial chemical facilities to verify that only non-prohibited activities occur there. The most radical verification tool created by the CWC—the right to request a "challenge inspection" of any facility suspected of violating the treaty, without right of refusal—is available to any state party. Departing from the experience of older multilateral arms control regimes, the OPCW has taken a hands-on role in persuading new states to join and helping them to develop domestic implementing legislation and regulations while taking into account their specific political, legal, and economic conditions.[10] The OPCW has developed an ambitious national implementation program, complete with national implementation packages, a checklist, and model legislation. It has also set up a roster of legal experts with in-depth knowledge of the national implementing legislation called for by the Convention. The OPCW action plan on implementation of CWC obligations is divided into four parts:

1. Identification and analysis of problems and needs
2. Resources for implementation support
3. The overall timeframe, intermediate steps, and target dates for implementation
4. Oversight by the Conference of state parties and the Executive Council

Engaging—and Profiting from—International Help

States also can get help for the implementation of the obligations of other conventions into national law.[11] If they want to profit and make the best use of such help for the preparation and adoption of domestic legislation, administrative regulations, and setting up functional national authorities, they have to discard the outdated assumption that lawmaking is strictly an internal matter that remains the prerogative of a sovereign state. With the help of multilateral institutions, a well-organized and transparent system of national implementation can be built, which strongly reinforces compliance mechanisms and provides an additional level of assurance to other parties regarding national compliance.

There is a need to revitalize and strengthen multilateral cooperative approaches, because of both their legitimacy and their potential effectiveness in addressing WMD threats. There is an equal need to instill a sense of collective responsibility and solidarity among governments for achieving the nonproliferation and counterterrorism goals that their official policies nominally support. The UNSC, in close contact with the members of the UN, should be the focal point for the world's efforts to reduce the threats posed by existing and future WMD, and to help harmonize, supplement, and enforce the many efforts that are made.

A lowering of the WMD threat requires many parallel and reinforcing approaches in the field of arms control, disarmament, nonproliferation, and antiterrorism at all levels—unilateral, bilateral, multilateral, regional, and global. Progress has been made over time and further progress is possible. Shortcomings in existing rules and regimes can be easily identified. They can and must be remedied. Gaps must be filled and what is broken must be fixed. This should be done, however, without breaking the consensus that brought the rules and regimes into being. While leadership and initiative by individual nations have much to contribute in the efforts to counter WMD, all states are stakeholders and must be included in the effort. Just as peace and order in a nation are best maintained if the consent and participation of its citizens are secured, international progress towards peace, order, and the reduction of arms, including WMD, can best be attained through the participation and cooperation of all governments. Implementation of the required measures may not end proliferation, but it will raise the risks to a level that even most inveterate proliferants may no longer tolerate. And those who continue the proliferation gamble will know that the odds have changed in an unforgiving form.

Taking Stock, Establishing an Inventory, and Assessing the Nation's Current Standing

In order to establish what has been done so far in national legislation and how the measures currently in force work, a review with audits must take place. Such a review has to start with the UNSC taking stock, establishing an inventory, and assessing the nation's current position and standing as a member of all ratified international conventions related to WMD and terrorism.

For this, the NSC will have to establish a temporary commission of representatives of all relevant ministries and agencies, mandated with a thorough review of the implementation of all international obligations serving the prevention of WMD proliferation, and the countering of terrorism into national laws and regulations. This review should take place with the triple aim:

1. To achieve, wherever possible, full conformity of national laws with all obligations contained in the ratified international conventions
2. To explore and evaluate all international conventions or multilateral agreements that serve the prevention of proliferation and the countering of terrorism to which the state is not yet a party, and submit proposals with all arguments for adherence
3. To single out problem areas for which more effective and efficient solutions have yet to be found to fully fulfill national obligations

The problem areas for which more effective and efficient solutions have to be found require the constitution of another temporary commission of experts and specialists that should be able to do in-depth analysis of the problems, seek to identify desirable and achievable processes through which the problems can be optimally solved, and give directions for interdepartmental and interagency cooperation. They should present realistic proposals aimed at the greatest possible reduction of the dangers of the proliferation of WMD and terrorism, which should comprise both short-term and long-term solutions. The scope of the investigations should be comprehensive and include nuclear, chemical, biological, radiological weapons, and the means of delivering them, as well as the possible links between these issues to terrorism and organized crime. These findings will then form part of the basis from which the security policies and national strategies can be developed to counter proliferation of WMD and to fight terrorism and organized crime.

Review of the Measures in Place

Along with taking stock and reviewing the implementation of international obligations serving the prevention of the proliferation of WMD and the countering of terrorism into national laws and regulations, the NSC has to establish interdepartmental and interagency commissions of experts mandated with a review and the conduct of audits of the measures, regulations, and practices currently in place in the following domains:

1. The nation's export-import licensing and control system
2. Materials control lists relating to nuclear, biological, chemical, radiological weapons, means of delivery, and dual-use goods
3. The counterproliferation activities of export-import control enforcement agencies: customs, police, border guard and coast guard, and the armed forces
4. The security of all nuclear sites and facilities
5. The secure location and transfers of nuclear, biological, chemical, and radiological materials
6. The surveillance and inspection of all academic institutions and companies that have stocks of pathogens listed in the Biological and Toxin Weapons Convention (BTWC), and have high-level microbiological containment facilities, fermenters, and bioreactors
7. The surveillance and inspection of the pharmaceutical sector and bio-engineering companies that have expertise in genetics and molecular biology, and consultant firms that offer services in the industrial microbiological process

This review should be conducted with the aim that the government could establish a universal system of export controls that provides harmonized standards, enhanced transparency, and practical support for implementation. In addition, the government should encourage the members of the five export control regimes to widen membership and improve implementation in view of current security challenges, without impeding legitimate trade and economic development. In addition, it should establish a national legal framework.

The National Legal Framework and Implementation of Legislation

Appropriate and effective national implementation requires that the conventions are enforceable in domestic courts. For this, the state must establish supporting civil and criminal laws and penalties as well as fiscal, administrative, export-import, customs, border guard, and coast guard rules. It must also put in place all that is needed to enforce the legal framework.

The national legal framework to implement international obligations relating to WMD, terrorism, and organized crime, must cover the following:

1. The national authority to lead and coordinate implementation
2. The organization responsible for proliferation, safety, and security risk assessment relating to WMD, means of delivery, and related and dual-use materials
3. Cooperation with, as well as access to and powers of, international organizations as mandated by the conventions
4. Civil and penal legislation related to WMD proliferation, terrorism, and organized crime
5. Judicial and law enforcement powers
6. Export-import controls and licensing system
7. Materials control lists relating to proliferation of WMD, delivery means, and related and dual-use materials
8. Security of facilities, sites, and transfers related to WMD and delivery means
9. Inspection of sites and measures in place
10. Emergency measures and consequence management
11. Education, training, exercises, and outreach

Among the key elements to be considered in the implementation of legislation are:[13]

1. A national authority, a State System of Controls that should be set up for ensuring fulfillment of conventions' obligations comprised of: a system of obligatory licensing of allowed activities by an independent state regulatory body, a system of strict sanctions and penalties for activities that are carried out without a license, and individual and corporate site operator's responsibilities for safety and nonproliferation with respect to potential dual-use WMD activities.
2. The account that should be taken of the regulatory means that have proved to be most effective internationally in establishing WMD controls. Proper judicial safeguards should be applied to ensure against human rights abuses. Derogation due to "public emergency" should be allowed only under defined circumstances.

3. Punishments in criminal legislation should be appropriate to effectively deter potential violators. A term of imprisonment for less than five years, for example, may be insufficient. Proper judicial safeguards must be applied, especially regarding imprisonment on remand.
4. Criminal legislation needs to be backed by strict liability laws to create an economic deterrent. While this may not stop determined proliferants, it may deter individuals from intentionally or culpably aiding and abetting individuals in their WMD activities.
5. Administrative laws must allow for appropriate police investigation and public prosecution. Procedural law should allow for a fair, speedy and, to the extent possible, public trial.

However, to have legislation in place is not sufficient. States must also rigorously enforce it through investigations and prosecutions of suspected violators. While this is implicit in treaty provisions requiring national implementation, UNSCR 1540 specifically requires states to enforce national measures that implement the resolution. This requires states to properly fund, train, equip, and operate law enforcement personnel such as the police; prosecutors; control of finances and money laundering; customs; border guard and coast guard; environment, animal, plant, food and transportation inspectors; visa, immigration, and naturalization service personnel; and civil and military defense. This should be executed in a manner that enables them to properly detect, prevent, investigate, prosecute, convict, and punish individuals handling or seeking access to WMD. The establishment of a licensing system is essential, since it allows the State System of Controls to ensure that NBC activities and practices are in accordance with laws and regulations. State legislation should further delegate responsibility for NBC security to operators and private sector enterprises, which have individual responsibility for internal control systems.

The development of effective physical protection measures calls for intrusive auditing of state procedures for the handling and accounting of NBC weapons-usable materials at installations and in transit. In creating and maintaining capabilities for NBC detection and investigation, reference can be made to the German system, which has established the following principles:

■ Responsibilities and tasks assigned to each authority under the State System of Controls must be clearly specified.

- Rapid reporting of illicit trafficking events and distribution of all relevant information to the concerned authorities and agencies must be ensured.
- Law enforcement and NBC safety authorities and their experts must be available around the clock.
- Law enforcement and NBC safety authorities need to have the proper detection and analysis equipment at their disposal.
- Bodies coordinating separate branches of law enforcement and border security agencies should be formed to address serious cases.
- National and transnational training and sharing of experience must be provided.

Moreover, a need exists for international and national coordination among prosecutors, police, intelligence agencies, border control authorities, and customs. In the EU, this kind of cooperation is already in progress. Also, Interpol has been proactive in identifying its responsibilities and coordinating its response, especially on bioterrorism. Understandably, this has proved to be a large and complex task. In many cases, police and customs officers do not know what to look for and may not be able to recognize NBC weapons equipment or related materials. Thus, much more effort needs to be invested in ensuring that enforcement itself is an effective, efficient, and credible deterrent.

The results of the inventory of the nation's current position as a member of all ratified international conventions related to WMD, and the reviews and audits of the measures, regulations, and practices currently in place, will then serve as the basis for the planning of the reorganization of the national efforts to prevent proliferation, to counter terrorism and organized crime, and for the corresponding transformation and reform of the security sector.

Establishing an NBC Security Culture[13]

Every state should establish all the essential characteristics, principles, attitudes, and behaviors of individuals, organizations, and institutions that serve as means to support, enhance, and inculcate NBC security. The basis for an effective NBC security culture requires three features:

- Creation of a policy framework at the state level
- Creation of implementing frameworks by those organizations and agencies having NBC security responsibilities

- Adoption of attitudes and behaviors by individuals operating within these frameworks

These should be part of a comprehensive system, which is a necessary prerequisite for developing a healthy NBC security culture through overall coordination and dialogue.

THE ROLE OF THE STATE

In any major activity, the manner in which individuals act is conditioned by frameworks established at the national level. The responsibility for establishing, implementing, and maintaining an NBC security regime, including protecting the confidentiality of NBC security information, within a state, rests entirely with that state. This includes responsibility for establishing policies and associated legislative and regulatory frameworks to govern NBC security. Through these frameworks, the foundations for the creation of an NBC security culture are established and conditioned. In general, a state defines general protection objectives, taking into account the present threats, the international context, and the specificity of the national situation, and distributes responsibilities, including for contingencies and creating the framework for protecting the confidentiality of NBC security information.

A national NBC security framework depends on specific requirements that are exerted through the regulatory process. These prescribe such things as how to approach the problem (e.g., by providing schemes for categorizing the target or for specifying the threat levels) and also establish performance standards, reporting requirements, design requirements for physical protection systems, licensing of organizations for particular activities, accounting and record keeping requirements, warning and alert, and many other aspects. They form the foundation for the management system associated with an NBC security framework. Since the management systems are an integral part of the culture of any organization, regulation is therefore inextricably linked with an NBC security culture.

The state should clearly lay out its own responsibilities for NBC security as well as the responsibilities entrusted to other appropriate organizations. It is essential for this distribution of responsibilities to be clearly defined and well understood by all individuals within the relevant organizations.

State commitment should be specified in national legislation and regulations, which include independent competent regulatory authorities, that are supported by technical assistance bodies as appropriate. These independent competent regulatory authorities should have adequate personnel, financial resources, and supervisory powers. Recognition must be given to the agencies having appropriate authority to intervene in NBC security events on or off site during the transport of NBC material.

The need for coordination between state authorities and other organizations requires that the state develop mechanisms for the exchange of knowledge and data, particularly between law enforcement, intelligence, and response authorities. State authorities should also organize periodic inspections and exercises involving operators and national authorities to evaluate and improve NBC security.

The state must establish general principles for authorizing access to NBC facilities and to information that could compromise the protection of NBC material, related substances, and their associated facilities and transport, and ensure their application. NBC security culture promotes the awareness in all individuals of the sensitive nature of NBC security information, and the need to protect the confidentiality of that information. Such information must be prevented from circulating freely in the public domain since it could be used for malicious purposes.

THE ROLE OF ORGANIZATIONS

A state's NBC security policy framework is developed at the highest level of each organization concerned, and is based on the general security policies established by the state. The framework sets the conditions of the work environment and the behavior of individuals. The policy framework may differ from organization to organization, depending on the nature of the work and the duties performed by its staff. Likewise, the framework will manifest significant common characteristics.

Any organization conducting NBC security related activities should make its responsibilities and commitment to NBC security known and understood publicly in a statement of security policy issued by its director. The NBC security policy framework of an organization forms the foundation of the management systems that are an integral part of the culture of any organization and that influence all NBC security culture components.

The NBC security framework should include clear definitions and distribution of responsibilities within each organization. Through these definitions, strong links are forged for direct exchanges on matters of security.

Each organization should appoint its own security officer, reporting to an appropriate senior manager of the organization. This officer should have sufficient authority and resources to oversee the implementation of NBC security activities throughout each organization.

Each organization should establish procedures and levels of reporting for responsible safety and security officers to promote the earliest resolution of questions regarding the practical balance between NBC safety and security. In addition, personnel should have the necessary equipment, adequate work areas, and other forms of support to carry out their responsibilities.

All organizations should make arrangements for the regular review of their NBC security practices. This regular review necessarily takes into account lessons learned from feedback and changes in the threat level. In particular, the organizations must ensure that all detected discrepancies relating to the protection systems are comprehensively analyzed and corrected.

THE ROLE OF THE MANAGERS IN THE ORGANIZATIONS

The work environment has a powerful influence on the attitudes of individuals. Developing and maintaining an NBC security culture depends on policies that foster this environment and encourage attitudes that contribute to the effectiveness of NBC security. Senior management is responsible for defining and revising policies and protection objectives while operational managers are in charge of initiating practices that comply with these. Managers demonstrate their commitment to NBC security through their behavior and, in doing so, play an important role in promoting NBC security culture within each organization.

Managers are responsible for defining the scope of responsibilities for personnel under their supervision, for clarifying lines of reporting, and for documenting responsibilities in sufficient detail to avoid ambiguity.

The managers should verify that the personnel under their supervision are carrying out activities relating to NBC security. All relevant documents, updated as necessary and listed in order of importance from general directives to detailed work procedures, form the foundation for good working practices. Managers should enforce a system of verifying that activities are executed as defined.

Managers must ensure that regular contact with other organizations be maintained in compliance with the rules governing information confidentiality. Cross-organization relationships are necessary when coordinating intervention resources between state entities and operators. In this context, drills must be organized to test the organizations and the planned liaisons, train teams, and generally draw on the lessons learned to improve the intervention system.

Managers must ensure that their staffs have all the skills and authorizations required to perform their tasks relating to the protection of NBC material, relevant substances, and their associated facilities and transport. And they must ensure that temporary staff and any externally or self-employed service providers are made equally aware of the importance of NBC protection.

Managers must encourage personnel to report any event affecting or likely to affect NBC protection. And they must ensure that their staffs comply with established security practices, take advantage of them, and incite them continuously through attitude and example to achieve higher levels of individual performance in tasks relating to the protection of NBC material, facilities, and transport.

A healthy NBC security culture of behavior for individuals is characterized by:

- A rigorous, prudent approach
- Constant vigilance and a questioning attitude
- Speed of reaction when faced with an unexpected situation

Among other things, individuals should be expected strictly to apply procedures and official rules. They should be aware that security systems must be operationally compatible with the performance of other activities in the organization. In addition, individuals must adopt a circumspect approach toward research and the divulging of confidential information. They must also have a steady motivation regarding the protection of NBC material, facilities, and transport. They must also be ready to be responsive and critical of any event or action regarded as suspect. In such circumstances, the information is sent immediately up the chain of command, even if it appears to be of minor importance.

11
National Interests and National Security Policy

Establishing an overview of all existing and potential threats, dangers, and risks to national security is a prerequisite for the definition of the national interests, the establishment of a national security policy, and a national security strategy.

For this, the External Intelligence Service (EIS) should be mandated—assisted by all the intelligence agencies forming the national intelligence community—to provide:

1. A comprehensive assessment of the threats, dangers, risks, opportunities, and chances related to national security, the proliferation and means of delivery of WMD, and an assessment of the possible and probable developments of the strategic situation
2. A comprehensive assessment of the threats, dangers, and risks of WMD falling into the hands of non-state actors, organized crime, and terrorists; their possible or probable use against the nation, population, its national interests and presence abroad, and its neighbors, allies, and friends

These comprehensive assessments of the EIS must be such that they can serve as a common national estimate on the basis of which the the National Security Council (NSC) can find solutions for the following three issues:

1. To define and prioritize the missions and tasks of the intelligence agencies for strategic warning, and for countering proliferation of WMD, terrorism, and organized crime
2. To define the National Interests, and to develop the National Security Policy and the National Security Strategy with particular focus on countering the preeminent threats

3. To establish a National Vulnerability Assessment in detail that can help to prevent, mitigate, and more effectively respond to the preeminent threats and catastrophic terrorism

Define the National Interests

There are two prerequisites for the definition of the National Interests:

1. A clear vision of the future of the nation as a democratic state, well integrated in the international community, and which appeals to the desires of the majority of its population
2. Intimate knowledge of the strategic situation, the possible and probable developments, and the risks, dangers, threats, chances, and opportunities as well as their interdependencies

On that basis, the definition of the National Interests—initiated by the NSC with a centralized formulation process that encompasses input from a variety of security sector actors—is best done by looking at what is needed to fulfill the vision of the nation in the future, and then by comparing these needs with all the foreign facts, trends, and actors in the strategic environment, and with the domestic threats, which may have a direct or indirect impact on the vision. This can be done first top-down, starting with the assessment of risks, dangers, threats, and opportunities at the global level and ending with the assessment of those in the country's immediate neighborhood and domestically—beginning with the nation's obligations under international law and ending with local transborder issues and the problems of internal security. Subsequently, the results thus gained should be validated and corrected through a reverse bottom-up approach.

The processes of establishing the vision of the future of the nation—and of the definition of the National Interests—can be used to test the value, effectiveness, and efficiency of the different organs and organizations of the existing security sector administration in view of future use for state modernization, strategic decision making, and strategic leadership.

Ideally, a committee that is established for the same tasks should parallel the two tasks given to the administration of establishing the vision and defining the National Interests. The members of this committee should be selected individually from outside the administration: from political parties, the intellectual elite, ethnic and other minorities of the country—reflecting the diversity of the society by profession as well as by language, culture, and religion. This would have the advantages of:

1. Promoting transparency of the processes of nation-building
2. Initiating participation and empowerment of the population and civil society
3. Initiating broad discussions about the future orientation of a modern nation

Such a community is a good way of testing what society supports at large. At the same time, such processes can broaden the acceptability of the results within and outside of the country.

The defined National Interests, together with the vision of the nation in the future, and intimate knowledge of the situation and threats, are the prerequisites for the later sequence of:

- Development of an adequate National Security Policy
- Development of a sound National Security Strategy
- Determination of organs needed for strategic decision making and leadership

Develop an Adequate National Security Policy[1]

The constitution protects the liberty and the rights of the people, and ensures the independence and security of the country. This includes fostering the common good and internal cohesion, the cultural variety of the country, fair access to information, promoting equal opportunities for citizens wherever possible, ensuring the sustainable conservation of vital resources and the environment, and promoting a just and peaceful international order. From this, and from the vision and the defined National Interests, the mainstays, principles, and objectives of security and foreign policy can then be derived.

National Security Policy is a framework for describing how a country provides security for the state and its inhabitants. It has a present and future role, outlining the core interests of the nation and setting guidelines for addressing current and prospective external and internal threats and opportunities. It seeks to integrate and coordinate the contributions of national security actors in response to the national interests and threats deemed most important. And it provides benchmarks for aligning operational decisions with the short- and long-term goals of national policy.

There are five major reasons for states to have an integrated and detailed National Security Policy:

1. To ensure that the government addresses all threats and risks in a comprehensive manner
2. To increase the effectiveness of the security sector by optimizing contributions from all security actors
3. To guide the implementation of policy
4. To build domestic consensus
5. To enhance regional and international confidence and cooperation

National Security Policy has to provide a comprehensive evaluation of both the domestic and international environments, and has to define the nation's role in the international system, taking into consideration the state's interests and values, governance structures, and decision making processes. It should culminate in a long-term vision of where the state and society should stand in the future.

National Security Policy should reflect the volatile and complex range of threats, hazards, and opportunities while taking account of the diminishing importance of geographical distance, and technological developments relevant to security policy considerations. More than ever, the nation is also challenged by the world's growing interdependence. National Security Policy has to clearly highlight what the nation needs to do against the preeminent threats of terrorism, proliferation of WMD, and transnational organized crime. And it has to point out and specify what is best done against international, regional or local conflicts, violent political extremism, radicalization, and corruption. Moreover, it has to show what the nation can do against, and how it will overcome, hazards like natural and man-made disasters; manipulation or breakdown of critical national infrastructures; curtailment of free economic exchange or economic pressure; legal and illegal migration; the scarcity of resources; environmental degradation; and new types of threats like efforts to attack or distort electoral processes and constitutional setups with a view of regaining influence and control through use of anti-democratic clients.

National Security Policy has to classify threats and dangers according to the development of the situation, and to define the adequate means and approaches for managing them. It describes each implementing actor's area of responsibility. The centralized process allows for the optimal use of resources, and helps to avoid discrepancies, redundancies, and deficiencies in drafting and implementation. National Security Policy has to address circumstances where government activity and its results are affected only in individual sectors, and where there is a need for a tightening of procedures and for rapid concentration of assets. And it has to provide for circumstances felt by a majority of inhabitants of an area to be threatening, or which massively disrupt or prevent normal everyday life, thus possibly legitimizing emergency law.

There are four key challenges for a National Security Policy:

1. It must balance openness and secrecy. Some nations try to avoid this problem by using vague language, but this may reduce the effectiveness of the document. Others have both public and classified versions. If the National Security Policy is a subject of public debate, however, its contents will likely reflect general national security goals, and leave their implementation to subordinate strategies and doctrines.
2. Some perceive a conflict between the need to preserve freedom of action and limits placed on the actions of leaders. For this reason, many nations prefer to address specific issues rather than specific countries in their National Security Policy document, although in cases where security policy is designed to send a clear signal to other powers, these might be named.
3. The need to review the National Security Policy must be balanced against the cost in both human and material terms. While reviews are necessary when important changes in the strategic environment and in the threats occur, or if the current security policy is deemed inadequate—or if changes are mandated too frequently—this can put strain on resources, particularly since a good security policy requires the input of those officials who are involved in implementing policy.
4. National Security Policy must balance public debate with the input of experts. While public debate is necessary for ownership, if there is a perception that the security policy document has become captive to political interests, this can undermine its utility.

The development of the National Security Policy is normally initiated and directed by the NSC that specifies the drafting body—which can be a standing committee, an existing or an ad hoc body. This drafting body should consult widely with all relevant ministries, actors of the security sector, and may also consult with non-governmental actors, such as political parties, academia, civil society, and the media. The breadth of participation in the formulation of National Security Policy is key to ensuring broad ownership of the security policy, which can help enhance its implementation.

Here too, it could be beneficial to establish a temporary committee, formed by members from outside the administration, and tasked with the development of the security policy, in order to get a—non-binding—alternative or second opinion, again reflecting what society at large will support. Furthermore, approval by the legislature may be required.

A comparable approach, and similar instruments, are needed for the development of the National Security Strategy.

Develop a Sound National Security Strategy

Security policy provides the basis for the development of a Plan of Action designed to achieve the aims set by security policy. The National Security Strategy, if it is to reflect the art and science of developing and using in an integrated and comprehensive way all instruments of security policy, will have to address more than what is to be done with, and expected from, the nation's armed forces.

Thus, with respect to foreign policy, strategy has to outline, among other issues and priorities, how the state will:

1. Contribute to the promotion and preservation of peace, conflict prevention, and crisis management
2. Strengthen respect for human rights and basic liberties
3. Ensure compliance with the provisions of international law and international humanitarian law
4. Contribute to defuse radicalization and diminish extremism
5. Counter transnational terrorism
6. Prevent and control the proliferation of WMD, delivery systems, and critical technologies
7. Counter international organized crime
8. Increase military transparency, support measures for disarmament as well as for verification of agreements
9. Assist developing countries in their endeavors to improve the living conditions of their populations, and provide humanitarian assistance in case of disasters or armed conflict

With respect to the protection of the population, strategy has to outline, among other issues and priorities, how the state will:

1. Classify situations, and prepare for special and extraordinary situations
2. Organize a civilian integrated management, protection, rescue and

relief system of civil protection and assistance for the prevention of, and defense against, force of strategic magnitude or politico-military threats

3. Fight terrorism and prevent terrorist acts, in particular the use of WMD on national territory
4. Prevent and control proliferation of WMD domestically
5. Prevent and fight organized crime and corruption
6. Warn, and protect the population, the resources, and cultural assets in cases of natural or man-made disasters, and how it will overcome other emergencies
7. Prevent the spread of epidemics or pandemics, and how it will cope with these in the health sector
8. Achieve, through enhanced domestic cooperation of police, fire, health care, and special technical services, the emergency response organizations, and the services protecting the critical national infrastructures, a maximum of synergies, and how it will ensure the availability of the option to expand capacities and assets should this be required, while avoiding a costly permanent orientation towards the worst case

With respect to protection of the constitution and law enforcement, strategy has to outline how the state will:

1. Promote the rule of law and community-based policing, maintain public safety and security, enforce law and order, and combat crime
2. Counter violence of strategic magnitude affecting considerable parts of the country and the population
3. Identify at an early stage, and counter dangers from violent extremism, hostile intelligence and espionage activities, illicit trafficking in arms and humans, and illegal technology transfer
4. Support the law enforcement and prosecuting authorities with information about transnational organized crime, proliferation, and terrorism

With respect to economic policy, strategy has to outline, among other issues and priorities, how the state will:

1. Strengthen international competitiveness of its economy and thus contribute to prosperity and political stability
2. Promote sustainable economic growth while preserving and creating jobs

3. Maintain a social equilibrium
4. Preserve the natural environment
5. Liberalize the markets, and diversify exports and imports
6. Reduce, through significant structural reform, the vulnerability of the economy to external shocks, and reduce economic discrepancies as a significant source of problems in the area of security policy
7. Ensure supply with the essential commodities and services when the normal economy is no longer able to do so due to circumstances beyond its control

With respect to information and communications, strategy has to outline, among other issues and priorities, how the state will:

1. Ensure its functioning as an information society in normal situations, unimpeded by government control
2. Handle information in special, extraordinary or emergency situations, and how the population will be addressed and kept informed
3. Adequately secure the country's exposed ICT infrastructure at reasonable expense

NATIONAL AND INTERNATIONAL SECURITY COOPERATION

In its core, the National Security Strategy will have to bank on cooperation. This derives from the recognition that two kinds of efforts are required for the preservation of values and the protection of the nation and its people: national and international security cooperation. National Security Strategy will have to be based on the one hand on the will and capacity to counteract the threats and dangers with its own civilian and military means, and, on the other—wherever these means are insufficient—on the cooperation with other countries and international organizations. Present and foreseeable transnational threats and dangers cut across national borders. Mostly, they can be countered successfully only through international cooperation. Collaboration with international security organizations and friendly states should be sought to counter terrorism, proliferation, and organized crime, in order to contribute, through mutually reinforcing cooperation, to stability and peace in the extended geographic sphere. This serves to strengthen the solidarity that is expected from the nation, and is at the same time a judicious investment in its own security.

This results in a need for bilateral and multilateral security cooperation with foreign partners, covering such subjects as coordinating strategies, operations, tactics, and actions against terrorist groups, proliferators, and organized crime, and also military training, arms procurement, participation in peace support missions, and supporting humanitarian aid and disaster relief missions. Military interoperability will also increase freedom of action were the nation to be attacked militarily.

Determine the Organs Needed for Strategic Decision Making and Leadership

From the elements contained in the National Security Policy and the National Security Strategy the organs needed for strategic decision making and leadership can be derived and determined. Not only the NSC, but all the organs involved in decision making must be intimately acquainted with the National Interests, the vision of the future nation, the situation, and the risks, dangers, threats and opportunities in order to be able to provide the necessary and required contingency planning. This knowledge, contingency planning, and timely strategic warning are at the same time the prerequisites for efficient and effective national crisis management.

The development of the National Security Policy and of the National Security Strategy require intimate knowledge of the essence of combating proliferation of WMD and terrorism, and of what has been done so far in these fields by international organizations and major states.

What is the Essence of Combating Proliferation of WMD?

The essence of combating proliferation of WMD can be found in the many strategies existing.[2] These strategies seek to create a global environment hostile to proliferation, where everything is done to deny both states and non-state actors supply of nuclear, radiological, biological, and chemical weapons and the know-how, material, or other means to produce and deliver them. They provide guidance to orchestrate all instruments of national power while coordinating the collective efforts of the international community. The end-state of the strategies is invariably a world secure against proliferation, and a global environment in which threats with the world's most destructive weapons cannot succeed.

An effective strategy for countering WMD, including their use and further proliferation, must be an integral component both of the National Security Policy and the National Security Strategy. The strategy for countering proliferation of WMD must aim at denying these weapons to states and terrorists, and to build a layered defense against them. To succeed, the nation must take full advantage of today's opportunities, including the application of new technologies, increased emphasis on intelligence collection and analysis, the strengthening of cooperation with international organizations, coalitions of the willing, and individual states, and the establishment of new partnerships.

Enforcing security against proliferation threats always involves trade offs. Sanctions may harm economic interests of the sanctioning states as well as the citizens of the sanctioned state. Military action to destroy suspect weapon capabilities or threatening regimes and terrorist networks carry even greater risks to life, treasure, and political order. In weighing such trade offs, distinctions among the types of threat should be made. Nuclear weapons would warrant more costly and risky action than chemical weapon threats, with biological weapon threats somewhere in between, depending on the assessed nature of the agents, dispersal mechanisms, and actors involved.

Strategies generally have three principal pillars:

1. Counterproliferation to combat WMD use
2. Strengthened nonproliferation to combat WMD proliferation
3. Consequence management to respond to the use of WMD

COUNTERPROLIFERATION

Experience shows that efforts are not always successful in preventing and containing proliferation of WMD to hostile states and terrorists. Therefore, the armed forces and all appropriate agencies of the security sector must possess the full range of operational capabilities to counter the threat and use of WMD by states and terrorists through three measures:

1. Interdiction
2. Deterrence
3. Defense and mitigation

Interdiction: Efforts must be undertaken to enhance the capabilities of the armed forces, and of the intelligence, technical, and law enforcement communities to prevent the movement of WMD materials, technology, and expertise to hostile states and terrorist organizations. This means ensuring that all needed capabilities to combat WMD are fully integrated into the emerging defense transformation plan as well as into the homeland security posture. Moreover, counterproliferation must be fully integrated into the basic doctrine, training, and equipping of all forces in order to ensure that they can sustain operations to decisively defeat WMD-armed adversaries.

Deterrence: Today's threats are far more diverse and less predictable than those of the past. Hostile states and terrorists have demonstrated their willingness to take high risks to achieve their goals. As a consequence, new methods of deterrence are required. A strong declaratory policy, effective law enforcement and armed forces are essential elements of the deterrent posture, along with the full range of political tools to persuade potential adversaries not to seek or use WMD. In addition to the response and defense capabilities, the deterrent posture against WMD threats must be reinforced by effective intelligence, surveillance, interdiction, and domestic investigation and police capabilities. Such combined capabilities enhance deterrence both by devaluing an adversary's WMD and missiles, and by posing the prospect of an effective response to any use of such weapons.

Defense and mitigation: Because deterrence may not succeed, and because of the potentially devastating consequences of WMD use against the nation, the population, and the armed forces, the military and all appropriate agencies of the security sector must have the capability to defend against WMD-armed adversaries, including in appropriate cases through preemptive measures. Prerequisite for this are capabilities to detect and destroy an adversary's WMD assets before their use. In addition, robust active and passive defenses and mitigation measures must be in place to enable the military and relevant civilian agencies to accomplish their mission. Active defenses disrupt, disable, or destroy WMD en route to the targets, and include air and missile defenses. Passive defenses must be tailored to the unique characteristics of the various forms of WMD. And there must be an ability to rapidly and effectively mitigate the effects of a WMD attack against the armed forces. Finally, the military and law enforcement agencies must stand ready to respond against the source of any WMD attack. The primary objective of a response is to disrupt an imminent attack or an attack in progress, and eliminate the threat of future attacks. As with deterrence and prevention, an effective response requires rapid attribution and a strike capability. And there is a need to be prepared to conduct post-conflict operations to destroy or dismantle any residual WMD capabilities of the hostile state or terrorist network. This will also have a powerful deterrent effect upon other adversaries that possess or seek WMD or missiles.

NONPROLIFERATION

Every effort must be undertaken to prevent states and terrorists from acquiring WMD and missiles. The traditional measures of diplomacy, arms control, multilateral agreements, threat reduction assistance, and export controls must be enhanced that seek to dissuade or impede proliferant states and terrorist networks, as well as to slow and make more costly their access to sensitive technologies, material, and expertise. Moreover, compliance with international agreements must be ensured. New methods of prevention of proliferation activities and expanded safety and security measures must be identified and pursued. Nonproliferation comprises six elements:

1. Active nonproliferation diplomacy
2. Multilateral regimes
3. Nonproliferation as well as threat reduction cooperation
4. Controls of nuclear materials
5. Export controls
6. Nonproliferation sanctions

Active nonproliferation diplomacy: States must actively employ diplomatic approaches in bilateral and multilateral settings in pursuit of the nonproliferation goals. Supplier states must be dissuaded from cooperating with proliferant states, and the latter must be induced to end their WMD and missile programs. Countries must be held responsible for complying with their treaty commitments. In addition, enhanced cooperation with international organizations and states must be developed and coalitions formed to support nonproliferation efforts, as well as to seek their increased support for nonproliferation and threat reduction cooperation programs.

Multilateral regimes: Existing nonproliferation and arms control regimes play an important role in the strategy to counter proliferation. The government has to support the regimes in force, and encourage improvement of the effectiveness of, and compliance with, those regimes. Consistent with other policy priorities, the government will also have to promote new agreements and arrangements that serve its nonproliferation goals. Overall, an international environment has to be cultivated that is more conducive to nonproliferation.

Nonproliferation and threat reduction cooperation: A wide range of programs need to be pursued, designed to address the proliferation threat stemming from insecurities in other countries such as the large quantities of Cold War-legacy WMD and missile-related expertise and materials. Maintaining and supporting an extensive and efficient set of nonproliferation and threat reduction assistance programs is important for the strategy, as is the continuation to encourage friends and allies to increase their contributions to these programs, particularly through the G-8 Global Partnership Against the Spread of Weapons and Materials of Mass Destruction.

Control of nuclear materials: In addition to programs to reduce fissile material and improve the security of the arsenals that remain, the government must continue to discourage the worldwide accumulation of separated plutonium, help to minimize the use of highly enriched uranium, and work in collaboration with international partners to develop recycle and fuel treatment technologies that are cleaner, more efficient, less waste intensive, and more proliferation resistant.

Export controls: States must ensure that the implementation of export controls furthers their nonproliferation and other national security goals. States have to update and strengthen export controls, while at the same time improving the ability of the export control system to give full weight to both nonproliferation objectives and commercial interests. The overall goal must be to focus national resources on truly sensitive exports to hostile states or those that engage in onward proliferation, while removing unnecessary barriers in the global marketplace.

Nonproliferation sanctions: Sanctions can be a valuable component of the strategy against WMD proliferation. At times, however, sanctions have proven inflexible and ineffective. Thus, a much more comprehensive sanction policy must be developed to better integrate sanctions into the overall strategy.

CONSEQUENCE MANAGEMENT

Defending the homeland is the most basic responsibility of government. The nation must be prepared to respond to the use of WMD against targets in the country, the population, the armed forces, or against neighboring states. Thus, a capability to reduce to the extent possible the potentially horrific consequences of WMD attacks must be developed and maintained. Homeland security has to work out programs to deal with the consequences of the use of WMD, whether by hostile states or by terrorists, and also offer planning, training, and assistance to regional and local authorities. To maximize their effectiveness, these efforts need to be integrated and comprehensive. The emergency response forces must have the full range of protective, medical, and remediation tools to identify, assess, and respond rapidly to a WMD incident on national territory.

INTEGRATING THE PILLARS

There are four critical enabling functions that serve to integrate the three pillars of counterproliferation, nonproliferation, and consequence management of the strategy to counter proliferation of WMD:

- Improved intelligence collection and analysis: A more accurate and complete understanding of the full range of WMD threats is, and will remain, among the highest national intelligence priorities, to enable the nation to prevent proliferation, and to deter or defend against those who would use these capabilities. Improving the ability to obtain timely and accurate knowledge of the offensive and defensive capabilities, plans, and intentions of opponents is key to developing effective counter and nonproliferation policies and capabilities. Particular emphasis must be accorded to three aspects:

  1. Improving intelligence regarding WMD-related facilities and activities
  2. Interaction among intelligence, law enforcement, and the military
  3. International intelligence cooperation.

- Research and development: States have a critical need for technology that can quickly and effectively detect, analyze, facilitate interdiction of, defend against, and mitigate the consequences of WMD. Numerous ministries and agencies have to engage in research and development to support the strategy against WMD proliferation. These efforts have to be coordinated; priorities, gaps, and overlaps in programs have to be identified; and options for future investments have to be examined.
- Strengthening international cooperation: WMD represent a threat not just to the nation, but also to neighbors, friends, allies, and the broader

international community. For this reason, it is vital to cooperate closely with like-minded countries on all elements of the strategy against proliferation.

■ Targeted strategies against proliferants: All elements of the strategy must be brought to bear in targeted strategies against supplier and recipient states of WMD proliferation concern, as well as against terrorist groups which seek to acquire WMD. Because each of these actors is different, country- and group-specific strategies have to be pursued that best enable the nation, friends, and allies to prevent, deter, and defend against WMD and missile threats from each of them. These strategies must also take into account the growing cooperation among proliferant states— the so-called secondary proliferation—and the current and potential future linkages between terrorist groups and state sponsors of terrorism, as well as those between terrorist and organized crime groups.

What is the Essence of Combating Terrorism?

Terrorism is the societal evil of our time that must be abolished as slavery and piracy were in the nineteenth century, and fascism and apartheid in the twentieth century. Efforts to disrupt and destroy terrorist organizations can occur in many ways, including: diplomacy in both bilateral and multilateral forums; law enforcement efforts to investigate, arrest, and prosecute terrorists; financial and related measures to eliminate terrorist support; military actions against terrorist training or support facilities in countries harboring them, as well as covert operations by intelligence services.

The essence of combating terrorism can be found in the many strategies already in existence.[3] Most are comparable to the U.S. National Strategy for Combating Terrorism,[4] which claims leadership in the worldwide effort and is—by admonishing preemptive strikes and preventive war—the most offensively oriented. For the United States, the best defense is an aggressive offensive in which traditional counterterrorism,[5] antiterrorism,[6] intelligence collection, and covert action are seamless and integrated. All strategies seek to create a global environment hostile to all terrorist groups, whether they operate globally, regionally, or within the boundaries of single states. They provide the guidance necessary to orchestrate all instruments of national power while coordinating the collective efforts of the international community. The end-state of the strategies is a world free of terrorism as an instrument of societal change, and a global environment in which terrorism can never again flourish.

Since the fight against terrorism requires a multidimensional, multinational approach aimed at the entire spectrum of terrorism, strategies call upon states, international and regional organizations, private and public entities, and individuals to collaborate in combating terrorism at all levels simultaneously. The United Nations should lead the effort while facilitating regional responses and assisting individual partner states.

All strategies place primary responsibility on sovereign states that have jurisdiction over terrorist activities within their borders. Many states are well equipped to combat terrorism. Other states are weak and require assistance, or are reluctant and require motivation. Some states still support or sponsor terrorists and must be compelled to stop. The United Nations, the United States, NATO, and the EU encourage all civilized societies to pool diplomatic, informational, military, and economic capabilities to defeat terrorist organizations wherever they exist, deter future acts of terrorism, and ultimately diminish the underlying causes of terrorism through a concerted effort at the global, regional, and sovereign state level. At the same time, individual states are called upon to provide a robust defense for their citizens both at home and abroad.

Strategies generally have four principal pillars:

1. Defeating terrorist organizations
2. Deterring future acts of terrorism
3. Diminishing the underlying causes
4. Defending the state at the home front

DEFEATING TERRORIST ORGANIZATIONS

The first element of abolishing terrorism as an instrument of change aims to defeat existing terrorist organizations at the global, regional, and state level. Terrorism will only be defeated by solidarity and collective action.[7] Through direct and indirect use of diplomatic, informational, military, and economic instruments of power, the international community should seek to defeat terrorist organizations by attacking their centers of gravity while directly compelling or indirectly influencing states that sponsor terrorists. The centers of gravity of terrorist groups include leadership, supporting ideology, finances, command and control network, and sanctuaries. To defeat existing terrorist groups requires:

1. Identification and isolation of terrorist organizations at each level
2. Disruption of support infrastructure and sanctuaries

3. Discrediting of ideology or reasons for committing acts of terrorism
4. Destruction of networks and leadership

While it is unrealistic to hope to eliminate every single terrorist who threatens innocent individuals, it is possible to eliminate the synergy created by cooperation of disparate terrorist organizations. This effort will reduce the operational scope and capabilities of global and regional terrorists to the point that they become threats only at the individual state level. At this level, the threat can be combated as criminal behavior, which will allow a narrower focus to attack their centers of gravity and allow full engagement of law enforcement mechanisms.

DETERRING FUTURE ACTS OF TERRORISM

The second element of the strategy focuses on deterring future acts of terrorism. To establish a credible deterrent, the international community should develop and maintain a set of capabilities and mechanisms that clearly communicate to potential terrorists and their supporters that the costs of engaging in terrorism far outweigh any perceived benefits. The deterrence message should be sent not only to terrorist organizations, but also to states that sponsor them, non-state actors that provide a front for their activities, and individuals who contemplate joining or supporting them. The goal of deterring terrorism supports the strategic aim of abolishing terrorism by convincing individuals, organizations, and states to seek alternate methods of political change because terrorism is no longer a viable option. Each of the four audiences associated with terrorism needs to be provided with the deterrence message.

- Deterring terrorist organizations: Terrorist groups believe that they can conduct operations with impunity. Capabilities, particularly improved intelligence, should be acquired to detect, thwart, and destroy such groups and bring their members to justice. Actions should be taken to create certainty that terrorists will be captured and imprisoned rather than becoming martyrs for their cause. Political, social, and religious leaders must understand that their organizations will be destroyed if they choose terrorism to advance their aims.
- Deterring state actors: States must be deterred from providing support or sanctuary to terrorist organizations. This can be done by broadening international norms against terrorism and demonstrating the resolve to hold accountable the leadership of any state that continues to sponsor

terrorism. States must clearly understand that the costs of engaging in acts of terrorism will far outweigh any perceived benefits.

▪ Deterring non-state actors: Non-state actors must be deterred from providing a front, aid, and assistance to terrorist organizations. This can be achieved by establishing an international environment of greater financial transparency, naming and shaming organizations involved in terrorist support, and lowering barriers to asset seizures and freezing of funds.

▪ Deterring individuals: Efforts to deter individuals from joining or supporting terrorist groups include educating potential recruits on the sinister nature of specific terrorist organizations and terrorism in general, dispelling the notion that terrorism results in positive gain, and demonstrating that terrorists will be brought to justice.

Although some believe that terrorists—particularly suicide terrorists— are undeterrable, arguments can be made to the contrary. State and non-state actors can be deterred from providing assistance. The tougher challenge applies to the actual terrorist organizations and their followers. Deterrence of these will take time. The bottom line is that terrorists must believe that ultimately their efforts would be futile.

DIMINISHING THE UNDERLYING CAUSES

Efforts to diminish the underlying causes of terrorism comprise the third element of the strategy of abolishing terrorism as an instrument of change. Through an aggressive long-term campaign, the international community should mitigate the underlying conditions to foster the formation of terrorist groups and their support elements. To do this, the international community should directly or indirectly engage vulnerable regions and disparate ideologies and peoples.

The major contributors to the underlying causes of terrorism are:

▪ Economic and social inequity in societies marked by both abject poverty and conspicuous affluence
▪ Poor governance and economic stagnation or decline that alienates many segments of a state's population
▪ Illiteracy and lack of education that lead to widespread ignorance about the modern world and resentment towards Western values
▪ U.S. and Western foreign policies, particularly regarding the Middle

East, that have caused widespread resentment toward America and the West

To mitigate these underlying causes, the international community should renew efforts to address the causes by the following actions:

- Increase foreign development assistance and use it, together with soft power, to promote accountable and participatory governance along with an environment favorable to sustained economic growth.
- Promote literacy and education in the Islamic world and under-developed nations.
- Engage in information operations to denigrate the concept of terrorism and discredit supporting ideology.
- Stop supporting authoritarian regimes and reenergize efforts for peace and stability in the Middle East.

DEFENDING THE STATE AT THE HOME FRONT

On the home front, states should remain vigilant and ready by establishing collaborative relationships between the ministries, agencies, law enforcement, public health and emergency management entities, professional associations, and private partners. To that end, states should use every power available to defend their citizens against terrorist attack. States should be postured to provide an effective defense in three areas:

- Prevent terrorist attacks: To the maximum extent possible, would-be terrorists and the weapons they intend to use must be denied entry into the country through increased control of the borders, transportation, containers, etc. WMD must be detected and intercepted before they can be employed. Collaboration at all levels of government, along with the private sector and individual citizens, is essential to disrupting terrorist aims.
- Protect critical assets: To minimize the probability of a successful terrorist strike, states should harden critical infrastructure and other potential terrorist targets. Cyber-based attacks are a real threat to the nation's critical computer-supported infrastructures, such as telecommunications, power distribution, financial services, national defense, and critical government operations.
- Prepare responses: To reduce the impact of terrorism, states should be

prepared to mitigate the consequences of an attack. This is particularly critical when responding to attack from WMD. Collaboration among all ministries and agencies at the national, regional, and local level is essential. States should be safe and secure at home to preserve the way of life, maintain economic growth and stamina, and remain engaged in the international effort against terrorism.

However, while there are strategies for combating terrorism and countering proliferation of WMD, the strategies by themselves, no matter how cohesive and comprehensive, will not ensure an integrated and effective set of programs to combat terrorism and proliferation. Such programs will have to be developed with the reform and transformation of the security sector.

12

The Modern Security Sector

Reform and reorganization of the security sector is of increasing interest in all regions of the world. This is a result of a reassessment of the threats to national security.

Security Sector Reform (SSR)[1] is a complex process. Depending on a country's specific needs and requirements, it may aim to address the following enhancements of:

1. Effectiveness and efficiency of the security sector to meet the needs of national security
2. State-building
3. Civilian control and the capacity to control the security sector architecture
4. Democratic control and oversight, especially in states of transition from one-party or military rule to participatory and democratic forms of government
5. State and security sector legitimacy
6. Transparency and accountability in public affairs
7. Possibilities to allocate more resources according to societal priorities by right-sizing the security sector
8. Conflict prevention or post-conflict reconstruction

The first and foremost role of the state is that of security provider. A state's capability to provide security is the foundation of its legitimacy. National governments have to earn the right to govern by providing security, law and order, and justice. Security is not limited to territorial security of the state or to the security of a particular regime; it includes both the external and internal security of a state and its people. Focusing on human security,[2] SSR must put the security of citizens at the center, thus complementing state security. Citizens should be able to expect the state to be capable of maintaining peace and guaranteeing the strategic and national security interests of the country, as well as ensuring that their lives, property, and political, economic, and social rights are safeguarded. The state has to be able to protect citizens from the threats of insecurity, including violent conflict, terrorism, and organized crime while protecting rights and institutions from being undermined by these threats.

The security system comprises all actors that have the capacity to use force, as well as all the institutions that are involved in the management, oversight, and delivery of security within the state. Thus, the security system can be defined as: All state institutions and other entities that have a role in ensuring the security of the state and its people.[3] Under its broadest definition it includes:

- Core security actors and law enforcement institutions entitled to use force: armed forces, law enforcement and special police, gendarmerie, paramilitary forces, border guard and coast guard, guards for homeland defense and protection of the critical national infrastructure, intelligence and security services, customs authorities, export-import and money laundering controls, reserve or local security units, etc.
- Civil security management and oversight bodies: parliament or committees of the legislature; government or the executive; ministries of defense, homeland defense, internal affairs, foreign affairs, finance or treasury; national security advisory bodies; customary and traditional authorities; and financial audit and management bodies
- Justice institutions: the judiciary with courts and tribunals, the ministry of justice; criminal investigation and prosecution services; implementation justice services; prison services; human rights commissions, ombudsmen, etc.
- Non-statutory security forces: private military and private security companies, liberation and guerilla armies, private investigation, intelligence and bodyguard units, etc.
- Non-statutory civil society groups and organizations: political parties, the media, academia, NGOs, professional associations, including human rights organizations, etc.

SSR means transforming the security sector through working together to manage and operate the system in a manner that is consistent with democratic norms and sound principles of good governance, thus contributing to a well functioning security framework. The objective is strengthening good governance, democracy, rule of law, protection of human rights, and the efficient use of public resources. In this respect, civilian control and Parliamentary oversight are key aspects of SSR.

In the context of this paper, the focus of SSR will be limited to the preparation of the nation to better cope with the preeminent threats. In many countries problems in countering terrorism, proliferation, and organized crime arise because of duplication, redundancies, and stove-piping among the various institutions and organizations with security responsibility. Organizations may not be aware of each other's missions, policies, and behavior, and senior decision makers may find themselves in the dark about the activities of other branches and agencies of their own government. This can have significant negative repercussions.

Principles that Must Guide SSR

Each security sector organization must have:

1. A clear vision on where it will have to go in the next two years for being capable to optimally fulfill its mission
2. A strategy[4] with mission objectives and enterprise objectives[5] for the transformation[6] of its capabilities faster than the evolving preeminent threats emerge
3. Standards[7] as well as standing operational procedures (SOP) built on best practices, which are continuously reevaluated and improved, and are internationally compatible
4. Plans for performance enhancement that recognize its core strengths and competencies and are written in consultation with the relevant ministries and agencies
5. A comprehensive resource allocating mechanism that is tailored to the preeminent threats and aimed at the enhancement of its agility and flexibility, improving its responsiveness and priority-setting procedures—the prerequisite for which is the establishment of a permanent risk assessment that allows resources to be distributed faster to areas that need them most while ensuring that they generate future capabilities as well as present results

The preeminent threats of transnational terrorism, proliferation, and organized crime can only be counteracted and preempted effectively when the activities and engagements of all security sector organizations are intelligence led or intelligence driven. This requires a radical new approach of more intensive collaboration—intimate interaction and information exchange of all security sector organizations with the agencies of the intelligence community. For the exchange of information, classified and protected communication means must be provided. For some organizations it may require the establishment of a cell with intelligence collection capabilities, or at least the dispatching of liaison officers to the intelligence agencies.

At the same time, much closer cooperation and information exchange between all other security sector organizations must be established. In the interest of information exchange and efficient burden sharing, all national agencies must cooperate more closely among themselves. They also must become more interoperable. The border guards, for example, cannot function effectively without integrating efforts of the police; customs; passport, visa, immigration and naturalization services; export-import, money laundering and financial controls; the health and migration services; the armed forces and their reconnaissance, surveillance and observation means; NBC, environmental, agricultural and food inspectors; agencies of the ministries of transport and communications; air traffic control; and many others, including private sector enterprises.

All security sector organizations must enhance cooperation, exchange of information, and interoperability with all relevant foreign partner organizations near and far abroad. In this, they must aim to harmonize practices by utilizing common standards and common risk assessment techniques, and selecting equipment and logistics that facilitate joint operations. For the border guards, for example, enhanced cooperation and exchange of information must stretch from countries of origin for immigration to countries of transit as well as to countries of destination, and involve close cooperation with other national agencies in these countries.

Since all main intergovernmental institutions of the Euro-Atlantic area play an active part in SSR, there are sufficient norms, standards, principles, best practices, and lessons learned that could guide SSR. At the normative level, the Organization for Security and Cooperation in Europe (OSCE) played a pioneering role in 1994 through the adoption of the Code of Conduct on Politico-Military Aspects of Security.[8] NATO adopted the Partnership for Peace: Framework Document, committing the member states to exchange information on promoting transparency in defense planning and budgeting, and to ensure democratic control of the armed forces. Next to be adopted was the Partnership for Peace Working Program for 2000–2001, focusing on democratic control of forces and defense structures, and the 2004 Partnership Action Program for Defense Institution Building,[9] focusing on capacity building in the defense sector from the perspective of personnel management and budgeting.

Relevant norms and practices on policing are contained in the following documents: UN Code of Conduct for Law Enforcement Officials;[10] UN Civilian Police Principles and Guidelines; OSCE Code of Conduct on Politico-Military Aspects of Security; OSCE Strategic Police Matters Unit (SPMU) 2006 Guidebook on Democratic Policing; and Council of Europe European Code of Police Ethics.[11] These cover five sets of issues:

1. Key principles of democratic policing
2. Upholding the rule of law
3. Ethics and human rights
4. Accountability and transparency
5. Organizational and managerial issues

Relevant norms and best practices for border management can be found in the OSCE Border Security and Management Concept that was adopted in 2005.[12] EU integrated border management rules are spread across a number of legal and administrative instruments, representing a multilayered compilation of provisions, with only the basic ones found in the formal legal texts such as the Treaty on the European Community or the Schengen instruments of 1985–90. Much of the rest have been adopted through informal arrangements like the Common Manual[13] on external borders adopted by the Schengen Executive Committee, and the Catalogue of Best Practices drawn up by the Working Party on Schengen Evaluation.[14] In 2005 the central event in border management was the establishment of the European Agency for the Management of Operational Cooperation at the External Borders of the Member States of the EU (FRONTEX).[15]

As they did in the 1990s, the Parliamentary Assembly of the Council of Europe adopted several texts on human rights of the professional staff of the armed forces, control of internal security services, and democratic oversight of the security sector.[16] The Organization for Economic Cooperation and Development (OECD), a forum where governments of thirty democracies work together to address the economic, social, and environmental challenges of globalization, is also heavily engaged in SSR-related support, providing an important basis in terms of norms, principles, and operational guidance.[17]

The Stability Pact for South Eastern Europe addressed SSR-related topics related to: fighting organized crime and corruption, migration, integrated border management, and defense conversion. The EU adopted a Concept for European Security and Defense Policy Support to Security Sector Reform, and a Concept for European Community Support for Security Sector Reform. It then adopted the Policy Framework for Security Sector Reform.

The general principles on which all Euro-Atlantic organizations agreed upon are:

1. Addressing SSR issues from the perspective of global security
2. Professionalism of the security sector
3. Transparency of the security sector in terms of public information and decision making
4. Democratic oversight of the security sector and its accountability to civilian authorities
5. Compliance of the security sector actors with internationally recognized values and standards
6. Rights and duties of the security sector actors
7. Appropriate funding of the security sector to guarantee functionality
8. National ownership of SSR projects

The European Community (EC) is engaged in SSR-related support in over seventy countries through geographical and thematic programs. This includes SSR support for Eastern Europe, North and South Caucasus, Central Asia, Western Balkans, Africa, Caribbean and the Pacific, South Mediterranean, the Middle East, Latin America, and Asia.[18] But the applied norms of a politically binding nature produced by the OSCE or those issued by other organizations in the form of programs of action, guidelines, and best practices, pertain to the category of soft law. No legally binding norms presently exist in regard to SSR and security sector governance. Also, there is no full-fledged SSR concept, except in the EU, which framed a "Policy Framework" directly inspired from the OECD's approach and policy guidelines.[19]

Establishing Strategic Leadership for the Planning and Reorganization of the National Security Efforts

Given that today's preeminent threats challenge the basic principles of the international order and national security, and pose special problems for establishing and maintaining procedures that are effective in carrying out their missions as well as consistent with democracy and the rule of law, strategic leadership has to be established. This leadership must be able to provide whole-of-government strategic direction for the planning and reorganization of the security sector. It will have to monitor and coordinate the implementation of national strategy and policy decisions, lead the reform and transformation of the security sector, and emphasize a cross-sector approach towards improving security by linking security with long-term governance and development programs. It will also have to conduct gap analysis that focuses on the threat of terrorism, malicious use of NBCR materials against the nation and the population, and organized crime.

For this, a Permanent Government Strategy Group (PGSG) can be formed of prominent and recognized experts in national security and all issues of nuclear, biological, chemical, radiological proliferation, terrorism, and organized crime. In addition, the PGSG composition can comprise a chief coordinator, an organizational development adviser, a security sector reform development adviser, a communications adviser, and a governance and accountability adviser. This group may be directly subordinated either to the president, the prime minister, or the NSC, to whom it is accountable and has to report. A general mandate to establish a National Action Plan that is long term, sustainable, and economically affordable for ensuring the security of the nation, the prevention of proliferation of WMD, the countering of terrorism, and organized crime in an all-encompassing national effort is also necessary. At the same time, the PGSG should help to stimulate an informed public debate about national and international efforts against the preeminent threats. They should therefore undertake outreach activities within their capacity to engage civil society, NGOs, academics, and experts.

For the establishment of a National Action Plan, an approach in three phases seems most promising:

1. Organize the first and second priority tasks at the national level.
2. Establish a temporary organization tasked with a comprehensive performance review of the whole security sector in light of the results of the first priority tasks.

3. Analyze and assess the results of the performance review of the security sector and derive from them the targets for the reform, transformation, and reorientation of the security sector that will ensure democratic control and accountability.

Organization of the First Priority Tasks

With the establishment of the National Security Policy and the National Security Strategy, and the establishment of the organs needed for strategic decision making and leadership, the government, supported by the NSC, can proceed with giving direction to the PGSG, and providing guidance for the implementation of security sector reform and transformation.

The PGSG has to set the first priority tasks: the development of a Security Sector Strategy and of a National Defense Strategy, which will then serve as the basis for the reform of the organs and forces responsible for domestic security, and of the armed forces. This requires the constitution of two separate groups of experts working simultaneously, one covering the nonmilitary security sector, the other the armed forces. For the development of their strategies, both groups will have to take into account the developments in the Euro-Atlantic area, and the latest developments and trends in the fields of internal security and the armed forces.

Developments in the Euro-Atlantic area

The EU has undertaken efforts to develop a stronger institutional approach to internal security matters by formulating a Common Action Plan; enacting measures to enhance cross border police and judicial cooperation; harmonizing policies for defining, responding to, and sentencing terrorists; and enhancing police-intelligence cooperation, including joint investigative teams of police and magistrates. The EU established Eurojust; improved border control as well as the asylum and immigration systems; introduced wide application of the European Arrest Warrant; improved air transport security throughout Europe as well as emergency preparedness; and has taken steps in economic and financial policy to eliminate sources of terrorist financing and to fight money laundering more effectively.

However, the EU will win the fight against the preeminent threats only if its member states work more closely together. In 2007 further improvements were planned through six major programs:

1. Fighting international terrorism and cross border crime
2. Managing migration together

3. Shaping the dimension of external relations
4. Strengthening administrative cooperation
5. Promoting integration and intercultural dialogue
6. The future of European domestic policy

For fighting international terrorism and cross border crime more effectively, the EU planned nine improvements:

1. To strengthen Europol
2. To transpose the Treaty of Prüm into European legislation
3. To fight threats on the Internet
4. To make information systems more secure
5. To connect new member states to the Schengen Information System II
6. To use biometrics to make identity documents more secure
7. To protect critical infrastructures
8. To enhance disaster management and civil protection
9. To transfer airline passenger data

In order to manage migration together, the EU planned improvements in five fields:

1. Fighting illegal migration and preventing visa fraud
2. Improving returns of illegal immigrants
3. Protecting refugees by uniform application of the law on asylum
4. Better managing legal immigration
5. Protecting the external borders by significantly strengthening the European Border Management Agency FRONTEX

Shaping the dimension of external relations comprises six major plans:

1. To strengthen further the strategically important transatlantic relationship
2. To deepen partnership with Russia within the context of the Road Map to the Common Space of Freedom, Security and Justice that was adopted in 2005
3. To seek close trilateral cooperation in areas where the United States, Russia, and the EU have common interests
4. To improve cooperation with Ukraine and Moldova
5. To strengthen domestic policy collaboration with all the remaining

states involved in the European Neighborhood Policy, stretching from the eastern borders of the EU to the Mediterranean Sea

6. To continue consistently to pursue the Global Approach to Migration, because illegal migration and human smuggling can be combated effectively only through real partnership between countries of origin, transit, and destination

Strengthening administrative cooperation comprises three plans:

1. Efficient administration that is responsive to citizens' needs by expansion of the European Public Administration Network (EUPAN); implementing the i2010 eGovernment Action Plan; creating a European framework for secure electronic identification; and promoting open and standard document formats for file sharing in Europe
2. Taking action against doping by strengthening cooperation among the national anti-doping agencies and by building a network to create minimum standards for anti-doping efforts
3. Simplifying the application of the EU Data Protection Directive, and the provisions on reporting requirements; making costs of European statistics more transparent; reducing the administrative effort required for elections to the European Parliament; and consultations on the European census planned for 2010/11

Promoting integration and intercultural dialogue comprises two plans:

1. Further developing integration policy because integration will be a lasting success only when all migrants are able to: learn the language of their country of residence, complete their education, and accept the basic rules of coexistence
2. Promoting intercultural dialogue because sharing views on a regular basis is crucial for different cultures and religions to be able to live together in peace and understanding

The future of European domestic policy is a plan that aims for European domestic policy cooperation that is more efficient, coherent, and easier to understand. It includes law enforcement, border management, freedom of movement and visa, asylum and migration issues. Since 2004 the aims and guidelines for European internal policy have been dealt with in the Hague Program on Strengthening Freedom, Security, and Justice in the EU. The program ends in 2009. For the establishment of a new multi-annual program, discussion is needed to explore where the member states can work together more closely in Europe, because doing so provides added value to national measures. Analysis is then needed of where national measures are sufficient and where member states should retain policy discretion. Finally, it should be determined what can be managed more simply and clearly at the European level.

All these efforts must not only be reinforced in individual states, but also more comprehensively coordinated and synchronized at the multilateral level. Nearly all agencies participating in collaborative regional processes and information exchange recognize that coordination problems exist; many have first hand experience in the difficulties that arise when these problems are not addressed. Many have also learned important lessons over the past several years and have developed innovative techniques to improve interagency coordination and accountability. States must focus on implementing these lessons learned and making more integrated planning a formal part of the interagency process.

As far as trends and developments relevant for a Security Sector Strategy are concerned, law enforcement and the police, border management, money laundering, and customs will be addressed in what follows.

Law Enforcement and Police

The functions of security forces are to protect the individual and the community at large from any dangers that pose a threat to public security, safety, and order, and to eliminate any disturbance of public security and order wherever the public interest so requires. In particular, the police have to safeguard the constitutional order and to make sure that citizens may exercise their civil rights without any restrictions. In practice, no single model of democratic policing and law enforcement exists. Law enforcement and policing are deeply engrained in the legal, social, political, and cultural traditions of a country, resulting in a wide variety of policing systems and styles.

In a democratic legal system, courts and magistrates or judges must be kept separate from, and independent of, the police. Prosecutions are normally brought by the staffs of the Public Prosecutor's or Attorney General's

Office, which are completely independent of the courts themselves. The individual members of the Public Prosecutor's Office attached to the lower courts report to senior Public Prosecutors, who, along with the Attorney General at the Supreme or Federal Court, report to the Ministry of Justice. In carrying out their duties, Public Prosecutors are authorized to have direct contact with, and enlist the support of, police authorities or other state or local authorities.

In a state, regular police are responsible for providing law and order, public safety. and fighting crime.[20] Increasingly, they also have to deal with the problems associated with illegal trafficking of drugs, arms, and persons, smuggling, and illegal migration. Though the situation may vary by country, national security is no longer the main purpose of regular policing. It has become more relevant for special police units, which are needed to deal with transnational terrorism, proliferation, and international organized crime in a centralized fashion at the national level.

The foundation on which police organizations should be built is the conviction that the police can contribute to democratic political development most directly by acting in accord with the following four rule sets:[21]

1. Police must give top operational priority to servicing the needs of individual citizens and private groups.[22]
2. Police must be accountable to the law rather than to government.
3. Police must protect human rights, especially those that are required for the sort of unfettered political activity that is the hallmark of democracy.[23]
4. Police should be transparent in their activities.

The nature of the work, and their powers to arrest, search, seize, and interrogate, means that they have substantial scope to limit people's rights and freedoms. Today the common view among experts is that the fundamental purpose of the regular police is to protect human rights and uphold the law, both by preventing the infringement of people's human rights by others, and also by respecting human rights in the exercise of that duty. Respect for human rights is thus essential for good and effective regular policing. Since the credibility of the police depends on its professionalism, more training is needed for police officers. This training must cover humanitarian principles, constitutional safeguards, standards deriving from existing codes of ethics, and operating in accordance with democratic rules.

A major role of the police is to discourage and investigate crimes with particular emphasis on crime against persons or property, the maintenance of public order, as well as the apprehending and detainment of suspected perpetrators. Moreover, police are often used as an emergency service and may provide a public safety function at large gatherings, in emergencies, disasters, and search-and-rescue situations. To provide a prompt response in emergencies, the police often coordinate their operations with fire and emergency medical services. In many countries there is a common emergency service number that allows the police, firefighters, or medical services to be summoned to an emergency.

In order for police officers to do their job well, they are vested by the state with a monopoly in the use of certain powers. These include the powers to arrest, search, seize, interrogate, and kill. In all democratic nations, the law of criminal procedure has been developed to regulate officers' powers so that they do not exercise them arbitrarily and ruin the lives of innocent people.

In many countries, police carry firearms in the normal course of their duties. They can also be equipped with nonlethal weapons, particularly for riot control. These include batons, shields, water cannons, tear gas, pepper spray, Mace, tasers, rubber bullets, beanbag rifles, and stun guns. The use of firearms or force is typically the last resort, used only when necessary to save human life.

Modern police forces make extensive use of radio communications equipment, carried both on the person and in vehicles, to coordinate their work and share information. Vehicle-installed computers have increased the ability of police communications, enabling criminal background checks on persons of interest to be completed in matters of seconds as well as updating the officer's daily activity log and other required reports on a real-time basis.

In most countries, there are multiple levels of police agencies. There may be several police or law enforcement organizations, each serving different levels of government and enforcing subsets of the applicable law. Most police forces also contain subgroups whose job it is to investigate particular types of crime. In police forces of western countries, the most significant division is between uniformed police and detectives. Uniformed police are involved in overt policing operations, traffic control, and more active crime response and prevention. Detectives, by contrast, wear business or other civilian attire when their job is to more passively investigate crimes, usually on a longer-term basis. In some cases, police are assigned to work undercover for long periods of time to investigate crime, most often organized crime, that is unsolvable by other means. This type of policing shares much with intelligence or espionage.

One of the main problems in the post–9/11 environment is that the emphasis on policing in most states has shifted to counterterrorism, proliferation, and organized crime, which tend to be covert and involve increased interaction with intelligence agencies and security services. This is resulting in the blurring of the lines between police and security or intelligence services, and has the potential to degrade transparency and accountability. The key concern in counterterrorist policing is maximizing efficiency, which may come at the expense of legal and procedural safeguards. Thus, it is important that legislation is reviewed, distinguishing more clearly between security and intelligence services and specialized law enforcement agencies. At the same time, legislation must take better account of developments in all relevant modern technologies, communications, Internet and cyber crime, and must be more regularly updated.

Specialized groups exist within the branches either for dealing with particular types of crime—traffic policing, murder, or fraud—or because of specialized skills they have, such as diving, piloting helicopters, explosive or bomb disposal, drug enforcement squads, etc. Larger jurisdictions also retain specially trained quasi-military squads with small arms for the purpose of dealing with particularly violent situations. These are sometimes called SWAT (Special Weapons and Tactics) teams.

The criminal investigation service is responsible for obtaining information, investigating crimes, shadowing suspects, and tracing wanted persons. It operates central specialists units investigating general crime, drug-related crime, organized crime, immigration crime, and human trafficking, as well as units dealing with proliferation, terrorism, fugitive apprehension, surveillance operations, pornography, and forensic science. Normally, only specialized groups of the criminal investigation service conduct special investigation activities like telephone tracing and tapping; bugging of public or other premises, and homes; electronic surveillance; pseudo-buying; controlled delivery; infiltration; and witness protection. The units of the national criminal investigation service often have full authority over subordinate services in criminal investigation matters.

POLICE ACCOUNTABILITY

Police units are notoriously closed institutions, reluctant to open themselves to outside scrutiny. Consequently, it is imperative to establish an accountability system. Police accountability refers to how law enforcement agencies exercise their policing powers and fulfill their obligations to provide a fair, equitable, and rights-respecting public service. Police accountability encompasses more than just issues of alleged police malfeasance and misconduct. It pertains to all aspects of police performance, from policies to operations, strategies, and tactics. As effective policing requires a police-community partnership, police accountability needs to measure, evaluate, and regulate the quality of that relationship.

In democracies it is widely accepted that a sound accountability system must integrate multiple and overlapping internal and external mechanisms of control and oversight. Since the success of police accountability lies initially with the police themselves, the heart of a good accountability system is the establishment of a fair and equitable internal affairs regime within the police, based upon a publicly acknowledged code of conduct.[24] In the security sector, well-functioning internal accountability systems are grounded on internal police mechanisms, processes, and procedures, and are based on the public availability of pertinent police information. Internal mechanisms cover a broad spectrum of disciplinary procedures, administrative rules and regulations, functions like the Inspector General, and other controls.

Among other issues that need to be addressed are: how allegations of malfeasance are lodged against police personnel; the anonymity of those lodging the allegations; who is allowed to lodge allegations; the process of subsequent investigation; due process safeguards for those against whom allegations have been lodged; and who determines and judges the veracity of the allegations, and how they determine it.

Another important component in internal affairs regimes is the method by which internal affairs departments are staffed and investigators recruited and selected. Within the police services, many possibilities exist for ancillary initiatives that can support the operations of a police accountability system, among which are: rigorous training and enforcement of a use of force and a use of firearms regime by police personnel; continuous refinement and improvement of personnel performance; evaluation systems within the police; and the strengthening of police promotion processes and procedures.

External accountability refers to the role of the executive, legislative, and judicial branches of government. Control of the police by the executive is exercised at the central ministerial, the regional, and, in some countries, at the local level of government. The executive level determines budgetary allocation, issues general guidelines and priorities for policing, and regulations for police action. The legislative level exercises control of the police by scrutinizing legislation in committees; passing laws regulating police and their powers; approving budgetary allocations; establishing parliamentary ombudsmen, and commissions to investigate complaints by the public. The judicial level monitors the police and prosecutes them through civil and criminal proceedings when necessary. Depending on the context, external accountability may include organs that receive and investigate citizen complaints; commissions that review police complaint investigations; boards that hear appeals of complaint investigations and their disposition; and councils that audit and monitor complaint procedures, police policies, and performance.

External civilian oversight over police is necessary to enable victims of alleged abuses to have these allegations investigated by an independent body. Allegations should be made to an independent "complaints committee" or to police ombudsmen. It is important that independent outsiders investigate the complaint, not only members of the police services.[25] Ombudsmen, grassroots initiatives from civil society, community consultation groups, and responsible media all can play a role in external oversight. Democratic oversight of police may also be exercised in informal bottom-up mechanisms from the grassroots levels of local communities. These civil society organizations can help to ensure that police forces enjoy public confidence.

ORGANIZATIONAL ASPECTS OF LAW ENFORCEMENT AND POLICING

The challenges in building police forces are:

1. Training and equipping individual officers and the forces, which is always a time-consuming and expensive process
2. Establishing accountable and rights-respecting institutions
3. Establishing adequate managerial structures and systems
4. Ensuring that the police forces operate as part of a wider fabric of self-enforcing rule of law

There are seven principles that should guide the organization of the police:

1. To have a mission statement that clearly sets out the priorities and role for the police services, and which needs to be matched to extant capabilities and finances.

2. No policing system can be understood apart from the social and political system in which it works. Thus, any police reform will falter and wither without concomitant introduction and refurbishment of other institutions whose work impacts on the police, such as the criminal justice system and the penal system.

3. The objective of police accountability is to enhance and maintain police effectiveness, and to establish a system that ensures continuous transformation and professionalization.

4. Improvement of the management of policing—skills and systems, human resource management, budgeting, planning, information, and communication management—will have significant positive effects on strengthening accountability.

5. Because police accountability rests on the measurement of police performance, it is imperative to define what types of police performance statistics, quantitative and qualitative, are to be measured and how these measurements will be updated and modified over time. Concurrently, decisions must be taken on how those measurements are collected, analyzed, and which ones are made publicly available, and who will be responsible for these tasks.

6. As police accountability is information driven, access to policing information must be secured, optimally by enshrining public access in legislation, and the subordinate directives and regulations specified.

7. Given the interlocking nature of police accountability—internal and external—planning is crucial to: assess the capabilities of the various institutions involved, strengthen those capabilities, and determine the proportions of resources dedicated to accountability activities within these institutions.

The democratic police ideal[26] can be supported by organizational means such as: a clearer division of labor between those who investigate, arrest, try, and punish; a military-like bureaucratic structure that limits discretion and tries to create audit trails; the creation of competing police agencies rather than a single monolith; external agencies that monitor police behavior and that must give permission for certain highly intrusive actions; regular police who can be readily identified by uniforms with identification numbers and clearly marked cars; specialized undercover police whose identity is hidden and well protected; more rotation in assignments; adequate compensations and working conditions at least at the average level of the society, and living in the community they serve, not in barracks. These efforts involve the belief that liberty is more likely to be protected if: power is diffused, competing agencies watch each other, identities and actions of the regular police are visible while actions of the specialized police are accountable to parliament, and the identities of those taking part in covert police operations are well protected.

Most countries are members of the International Criminal Police Organization (Interpol) that was established to detect and fight transnational crime and provide international cooperation and coordination of other police activities. Interpol does not conduct enquiries or arrests by itself; it serves as a central point for information on crime, suspects, and criminals. Political crimes are excluded from its competencies. Countries normally maintain a Single-Point-of-Contact office in the headquarters of the national criminal investigation service that is available twenty-four hours a day, providing the gateway for international law enforcement enquiries and cooperation as well as the exchange of intelligence and information. It also serves as the point of contact for foreign liaison officers posted in the country, and it sends its own liaison officers abroad—to Interpol, Europol, and other international or regional organizations, as well as to different countries. Access to files is normally granted for enquiries about the following: wanted or missing persons; stolen vehicles or stolen property; criminal records; fingerprints; photographs of criminals; prisoners; listed or unlisted telephone subscribers; vehicle owners and registrations; driving licenses; passports; company registers; national register; electoral roll; bank accounts; and tax information.

Border Management

Border policing is a specialized police function normally performed by personnel specifically trained and equipped for that purpose. An integrated border management consists of five distinct functions:[27]

1. Border control—checks and surveillance—as defined in the Schengen borders code, including relevant risk analysis and crime intelligence
2. Detection and investigation of cross border crime in coordination with all competent law enforcement authorities
3. The four-tier access control model—in third world countries it measures cooperation with neighboring countries, border control, and control measures with the area of the free movement including return, as described in the Schengen Catalogue

4. Interagency cooperation for border management—border guards, customs, police, national security, and other relevant authorities—and international cooperation
5. Coordination and coherence of activities of member states, institutions, and other bodies of the Community and the Union

All border police organizations should have a public security mission that ensures effective and citizen-oriented protection of borders for the benefit of preserving and strengthening the safety of the population, and carries out its mission within a national and international security alliance. Border police objectives are:

1. Preventing and precluding illegal entries and trafficking in human beings
2. Detecting and warding off other crimes and dangers relevant to border police
3. Preventing and warding off risk within the scope of its jurisdiction
4. Repatriating foreigners who have entered the country illegally or legally, or who have to leave the country
5. Providing legally guaranteed assistance and protection to other authorities
6. Representing a border police service center for citizens

Moreover, border police must carry out customs inspections in areas where the Customs Administration does not normally operate. Military units, gendarmerie, or civil police should not be expected to perform duties related to border security without receiving specialized training and relevant equipment.

Border areas represent a coherent and complex operational environment that must be managed by flexible and easily adaptable methods. Specific offenses that may occur in border areas include:

1. Use of forged and falsified personal documents
2. Offenses covered by laws pertaining to aliens or asylum
3. Trafficking in human beings
4. Commission of drug crimes
5. Property offenses such as transferring stolen vehicles, art, and other goods to other countries

6. Arms and ammunition smuggling
7. Proliferation of WMD, radioactive, and dual-use technology
8. Illegal alteration of the border or of border markers and installations

To counter these offenses and investigate border-related crimes, special criminal investigation units must be incorporated into frontline service stations as well as in the chain of command.

Border security, in all its complexity, is no longer only a national security concern; it plays an important role in confidence building among European and international actors, and in the creation of international alliances, and should thus work hand in hand with foreign policy. Thus, border security systems should be built on the same principle and designed with wider European and international dimensions of modern border police work and cooperation in mind. Cooperation based on shared responsibility and mutual trust can serve a number of purposes, such as increasing effectiveness, improving the level of interoperability, and sharing relevant information and operational lessons. Cooperation is at its best if it is based on common operational principles. Cooperation is required at all levels. The work of units such as headquarters and ministerial agencies within national authorities must be included because cooperation must extend to all border-related threats and activities—encompassing political, economic, and fiscal security, social and health security, environmental and military security, and foreign policy. It must also involve transit countries, migration-affected countries, as well as internal and external border areas.

Effectiveness and efficiency can be achieved only if proper coordination is in place—nationally, bilaterally, and regionally. Coordination is important in both national and international cooperation as the ultimate aim can be achieved faster and more easily if all efforts are targeted in a common direction. The overall objective should be the development of internationally coordinated actions by border police and other law enforcement agencies.

In Europe, the basic guidelines regarding border control have been laid down in the Schengen acquis that was integrated into the EU framework in 1999 when the Treaty of Amsterdam came into force.[22] These basic guidelines are:

1. Movements across the EU external borders must take place at official border crossing posts guarded by member states.

2. Control of persons crossing the external border shall be the responsibility of authorized and competent officials of member states.
3. Crossing the external border at a point other than an official border post without special permission is illegal.
4. Crossing the border outside the operating hours of the border post is not permitted (locations and operating hours of border posts are to be determined by each state independently).
5. Effective control of border sections in between border crossing posts shall be ensured by mobile patrol or other suitable means, and the external borders shall be guarded along their entire length by the member states.
6. Effective control of the external borders presupposes the cooperation of borderguard personnel.

Border management is best achieved by entrusting the task to a specially trained, professional, and multipurpose police force operating under the Ministry of Interior—a unified law enforcement organization with its own clear and unambiguous command line over the organization, where all organs involved must have precisely defined responsibilities as well as means to act. However, a centralized management structure cannot be effective if regional branches in possession of deeper knowledge and better situational awareness of regional problems and characteristics are not empowered to tackle problems and solve issues themselves. Thus, certain decision making processes may require decentralization.

Moreover, an effective border control system requires the following:

1. A command, control, communication system with intelligence exchange, risk analysis and assessment, a permanent state of readiness, and the skills and the capability to raise the readiness level and to concentrate forces at critical locations
2. Units for border surveillance between border checkpoints on the land and sea borders with a tactical coordination center for maritime borders
3. Units carrying out passport control at border checkpoints, airports, and harbors
4. Units with legally guaranteed and regulated criminal intelligence investigation capacities and means
5. Units for education and training

6. Aircraft, helicopters, vehicles, and the establishment of an electronic and visual observation network that is integrated into a uniform border control system with passport checkpoints and border guard sectors
7. Uniform basic training for all forces responsible for border control tasks
8. Close cooperation between the various levels of internal security sectors because border control, immigration, and policing underpin law and order
9. A national point of contact with liaison officers and centralized and effective official contacts with neighboring countries
10. Legal and document advisers in the frontline service stations and in the chain of command

Furthermore, the command system in place should allow border guard units to be engaged in crisis and emergency situations, and to be easily integrated into the national civil protection structure.

Money Laundering

Money laundering is the process by which criminal proceeds are "cleaned" so that their illegal origins remain hidden. Processing its dirty money is the way organized crime disguises its activity. Though it is not possible to measure it in the same way as legitimate economic activity, the scale of the problem is considered enormous. The International Monetary Fund has estimated that the aggregate size of money laundering is anywhere between 2 and 5 percent of the world's gross domestic product.

Since money laundering is at the heart of practically all criminal activity, it has been given strategic priority at the EU level. A decision has been adopted by the EU Council of Ministers concerning arrangements for cooperation between financial intelligence units of all member states. The Europol convention was extended to money laundering in general, not just drug related money laundering. Also, a framework decision has been adopted on money laundering, dealing with the identification, tracing, freezing, and confiscation of criminal assets and the proceeds of crime. The EU members have signed the protocol to the convention on mutual assistance in criminal matters between the member states. A second anti-money laundering directive was agreed upon, widening the definition of criminal activity giving rise to money laundering to include all serious crimes, including offenses related to terrorism.[29] A framework decision has been added on the execution in the EU of orders freezing property or evidence, the scope of which was extended to terrorist-related crimes.

All of this builds on earlier work, such as that which led to the 1995 Convention on the Protection of the Financial Interests of the European Communities and to a number of joint actions on aspects of money laundering. A third money laundering directive[30] introduced an EU-wide common approach to controlling cash movements into and out of the EU, and complements the directive which had already introduced a monitoring of transactions made through credit and financial institutions. Since June 15, 2007, travelers entering or leaving the EU are required to make a declaration to customs authorities if they are carrying €10,000 or more in cash or its equivalent in other currencies or easily convertible assets such as non-crossed cheques. Under the new rules, customs authorities are empowered to undertake controls on people and their luggage, and detain cash that has not been declared. They are required to initiate proceedings against people who fail to declare cash of 10,000 or more. As for penalties resulting from such proceedings, it is up to member states to ensure that they are proportionate to the offense. Member states must record information obtained through declaration or through control and make it available to the authorities competent for fighting against money laundering and financing of terrorism. Where there is evidence that cash is being carried for the purpose of money laundering or terrorist financing, member states may exchange information. The new regulation takes into account the 2002 Commission report on cash movements into and out of the EU. This report revealed that between September 1999 and February 2000, EU customs authorities observed a considerable amount of cash and other assets such as cheques, securities, gems, and precious metal moving in and out of the EU—a total of €1.6 billion of which €1.35 billion was cash.

More generally, the European Commission is a member of the Financial Action Task Force and participates fully in international bodies such as the OECD and the Council of Europe. The Commission has also negotiated on behalf of the EU in respect of the relevant money laundering provisions of the UN Convention on Transnational Organized Crime.

Customs

In the EU, which is becoming a genuine single market, national customs authorities have a crucial role to play in fighting cross border organized crime. The single market can only function properly when there is a common application of common rules at its external borders. This implies that the twenty-seven customs administrations of the EU must act as though they were one. These common rules go beyond the Customs Union with its common tariff and extend to all aspects of trade policy, such as preferential trade, health and environmental controls, the common agricultural and fisheries policies, the protection of economic interests by non-tariff instruments, and external relations policy measures. Cooperation between the different services must be reinforced. Several measures have been put in place at the EU level to help them work together quickly and efficiently.[31]

Together with police cooperation, customs cooperation was introduced into the intergovernmental part of the Maastricht Treaty on the EU in February 1992. Article 29 provides for closer cooperation between police forces, customs authorities, and other competent authorities in the member states. Within their national competencies, customs administrations of the member states contribute to the fight against cross border crime through prevention, detection, investigation, and prosecution of activities in the areas of irregular or illegal movement of goods; the trafficking in prohibited goods; money laundering; and the protection of the financial, cultural, and environmental interests; and the health, safety, and security of EU citizens.

The competencies of customs administrations differ widely between member states. In some states, they have much greater competence and are law enforcement agencies with powers of criminal investigation and prosecution. EU customs provisions are generally wholly within the jurisdiction of national customs administrations. However, recent events in the EU have revealed the abhorrent nature of activities involving illegal movements across borders. International organized crime does not recognize national borders or competencies. Therefore, a multinational and multi-agency approach and cooperation are imperative. Criminal gangs profit from the illegal trafficking and sexual exploitation of human beings or smuggle outlawed drugs or arms. Soccer hooligans trade in hatred and violence. A black market in legal goods like alcohol and tobacco persists. The member states of the EU must be able to match and surpass the ability of criminals to work across national boundaries.

The most effective tool available to law enforcement agencies is accurate and detailed information. Professionals working at the borders need instant access to information and events on the ground. They also need to be able to act quickly on the basis of this information, often in close coordination with other national authorities. In recognition of the need for effective, clearly defined mechanisms, the EU is developing:

1. A customs information system to allow national customs services to share information on movements across borders
2. A customs files identification database to enable the national authorities responsible for carrying out customs investigations to identify competent authorities of other member states that are investigating or have investigated those persons or businesses
3. Mutual assistance, launched by the Naples II Convention, to improve the effectiveness of customs cooperation and law enforcement in the EU. Mutual assistance establishes the principle of institutional assistance in criminal matters, and cross border cooperation comes within its ambit

Illegal activities that are covered by the customs cooperation procedure include the following:

1. Drugs and other psychotropic substances
2. Firearms and other explosive materials
3. Dangerous or toxic goods
4. Nuclear goods
5. Any other trade in prohibited goods
6. Pornography and other indecent material

These cooperation efforts also cover the smuggling of goods liable to non-harmonized excise duties, such as cigarettes, tobacco, and alcohol.

Although law enforcement activities undertaken by national customs are deemed to be the responsibility of the member states, the European Commission is "fully associated" with the work as stated by the Maastricht Treaty. The Commission shares the right to initiate proposals with member states on police and judicial cooperation in criminal matters. The Customs Cooperation Working Party (CCWP) is the coordinating group within the Council structure with responsibility for taking forward initiatives in the field of customs cooperation. The group undertakes several joint operations a year focusing on specific issues such as methods of drug smuggling or illegal trade in other goods.

Until recently, the role of customs consisted primarily of collecting customs duties and indirect taxes at import. Numerous developments, including the development and enlargement of e-commerce, the threat of terrorist attacks, and the role of organized crime, have altered the environment in which customs operates. Customs is in a unique position today to be able to facilitate trade, oversee the entire supply chain, and protect the interests of the European Community and its citizens. Customs authorities implement Community policies in almost every field connected with international trade. They are in the frontline in the fight against fraud, terrorism, and organized crime. In July 2003 the European Commission adopted a package of measures covering:

1. The role of customs for the integrated management of the external borders
2. A paperless environment for customs and trade
3. Proposals for amending the Community Customs Code

With the amendments of the Code, the EU will introduce a number of measures to tighten security around goods crossing international borders. The measures will mean faster and better-targeted checks—a positive development for customs authorities, the public, and industry. The European Commission has also adopted two proposals[32] to modernize the EU Customs Code and introduce an electronic, paper-free customs environment in the EU. The first proposal aims to simplify and streamline customs processes and procedures. The second is designed to make member states' electronic customs system compatible with each other; introduce EU-wide electronic risk analysis and improve information exchange between frontier control authorities; make electronic declarations the rule; and introduce a centralized customs clearance arrangement. The result should be to increase the competitiveness of companies doing business in Europe, reduce compliance costs, and improve EU security.

The European Council on March 25, 2004, called for the protection of all forms of transport systems in order to ensure effective border control and facilitate the adoption and implementation of the strategy for customs cooperation. On an annual basis, 1,600 million tons of cargo are transported by sea, and 8 million tons of cargo are transported by air in and out of the EU. Worldwide container traffic is projected to grow from 104 million containers in 2005 to 400–460 million containers in 2010, and increase to 510–610 million containers in 2015. A particular security concern is the potential misuse of a container to smuggle a nuclear or radiological device.

Customs expertise in controlling goods, backed by the use of modern IT systems, and an efficient risk assessment, is vital to detect illegal goods such as drugs, explosive materials, or nuclear and chemical weapons. The security amendments to the Community Customs Code[33] provides the legal framework for the measures introduced in the EU Customs Security Program:

1. Traders are required to provide customs authorities with information on goods prior to import or export from the EU—Pre-Arrival and Pre-Departure Declarations, mandatory as of July 2009
2. Reliable traders will benefit from trade facilitation measures through the Authorized Economic Operator (AEO) program, which entered into force in 2008
3. Introduction of a mechanism for setting uniform Community risk-selection criteria for controls, supported by computerized systems, fully ready by 2009

These three approaches are interlinked and provide enhanced security through a combination of measures.

Customs in the EU handles 19 percent of the world trade, equating to more than 2 billion tons of goods per year. 1,600 million tons of inward seaborne cargo pass through customs. Trade made more than 120 million declarations to customs in 2004. 7.5 million international transit movements were made through the EU in 2005. In 2004 about 12 billion was collected in customs charges. Around 6,000 kilos of heroin and ninety tons of cocaine are seized in the EU each year. Thousands of seizures of endangered species are made by customs in the EU each year.

The statistics for 2006 show that the number of cases treated by customs involving goods infringing intellectual property rights—as well as the number of articles seized—had never been so high. Customs intercepted more than 250 million counterfeit and pirated articles, representing a 330 percent increase. Particularly worrying is the increase in medicines[34] and products for personal care, as these products could potentially harm the health and safety of consumers. The more traditional sector of counterfeit goods—clothing and luxury goods—have shown again a big increase. A decrease in goods seized occurred in the food and the computer equipment sector. More than 60 percent of the articles seized were cigarettes. In terms of overall quantities seized, China remains the main source for counterfeit goods with over 80 percent of all articles seized. In the medicine sector, India is the number one source, followed by the United Arab Emirates and China. Turkey remains the main source in the food sector, and Malaysia has become the main source in the electrical equipment sector. The breakdown by means of transport shows that air and postal traffic accounted for almost 80 percent of all cases treated by customs. It is conservatively estimated that the 150 million packets of cigarettes seized represent potential losses in customs duties of more than 460 million. The Commission is building up a close cooperative relationship with the United States, and is further strengthening cooperation with China. It is also working on a specific Supply Chain Security Pilot Project with the aim of tightening and securing "end-to-end" supply chains between Asia and Europe. Particular emphasis will be laid on having "secure lanes" for sea containers moving from China to Main European Maritime ports.

Developments and Trends Relevant for the National Defense Strategy

New military organizations and structures are required. They must be smaller in number and size, but more capable. Tomorrow's armed forces will need to have a much broader range of competence. As armed forces need to become more flexible, versatile, and capable of being deployed and sustained abroad, their cost will increase. As a result, the size of force that can be afforded will drop. For smaller countries, this means that they will no longer be able to field balanced national armed forces capable of conducting all the functions needed in combined-arms operations. This will require concentration on core capabilities and mission-critical or emergency essential functions. It will also require a more developed multinational division of labor, more role sharing, and more specialization. It will result in less combat support, less combat service support, and more outsourcing.

Hence, countries will have to cooperate more fully in collective security agreements because fewer states will be able to meet all the security requirements alone. This makes interoperability of the armed forces with foreign forces imperative—with an alliance like NATO at both the highest political-military levels of decision making and at the military operational and tactical levels. Moreover, within the last few years, there has been a growing tendency towards military and industrial integration as well as multinational military coalition structures. The whole aim of NATO, and in particular also of the EU, is to avoid "nationalized" defense and security policy in order to deepen integration.

It is obvious where the development of armed forces will have to go: manpower will have to give way to firepower, and quantity and mass will have to give way to quality of personnel and training, precision of weapons, better equipment, and better protection. The future battlespace will be relatively empty as military operations become more dispersed. Land forces disperse in response to increasing lethality of weapons, especially the threat from aircraft and long-range missiles. Long-range precision fires can now be delivered by a variety of means because of recent improvements in command and control, and in sensor technologies. Even direct fire is now much more lethal.[35] Warfare is becoming a hide-and-seek struggle where units must remain elusive in order to survive.[36]

Given this kind of battlespace, much of the current discussion about future warfare focuses on dispersed yet integrated operations, nonlinear tactics, networking, small autonomous units operating independently and swarming,[37] and a greater reliance on aerospace firepower.[38] There will be a premium on force projection as well as on reach, range, and speed of operations, deployment, engagement, and sustainability. Of predominant importance will be the modernization of the information, intelligence, and decision making process, which will create the capability to act preemptively because the new security environment will require more preventative actions.

At the same time, the new threats entail more military support to civilian authorities and police to cope with serious situations such as terrorist attacks, organized crime, drug trafficking, and smuggling. In addition to military interventions to bring about, restore or maintain peace, today the defense sector is called upon to carry out a greater number of security related roles. Occasionally, this can be direct action by the armed forces such as the engagement of special forces to interdict and destroy terrorists; the protection of state institutions and the critical national infrastructures; reconnaissance, surveillance, and subsidiary reinforcement of the border management services; patrols; or aid and humanitarian action. It can also involve the use of defense capabilities such as intelligence; air and ground transport; communications, bridges, and military and engineering equipment.

Thus, the essence of the problem with today's armed forces is that they are confronted with a revolutionary change in requirements that has resulted in two contradictory ends in the strategic frame of the classic interaction between ends, ways, and means: defense and security—and as such a problem of the division of labor. Because war does not seem to be imminent, the dominant trend is to rationalize this problem by addressing both these ends in sequence: by putting defense on the backburner in order to concentrate now on meeting the needs of security. However, there are dangers in reorganizing the means to meet these ends without addressing the ways. In theory, the way defense is dealt with has not changed. States still think of defense as requiring mass armies. It is true that, as weapons have become more capable, the density of forces needed in open battle is diminishing. But it is equally true that the future will witness increasing dislocation of the new threats, insurgencies, and combat into urban areas, requiring a much higher density of forces. It is even truer for peacekeeping operations and out-of-area interventions. For such operations, land forces need to have more manpower of the actual battalions and brigades making up the force structure deployed to sustain the operations. They also need this manpower to generate sufficient periodic replacements of the forces engaged.[39] However, because of diminishing finances and defense budgets, states continue with the downsizing of their armed forces. Hence, it is no longer clear what the way should be either for defense or for security. The only thing that is clear is that the existing means are far from being optimized either for defense or security. The most critical problem is to find new ways to satisfy both ends of defense and security with the means affordable—solving the challenges of the dual role of the military through greater participation of the whole security sector, and more precisely defined fields of division of labor.

FUTURE WAR

War may no longer be what it was originally, nor will it be carried out in the ways with which we are familiar. War is ever more war among the people,[40] which has six defining characteristics:

1. The different ends of military action in such conflicts: to create conditions in which other means and levers of power may be brought to bear to achieve the decision, one generally having to do with the individual and societies that are not states. In Bosnia, the UN did not use military force to resolve the issue by destroying Bosnian Serb forces outright, but instead deployed it selectively to create a condition in

which humanitarian activities could take place, and negotiations or an international administration could lead the desired outcome.

2. Given the nature of the new objects of war, Western armed forces fight amongst the people instead of on the battlefield. People become an object of war because of their close proximity and the fact that they may be the support base of the opposing force. Guerillas and terrorists conceal themselves among the people rather than separating themselves in the manner of mechanized divisions, fleets of combat ships, and squadrons of combat aircraft. Additionally, modern media bring the war home to those not directly involved, and whose opinions may also be relevant to policy making, such as national electorates.

3. Conflicts tend to become timeless because the conditions that are the purpose of military action are ones in which it may take those other "means and levers of power" years or decades to attain a definite outcome. While American troops remained in Germany and Japan six decades after the war, this quickly ceased to be motivated by fears of renewed aggressiveness on their part. It was instead driven by the exigencies of the Cold War. In fact, for decades the United States had encouraged Germany and Japan to develop their own military capability more than they have, first to contribute to the Cold War, and later to peace operations and other missions. U.S. troops, however, remain in South Korea precisely because the Korean War remains unresolved.

4. A premium is placed on preserving the forces performing the mission rather than achieving the aim at any cost. This is a function not only of the oft-cited political sensitivity to casualties, but also of the difficulty and expense of replacing professional soldiers and advanced equipment. A commander in World War II knew there were reserves of equipment elsewhere in the service, and an industrial base behind them capable of rapidly producing replacements. This is no longer the case.

5. Established organizations and weapons systems are constantly being put to new, unforeseen uses. The conventional weapons of today's major militaries were generally designed to fight industrial war in Central Europe against the Warsaw Pact. Those capabilities, however, have been of decreasing relevance. In practice they have been used with varying levels of effectiveness for other purposes such as patrolling no-fly zones and counterinsurgency in Iraq and Afghanistan.

6. Increasingly, combatants on both sides tend to be non-state. Not only is it the case that non-state actors like warlords, terrorists, and guerillas

play a more prominent role, but the states fighting them tend to come together in some form of multinational grouping such as NATO or the UN when they combat them. While non-state actors did participate in World War II as guerillas, and the UN emerged from the conflict, few would contest that it was a conflict between states in a way that more recent wars have not been.

ANNIHILATION AND EXHAUSTION

The metamorphosis of war may have a more complex backdrop. Until recently, technology and tradition have relegated the use of military power to the same general functions on which all powers throughout history usually relied: battle was engaged to annihilate the enemy or to exhaust him by wearing down his military forces, reducing enemy power before one's own forces were exhausted. Annihilation consisted of a single option, the battle, while exhaustion made use of the combination of battle and maneuver.[41] Attrition and exhaustion were manifest when two forces pounded each other until one no longer could continue. Then, the marginal victor would impose his will on the vanquished.

Attrition has always been the least economical way to fight. The political reality of war today and in the future is that, for democracies, destruction, seizing, and holding territory or conquest for territorial aggrandizement are unlikely endeavors. Influenced by human rights and new political concepts, the integrative trends in international economics, the interlocking demands and political positions encompassing the interests of various social and political forces, ecological environmental concerns, and the value of human life have resulted in misgivings about killing and destruction, forming a new value concept for war as well as new ethics for warfare. Even those who opt for preemption—like the United States in Afghanistan and Iraq—would use it as a proactive defensive measure for limited ends and self-defense, without the intent to crush a population. Thus, attrition or the wanton destruction of enemy forces may become politically less viable.

COERCION AND MANAGEMENT OF VIOLENCE

Now, in order to limit the objectives in war, democracies tend to engage their armed forces in two modes of operation: coercion and management of violence. Coercion aims at putting an opponent's forces out of action and dismantling the military system. As a direct strategy—seeking military victory through forcing an opponent to end his aggression—coercion is conducted primarily against opponent's forces and the areas of space they are likely to use for maneuver or support. It is also primarily conducted against discrete targets leading to the collapse of key centers of gravity and overall system failure. In the decisive phase of the operation, surgical action is taken against the opponent's decision making processes, centers, and nodes until he loses his determination. Coordinated with the operations, other actions are conducted to deceive the opponent, lower his morale, and affect the perception of third parties about the situation.

Management of violence, the second major mode of operations at the operational level, falls within the strategic framework of limiting a crisis, containing a conflict, or stopping the war. The objective is to ensure or restore security in an area affected by violent hostile actions without destruction of an opponent's decision making centers. It aims to create the conditions for a peaceful settlement of the crisis.

Other Developments that May Lead to Other Changes in War

There are other developments that may lead to other changes in warfare. During the Cold War, armed conflict was generally portrayed as a graduated linear model encompassing general nuclear and limited war. Now, armed conflict embraces a wider range of situations in which military forces may be required to operate from peace to nuclear war. Although this variety defies simple categories, recurring factors emerge. They include:

1. The degree of national interest involved
2. The nature and extent of any limitations imposed
3. The character of the forces engaged
4. The level of intensity
5. The projected or actual duration

Each of these factors can vary in scale according to the circumstances. But they determine the dimensions and character of a particular conflict at a certain time. Moreover, during the course of a conflict, circumstances or policy may change and alter the relationship between factors.

National interests can be differentiated as being vital, important, humanitarian, or other. If a vital interest, such as the physical integrity of the state, is threatened, the armed forces are the appropriate response. In case of important but not vital interests, armed forces should only be used if they advance national interest, if they are likely to accomplish their objectives, if the costs and risks are commensurate with the interests at stake, and if non-military means are incapable of achieving the objective. With humanitarian and other interests, the focus should be on the "unique capabilities and resources" rather than the "combat power" of the armed forces when the military are called up to assist. More specifically, the armed forces should be used when there is a need "to establish the preconditions necessary for effective application of other instruments of national power." This clearly calls for the employment of the armed forces in those instances in which traditional diplomacy, public diplomacy, aid, and assistance are unable to function because of an insecure environment. The ability of Western democracies to sustain major military ventures over time, particularly in the face of casualties suffered for less than truly vital stakes, represents a real vulnerability. The sheer cost of maintaining large fighting forces in action at great distances from the homeland is a liability that can be exploited by opponents able to tie down Western forces in extended insurgencies and conflicts.

Limitations on the scale of conflict may be imposed by the selection of objectives, restrictions on the type of forces and weapons involved, how they can be employed, and by confining operations to specific geographic areas. They can be articulated as a set of rules of engagement, which detail the degree and manner in which force may be applied by means of prohibitions and permissions, or they may appear as constraints set out in strategic guidance to the forces involved. Limited objectives are pursued by limited means. In a war of national survival there may be little strategic choice in the objectives that must be pursued. In alliance or coalition operations, however, the political and military objectives need to be agreed to by all the members, which may constrain what is achievable. In most conflicts, the degree of force employed will be influenced by what is considered acceptable by public or international opinion, which may shape military objectives. Geographic limits may be defined in an attempt to ensure that the conflict does not draw in other participants or involve neutral parties. Certain areas may be designated as out of bounds to avoid civilian casualties or damage to sites of cultural or religious significance. In the air, "no fly zones" are increasingly used as part of control regimes imposed by the UN.

As to the character of the forces engaged: modern war as practiced by Western democracies trades on technology and wealth, not manpower and ideology. Western militaries are mostly smaller, professional organizations, officered by the middle class, and the ranks filled by working-class volunteers.

Their wars are "out of area," and hence not fought in defense of national sovereignty and borders, placing a premium on short, sharp campaigns won with relatively few casualties. While land forces remain indispensable, whenever possible Western militaries fight at a distance using standoff precision weapons. Accuracy and lethality of these weapons make it difficult or impossible for less sophisticated adversaries to fight conventionally with much chance of success. Increasingly, the Western advantage in rapid data transmission throughout the battlespace is changing how American and NATO militaries wage war as control and use of information assumes decisive importance. The qualitative gap between Western armed forces and their likely opponents is not likely to narrow in the foreseeable future. Although challengers may pursue niche technologies like hacker and computer attack systems, cruise or theater ballistic missiles, or anti-ship weapons, their inability to match the capital expenditures and technological sophistication of the U.S. armed forces and their NATO allies will make military parity highly doubtful, even when they act in coalitions. Nor will nuclear weapons easily change this calculus.

The gap in economic and technological capacity suggests other approaches for weaker opponents. Here is the real danger. The experience with protracted insurgencies since the end of World War II is not encouraging. In Vietnam, Laos, Algeria, and Congo, the West or its surrogates struggled for years and lost. The same may be the case in Iraq and Afghanistan. Russia has been confronted with that in Afghanistan, and still is experiencing it in Chechnya. Even Western "successes" in Malaya, Aden, Nicaragua, and El Salvador proved painful and debilitating.

The level of intensity. Despite a terrifying increase in its scope, scale, and lethality, war persists as a political genre. This is because it mobilizes and unifies the state behind its leaders as nothing else can, and also because states so often persuade themselves they can win. Rarely do states accept battle with no hope of victory.

Projected or actual duration. Except in very short conflicts, mounting impatience soon permeates the conduct of war, enhancing and emphasizing its inherent emotional component. War's ebb and flow may lead to changes in its aims and objectives in mid-course, either from the thrill that accompanies success or the dismay that follows defeat or stalemate. In either case, the rational and sober conduct of the war is constantly challenged and influenced by passionate and elemental currents closely related to the character of war itself. The passion and emotion generated by war unquestionably account for its durability and its tendency to spawn new and more vengeful conflicts afterward, for wars are difficult to win conclusively. The costs of waging long, drawn-out conflicts will be counted in more than dollars and lives. By a curious logic, the loss of many Americans in a single event or short campaign is less harmful to their political and military institutions than the steady drain of casualties over time.

By necessity, the military adapts to the narrowed exigencies of the moment, focusing on the immediate fight at some cost to the future investment, professional growth, and broader warfighting competencies, which can be vital in other potential conflicts of greater import. A subsidiary effect is loss of confidence in the military as an institution when it is engaged in protracted operations involving mounting losses without apparent progress. The experience of the Vietnam conflict, and now that in Iraq and Afghanistan, suggests that very long and enervating campaigns, fought for less than truly vital objectives, delay necessary modernization, absorb military resources earmarked for other contingencies, drive long-service professionals out of the force, and make it harder to recruit qualified personnel. These direct effects may then be mirrored more indirectly in declining popular support, more strident domestic political conflict, damage to alliances and mutual security arrangements, and economic dislocation. There are limits to the power of any state, and those limits must be carefully calculated before, and not after, the decision to go to war. In future wars, the United States and its Western allies will attempt to fight short, sharp campaigns with superior technology and overwhelming firepower delivered at standoff ranges, hoping to achieve a decisive military result quickly with few casualties.

Organization of the Second Priority Tasks

The second priority tasks consist of the following:

Group 1, covering internal security, has to:
1. Determine the organs needed for the safeguard and enforcement of internal security
2. Determine the missions, responsibilities, and accountabilities of the security services, law enforcement, and internal security forces
3. Determine the missions, responsibilities, and accountabilities of the organs and forces for homeland defense, critical infrastructure protection, and emergency response

4. Set directives for the coordination, cooperation, control, and accountability of all the organs and forces needed for the safeguard and enforcement of internal security

Group 2, covering the armed forces, has to:
1. Determine the missions of the armed forces
2. Determine the shape, size, structure, and organization of the armed forces
3. Develop plans and programs that take full account of the need for the transition of the armed forces to core capabilities
4. Establish military doctrine

Establishing an Organization Tasked with a Comprehensive Performance Review of the Defense and Security Sector

Teams of specialists have to comprehensively review performance, planning, and budgeting of the defense sector—the army, the air force, the navy, and reserve system—and the security sector—security and intelligence services, the border and coast guard, the customs services, security and paramilitary forces, police and law enforcement forces, homeland defense and emergency response forces, and the civil authorities mandated to control and oversee these institutions.

The task of these teams of specialists, which can be reinforced by specialists from outside state administration, is:

1. To find duplication and unnecessary redundancies in missions, operations, and resources
2. To find weaknesses, shortcomings, waste, and failure in the work of the existing state administration, organizations, and agencies
3. To highlight where and why accountability, efficiency, and effectiveness are lacking
4. To provide reports on their review and findings with recommendations for reform and transformation

After having analyzed and assessed these performance reports and briefed the state leadership, the PGSG must elaborate guidelines, define priorities, and establish timetables for reform and transformation of the defense and security sector. This with a view to:

1. Secure and maintain public consent for the new organizations and activities of the state and the government
2. Eliminate parallel organizations, redundancies, overlap, or duplication of missions and tasks, particularly in the domain of security and intelligence agencies
3. Demilitarize border and coast guard, internal security, and homeland defense services
4. Reduce state expenditures
5. Streamline budgeting processes and impose transparency
6. Firmly establish democratic control and oversight over, and to impose accountability in, the whole security sector

Security Sector Reform Implementation

Viable reform can take place only in an atmosphere of support from government, including the leadership of key ministries. Sustained and committed leadership by top policy makers, including ministry of interior and defense officials, is critical both for improving the effectiveness and accountability of police, law enforcement, internal security forces, and the armed forces. Significant reform cannot be implemented from below against the indifference or hostility of senior managers. The need to establish commitment and ownership of the process and outcomes by those responsible for implementing and sustaining the underlying principles of reform and change programs has been demonstrated by experience. It is important that broad stakeholder participation is encouraged and utilized to guide, test, and validate the reform process and provide recommendations at critical points. Expertise drawn from within and outside the security sector will make important contributions to inform the wider debate.[42]

Effective oversight and accountability measures, and review mechanisms that serve the interests of all communities need to be developed both through formal authorities, such as parliament, and more broadly, with the general public, through the media, academic institutions, and wider civil society. Genuine debate in these arenas, rather than carefully managed public information events, are the precondition for effective oversight and accountability of those who will attain new powers as a result of security sector reform implementation.

Transformation of the Armed Forces

Transformation requires a strategic approach. At issue is creating capabilities to defend and promote national interests in a new environment where threats are both diffuse and uncertain, and conflict is inherent, yet unpredictable. These new patterns of uncertainty combined with declining resources pose difficult challenges to defense reform and national security. This is also because the combined revolutions in technology and global affairs have shattered traditional boundaries, merging the strategic, operational, and tactical levels of war into a single, integrated universe in which action at the bottom often has instant and dramatic impact at all levels.

Transformation of the armed forces[43] has to correspond to the changing face of war. Although the direction, consequences, and implications of a revolution in military affairs (RMA) are largely unpredictable, it is the professional duty of military leaders to design and implement a change process as well as a fresh military culture that will produce superior armed forces relative to any prospective challengers to national security.

The challenge of armed forces transformation is to respond to change in such a way as to enhance the overall effectiveness of the armed forces to perform all assigned defense and security missions. This does not imply that the military performance of technological innovations will be maximized. It means that overall military effectiveness will be improved by the successful integration of the innovation with all aspects of military effectiveness: technology, doctrine, organization, leadership, and training.

Transformation of the armed forces, to become continuous, will have to integrate science and engineering research with studies of doctrine, organization, leadership, and training to appreciably enhance the overall military value of technological innovations. Such a continuous transformation process requires an entirely new approach to thinking about and improving the effectiveness of the armed forces. Continual transformation is key to maintaining a top modern military force in the face of accelerating technological change. Developing an unsurpassed process of unending transformation of the armed forces will be the single most important factor in protecting the nation in the future.

The greatest challenge is to reorient the technology design process so that all components of military effectiveness are synergistically blended into an integrated design methodology to produce the optimal overall increase in effectiveness. This process will involve tradeoffs among all the components of military effectiveness to optimize the full integration of capabilities to produce a modern military force.

The professional military culture places great value on action and generally disdains process. Only comfortable when acting, military leaders feel guilty if too much time is given to reflection. But if the armed forces are to progress successfully, the balance between product and process needs to shift toward process, and the leaders need to trust that a high-quality process will produce a high-quality product or performance.

Defense reform and transformation of the armed forces will have to aim more at a capabilities-based rather than a threat-based approach, focusing on how an adversary might fight instead of focusing on who the adversary might be, and when or where war might occur. Accordingly, planners will have to concentrate on the growing array of capabilities that adversaries might possess as well as determining the capabilities needed. It is sound strategy to prepare broadly for a range of threats that cannot always be specified exactly in advance.

Transformation will have to focus on greatly improving intelligence, surveillance, and reconnaissance, and on fast response, long-reach precision attack. These capabilities will be the hallmarks of modern armed forces. Aerospace power will be the primary military tool allowing to scale up and down from small operations to major theater conflicts and to respond with agility to all of the obligations in between. With adequate aerospace power, new and unforeseen operations can be handled rapidly and successfully.

A major consequence of an inadequate transformation process would be the inability to protect against advanced technology in an opponent's hands that could be brought to bear against the nation. Only by making the effort to remain at the cutting edge of science and technology advances across all fields can the armed forces understand what is currently possible and what the near future may hold in terms of weapons that can threaten national security.

As technologies are being adapted for military use, the protections or counters to the employment of these technologies have to be developed in parallel. That means that the design of any military technology is not complete until a defense against it, or a way to neutralize it, has also been created. Designs must consider the possibility of deliberate attempts to convert the new tools into impromptu weapons.

A further consequence of inadequate transformation would be the loss of the genuine dissuasive power. Conventional wars normally occur only between nations or entities that have comparable military capabilities, and a potential opponent would be very hesitant to trigger military action with the sure knowledge that he is inferior in terms of military effectiveness. This embodies all areas of technology because potential opponents cannot be allowed to discern any vulnerability in military capabilities prone to asymmetric exploitation.

Nowadays, technologies, economy, and society are so complex that it seems impossible for any single individual to fully understand them. Yet, modern leaders can still effectively function, compete, and improve their abilities to achieve objectives. The principal reason for their success is organizational networks that can blend the diverse knowledge of all members into skillful solutions, and, even more important, continuously adapt to changing knowledge requirements. Only networks can provide access to the wide-ranging knowledge domains required, and only self-organizing networks can provide the intimate interactions among the participants that permit the synthesis of this knowledge. Defense reform thus must recognize the dysfunctional nature of traditional barriers that separate organizations and roles. Complexity has generated many new ways to consider how organizations operate and how innovation is developed. The most successful future policies will be those that pursue adaptation and innovation through trial and error.

The authoritarian military command culture, while indispensable in combat, can impede open discussion of fundamental issues at all levels of the organization. To overcome this impediment, all armed forces personnel and the public will have to become stakeholders in this process. They must be given the opportunity to contribute to the discussion in a systematic manner.

The one indispensable aspect of a continuous process most difficult to achieve is the close collaboration of scientists, engineers, strategists, historians, national security experts, operators, doctrine creators, trainers, logisticians, soldiers, and the public. If each community brings its own particular goals and objectives to the process in a defensive manner, the collaboration and continuous transformation will fail. However, if all participants earnestly agree that the vision and goals of the armed forces are more important than their personal or individual community goal, then serious constructive collaboration should become possible.

Moreover, with professionalization and specialization, a particular culture with its own jargon is developing within the armed forces. These reflect an important development in national security policy: the growing distance between the military and the public. Thanks to technology, armed forces require fewer people. Yet, they also need people to remain in the force for years. Otherwise training costs explode and units lose the opportunity to learn how to work as a team.

The problem is that, as the military becomes more professional and specialized, it also grows more distant from civil society at a time when increased cooperation is needed between the military and the public. Hence, with force transformation, ways have to be found to reverse these trends. Society is changing at an increasing pace, and the armed forces that safeguard the society must change in parallel to avoid becoming irrelevant to the citizens they are pledged to defend.

13

Homeland Defense, Critical National Infrastructure, and Emergency Preparedness

The best approach to making the nation safer from the preeminent threats is to identify the current threats to the nation, understand the most likely vulnerabilities in the face of these threats, and identify highly leveraged opportunities for science, technology, and health care contributions to counter the preeminent threats in both the near term and the long term.[1]

Modern Western societies are too complex and interconnected to defend against all possible threats. As some threats are diminished, others may arise; terrorists, proliferants, and organized crime groups may change their goals and tactics. The important conclusion is that the nation needs a well organized and disciplined ability to respond as circumstances change. There is not a single enduring plan for the efforts to strengthen homeland security, but rather a starting point from which the nation can create defense-in-depth against the preeminent threats. For that reason, the strengthening of the national effort in long-term research that can create new solutions should become a cornerstone of the strategy for countering proliferation, terrorism, and organized crime.

The vulnerability of societies to terrorist attacks results, in part, from the proliferation of WMD, but is also a consequence of the highly efficient and interconnected systems that are relied on for key services such as transportation, information, energy, and health care. Efficient functioning of these systems reflects the great technological achievements of the past century. However, interconnectedness within and across systems also means that infrastructures are vulnerable to local disruptions, which could lead to widespread or catastrophic failures. As terrorists seek to exploit these vulnerabilities, it is fitting that the nation harnesses its scientific, technological, and health care capabilities to counter proliferation and terrorist threats.

Key elements or infrastructures of society can be means of attack, targets, and means of response. While some systems and technologies can be classified roughly in one of these categories—for instance, nuclear weapons are primarily means of attack; energy systems are primarily targets—most systems and technologies fit into multiple categories. For example, air transportation is both a target and a means of attack, and information and telecommunications systems are both targets and means of response.

The Scope of Domains that Must Be Addressed

Overall, there are nine domains that must be addressed to make the nation, the population, and homeland security safer from the preeminent threats:

1. The nuclear and radiological domain
2. The domain of toxic chemicals and explosives
3. The biological domain
4. The domain of information technology
5. The energy systems
6. The transportation systems
7. Cities and fixed infrastructure
8. The response of people to terrorism
9. Complex and interdependent systems

The actions and measures to be taken, and the needs for research and development, cover a wide assortment of approaches, fields, and systems. They range from immediate applications of existing technology to development and deployment efforts to long-term basic research programs. The actions include support for all phases of countering proliferation and terrorism as well as ways to improve the ability to perform analysis and invent new technologies. The different phases have varying importance in each of the nine areas examined. For example, the nuclear threat must be addressed at the earliest stages. That is when intelligence and surveillance based on international cooperation are critical for preventing the manufacture and use of nuclear weapons by terrorists. For biological threats, the situation is reversed. An attack is relatively easy to initiate and difficult to prevent, but there are many opportunities for technological interventions to mitigate the effects. In other cases, such as an attack on the electrical power system, it is possible both to make the attack more difficult and to ameliorate its effects after it has been initiated. Despite such fundamental differences in the approaches needed for countering the different classes of proliferation and terrorist threats, some general principles and strategies can be applied in all of these domains:

- Identification and repair of the weakest links in vulnerable systems and infrastructures
- The use of defenses-in-depth instead of sole reliance on perimeter defenses or firewalls
- The use of "circuit breakers" to isolate and stabilize failing system elements
- To build security into basic system designs where possible
- To build flexibility into systems so that they can be modified to address unforeseen threats
- To search for technologies that reduce costs or provide ancillary benefits to civil society to ensure a sustainable effort against proliferation and terrorist threats

The Ways to Respond to the Preeminent Threats

A multifaceted approach is needed for responding to the threats of proliferation of WMD and terrorism. This includes the following capabilities, organized according to a timeline that extends from before a proliferation or terrorist incident to their aftermath:

- Intelligence and surveillance, which involves the observation of persons, groups, and motives as well as of potential means of destruction, such as nuclear and radiological materials, toxic chemicals, and biological agents.
- Prevention, which involves disrupting the networks of proliferators and terrorists, and keeping WMD out of the hands of would-be terrorists, as in safeguarding fissile materials or foiling plans for the hijacking of airliners.
- Protection is needed should detection and prevention fail. Protection means securing WMD and materials from diversion or theft, as well as "hardening the target" so that destruction or disruption becomes more difficult for the terrorist. It includes systems and procedures for making borders, buildings, and critical infrastructures more difficult to breach. It also means use of vaccination and other public health measures to make people more resistant to disease.

- Interdiction, or crisis management, seeks to detect illicit proliferation activity—particularly an imminent terrorist attack and prevent its occurrence either by disrupting and destroying potential terrorist perpetrators before they can mount an attack, or, when an attack is imminent, by identifying the attackers, preventing their access to the target, or frustrating the attack itself by technical and other means.
- Response and recovery, also called consequence management,[2] means containing and limiting the level of damage and the number of casualties by organizing emergency responses and public health measures, and restoring critical functions in the aftermath of a terrorist attack.
- Attribution refers to the ability to identify proliferators—especially the perpetrators of a terrorist act—by typing a bioagent or performing radiochemical analysis of nuclear bomb debris—which is also key to the choice of responses, such as retaliation or prosecution.

In addition, all of these phases benefit from analysis and invention, which involve systematic learning from incidents that do occur, studying proliferators and terrorist tactics, and devising countermeasures through "red team/blue team"[3] and wargaming exercises. It also involves understanding motivations and factors that influence deterrence and developing systematic plans for ongoing operations, future investments, and scientific and technological innovations.

The Nuclear and Radiological Domain

A multilayered systems approach is needed for defending the nation against nuclear weapons, improvised nuclear devices, and radiological dispersion devices. Next to good intelligence and security services—the first line of homeland defense—robust systems have to be established for the protection, control, and accountability of nuclear weapons, nuclear installations, and special nuclear and radiological materials at their sources, nationwide.

Protection, control, and accountability of nuclear weapons, nuclear installations, and special nuclear and radiological materials must also be improved in many other countries worldwide. For this, the government should provide encouragement as well as technical and financial assistance to the International Atomic Energy Agency (IAEA) to raise the levels of international norms for protecting these, and also civilian special nuclear materials, particularly highly enriched uranium (HEU) from research reactors, and civilian plutonium from intact and reprocessed spent nuclear fuel.

The United States and other countries have already heavily invested in research and development of nuclear detection systems. One promising sensor is the Arktis Radiation Detector that has been developed from techniques used to explore dark matter in space. Such systems, which can detect the movement of illicit weapons and materials, should be deployed at strategic transportation choke points, such as critical border transit points, major cargo-container ports, major airports, train crossing sites, and pinch points in the national highway system. In addition, a focused and coordinated effort should be made to evaluate and improve the efficacy of special nuclear material detections systems—especially for detecting HEU.

The government has to assess its strategic readiness to deal with nuclear contamination, and to plan and organize responses to nuclear and radiological attacks. These fall into two distinct categories that require different types of governmental actions:

1. Attacks involving the detonation of a nuclear weapon or an improvised nuclear device, especially on a city
2. Attacks involving radiological dispersion devices.

Responses to a catastrophic detonation of a nuclear weapon have to address the following needs:

- Rapid, nationwide mobilization of medical resources to cope with burns, physical trauma, and poorly characterized outcomes of exposure to radiation
- Rapid deployment—or airlift when possible—of field hospitals to the affected area, as well as support by the armed forces
- Means to provide the affected public with basic information on protection against radiation and fallout
- Technical procedures for decontaminating people, land, and buildings

Physical and operational changes may have to be made to the nation's nuclear power plants and research reactors to mitigate vulnerabilities to attacks from the air with a commercial airliner or smaller aircraft loaded with explosives, and attacks from the ground using high-explosive and other projectiles. Analyses should be carried out on a plant-by-plant basis to better understand the effects of such attacks on reactor containment buildings and essential auxiliary facilities, spent fuel storage facilities, spent fuel transportation casks, and on the security of transports to clearly identify vulnerabilities. Nuclear power plants must be required to train and prepare security personnel against these threats, and they must periodically test the level of training and measures in force to ensure readiness to meet these threats.

The likely aim of a terrorist attack with a radiological dispersion device—or the surreptitious placement of radiation sources—is to spread fear and panic and cause disruption. Recovery from an attack would therefore depend on how the attack is handled by emergency responders, political leaders, and the media, all of which help to shape public opinion and reaction. Thus, technically credible spokespersons at the national level, who are perceived as being outside the political arena, should be prepared to provide accurate and usable information to the media and public concerning public health and safety risks, as well as the appropriate response actions for the case of such an attack.

Although a radiological attack would be unlikely to cause large numbers of casualties, the potential for inflicting economic loss and causing terror or panic warrants increased attention to the control and use of radiological sources by the regulatory agency and materials licensees. The agency should tighten regulations for obtaining and possessing radiological sources that could be used in terrorist attacks, including requirements for securing and tracking these sources. In addition, licensees possessing large sources should be encouraged to substitute nonradioactive sources—compact accelerators, electron beams, and X-ray generators—whenever economically feasible.

Training should be provided to emergency responders on how to assess on-the-ground hazards from radiological attacks. As part of this training, responders should be provided with simple but effective radiation-monitoring devices, trained in their use, and told whom to contact for expert assistance, if needed.

Given the potential importance of attribution to deterring nuclear attacks, efforts should be undertaken to develop and organize an attribution capability. The technology for the needed attribution capability exists, but it has to be assembled and organized as quickly as practicable.

A single governmental agency should be designated as the nation's lead agency for nuclear and radiological counterterrorism. This agency should develop a focused and adequately funded R&D program, and ensure that effective mechanisms are in place for the timely transfer of results to the homeland defense effort.

The Domain of Toxic Chemicals and Explosives

The toxic, explosive, and flammable properties of some chemicals make them potential weapons in the hand of terrorists. Many chemicals—such as chlorine, ammonium nitrate, liquefied gas, and petroleum products—are produced, transported, and used in large quantities. These, as well as chemical agents of extremely high toxicities, can become available to terrorists through purchase or theft; and facilities, transports by truck, railroad tank cars, ships or boats, and pipelines can be attacked and exploded.

The most plausible use of chemicals as weapons is in attacking aggregations of people in enclosed spaces—such as subways, airports, and financial centers—in ways that would cause disruption to crucial infrastructure services or render them unusable. Other ways to use chemicals as weapons include attacking people indirectly by contaminating facilities. Since both could potentially cause widespread loss of confidence in the government's ability to protect its citizens, such attacks must be prevented through better physical protection, improved surveillance, limiting access, or relocation and reduction of stocks of hazardous chemicals and manufacturing sites, as well as by much more restrictive regulations. Furthermore, plans for regulating the movement of hazardous materials through and near cities must be developed. They should incorporate technologies that allow detection of anomalies in handling and movement.

In principle, a number of technologies can be brought to bear for the rapid detection and characterization of a chemical attack, or for detecting explosives before they are used. For the latter, new and emerging techniques can augment detection capabilities already existing in airports, including X-ray diffraction, which detects several types of explosives; microwave-millimeter wave scanners; and nuclear quadrupole resonance. Methods to detect explosive vapors seem to be particularly promising.[4] Investments have been made in research on sensor technologies. However, if research is to move forward efficiently, mechanisms to focus and exploit the highly fragmented array of existing R&D programs will be needed to continue the search for promising new principles on which better sensors may be based. Mass spectroscopy offers the possibility of rapid and specific identification of volatile agents. Research on how animals accomplish both detection and identification of trace chemicals could yield new concepts that allow manufacture of better sensor systems. This also reduces dependence on trained dogs, which currently have the best broad-spectrum high-sensitivity sensory systems.

Toxic chemicals could also be used by terrorists to contaminate food production facilities or water supplies. Although much attention has been paid to ensuring safety and purity throughout the various stages of food production, processing, and distribution, protecting the food supply from *intentional* contamination has not been a major focus of the food industry.[5] Thus, the agencies for veterinary services and food inspection should develop criteria for quantifying hazards in order to define the level of risk for various kinds of food-processing facilities. The results can be used to determine the minimal level of protection required for making each type of facility secure. These agencies must also act promptly to extend the current quality control approach so that it may be used to deal effectively with deliberate contamination of the food supply.

One of the best ways to secure the safety of the water supply is to ensure an adequate residual concentration of disinfectant downstream of water treatment plants. Moreover, several filtration technologies are available for the treatment of contaminated water, including: micro-, ultra-, and nanofiltration membranes. But environmental protection agencies should direct additional research on determining the persistence of pathogens, chemical contaminants, and other toxic materials in public water supplies in the presence of residual chlorine.

Once a release of toxic chemicals occurs, proper protection of people and buildings can do much to reduce injury as well as facilitate cleanup and recovery. Absorbers and filters can be used both to prevent toxic chemicals from entering a facility through the ventilation system. They can also be used to decontaminate a building after an attack. Universities, companies, and government agencies need to work together to advance filtering and decontamination techniques by improving existing technologies and developing new methods for removing chemical contaminants from air, ground, and water. Research is especially needed on filter systems capable of treating large volumes and novel media that can help prevent toxic materials from entering facilities through ventilation equipment and ducts. Sensors for ventilation systems capable of detecting deviations from normal condition and monitoring for agents can be coupled to rapid shutdown procedures. New methods should be found for mapping the extent of, containing, and neutralizing clouds of airborne toxic materials such as ammonia, chlorine, hydrogen fluoride, hydrogen sulfide, and sulfur dioxide. Work to date has shown that large quantities of water must be sprayed in the air to "knock down" any significant portion of such airborne chemical clouds. Also, the use of reactive foams in existing fire suppression systems to counter chemical agents should be explored. Furthermore, new approaches to decontamination, including hardened structures, must be found, as well as environmentally acceptable ways of disposing of contaminated material that cannot be cleaned.

The existing capacity to respond to chemical attack should not be underestimated. The military is trained and equipped for chemical warfare. It maintains large supplies of relevant equipment; industrial and academic chemists have significant expertise in dealing with toxic chemicals; and cities and industries have a broad capability in responding to their accidental releases. Among the first responders, fire departments can be a major resource. They have personnel who are trained and equipped to work with respirators and protective gear, and are accustomed to engaging in, and dealing with, emergencies. While this collective know-how is not yet organized to handle the threats of chemical terrorism nationwide, it is an excellent starting point for building a reasonable level of preparedness—one which is more tractable than for nuclear and biological terrorist attacks.

The Biological Domain

The traditional public health response of intelligence and surveillance, prevention, detection, response, recovery, and attribution is the paradigm for the national response not only to all forms of terrorism, but also to emerging infectious diseases. A comprehensive approach to coping with bioterrorism must incorporate efforts to prevent the proliferation of biological agents; methods for detecting covert biological weapons programs; strategies for deterring their use if biological agents do proliferate; and mechanisms for protecting the civilian population and the armed forces if deterrence fails.[6] The emphasis in this multi-tiered approach should be on defense because the proliferation of biological agents is difficult to control, covert bioweapons programs are difficult to detect, and deterrence will likely be less effective against suicidal terrorist groups than against states.

The government must plan and organize defense and responses against bioterrorism as well as against pandemics. Investment in research on bioterrorism has enormous potential for application in the detection, prevention, and treatment of emerging infectious diseases or pandemics that are unpredictable. Investments made to protect the nation against bioterrorism will help protect and improve the public's health and food supply from naturally occurring threats as well.

The deciphering of the human genome sequence, the complete eluci-dation of numerous pathogen genomes, rapidly increasing understanding of the molecular mechanisms of pathogenesis and of immune responses, and new strategies for designing drugs and vaccines all offer unprecedented opportunities to use science to counter bioterrorist threats. However, these same developments also allow science to be misused to create new agents of mass destruction. Hence, the effort to confront bioterrorism must be a global one. Together with intergovernmental agencies related to the UN such as the World Health Organization (WHO), the Food and Agriculture Organization (FAO), the International Civil Aviation Organization (ICAO), and the World Meteorological Organization (WMO), the government must encourage, and contribute to, the creation of a global network for detection and surveillance of bioagents and pandemics, making use of computerized methods for real-time reporting and analysis to rapidly detect new patterns of disease locally, nationally, and internationally. The use of high-throughput methodologies that are currently being increasingly utilized in modern biological research should be an important component of an expanded and highly automated surveillance strategy.

A multifaceted approach is required. It should strengthen the multi-lateral normative and legal prohibition regime while linking it with other kinds of governmental and nongovernmental, national, and international measures. The nuclear and chemical industries cooperate actively with governments, and have found this to be in their interests. Bioindustry can and should do likewise. It has much to gain in credibility and respectability by cooperating in preventing abuse of biotechnology, as the nuclear and chemical industries have in their respective fields.

Periodic inspections of the pharmaceutical and biotechnical industry must be established. Industry must be required by law to establish and maintain control over personnel, facilities, and materials, including all raw materials, intermediates, and final products. Controls must include physical management of material movement and use, especially inventory reconciliation; workers training and qualification for assigned tasks; and strict monitoring of water and air systems within the production environment. Also, government must periodically review the security and inventory controls applied in facilities that are equipped with bioreactors and fermenters—as well as those used by manufacturers of drug excipients and health supplements—to determine if the methods and standards in place need to be improved.

New tools for detection and diagnosis of bioagents must be developed and deployed. Knowledge of the genome sequences of major pathogens allows new molecular technologies to be developed for the sensitive detection of pathogens. These technologies offer enormous possibilities for the surveillance of infectious agents in the environment, the identification of pathogens, and rapid and accurate diagnoses. For these technologies to be used effectively to ensure early warning, improved communications are needed. This communication must be improved everywhere from the doctor's office and hospital emergency rooms to public health agencies at all levels of government, including those dealing with animal health. These capabilities will be important for responding to attacks on agricultural systems—animals and crops—and for protecting humans. All incidents require careful evaluation and standards. In addition, there is a need for an integrated system to protect the food supply.

To be able to respond to current and future biological threats, the government needs to expand research programs aimed at increasing knowledge of the pathogenesis of, and immune responses to, biological infectious agents. The development of therapeutics and vaccines will require more research on pathogenesis and protective host responses. Financial incentives, indemnification, and regulatory changes may be needed to allow the pharmaceutical and biotechnical industry to pursue such efforts. Because markets are very limited for vaccines and drugs for countering potential bioagents, special institutes may have to be established for carrying out biohazardous research, and producing drugs and vaccines. The National Health Department must investigate strategies, including the modification of regulatory procedures, to encourage the development of new drugs, vaccines, and devices to address bioterrorist threats.

Research efforts critical to deterrence, response, recovery, and attribution,[7] particularly bioterrorism forensics, should be strengthened. Without attribution, deterrence measures will likely fail. Nucleic acid sequence databases for pathogen strain types, advances in chemical-trace analysis, and the use of taggants will help the process of attribution, thus discouraging terrorism, but they may not guarantee that perpetrators can be identified.

Appropriate scientific expertise should be integrated in the government agencies with principal responsibilities for emergency response and postevent investigations. Modeling tools for analyzing the health and economic impacts of bioterrorist attacks are needed in order to anticipate and prepare for these threats. Techniques for protection of individuals and buildings should be developed along with efficient methods of decontamination in the event that such defenses are breached.

The government must improve preparedness for bioterrorist attacks by creating a public health reserve system as well as developing and organizing a surge capacity to deal effectively with terrorist attacks and natural catastrophes. New strategies must be developed and implemented for assuring security, usability, and accurate documentation of existing stocks of supplies at research facilities, hospitals, veterinarian facilities, and other host sites. The potential for a major infectious threat or pandemic to kill and disable thousands of citizens requires a level of preparedness lacking in almost all countries—a surge capacity to mobilize the public health response and provide emergency care, particularly in all health systems that have been downsized to cut costs.

There are immediate needs and opportunities for training first responders, medical nursing, health professionals, certified laboratory personnel, and communities as a whole in how to respond to biological threats. Also needed is a well trained, professional public health reserve, modeled on the military reserve system—including laboratories and health care professionals—that can be mobilized when the health care system becomes overloaded. The establishment of standardized protocols for public health responses to bioterrorist attack is critically important.

National security depends on public-private sector cooperation and communication, and on an increased willingness to collaborate for creating capacities to produce diagnostics, therapeutics, vaccines, and devices to counter terrorism. A much more inclusive effort is needed to build a seamless system of preparedness and response. Equally critical is to have in place agreements between public health and emergency response agencies across jurisdictions.

The Domain of Information Technology

Information Technology (IT) is essential to virtually all of the nation's critical infrastructures, which makes any of them vulnerable to terrorist attack. IT plays a critical role in managing and operating nuclear power plants, dams, the electric power grid, the air traffic-control system, and financial institutions. IT can also play a major role in the prevention, detection, and mitigation of terrorist attacks. However, IT is both a target and a weapon. The three counterterrorism-related areas of highest priority in IT are information and network security, IT for emergency response, and information fusion and management. In particular, actions must be taken on the critical need to improve the telecommunications and computing infrastructure of the first responders, and to promote the use of best practices in information and network security, especially by emergency response agencies and telecommunications providers.

A terrorist attack that involves the IT infrastructure can operate in one of three different modes:

1. The attack can come in "through the wires" alone.
2. It can include the physical destruction of some IT elements, such as critical data centers or communications links.
3. The attack can rely on the compromising of a trusted insider who, for instance, provides passwords that permit outsiders to gain entry.

All of these modes are possible and, because of the highly public nature of the IT infrastructure and of society in general, impossible to fully secure. Given IT's critical role in many other elements of the national infrastructure, and in responding to a crisis, the targeting of IT as part of a multipronged attack scenario could have catastrophic consequences. Attacks on IT can amplify the impact of terrorist attacks and diminish the effectiveness of emergency responses. Reducing such vulnerabilities will require major advances in computer security with the objective of improving information and network security. Moreover, reliance on the Internet as the primary networking entity means that severe damage through cyber attacks is more likely. Hence, an agency has to be made responsible for promoting information security in the government through adoption and use of what is currently known about enhancing security practices. To the extent that the government is successful in improving its procedures, it should make these best practices available to the local authorities and private sector.

Command, control, communications, and information systems for emergency responders are critical for coordinating their efforts. They also increase promptness and effectiveness of the response. Unfortunately, such systems are vulnerable to attack. Because emergency-response units often do not have the expertise to review and revamp the telecommunications and computing technologies used for emergencies response, it is necessary to provide them with authoritative knowledge and support. In addition, designated emergency-response agencies should use existing technology to achieve short-term improvements in telecommunications and computing infrastructure for first responders.

All phases of counterterrorism efforts require that large amounts of information from many sources be acquired, integrated, evaluated, and interpreted. Given the range of data sources and data types, the volume of information each source provides, and the difficulty of analyzing partial information from single sources, the timely and insightful use of these inputs is very difficult. Thus, new information fusion and management techniques promise to play a central role in future prevention, detection, and remediation of terrorist acts. For detection of an attack, fast and scalable methods for high-confidence authentication must be developed, and approaches should be explored for the self-monitoring of traffic and users to detect either anomalous users or unusual traffic patterns. Moreover, intruder-detection methods should be developed to that scale to function efficiently in large systems. For the containment of an attack, tools and design methodologies for systems and networks that support graceful degradation in response to an attack should be developed, as well as mechanisms to contain attackers and limit damage rather than completely shutting down the system once an intrusion is detected. For recovery from an attack, schemes for backing up large systems, in real-time and under "hostile" conditions, should be developed that can capture the most up-to-date snapshot of the system's state. Furthermore, new decontamination approaches must be created for discarding as little good data as possible, and for removing active or potential infections on systems that cannot be shut down for decontamination.

Unlike some other sectors of national importance, IT is a sector in which the government has little leverage. Thus, constructively engaging the private sector by emphasizing market solutions seems a desirable and practical way for the government to stimulate advances that can strengthen the nation's IT infrastructure. The challenge for policy makers is to change the market dynamics by encouraging the private sector to pay more attention to security-related issues, and facilitating the adoption of effective security.

Within government, some ministries, numerous agencies, and institutions like the armed forces, intelligence services, and police play important roles in funding and performing telecommunications and computing research, and many other agencies are major users of IT. Thus, a strategic long-term R&D agenda should be established to address the three primary counterterrorism-related areas of IT:

1. The R&D efforts in information and network security would include

architectures for the prevention, identification, and containment of cyber intrusions, as well as recovery from them.

2. The efforts to address IT needs of emergency responders would include ensuring interoperability, maintaining and expanding communications capacity in the aftermath of a terrorist incident, communicating with the public during an emergency, and providing support for decision makers.

3. The R&D efforts in information fusion for the intelligence, security, law enforcement, and emergency response communities should include data mining, data integration, language translation technologies, and processing of image and audio data.

The government's efforts should focus on multidisciplinary problem-oriented research that is applicable to both civilian and military users, yet is driven by a deep understanding and assessment of vulnerabilities to terrorism. To achieve long-term advances, research must extend beyond improving existing systems and investigate new approaches to secure and reliable operations that do not directly evolve from the IT of today.

The Energy Systems

The national economy and quality of life require a plentiful and continuous supply of energy. Energy systems include the nation's electrical power supply system as well as its oil and gas facilities. Because reliance on energy is so great, the vulnerability to an interruption in its supply is equally great. There is great dependence of major infrastructural systems on the continued supply of electrical energy, oil, and gas. Telecommunications, IT, the Internet, food and water supplies, homes, and worksites are dependent on electricity. Numerous commercial and transportation facilities are equally dependent on natural gas and refined oil products. These and many other interdependencies need to be better understood in order to determine which nodes of the various energy systems should be given the highest priority for increased security against terrorism. Simulation models of interdependent infrastructure may help provide such understanding and prove vital to post–event recovery. Therefore, new and improved simulation design tools should be developed to model and analyze prevention, response, and recovery for energy systems under a variety of terrorist threat scenarios. Such efforts would include simulations of the interdependencies between the energy sector and key infrastructures such as the communication, transportation, and water supply systems.

Improving protection of energy systems must first be accomplished with available technology, including:

1. Increased surveillance of critical sites and equipment
2. Hardening of specific sites
3. Installation of barriers to prevent vehicle or other intrusion
4. Masking the thermal signatures of selected sites and equipment

Surveillance technologies developed for the armed forces and intelligence agencies should be investigated for their usefulness in defending against terrorist attacks on the widely distributed oil, gas, and electric transmission assets. These can include UAVs, satellite surveillance technology, intelligent software-based analysis of surveillance images to scan for unwanted activity, change-detection sensors, and intrusion-detection devices designed to sense unusual movement, vibrations, or noises. Energy system assets should be hardened against blast-shock and fire with material coatings and surface-applied structural enhancements. Integrated multisensor warning systems should be deployed in the oil and gas industries in order to enhance response, control, and post–event analysis. Moreover, smart controls should be deployed that limit the manipulation of systems outside normal operating settings, utilizing artificial intelligence or redundant controls.

The government and the energy industry should cooperate to establish appropriate security goals. Building on this alignment, government should cooperate with industry to establish joint security performance expectations and define the roles and responsibilities of each in ensuring such performance. Industry should design the security measures and procedures needed to achieve the established security goals. Also, government should identify statutory authority that will permit emergency actions to be taken, and temporary changes in regulations to be adopted, after an attack to reestablish service.

The electrical power supply system warrants special attention because a prolonged loss of service to a region would probably cause extensive hardship, economic loss, and many deaths. Outage of an entire regional transmission grid might occur if the damage or destruction of important components of that grid were followed by a cascading failure of interconnected components. In order to reduce near-term vulnerability to such a loss and improve the resilience of the nation's power system, those parties responsible for critical components of the electric power grid should be urged to install additional physical barriers to protect these components.

In the longer term, the National Energy Department, supported by other government agencies and significant industry participation, should take the lead in developing, testing, and implementing an intelligent, adaptive electric power grid. Such an intelligent grid would provide the system with the ability to fail gracefully, minimizing damage to components and enabling more rapid recovery of power. A key element would be adaptive islanding, a concept employing fast-acting sensors and controls to isolate parts of the power system. Operations models and intelligence are needed to differentiate between failure of a single component, and the kind of concurrent or closely coupled serial failures at several key nodes that could indicate the onset of a concerted attack.

Another vulnerability of the power grid is its extra-high-voltage transformers, for which almost all nations stock limited numbers of replacements. Today, replacement of a seriously damaged or destroyed unit could take months or years. To counter this vulnerability, the Department of Energy and the electric power industry should acquire, stock, and deploy modular, universal, extra-high-voltage transformers to provide temporary replacement when key components are damaged. Such replacement transformers must be relatively small, easily transportable, and capable of being used individually or in sets to replicate the unit being replaced.

Yet another challenge is the vulnerability of the power grid's control systems to cyber attack. In particular, the Supervisory Control and Data Acquisition (SCADA) systems pose a special problem. As a result, the manner in which data are transmitted between control points or SCADA systems used in the grid should be reviewed. Encryption techniques, improved firewalls, and cyber-intrusion detection technologies should be used to improve security and reduce the potential for hacking and disruption. This should apply to oil and gas system facilities as well because they are similarly vulnerable. Moreover, government support for energy sector information sharing and the establishment of analysis centers is essential.

The Transportation Systems

Transportation systems, while often indispensable for proliferation and the delivery of terrorists weapons, are recurrent targets of terrorist attacks. Many transportation facilities and structures are strategically important, serving as key nodes in networks and corridors that handle the movement of large volumes of people, goods, and services. They are international in scope and intertwined in economic and social activities. Airline service is essential to areas of the country that depend on business travel and tourism. Sea ports handle a major share of the goods moved in international trade. Commuter and rapid rail transit systems are the circulator systems of urban environments, critical to the functioning of some of the largest cities. Pipelines, waterborne modes, and trucks move products and commodities over long distances. The highway system pervades the lives of all those who use cars for most daily activities. It is also used by emergency responders to move critical services and supplies as well as to evacuate people. Mail and package services reach nearly every household, business, and government office in the country. However, much of the transportation infrastructure was designed and built long before the advent of concerns over security and terrorism. Disruptions to these systems can have potentially far-reaching and long-lasting economic and social repercussions.

Transportation security is best achieved through well conceived security systems that are integrated with transportation operations. A layered security system, in which multiple security features are connected and provide backup for one another, has particular advantages. Perfect execution by each element in the system is not crucial because other elements can compensate for human, technological, or other shortcomings, and, correspondingly, enhancements to one element can boost the performance of the system as a whole. Hence, defeating a single layer cannot breach such systems, and the difficulty of calculating the overall odds of success may thus deter or impede terrorist attacks. Moreover, layered security features that are well integrated with operations and confer multiple benefits—such as enhanced safety and operating efficiency—have a greater chance of being maintained and improved over time.

Many actions are being taken by governments to strengthen air transportation security—including the deployment of explosives detection systems for checked baggage, the strengthening of cockpit doors, and the use of air marshals. Some of these measures are providing much-needed security layers, though not yet as part of a preconceived system designed to address multiple threats and ensure continued improvement over time.

The prevention of future airline attacks may be made possible by systematically identifying and defending against all or most vulnerabilities. Access to airfields and aircraft can be closely guarded, passengers and luggage can be screened with great care, and airline and airport workers can be monitored. By comparison, the more open and decentralized maritime and land transportation systems are less amenable to such a defensive approach. The intensive inspection and screening methods used for air transportation security, for instance, are impractical for transportation modes that require more convenient user access and have a myriad of entry points. Means of deterrence in those systems are therefore critical, as are means to contain and respond to attacks that do occur. Indeed, it is possible that good mitigation, response, and recovery preparations will themselves dissuade terrorists from attacking these targets since ensuing damage and disruption may be limited.

New security approaches have also been taken for marine shipping containers with the Container Security Initiative (CSI),[8] launched in 2002 by the United States. It is now operational in forty-seven foreign ports. It has moved inspections out from the U.S. ports of entry to ports overseas. Its purpose is to increase security for container cargo shipped to the United States. In 2002 the World Customs Organization unanimously passed a resolution that will enable ports in all 161 of the member nations to begin to develop programs along the CSI model. In April 2004 the EU and the U.S. DHS signed an agreement that calls for the prompt expansion of CSI throughout the European Community. Also the 2003 Proliferation Security Initiative (PSI) represents a new approach. Launched by the United States, it has gathered a coalition of states that have agreed to use their national resources, including force if necessary, to interdict and seize international shipments of goods believed to be illegally destined for use in WMD programs. Currently, the PSI is targeted at an undisclosed set of "states or non-state actors of proliferation concern." While the number of states participating in the PSI has expanded significantly since, the initiative has also generated criticism over issues relating to its consistency with international law, lack of transparency, and other concerns.

An understanding of operations and economics of transportation systems is crucial for finding ways to integrate security with other transportation system objectives. For example, shippers and other commercial users of transportation may be willing to accept outlays for blast-resistant containers, electronic tamperproof seals, and real-time recording of shipment manifests if they facilitate the general movement of cargo, and better secure it against theft and loss. However, while opportunities exist for using information generated by operations—ticket reservation records, shipment manifests, passenger identification—to devise layered security systems in air and maritime transportation, similar information is not available for many land transportation modes, such as public transit, where users are much more anonymous. Nonetheless, security in surface transportation modes can be layered though other means while also capitalizing on dual-use applications.[9] When new stations are designed or existing ones remodeled, many cost-effective protective features can be added, such as good lighting, blast-resistant structures, air filtration systems, emergency evacuation routes, and open spaces that provide a broad field of vision. The well placed application of surveillance cameras and sensors that detect chemical or biological agents can further strengthen the overall security by adding an element of deterrence as well as an early diagnosis and response capability. As facial recognition technologies become more mature, these may have strategic application in some public transportation setting, thereby strengthening deterrence and detection capabilities.

Many of the R&D efforts already mentioned—such as improved sensors, the ability to mine data more effectively, and a capability for unconventional, broad-based thinking on terrorist threats and responses—are also of great value in boosting security for other transportation and distribution. The most critical need in the transportation sector is a systematic approach to security. In the United States, the Transportation Security Administration (TSA) meets this need by serving as a focal point of responsibility for devising effective and coherent security systems for each transportation mode as well as by supporting and marshalling relevant R&D. The TSA has created a multimodal, strategic research and planning office to increase the utility of sensing, screening, decontamination, and other security-related technologies being developed. By working closely with the agencies of the U.S. Department of Transportation, such as the Federal Aviation Administration, the Federal Highway Administration, other federal entities, state and local governments, and the private sector, it serves as a focal point for research, planning, evaluation, and collaboration. It identifies and evaluates promising security systems concepts and promotes the development of knowledge, technologies, and processes for implementing them.

Evaluations help gauge the need for changes in law, regulations, and financial incentives, as well as the division of responsibility among public and private entities. Some of these changes may be practical to achieve while others may not. Deployment of many new technologies, from biometric ID cards to cargo and passenger-screening devices, and processes in support of security systems, this also raises many difficult social issues—concerns over legality, personal privacy, and civil rights, for example. Concerns that may constrain or even preclude implementation must be appreciated early on, before significant resources are devoted to furthering impractical or undesirable concepts.

Considerations of human factors are critical. Human factors expertise is necessary for crafting a layered security system that, as a whole, increases the perceived risk for terrorists of getting caught and maximizes the ability of security personnel to recognize unusual and suspicious patterns of activity and behavior. Recognition of human factors is important for ensuring that the role of people in providing security is not determined by default or on the basis of what technology promises, but rather as a result of systematic evaluations of human strengths and weaknesses that technology can both complement and supplement. In the United States, TSA ensures that human factors are fully considered at the earliest possible stages in all security initiatives.

The restructuring of transportation security technologies, techniques, and procedures to form coherent systems is not easy. It requires an ability and willingness to step back and define security goals and performance expectations, to identify the layered systems best suited to meeting them, and to work with many public, private, and foreign entities to implement them. Security planners must be willing to question many existing security rules, institutional relationships, tactics, and technologies. This will require much strategic planning, supported by well-targeted, systems-level research and analysis.

Cities and Fixed Infrastructures

Cities are a target-rich environment for terrorists, whether the aim is people or economic damage. The urban setting provides access to a set of highly integrated infrastructure systems—such as water, electrical power, oil and gas supplies; digital or voice communications; mass transit; sewage collection and transport; conduits for utilities, tunnels, and bridges—as well as to major buildings, shopping arcades and centers, universities, research centers, monuments and icons, and other places of public assembly.

Major buildings present especially attractive targets. They have also become the subject of structural reexamination to determine what weaknesses must be corrected to prevent catastrophic collapse following an attack as happened with the twin towers of the World Trade Center in New

York. Information coming from the failure of those buildings shows a need for improved blast and fire resistant designs.

Major buildings are also vulnerable to infectious or toxic materials being circulated by heating, ventilation, and air conditioning systems after their release into the air. To counter this threat, the air handling ducts should be equipped with sensors that can determine whether air is safe or not. Also, allied controls could adjust the functioning of these systems and provide for rapid shutdown.

The heart of a city's response to a terrorist attack is an Emergency Operations Center (EOC)—the crisis command center for a city. The EOC must coordinate, by prearranged plan and agreement, the efforts of key leaders beginning with the mayor, city hall staff, and the directors of police, fire, and emergency medical services. Also integral to the EOC mission is interaction with senior officials from public works and public health departments, utilities, and mass care and mortuary facilities. The EOC must also have direct communications links with the control centers intrinsic to the railroad, subway, highway, and transit systems, public utilities, communications facilities, and various neighboring and mutual support organizations. For this, a common frequency has to be established in the area of the broadcast spectrum that is best for emergency-use radios.

An EOC is a complex organization whose success is directly related to the capability of its communications systems and the competence of its staff. The EOC engages the first responders—those who are dispatched to the scene of a problem to assess and report, before the EOC can determine its nature, size, and cause. For such cases, credible terrorist threat scenarios must be developed that serve the EOC and first responder teams to prepare to meet. Furthermore, a technical assessment of the adequacy of an EOC's physical facilities to address and survive these threat scenarios should be performed.

The ability of first responders to quickly determine if the dust and smoke at a site contain toxins will likely mean the difference between life and death. It is important that R&D efforts are undertaken with the aim of producing new, small, reliable, and quick-reading sensors of toxic materials for use by first responders. These devices might be based on the same core element as the sensors needed in air handling ducts to determine whether the air is safe.

EOC crisis management teams may have experience in dealing with natural disasters and perhaps some manmade threats to cities, such as riots.

However, very few have ever experienced a terrorist attack. This lack of experience and the potential problems it implies for attack recognition, response, interagency operations, public information management, and media relations, constitute a real vulnerability. Homeland Security and the National Emergency Management Agency, in conjunction with province, district, and local officials, should collaborate to develop and deploy threat-based simulation models and training modules for EOC and first responders training. This will help with identifying weaknesses in systems and staff, and for testing and qualifying EOC teams. This should lead to certification, according to national standards, of EOCs and their crisis management teams throughout the country.

The Response of People to Terrorism

Because good intelligence on terrorists' intentions and targets is extremely difficult to acquire, it is exceedingly difficult to foresee and plan to cope with any specific terrorist act. Thus, the nation must make efforts to deter such acts and to counter and minimize terrorists' actions through adequate responses. Since people are the primary target of terrorists, the focus must be on the response of people to terrorism. More precisely, the focus must be on the fact that all terrorist attacks generate behavioral, attitudinal, and emotional responses in the population affected. The human response to crisis situations can be influenced by factors such as adequacy of preparedness, effectiveness of warnings, confidence in effective national crisis management and in agencies designated to deal with crises response. However, because it involves attitudes and feelings, it cannot be fully controlled by the government, planning, crisis management authorities, and other agencies. Nor should it be. In a democratic society, such total control is unwanted because it would constitute unacceptable intrusions on citizens' freedoms. Human responses need to be examined at four distinct stages of the attack process:

1. Anticipatory attitudes, emotions, and behavior
2. Responses to warnings
3. Immediate responses to the attack itself
4. Recovery

Most thinking and planning related to preparedness, warning, and response against terrorist acts rests on the assumption of an undifferentiated community or public. Research on disasters, however, reveals that individuals and groups differ in both readiness and response according to previous disaster experience, ethnic and minority status, level of education and economic resources, and gender. In addition, individual households vary in their responses to crises, depending on factors such as perceived risk, credibility of the warning system, and concerns about the family and property. Thus, the behavioral and social sciences can make important contributions to understanding group responses to crises. A program of research should be established to understand how differences based on cultural background, experience with previous disasters or emergencies, and other factors should be taken into account when systems are designed for preparedness, warning, and response to terrorist attacks and other disaster situations.

While research will lay the groundwork for long-term improvements in the quality of preparedness, warning, and response communications, in the near-term, the government must be preparing to communicate as best it can in the wake of a terrorist act and crisis. Appropriate and trusted spokespeople should be identified and trained so that, if a terrorist attack occurs, the government will be prepared to respond by supplying emergency services and providing important, accurate, trustworthy information quickly and authoritatively.

To strengthen the government's ability to provide emergency services, in-depth research should be conducted to characterize the structure of agencies responsible for dealing with attacks and other disasters. These studies should focus on discovering optimal patterns of information dissemination and communication among the agencies, the most effective strategies for coordination under extreme conditions, ways of responding to the need for spontaneous, informal rescues, and approaches to dealing with citizen non-cooperation. Research should also focus on the origins and consequences of organizational failure, miscommunication, lack of coordination, and jurisdictional conflict. Moreover, comparative work on cases of successful coordination should also be prominent on the research agenda.

The interface between technology and human behavior is an important subject for investigation. The research agenda should be broad based and include topics such as decision making that affects the use of detection and prevention technologies; the ways in which deployment of technologies can complement or conflict with the values of privacy and civil liberty;

and factors that influence the trustworthiness of individuals in a position to compromise or thwart security. All the agencies creating technological systems for the support of first responders and other decision makers should base their system designs and user interfaces on the most up-to-date research on human behavior, especially with respect to issues critical to the effectiveness of counterterrorism technologies and systems.

Complex and Interdependent Systems

There is a need for an overall systems approach to counter terrorism. Unfortunately, many government ministries and agencies do not have the capabilities needed to assess the preeminent threats, infrastructure vulnerabilities, and mitigation strategies from a systems perspective. For example, in order to perform the analyses needed to identify vulnerabilities in complex systems and weaknesses due to interconnections between systems, various threat and infrastructure models must be extended or developed and used in combination with data from intelligence agencies. The systems approach is especially necessary for understanding the potential impacts of multiple attacks occurring simultaneously, such as a chemical attack combined with cyber attack on first responder communications designed to increase confusion and interfere with the response.

The required range of expertise is broad. Information about threats must come from communities knowledgeable about chemical, biological, nuclear and radiological weapons, information warfare, and computer network attack, while vulnerability analysis will depend on information about critical infrastructures such as the electric power grid, telecommunications, gas and oil, banking and finance, transportation, water supply, public health services, emergency services, and other major systems. In all these areas, threat assessments, red-team activities, regular exercises and tests are essential.

A large volume of data and information must be collected and analyzed by intelligence services and in industries that are relevant to assessing terrorist threats and system vulnerabilities. However, to maximize the usefulness of this data and information, and increase the ability to cross-reference and analyze it efficiently, counterterrorism-related databases have to be identified. In addition, metadata standards for integrating diverse sets of data must be established.

Important information about vulnerabilities can also be gained by modeling of critical infrastructures. Computational or physical-analog models of infrastructure for use in simulating various counterterrorism activities can help with identifying patterns of anomalous behavior, finding weak points in the infrastructure, training personnel, and learning how to maintain continuity of operations following terrorist attacks. Existing modeling and analysis capabilities, as well as new methods, can allow the use of integrated models to determine linkages and interdependencies between major infrastructure systems. These results, in turn, can be used to develop sensor deployment strategies and infrastructure defense approaches in all relevant areas of major vulnerabilities.

The basic tools of system analysis and modeling are available, and widely used in military and industrial applications. However, these tools have severe limitations when applied to interdependent complex systems, and R&D is required to extend them. Thus, government should establish a long-term research agenda in systems engineering. Relevant research projects will involve many domains of expertise; a single disciplinary perspective should not dominate the agenda.

Countering terrorism requires insights and approaches that cut across traditional boundaries of scientific and engineering disciplines. Seven crosscutting challenges can be identified:

1. Systems analyses, modeling, and simulation
2. Integrated data management
3. Sensors and sensor networks
4. Autonomous mobile robotic technologies
5. Supervisory control and data acquisition systems
6. Control of access to physical and information systems using technologies such as biometrics
7. Human and organizational factors

All the technologies are critically important, but none of them is the sole solution to any problem. Because technologies are implemented and operated by human agents and social organizations, their design and deployment must take human, social, and organizational factors into account.

Essential Partners in a National Strategy

Since homeland security's principal function is to protect the nation, government has a vital role to play. However, eliminating every risk to the country's critical national infrastructure is impossible. The government does not have the financial resources to shoulder all homeland security responsibilities nor can it supply sufficient personnel to guarantee a massive reduction in the vulnerabilities. Moreover, many of these infrastructures are owned and operated by private businesses that have a natural incentive to protect them. Thus, a partnership model is called for that seeks to have businesses share in the burden of security enhancement: A partnership with the objective to leverage private-sector capabilities and incentives with government know-how in an effort to achieve maximum risk reduction based on the most efficient use of resources.

The government must take the lead in the national counterterrorism effort, but effective use of existing technologies, R&D activities, and deployment of new approaches to mitigating the nation's vulnerabilities depends on close cooperation with other entities—such as province and local government and agencies, industry, universities, laboratories, non-profit organizations, and other institutions.

Primary responsibility for response to, and recovery from, terrorist attacks falls to cities, districts, and provinces. The first responders— police, firefighters, medical emergency or first-aid personnel, and rescue teams—and local governments possess practical knowledge about their technological needs and relevant design limitations that should be taken into account in the national efforts to provide new equipment—such as protective gear and sensor systems—and help set standards for performance and interoperability. Government agencies must develop collaborative relationships with local governments and national organizations of emergency services providers to facilitate technological improvements and encourage cooperative behavior.

Private companies own many of the critical infrastructures that are targets for terrorism. Inducing industry to play its critical role in homeland security activities—to invest in systems for reducing their vulnerabilities, and to develop and manufacture counterterrorism technologies that may not have robust commercial markets—demands new regulatory requirements, financial incentives, and voluntary consensus agreements. Thus, a public-private dialogue is needed to define the best approach for particular industrial sectors and types of vulnerabilities.

The scientific enterprise is complex and highly fragmented, consisting of universities, industry, private sector organizations, government, and pro-fessional societies. The institutional, managerial, and public policy problems that must be solved are daunting. They include:

1. Defining criteria for setting the nation's research priorities
2. Identifying those research priorities
3. Proposing new institutional arrangements and entities that will enable a stronger interaction between the nation's science, technical, and health care enterprises, and its security apparatus

R&D requires considerable finances. However, technology is a key driver for change in the modern world, and investments in R&D are important for the competitiveness of a country, because they create economic offsets for the whole system. Data show a positive influence of investments in defense R&D on total factor productivity. By increasing 1 percent the investments in R&D, a 0.5 percent increase in labor productivity follows. Defense R&D still remains the third largest investment sector—after energy and health—accounting to €400 billion, or 1.1 percent of the world's gross domestic product. Aerospace and defense count about 1.7 percent of world output, but the amount of technological innovation produced in these fields positively influences more than 50 percent of world output. The multiplier of national income related to investments in defense is one of the largest among different sectors. In the United States it is 1.87 to 1.9, while in Italy, for example, it is 1.83.

A strong public effort in defense R&D is needed. Public spending helps private investments to reduce risks, and to pursue collective interests that transcend the private incentives. Public demand boosts the private sector to invest in defense R&D more than the private sector demand does. The best value for money is to avoid duplications. This should also be the priority for Europe. Too many defense programs are duplicated at the national and international level. Introducing a subsidiary principle—like in EU law—will allow deciding whether a program should best be developed at national or supranational level in order to fund it properly, and to avoid duplications. This approach would also allow a more effective division of labor by developing single programs that fit into a bigger picture for common coordinated programs.

The security threats the nation faces affect every phase of domestic life and demand that technical solutions that might be deployed relatively quickly be readily accessible to local, district, province, and government entities. The challenge is to identify the threats and the nation's vulnerabilities, responses to these threats, and to properly organize the nation's science, engineering, and health care capabilities to meet both short- and long-term needs.

Sustaining a long-term national effort against terrorism requires minimizing the costs of security efforts and avoiding placing extra burdens on accustomed conveniences or constraints on civil liberties. Many of the measures explored above not only make the nation safer from terrorist attacks, but can also make it safer from natural or manmade disasters, infectious diseases, hackers disrupting the Internet, failures in electric power distribution and other complex public services, and human error causing failures in such systems. This helps sustain the public's commitment to addressing the preeminent threats.

14

International and Interagency Collaboration

The change in the nature of the threats requires more intelligence exchange and sharing as well as much closer cooperation between intelligence services and their counterparts in security services, policing organizations, and many other security sector entities. Over the years, and for good reasons of separation of power and internal-external division of labor, a different attitude to intelligence handling between all these organs developed. This makes it difficult for them to work together with the degree of interaction now needed. It may be less of an issue of trust or "turf battles" between rivals seeking to protect their little "empires" than it is a deep philosophical and cultural difference that is not easy to overcome. But the issue of intelligence exchange and sharing of information not only affects national agencies or bilateral collaboration; it affects multilateral cooperation and international organizations to an even greater degree. The importance of international cooperation between intelligence and security services was emphasized after 9/11 by UN Security Council Resolution 1373, which called on all states to work ever closer in the fight to combat terrorism.[1] Sharing of information means using information together and allowing others to use someone's information. There may be a corollary to it: the sharing of an activity, where each participant has to perform a task—like the collection, processing, integration, analysis, evaluation, assessment, or interpretation of available and multilaterally relevant information. However, sharing needs to be systematically developed (see Annex 1).

The benefits of sharing are obvious. Sharing can:

1. Improve crisis management and coordination of the overall operation
2. Enhance unity of effort, efficiency and efficacy of collective action
3. Lead to better risk assessments

4. Diminish the likelihood of unpleasant surprises
5. Enhance the possibilities of targeted prevention and more effective preparedness activities
6. Enable more effective use of resources
7. Reduce duplication and improve targeting of sectoral activities
8. Increase accountability
9. Allow a more balanced burden-sharing and better division of labor among participants
10. Allow for greater redundancy of scarce capabilities
11. Reduce casualties and collateral damage
12. Increase sustainability

In a multilateral environment, intelligence and information sharing is at the heart of unity of effort. Collecting and sharing timely, reliable, and accurate information during a crisis is improving the response, maximizing the engagement or allotment of resources, and minimizing human suffering. In a sudden-onset emergency, the quick assessment of needs, the creation of emergency maps, and matching of needs with available resources all improve efficiency and efficacy of the reaction. During protracted conflicts, the ongoing assessment of political, economic, and social changes and the dissemination of this information at headquarters and on the ground ensure that planning, funding, and assistance stay ahead of events. This may eventually lead to a shortened need for international presence in the crisis area implying significant cost savings. Moreover, for governments of smaller nations with fewer intelligence, reconnaissance, and surveillance resources, intelligence received from states with these resources is very often invaluable—another one of the major benefits of sharing.

Information sharing basically occurs in two dimensions. Vertical sharing top-down and bottom-up occurs within a state's administration or government, an alliance or coalition, an international organization or within an organizational entity in the hierarchy. Horizontal sharing occurs among different states, members of an alliance or a coalition, force contingents, international organizations or agencies, or among various organizational entities of all kinds, irrespective of their individual size, influence, power, or importance. Conventional wisdom assumes that vertical information sharing, however differently it might be handled, poses few problems—since it is practiced. procedures are established and known in all organizational entities—whereas horizontal information sharing is generally said to be much more difficult. However, in practice, many hurdles accrue to both vertical and horizontal information sharing, which can be subdivided into five basic groups of obstacles:

1. Technical and infrastructural
2. Functional and operational
3. Legal
4. Political and institutional
5. Classification and security obstacles

Technical and Infrastructural Obstacles

The main technical and infrastructure-related obstacles to information sharing reside in the fact that the actors and organizations already have their own systems in use, which they also bring to bear in crisis management and in their own operations. However, these systems often neither unify information and communications technology, nor can they easily be integrated into a single, standardized entity. Non-interoperability of systems and the intricacies resulting from the need to share resources such as a frequency spectrum or public networks, pose the greatest technical and infrastructural obstacles to information sharing.

The spectrum suitable for wireless and mobile communications is finite and bound by both physics and technology. In particular, the spectrum from 200 MHz to 3 GHz is needed not only by military systems, but also by increasing numbers of new civil devices and services. Cell phones, wireless, e-mail, digital audio, high definition TV, and more all compete for the same spectrum crisis management, also required by the military for their most advanced tools. The result is a difficult, unsustainable situation. Also, when operating in foreign countries, whether in conflict or peace, all actors are always subject to the host nation national sovereignty, and regional spectrum usage patterns. This is true in both friendly and hostile environments. There is no guarantee of the availability of the required spectrum. Even if it is available, the existing management process for locating and assigning frequencies in advance is lengthy, difficult, and uncertain, and therefore unsupportive of the rapid response capability crisis management and interventions should develop.

The technologies making the greatest impact on the delivery of information are many and varied, ranging from computers and networks, online services, the Internet, intranet, television, videoconferencing, satellite transmissions, cellular phones, compression technologies, access to, and supply of, electric power, and the miniaturization of everything from laptop computers to satellite dishes. More changes will occur because of a disarmingly simple idea: the flow of digital information. This flow greatly depends on the digital network in an organization, which must be based on good solutions aimed at solving the "how" problem of information sharing. The ultimate goal is to ensure the authentication, confidentiality, availability, and integrity of sensitive and important information.

The priority for crisis management is to be able to communicate as quickly, accurately, and securely as possible. Technical systems and infrastructure[2] should be able to supply the right information to the right place at the right time. To do so, they depend, in ascending order, on four levels of standardization[3] defined as:

- Compatibility: the capability of two or more items or components of equipment or materiel to exist or function in the same system or environment without mutual interference
- Interoperability: the ability of systems, units, or forces to provide services to and accept services from other systems, units, or forces, and to use the services so exchanged to enable them to operate effectively together
- Interchangeability: a condition that exists when two or more items possess such functional and physical characteristics as to be equivalent in performance and durability, and are capable of being exchanged without any alteration of the items except for adjustments, and without selection for fit and performance
- Commonality: a state achieved when groups of individuals, organizations or nations use common equipment and procedures

Insufficient, uneven, or the lack of standardization—which is particularly critical for IT, authentication schemes, encryption, and formatting—pose the greatest technical obstacles to information sharing. Information may come from a variety of sources that need to be integrated into a system that is appropriate for the environment in which it operates. Within crisis management and a multilateral mission, the core processes should not be confined inside each individual organization but instead flow without any friction among all the players. However, it is not feasible to oblige different organizations to commit to a single, monolithic system. Different organizations have different needs and they must be able to address their particular needs with the most suitable products. This depends not only on the good intentions of the creators of new and advanced technologies, but also on the appropriateness and the affordability of the latter.

A good insight into the kinds of technical and infrastructural obstacles presently encountered, and plaguing connectivity in the armed forces, can be gained from the Advanced Concept Technology Demonstration (ACTD) Program[4] in the field of Joint C4ISR[5] architecture of the U.S. Department of Defense. For the U.S. Armed Forces—which are way ahead of all other armed forces in terms of interconnectivity and digitization of the battlespace—the Joint C4ISR digital network poses a challenge because of the number of incompatible systems to be linked. To break interoperability barriers, two key networks had to be rendered compatible: the Tactical Data Link Network used by the U.S. Navy and the U.S. Air Force, and the Joint Variable Message Format Network used by the U.S. Army and the U.S. Marine Corps. Link 16 now provides a translator, fuses air and ground pictures, and allows commanders in Afghanistan to see E-8 Joint Surveillance and Target Attack Radar System (JSTARS) ground targets and air targets in one precise and accurate picture.[6]

Sensors and reconnaissance are integrated under the Joint Intelligence, Surveillance, and Reconnaissance ACTD. To solve the problem of sensor fusion, the two-way links between firefinder radars, millimeter wave radars on Apache helicopters, and remote battlefield sensors had to be integrated— meshing sensor data into one picture, which is needed to reduce targeting time as well as errors. The Network Centric Collaborative Targeting ACTD links sensors with machine-to-machine front-end processing on the RC-135 Rivet Joint, E-8 JSTARS, E-3 Airborne Warning and Control System, Global Hawk, Predator, U-2, and EP-3.[7] Fusing multiple intelligence sources enables a time-sensitive designation of mobile targets, reduces target location error on mobile threat emitters to 10 meters, and provides warfighters with a targeting solution.

Another organization that had to overcome comparable problems is the Geneva International Centre for Humanitarian Demining. It succeeded combining satellite and aerial imagery with the Geographic Information System (GIS), and with various other data of different standards in one Information Management System for Mine Action (IMSMA), which, once deployed in Kosovo, placed the Mine Action Coordination Center (MACC) and the mine action community on the leading edge of information technology operations in humanitarian applications.[8]

Non-military organizations participating in crisis management and coalition operations will generally be confronted with technical and infrastructural obstacles, which, today, can be solved much more easily.

Functional and Operational Obstacles

The greatest functional and operational obstacles to information sharing arise from insufficient organization and coordination. Other major obstacles stem from an ignorance of the requirements of each stakeholder; incomprehension of who needs to talk to whom, when, and why; redundancy or duplication of efforts; and interoperability[9] problems due to lacking common language, terminology, and a process model. Moreover, organizational fragmentation, compartmentalization, and stovepipes[10] can be the cause of functional obstacles. Operational obstacles arise when information management knowledge is lacking. Other operational obstacles are often also related to a lack of common user culture, IT management knowledge, and appropriate application.

The essence of international collaboration lies in the principle that in response to crises, each country, international organization or specialized agency, and NGO should contribute according to its capabilities and fields of competence, and the contribution should be aimed at the substance of the crisis instead of the symptoms. Thus, the key to multilateral functioning is establishing leadership through coordination: combining cooperation responding to the substance while at the same time focusing on areas of specialization. A continuous exchange of pertinent, operationally important information is a prerequisite for the establishment of permanent, coordinated interaction, and encouragement of leadership in fields of competence and capabilities. To achieve this—and because coordination is dependent on the central function of communication—innovative ways and means of continuous exchange and sharing with appropriate processes and tools are required.

All stakeholders involved in crisis management may be better equipped than ever to deal with crisis situations in purely technical terms. But the activities of the different actors confronting the same problems might be hampered by a "command and control" instead of a "sense and respond" approach by the leadership of the crisis management and, more often than not, by a lack of organization and coordination. The effectiveness of crisis management is largely dependent on good coordination of the appropriate or assigned duties, responsibilities, missions, or tasks of the actors in a multilateral endeavor; on interoperability between the organizations or agencies they represent; and on the processes.

Where there is no organization or coordination, or where it is insufficient, multilateral actors tend to work in a wasteful fashion on the same problem, plan and take decisions without consulting other organizations, and do so without access to up-to-date information or adequate knowledge. Although competition between organizations is a normal part of life, the real challenge is to overcome these difficulties by first understanding the requirements of each stakeholder, particularly: What information is needed and used by whom, for what purpose, where, when, and in what form?

A key organizational obstacle, and the prerequisite for making coordination work, is the ignorance of who needs to talk to whom, when they need to talk, and why they need to talk. Before this is clear, they cannot provide access to critical, real-time decision making information, facilitating communication and the sharing of information among multiple organizations and agencies that can help to identify, and reduce, redundant efforts quickly—since there will always be duplicate efforts going on in parallel, usually with the best of intentions.

The interoperability problem of processes accrues when there is no decision on a common language, terminology, and process model. Without agreement on language and terminology, interpersonal, verbal interaction cannot work. In addition, without a process model that can provide a framework for identifying, defining, and organizing the functional strategies, functional rules, and processes needed for crisis management, and without that process model to support the way organizations work, processes will remain a big obstacle.

Organizational fragmentation, compartmentalization,[11] and the legendary stovepipes are other functional obstacles, all of which hinder information sharing since they usually lead to ignorance of requirements, information needs, and priorities of outside actors, and little understanding of cross-sector impact. Though functional difficulties may also be rooted in deeper differences of organizational culture, procedures, and operational concepts, it is the stovepipes that are not only quaint, but—where armed forces are involved—can also be dangerous. They hinder the ability to accelerate operations and take full advantage of technologies that promise greater effectiveness. Moreover, as the ability to accelerate the pace of operations rises, stovepipes enhance the danger of fratricide.

Operational obstacles can also arise because some organizations still operate through processes established before the information age. Vast amounts of information are stored in electronic media and exchanged over the Internet or intranets, but processes that allow this to actually be turned into useful information and intelligence are often still very much in their infancy. Moreover, most organizations do not know what they know. The technology to share information might be there, but the drivers of knowledge sharing are often still immature. Transforming data into intelligence is a function that is much more complex, qualitative, and requires a high degree of sophisticated human thinking. Thus, among the operational obstacles, one of the major challenges is that of knowledge management,[12] not of technology.

There are other operational obstacles that are related to the effective management of IT, a common user culture, and appropriate application. These often surface when a 24 hours/7 days operational capability is required, and continuity has to be ensured.

Legal Obstacles

Among the impediments to information sharing are the different legal authorities of intelligence and law enforcement, as well as restrictions on the release of case-sensitive information and rules of discovery, limiting exchanges between law enforcement and third parties in democracies. Also laws, rules, and regulations on data protection, privacy, and security can be obstacles to sharing. Other obstacles accrue because nations balance civil liberties with their need for security in differing ways.

The threats posed by terrorism, proliferation, and organized crime typify the new sort of security problem a state must confront. All are transnational, defying ready classification as foreign or domestic, either in origin, participants, or materials. Clandestine networks that are the carriers of these threats can combine citizens with resident aliens and foreign nationals, operating in and out of national territory over long periods of time. A greater danger may arise if a threat falls into one of the crevasses of overlapping jurisdictions, such as the divide between foreign or domestic terrorism, state or non-state sponsored terrorism, or terrorism that is classified as a problem for law enforcement or one of national security.

The increasingly menacing nature of the threats, previously viewed as law enforcement problems, have become national security matters. This has led to a growing number of agencies and services now having larger roles for protecting their own citizens and combating these transnational wrongdoers: customs, border and coast guard, immigration, visa, export-import and money laundering control, homeland defense, and other security officials who encounter the individuals. Sharing between all these critical interfaces must be developed and facilitated. Centralized databases must be established, containing intelligence by which individual names can be checked. Although there are many potential concerns about the establishment of centralized databases, there is a need to ensure that law enforcement and other agencies, including those of regions and localities, have better access to information acquired by intelligence services about potential terrorist activities.[13] Investigating today's terrorist groups requires interagency communication and collaboration. It is essential that law enforcement agencies and task forces be able to collect and analyze data from multiple data sources in order to monitor, penetrate, infiltrate, disrupt, and prevent terrorist activity. While each of these services' roles is important, their overlapping responsibilities have led to conflicts in mission and methods, most visible between the intelligence and law enforcement communities. The latter is often due to government relying too heavily on law enforcement as the primary response to these perpetrators. This reliance is to the detriment of other possible actions.

Law enforcement can be a powerful weapon against these threats, but may not be the most appropriate response in all circumstances. Often the perpetrators have sought sanctuary in other countries and cannot be brought to trial. It is, however, at the policy level that the decision needs to be made whether to give priority to law enforcement, to intelligence, or to other policy options. Since not all global crime constitutes a threat to national security, those groups or activities that do should be identified as specifically as possible. The various services should be alerted with respect to these threats and their operations coordinated.

Increasingly overlapping interests in the same foreign groups and activities have caused conflicts between law enforcement and the intelligence community. While intelligence is fundamentally predictive and based on assumptions, hypotheses, analyses, and forecasts, the fact that law enforcement is responsive is based on credible evidence. The national security paradigm fosters aggressive, proactive intelligence gathering, presuming the threat before it arises, planning preventive action against suspected targets, and taking anticipatory action. The law enforcement paradigm fosters reactions to information voluntarily provided, post–facto arrests, trials governed by rules of evidence, and general protection for the rights of citizens. These functions use different approaches and operating procedures, and there is great risk that marrying the two will sacrifice one or both. Thus, tensions may result, in part, from their very different missions, goals, and legal authorities.

The mission of intelligence services is to collect, analyze, and disseminate intelligence to their consumers. Human sources and technical collection systems can be only developed over long periods of time and often at great cost. They are easily compromised and then often unable to be replaced. Accordingly, intelligence agencies are, by nature, reluctant to permit consumers, including law enforcement, to use intelligence in any way that might result in the loss of a source or collection method. Moreover, they cannot present their evidence for the world to see and testify in court.

The mission of law enforcement, in contrast, is to investigate and prosecute individuals who violate national laws. It is their business to present evidence and prosecute in open courts. Like intelligence services, law enforcement agencies want information about global criminal activities, terrorists, and proliferants, but as a means to a different end: the arrest and conviction of criminals. Law enforcement's need for intelligence may not always be compatible with the methods of the intelligence community.

Among a number of specific areas of conflict between the two communities, three stand out: First, there remains a mutual reluctance to share sensitive information. Law enforcement complains that intelligence services, citing the need to protect sources and methods, do not disseminate important intelligence reports or, more often, disseminate them with such onerous restrictions on their use that they are valueless to investigators and prosecutors.

Similarly, intelligence services[14] complain that law enforcement refuses to share information about terrorists, proliferators, narcotics trafficking, and organized criminal activities collected during the course of domestic criminal investigations. With largely unfettered access domestically, and armed with enforcement powers, law enforcement can often collect information about individuals involved in global criminal activities more easily than intelligence services operating clandestinely abroad. Much of this information is potentially useful to intelligence services, but law enforcement agencies are reluctant to share it lest it leak out or be used in a way that would taint the prosecution's case.

A second source of conflict involves the intelligence services' refusal to accept direct collection tasking from law enforcement. Intelligence services' interpretation of their legal authorities is that they only permit them to engage in intelligence collection for "foreign intelligence" purposes. The legitimate concern with protecting civil liberties creates firewalls between the activities of the two communities. If a trail of conversation on which intelligence is eavesdropping becomes domestic—that is: involving citizens, corporations or even resident aliens—the trail must end. Accordingly, while they invite law enforcement to request information about specific targets, intelligence services will only begin collection if they independently determine that the requested collection has a valid "foreign intelligence" purpose. In almost all instances, requests for information about specific individuals involved in terrorism, proliferation, organized crime, and narcotics trafficking are deemed to have foreign intelligence value. The intelligence services' refusal to accept direct collection tasking, however, makes them appear to be unresponsive to the needs of law enforcement, which, in turn, makes it reluctant to make further requests.

A third source of tension is an increased effort by law enforcement agencies to expand their activities abroad, both to engage in liaison with foreign law enforcement agencies and to develop independent sources of information about global criminal activities that can be used more easily by investigators and prosecutors. Law enforcement agencies are hesitant to provide details about these activities abroad to intelligence and to their own diplomatic representatives or foreign ministry officials because of concerns about leaks and possible tainting of their investigations.

The need to combat transnational terrorist and criminal activities more effectively requires that the capabilities of intelligence services be harnessed to support law enforcement as efficiently and effectively as possible. Yet, forcing intelligence services to provide more direct support to law enforcement might open them up to stricter judicial scrutiny and criminal discovery procedures, which could ultimately hamper their collection activities and risk disclosure of their sources and methods. Although each has legitimate practical and legal concerns about how information it collects may be used—or can be misused—by the other, states cannot wage an effective fight against international terrorism and crime unless the two communities pool their information resources. Thus, government must establish procedures that allow the passage of relevant information in a manner that neither taints a potential prosecution nor jeopardizes sources and methods. Channels for transferring information must be clearly established and close oversight by both the executive branch and the parliamentary oversight committees is required to ensure a smooth functioning of transfer arrangements.

Decentralization of law enforcement activities can also be an impediment to information sharing. Moreover, due to fragmented justice information systems, law enforcement and public safety officials often do not have access to complete, accurate, and timely information. As a result, critical information is not always shared at key decision points in the law enforcement or justice process.[15]

In some cases, the duty of confidentiality owed to individuals, data-protection and privacy laws, compliance with the European Convention on Human Rights, and other statutory provisions[16] can prevent the sharing of information. Primarily for legal reasons, the intelligence community and the military do not maintain a database on the activities of organizations and actors of the humanitarian assistance and relief communities. Both sides are also sensitive to any charges that members of the humanitarian assistance and relief communities of the ICRC or other NGOs have become informers or intelligence sources. As a result, intelligence and the military frequently do not know which of these organizations are important, what information they possess, or how to access this information. This might not only hamper the sharing, but also closer and efficient cooperation in any coalition effort.

Political and Institutional Obstacles

Major obstacles may originate in an unwillingness to share or from institutional resistance or reluctance to cooperation. Moreover, they can reside in official or unofficial policy, or be caused by different cultures. Relationships are frequently marked by competition, rivalry for public attention and resources, differing priorities, and contradictory observations, all of which generate delays. One basic obstacle is that many governmental systems are just too slow to respond to a rapidly evolving crisis. Other obstacles stem from a lack of understanding on the issue, propriety of information, fear of embarrassment, or reluctance to ask permission from the originator to use his information.

The unwillingness to share can have different reasons. Organizations or individuals may not willingly share information with other organizations, agencies, or individuals because they believe that what they know provides them with an inherent advantage in crisis management, for bargaining, in negotiations, or as a competitor. Moreover, as evidence suggests, it is not unreasonable to view the unwillingness to share stemming from historical, ideological, ethnical, or even religious adversity between nations. It could, however, also be caused by uncertainty, which can exist in many areas. What mission will be needed? Which countries, organizations, agencies, or NGOs will participate? Under what conditions will allies or other partners join or leave the coalition? What are the dangers and implications? How do they react to bad news? Furthermore, the unwillingness to share could be a function of the willingness to accept or share risks and responsibilities.

Such organizational, institutional, or human concerns may often result in a lack of sharing. That said, even more critical than the absence of information is the propensity of sharing partial, inaccurate, or ambiguous information, and this leads to one of the most important obstacles—the lack of trust. The sharing, particularly of sensitive information, is dependent on the trust relationship established between the information sender and receiver. These relationships are fragile, often take a long time to establish, and cannot easily be replaced by changing mandates or reassigning responsibilities. Moreover, the fragility of these relationships is influenced by the fact that information sharing can hardly ever be a one-way street, or survive long as such, and by the fact that information sharing is only as valuable as the information shared.

The motivation of institutions, organizations, suppliers, and consumers of intelligence to share accurate and timely information is based on trust, despite the potential of use of information in unanticipated ways. This, in turn, depends on the overriding horizontal and vertical sharing cultures. As community and institutional paradigms increasingly intermingle, crisis management and coalition partners will be challenged to inspire trust and motivation for sharing needed information with those stakeholders over which they may often have little control. Given the lack of these enabling factors, it will be almost impossible to ensure that accurate information is available for integration, despite the presence of enabling technologies that can facilitate such integration.

There is a wide range of institutional obstacles that limit the sharing of information. They exist in both civilian and military communities. The military cannot disclose classified information. UN agencies and humanitarian relief organizations are reluctant to share information that may look like "intelligence" about the conflict, and thus threaten the security of their staff and operations in the field. At one extreme, there is the potential threat of jeopardizing humanitarian neutrality, which limits the willingness of the ICRC, some UN agencies, relief organizations, and NGOs to institutionalize information sharing, exchange staff, co-locate offices, or even share information in a mutual coordination structure to which the military has access. At the other extreme, there is the problem of differences in national intelligence cultures that is greater among some countries than it is among others. There have always been, and will continue to be, clubs within the intelligence community. A further reason for institutional tightfistedness is that intelligence collection, analysis, and exchange remains the most proto-national of a country's activities; its priorities are governed strictly by national political agendas.

Policy can be another big obstacle to the sharing of information and intelligence. A lack of policy can play a role. Thus, though intelligence services and the armed forces have met often with UN agencies, the ICRC, and NGOs to share information, no official policy on this relationship exists. There is also the problem of political bias: how to ensure that intelligence that comes from national sources is not slanted or used manipulatively? There have, for instance, been many accusations, most of them unfair and unsound, that UNSCOM was influenced in this way by Israeli intelligence. Moreover, political ambition or secret political intentions can play a role. When political motives are misaligned, no amount of interoperability—technological or otherwise—can mitigate the problem. A related challenge is balancing each actor's political needs against the requirements of the operation. This is particularly important when political guidance changes during the course of an operation. Such tensions can complicate command and control—the vertical dimension, and coordination—the horizontal dimension.

A further obstacle involves the fact that most current government systems are just too slow to respond to a rapidly evolving crisis or environment, and have not evolved much as overall information management capabilities have advanced and grown. Information and decisions must pass through many channels and specialist cubbyholes, each with their own priorities and pieces of the total picture, being filtered and massaged by any number of analysts, managers, and political operatives. The overall system then hopes that all of these "bits and bytes" will get put back together into a comprehensive picture higher in the chain of command. This prevents information from arriving in the hands of those who need it to manage a strategic or tactical situation in any sort of a timely manner. Since vital information is of little use until it is applied to the problems that actually exist on the ground, the delay existing in the processes of international organizations and NGOs is also an impediment to the sharing of information.

Security and Classification Obstacles

Major obstacles to vertical and horizontal information exchange accrue whenever security considerations work against the sharing: when the information, the documents, or other carriers containing the information have to be protected.

The reasons for protecting information can be manifold, but first and foremost is to prevent any knowledge of the information from being exploited by outsiders to the detriment of the actors, their activities, plans, and intentions in domains that need confidentiality or to remain unknown or secret to outsiders. The need for protection and security is widespread, and—after what was probably too overzealous openness since the demise of the Soviet Empire—in the wake of the terrorist attacks of September 11, 2001, again increasing. This need is unlikely to subside in the near term. New risks and vulnerabilities are most likely to reinforce the trend to expanding information protection to include more than the traditional sectors in need of security.

States, governments, and the armed forces traditionally have their own security needs in fields that include policy making; diplomacy; telecommunications; R&D; nuclear or other weaponry storage and installations; strategies, tactics, and engagement techniques for means of power projection; force deployments; and intelligence activities.

The public sector will want to protect information about the critical national infrastructure and its vulnerabilities: utilities; water purification and distribution; power generation and distribution; energy; pipelines; fixed and mobile telecommunication; transportation; ports, airports, and air traffic control; the health sector; emergency services; banking and financial services; etc.[17]

The private sector generally will want to ensure privacy in order to protect sensitive information about finances; R&D; proprietary information and intellectual property; patents; plans; marketing; economic agreements; manufacturing and trade secrets, and more.

Current and future developments are, however, opening areas where protection of information can only be ensured—to use military terminology—in a joint effort: areas in need of enlarged and overlapping cooperation between the private sector, the public sector at large, and the legitimate international/multilateral sector simultaneously. This is a result of technology having ushered in a new age filled with almost unlimited potential for communications, and with it, the new challenges of the Internet age. Ever more critical national infrastructures, enterprises, governments, and local administrations depend on the reliable functioning and security of complex IT systems. The public and private sector need to make sure that these essential systems are protected from all forms of attack—which is precisely the cause of tremendous problems finding a workable solution for information sharing.

The private sector is understandably reluctant to share sensitive proprietary information about intrusions, actual damage, theft, and crime, as well as prevention practices, with either government agencies or competitors because information sharing is a risky proposition with less than clear benefits. No company wants information to surface that they have given in confidence. Such an event could jeopardize their market position, strategies, customer base, or capital investments. Nor would they risk voluntarily opening themselves up to costly and time-consuming litigation. Releasing information about security breaches or vulnerabilities in their IT systems presents just such risks. Negative publicity or exposure as a result of reports of information infrastructure violations could lead to threats to investor and consumer confidence in a company's products. Companies also fear revealing trade secrets to competitors, and hence are reluctant to share such proprietary information. They also fear that sharing this information, particularly with government, may lead to increased regulation of the industry or of e-commerce in general.

Moreover, there might be a lack of trust towards law enforcement, or a concern that company systems may become caught up in an investigation and lose production or development time. Thus, many private sector enterprises, including banks, find it easier to keep quiet, and absorb the pain inflicted by computer attacks and intrusions, even at substantial cost. In addition, there is the need to protect individual customer's privacy. Industry fears that privacy breaches on innocent customers might inadvertently occur during investigations. Furthermore, few high tech companies are interested in being perceived by their customers as active agents of law enforcement. Government agencies, meanwhile, are often viewed as demanding this type of information from the private sector, but giving little back in return.

These and other comparable concerns are relevant whether we consider inter-industry, cross-industry, industry to government, local administration to federal government, or—since attacks can be launched from any point in the world—government to government or international information sharing. Hence, how should one protect the critical national information infrastructure? In many ways, solutions to information security challenges are no different than any other Internet-related policy issue. Regulation is not the answer. Industry leadership has been the hallmark of the ubiquitous success of the IT sector. It advocates a market-driven, industry-led, free market approach to the Internet and e-commerce. These same principles must be applied in the realm of information security.

However, IT security cannot be achieved without information sharing between the private sector and government agencies. Thus, there is need for an active, robust, and credible liaison of the government with the private sector. Government agencies have to respect the confidentiality as well as the value of the information and secrets that the private sector may give them to do their job. In order to do the job on both sides, real-time feedback of information sharing is essential. All partners engaged in ensuring IT security will not share information unless they have a high degree of confidence that this information will be protected from disclosure. Hence, all partners must take steps to protect the sensitive data as a precursor to information sharing. Only then will it be possible to form trust relationships and begin data sharing. Similar principles apply to information sharing between governments.

A nation's protection from terrorist attacks is another area where enlarged and overlapping cooperation is needed between the private sector, the public sector at large, and the multilateral or international sector simultaneously. A top-to-bottom review and reorganization of the U.S. Department of Justice found that America's ability to detect and prevent terrorism has been undermined significantly by legal restrictions that limit the intelligence and law enforcement communities' access to and sharing of the most valuable resource in the war on terrorism. That resource is information.[18] Homeland security stakeholders must work together more effectively to strengthen the process by which critical information can be shared, analyzed, integrated, and disseminated to help prevent or minimize terrorist activities. The success of a homeland security strategy relies on the ability of government's relations with foreign states, all levels of government, and the private sector to communicate and cooperate effectively with one another. Activities that are hampered by organizational fragmentation, technical or infrastructural impediments, or ineffective collaboration blunt a nation's collective efforts to prevent or minimize terrorist acts.[19] The challenges facing the homeland security community require a commitment to focus on transformational strategies, including strengthening the risk-management framework, refining the strategic and policy guidance structure to emphasize collaboration, integration, information sharing among all relevant stakeholders, and bolstering the fundamental management foundation integral to effective public sector performance and accountability.

Similarly, for combating international organized crime effectively, enlarged information sharing and overlapping, simultaneous cooperation between the private, public, and international sector is needed. All partners must ensure that sensitive data is protected as a precursor to information sharing. In this respect, Schengen appears to be the system that has solved the sharing problem convincingly.

Improving Sharing and Exchange of Intelligence

None of these obstacles presents a uniform aspect. As much time has to be spent in qualifying conclusions as making them. While legal impediments may restrict information exchange, the same exchange can be facilitated and assisted by technical proposals. Generally much harder to overcome are the political and institutional as well as the operational problems of what information to exchange, when to provide it, and for what aims and purposes. The two most important obstacles to sharing sensitive information and strengthening cooperation are those of protection and security. These can stem from technical and infrastructural, legal, functional and operational, or political and institutional obstacles, as well as from a combination of some or all of those. However, the prospects for overcoming many of these obstacles in due time through innovation are not too bleak (see Appendix B).

The immense importance of improving the exchange of information and intelligence cannot be overemphasized. Without urgently required improvements, national governments and international organizations will not be able to tackle the new threats to security comprehensively. Improvements are needed between national agencies and institutions, between countries, and between states and international organizations. To that end, networks of trust between individuals from different countries and different agencies have to be developed, since it is precisely on the basis of trust that information and intelligence is most readily shared. It is pointless for governments to legislate for information exchange if the basis of mutual trust is lacking. Instead, governments should think of how to make best use of models of informal trust-generating mechanisms as, for example, developed and working in NATO to improve their capability for intelligence exchange.

Intelligence services have cultural and bureaucratic incentives not to share their information with each other or with those outside the service. These include a natural impulse to hoard information to protect turf as well as an ingrained passion for secrecy. Security services and intelligence agencies traditionally have resisted sharing information with each other. The United States is by far not the only country that has learned that failure to share, coordinate, and connect available intelligence can have devastating consequences. If much more sharing is required—vertically and horizontally, internally and externally—intelligence management not only has to alter agency incentives and culture to require sharing, it also has to address the excessive emphasis on secrecy and classification that inhibits constructive, timely information flows while continuing to respect the need to protect genuine sources and methods.

Bilateral Intelligence Sharing and Information Exchange Still Predominant

Historically, states have been willing to reciprocate where they share common intelligence interests and concerns.[20] For the most part, these relationships have proven mutually beneficial. Even where the interests of two nations do not entirely converge, intelligence often supplies the *quid* for the other's *quo*. Bilateral cooperation normally involves the exchange and sharing of intelligence and analyses on topics of mutual interest. However, such bilateral relations will only be maintained and continued if both parties strictly respect the basic agreement underlying their intelligence sharing: that the origin and details of the intelligence provided by the partner service will be protected according to its original classification, and will not be passed on to third parties—the so-called Third-Party Rule.

Though countries with smaller intelligence resources are not always able to bring to the table capabilities equal to those of bigger services, they can reciprocate in other ways. In some cases, states can provide geographic or other access that would not otherwise be available. In others, intelligence services of smaller countries can provide skills, expertise, or languages that larger countries would otherwise have to develop. While some states spend a greater percentage on intelligence than others, it is often unreasonable to expect quantitative comparability in such relationships. Apart from access and capabilities states can provide, there is often great benefit in having close and enduring friends who can be counted on in times of trouble. Intelligence services provide tangible cement for such security relationships.[21]

With expanded missions, the requirements for intelligence contributions to international security have multiplied. These are no longer limited to crisis management and response, conflict prevention, and peace operations, but extend to other categories of worldwide and long-term security issues. The fight against terrorism is obviously one where intelligence is the most critical resource. International terrorism and the danger of a recrudescence of internal terrorism make it essential to achieve the broadest possible cooperation among different countries. The limitation of WMD and other arms proliferation is another. A third category is the fight against organized crime. The enforcement of international sanctions constitutes a fourth category of wide-ranging, intelligence-driven cooperation. A fifth category is the support of many agreements that now exist for arms control and other confidence-building measures. A sixth category is intelligence support for disaster relief and humanitarian assistance. Moreover, there is the growing need for critical national infrastructure protection against hacker and information warfare attacks, the challenges of which pose the problem of international intelligence cooperation in its most extreme form.

The preeminent threats, expanding international interventions, and multinational peace support operations account for the rapid expansion of requirements for intelligence contributions to international security. At the same time, they are opening the way for more advanced cooperation between security and intelligence organizations from participating and interested countries. Coalition forces deployed in peace operations require the full range of wartime intelligence support. The concepts of graduated force, surgical strikes, low casualties, and minimum collateral damage are all intelligence dependent.

Peace operations in Bosnia and Kosovo have already represented what appears to be the new pattern of intelligence support for international intervention of all kinds. All those responsible for such operations, from the UN Secretary-General downward, have emphasized the need for good intelligence. The UN, the EU, NATO, and other supranational organizations and their actions still largely depend on national intelligence inputs. National intelligence is relied on to fill gaps, validate other sources, and assess. International organizations will eventually develop machinery for supranational intelligence assessments, but it will be a long haul and will have to build on interstate exchanges. The United States and some other countries are committed to intelligence support for international organizations.[22] To some extent, this is already a de facto underpinning of international society. This is why intelligence networking increasingly also has to occur at the multilateral level. Multilateral networking can take care of the development of appropriate concepts, processes, communication, liaison arrangements, coordination, use of modern technologies and databases, mutual legal assistance, training, and other support.

Multilateral Sharing and Information Exchange

Multilateral cooperation still has many limits. In general, and despite some efforts at reform, information sharing across the UN and its affiliated organizations remains poor. All five groups of obstacles to sharing have a negative impact on sharing. Among the many problems of sharing, four are most visible: UN's adversity to intelligence, the issue of politics, the question of bias, and the dilemma of security.[23]

In the OSCE, information management is inadequate for its geographic scope, varied mandates, number of field missions, and activities of this organization. With fifty-five participating states, a headquarters in Vienna, an annually rotating chairmanship in one of the capitals, a principal institution in another city, other institutions in different capitals, seventeen long-term field missions with staff ranging from five to several hundred, and the annual deployment of several hundred strong election observation missions, the OSCE's capacity to manage information sharing is stretched beyond its limits. Information is often shared through electronic means of Internet and intranet within the headquarters, but hard copy sharing is prevalent with the rest. The Internet is primarily responsible for the smooth and efficient flow of information within and between the various components of the organization when the information pertains to routine matters. Information beyond routine matters, however, is all too often mismanaged to the detriment of the organization's effectiveness.

NATO and the EU have no integrated intelligence services of their own—they are entirely dependent on what intelligence services of the member states can or are willing to provide. As with other multilateral cooperation bodies, there is no requirement that member states share intelligence that might be of value or interest to other member states, NATO, or EU institutions. Sharing is explicitly voluntary. Voluntary sharing means there is no direct way for receiving states to ensure that a sharing state has divulged all the relevant intelligence in its possession or to determine that the intelligence exchanged has not been modified or distorted to serve the provider's interests. Multilateral cooperation agreements lack strong or effective mechanisms for monitoring or punishing a failure to disseminate relevant intelligence.

In Europe there are no arrangements in place for the sharing of very secret intelligence—though most requests for information are generally met. Multilateral cooperation bodies collate intelligence received from national intelligence services and provide analysis that is disseminated under their name so that recipients are not able to identify directly the country that has provided the original information. Multilateral cooperation bodies receive relatively little raw intelligence from the member states, instead they rely on finished intelligence from which sensitive details on sources and methods are eliminated. European intelligence cooperation to date has been hampered by emphasizing national sovereignty over intelligence sharing.

Mistrust and divergent policy interests between partners to an intelligence-sharing agreement is a key barrier to sharing. However, European intelligence cooperation is indispensable for the conduct of a Common Foreign and Security Policy (CFSP), and a European Security and Defense Policy (ESDP). This is why the EU Commission has decided that from January 2008 onward, any information available in one country should be available to all twenty-seven member states. Thus, it proposed to substitute the principle that data belong to state authorities, and can only be transmitted to another member state on conditions established by the state that holds the information, with the "principle of availability." Under this principle, any member state would have the same right of access to information held by another EU member state, whereby national settlement on collection and retention of data is transformed into an EU-wide "right of use of data."

Sharing in NATO

Though lacking a truly integrated intelligence structure, intelligence sharing within NATO works quite well. U.S., UK, French, German, and Italian intelligence services feed in most intelligence reports and assessments. Reports are sanitized so that references to sources and methods or sensitive pieces of information are removed. Some governments still withhold high-grade material from NATO because of open questions concerning the reliability of personnel of intelligence services of some of the new NATO members. Moreover, sharing is complicated by doctrinal inconsistencies, different military traditions, and the fact that some members have always been more equal than others. There are special relationships and continuing differences in intelligence cultures that impose consequential limitations on NATO. In addition, intelligence sharing is hampered in some cases by political sensitivities and occasional outright conflicts between some member states such as Turkey and Greece.

Throughout NATO's history, intelligence, unlike other aspects of defense, has not been organized in truly integrated structures.[24] NATO has no mandate or capability for intelligence gathering except when there are deployments of NATO or NATO-led forces. NATO depends on member nations for intelligence, which is then shared with allies and, as appropriate, with Partnership for Peace (PfP) partners and other countries contributing forces to NATO-led operations or participating in PfP activities. NATO headquarters' key focus of intelligence is the Intelligence Division of the International Military Staff (IMS). It acts as the central coordinating body for the collation, assessment, and dissemination of intelligence within NATO headquarters and the NATO commands, agencies, organizations, and nations. NATO Intelligence Division provides day-to-day strategic intelligence support to the NATO secretary general, the North Atlantic Council, the Defense Planning Committee, the Military Committee, and other NATO bodies such as International Military Staff elements, the Political Committee, and the WMD Proliferation Center. It maintains selected databases and digital intelligence information services. It performs strategic warning and crisis management functions, and conducts liaison with other NATO and national bodies performing specialized intelligence functions and related activities.

Established at the end of 2004 at NATO headquarters, the Terrorist Threat Intelligence Unit (TTIU) is the competence center for sharing intelligence related to terrorism, analyzing threats by drawing on information from member nations, and providing forward-looking assessments. TTIU has a permanent staff of seven from Germany, the United States, the United Kingdom, and Spain, plus additional experts and analysts on loan from other member nations. Allies have recognized the need to intensify exchanges of information and intelligence with other international organizations and partners, which is reflected in the Partnership Action Plan against Terrorism (PAP(T)). A joint IMS/IS EAPC-PfP Intelligence Liaison Unit has been established for the exchange of such information.

In addition to the Joint Operations Information and Intelligence System (JOIIS), NATO has the Linked Operations-Intelligence Centers Europe (LOCE) system in use, supporting combined intelligence operations by connecting users at all echelons, from the national ministry of defense to tactical levels. LOCE is the only intranet approved by ECJ6 to process NATO SECRET data, consisting of web-enabled PCs (over 400 workstations serving 2,700 registered and 10,000 e-mail users), a centralized set of servers, and dedicated communication circuits, providing multimedia e-mail, bulletin board, TACELIT, secondary imagery, order-of-battle databases, network services, and secure voice capability. LOCE is a U.S. owned intelligence system that serves as USEUCOM intelligence system for coalition warfare, and as the U.S. gateway to NATO's Battlefield Information Collection and Exploitation System (BICES), providing connectivity among U.S. and NATO forces.

Sharing in the European Union

Intelligence sharing within the EU and with other international organizations is underdeveloped and hampered by a lack of political will, institutional limitations, and compartmentalization within the EU administration. Despite motivating factors for increased cooperation, obstacles such as security and use of classified information, concerns over sovereignty, and the fear of damaging privileged NATO relationships affect intelligence sharing negatively. The problem of sovereignty and differences in national intelligence cultures probably will not soon lead to the creation of a truly integrated EU intelligence authority. One notable exception is the Schengen Information System where intelligence sharing works smoothly and efficiently.

The EU has established a Joint Situation Centre (SITCEN), which is located within the General Secretariat and produces external intelligence reports. Seven member states have seconded an intelligence analyst each,[25] which produce daily situation reports and general situation assessments of different regions and threats to EU deployments within the framework of ESDP. SITCEN obtains intelligence from the member states, directly from some intelligence agencies through the seconded analysts, and diplomatic reports from the Commission's various representatives in the field as well as from foreign ministries. It disseminates its products to the Political and Security Committee (PSC), the High Representative, the EU Military Committee, member states, and the Policy Planning and Early Warning Unit (PPEWU).

The EU also maintains a Satellite Centre (SATCEN or EUSC), set up in Torrejón that is dedicated to the exploitation and production of information derived from analysis of earth observation space imagery and collateral data, including aerial imagery. It neither owns nor operates satellites or other collection resources. It purchases commercial imagery and obtains some from the French-Spanish-Belgian *Helios II-A*, the German *SAR-Lupe*,[26] and the Italian *Cosmo-Skymed* satellite systems, but does not control the tasking of the satellites and cannot guarantee that relevant or timely images will be available. Under the supervision of the Political and Security Committee of the Council, and under operational direction of the secretary general, SATCEN supports EU decision making in CFSP and ESDP within the Council, the Commission, for member states, and third states or international organizations that have addressed a request to the secretary general.

Moreover, there is an Intelligence Division (INTDIV) in the EU Military Staff. An intelligence instrument within the EU Intelligence Community, it brings together information from various sources such as civilian services, law enforcement and police authorities, diplomatic, economic, political, and military intelligence reporting, but depends on information provided by EU member states and their defense intelligence organizations. INTDIV comprises thirty-three individuals from nineteen member states that work in three branches:

1. The Intelligence Policy Branch, which develops intelligence-related concepts, doctrine, and procedures, and manages personnel, infrastructure, and communications
2. The Requirements Branch, which fosters relationship with EU member states' defense intelligence organizations, handles the distribution of requests for information, and coordinates with the Satellite Centre
3. The Production Branch, which is organized into five geographic task forces and one transnational issues task force, develops the classified EU Watchlist—the common basis for intelligence exchange—in coordination with EU early warning bodies such as the Policy Unit, the Joint Situation Centre, and the EU Commission, and produces intelligence assessments for the Military Staff, the Military Committee, and the secretary general.

In addition, there is the Bureau de Liaison (BDL network), the EU's official encrypted communication system assisting officials in all twenty-seven member states, and in the Working Group on Terrorism in the transmission of information among EU member states law enforcement bodies, Europol, and security and intelligence services. A standard special bulletin form is sent through the network of liaison offices, marked either "urgent" or "flash," as appropriate. New rapid information exchange procedures aim to have reliable information on terrorist attacks that occur in other member states so that they can integrate it into their respective assessment of the level of the threat. Its origin is in the TREVI Group that brought together the Ministers of Justice and the Interior.[27]

Europol

Europol was created by convention signed by all member states in 1995 as the successor of the intergovernmental forum of the TREVI Group, with headquarters in The Hague. It began operations in 1999 as the EU law enforcement organization handling criminal intelligence. Europol is accountable to the Council of Ministers for Justice and Home Affairs, which is responsible for guidance and control, appoints the Director and Deputy Director, and approves its budget. Europol has a Management Board with one representative from each member state supervising the activities. A Joint Supervisory Body, made up of two data protection experts from each member state, monitors the content and use of personal data held by Europol. Europol is comprised of 590 people with ninety Europol liaison officers from different law enforcement agencies. Its mission is to make a significant contribution to EU's law enforcement action against organized crime and terrorism, with emphasis on targeting criminal organizations. Its mandate is to support law enforcement activities of member states against illicit drug trafficking, illicit immigration networks, terrorism, forgery of money and other means of payment, trafficking in human beings, child pornography, illicit vehicle trafficking, and money laundering. Other main priorities include crimes against persons, financial crime, and cybercrime—which apply where an organized criminal structure is involved, and where two or more member states are affected. Europol supports law enforcement of the member states by facilitating exchange of information in accordance with national law, providing operational analysis in support of operations, generating strategic reports and crime analysis, and providing expertise and technical support for investigations and operations.

Europol has operational agreements with the non-EU states of Canada, Croatia, Iceland, Norway, Switzerland, and the United States, and it concluded strategic agreements with Colombia, Russia, and Turkey. As far as EU bodies are concerned, Europol maintains an operational agreement with Eurojust, as well as strategic agreements with the European Central Bank, the European Commission, the European Monitoring Center for Drugs and Drug Addiction, and the European Anti-Fraud Office. As far as cooperation with international organizations are concerned, it concluded an operational agreement with Interpol and strategic agreements with the World Customs Organization and the UN Office on Drugs and Crime.

Member states are required to supply relevant intelligence to Europol through their European liaison officers on their own initiative or in response to a request from the organization. Liaison officers are also responsible for filing national requests for information from Europol. The key mechanism for intelligence sharing is the Europol Computer System (TECS) with three components:

1. An information system
2. An analysis system
3. An index system

The Europol information system contains information about individuals and groups suspected of having committed, or being likely to commit, a crime. The work files generated by Europol staff and liaison officers deal with details of specific offenses, including contacts of suspects, potential witnesses, and others that can provide information.

Interpol

Most countries are members of the International Criminal Police Organization, Interpol, established to detect and fight transnational crime and provide international cooperation and coordination of other police activities. Interpol does not conduct enquiries or arrests by itself, but serves as a central point for information on crime, suspects, and criminals. Political crimes are excluded from its competencies. Countries normally maintain a Single-Point-of-Contact office in the headquarters of the national criminal investigation service, available twenty-four hours a day, and providing the gateway for international law enforcement enquiries and cooperation as well as the exchange of intelligence and information.

Furthermore, there are multilateral bodies and institutions entrusted with intelligence cooperation efforts by EU members, such as the European

Council's Security Committee, the Terrorism Working Group (TWG), the Working Party on Terrorism (COTER), the Standing Committee on Internal Security (COSI), the Article 36 Committee (CATS), as well as an EU Counterterrorism Coordinator.

Other Multilateral Sharing

The most recent such body is that established by the *Treaty of Prüm*—a convention concluded in May 2005 between Belgium, Germany, Spain, France, Netherlands, Luxembourg, and Austria. Its aims are to further the development of European cooperation and play a pioneering role in establishing the highest possible standard of cooperation. They want to accomplish this by means of a much speedier exchange of information, particularly in combating terrorism, cross border crime, and illegal migration, while leaving participation in such cooperation open to all EU member states. The extended security cooperation measures comprise among other things: sharing of DNA and fingerprint data, common rules on flight security, vehicle registration databases, and cross border "hot pursuit" of officers without prior consent of the convention parties in urgent situations.

Some observers feared the convention would undermine efforts to facilitate sharing of information in the EU as a whole, since it involved only a handful of countries, ignored related initiatives by the European Commission, and created a new hierarchy within the EU and a new form of the Schengen process. But it turned out that the Prüm Treaty was the best way to encourage wider information sharing. Its members have acted as a laboratory, working out the complicated technical arrangements for querying each others' police databases quickly and effectively in a small group. The rapid progress has encouraged the rest of the EU to adopt the Prüm system and, in February 2007, the member states agreed to incorporate the information sharing bits of the treaty into the EU's legal order. If this agreement is implemented on time, every EU member state will have automatic access to others' DNA, fingerprint and vehicle databases by 2009, a quantum leap in cross-border sharing of information. The challenge for the future is to make the Prüm information sharing arrangement work well with twenty-seven countries. Overall, the Prüm experience is an important case study for the future of police cooperation in the EU.

In addition, there exist a number of groups of less formal character where intelligence problems are discussed and sharing takes place. So the *Club de Berne* formed in 1971 as a forum for security services of six nations. It has become a partnership of services of the twenty-seven EU member states, plus Norway and Switzerland. The Club operates outside of EU institutions. Its activities are not based on a formal charter, but the chair rotates in tandem with that of the EU. It serves as principal point of contact of the heads of national security and some intelligence services that meet annually to discuss intelligence and security matters as well as implementation of objectives of European Council declarations. There is no formal commitment or even expectation that participants will share all relevant intelligence with other members.

The Club de Berne also has a Counter Terrorist Group (CTG) as a sub-organization, established in 2001 to act as interface between the EU and the Heads of security and intelligence services of the member states as well as the United States on terrorist matters, doing "threat assessments" on Islamic terrorism and situational reporting for key EU policy makers, and providing a forum for experts to develop practical collaboration. The CTG is composed of twenty-nine security services from all EU member states plus Switzerland, Norway, and the United States. The chair is changing with EU presidency. The Heads of the Services (HoS) form the main steering instrument meeting twice per year while the Heads of Units (HoU) coordinate and implement HoS decisions, meeting four times per year or when needed.

The *Middle European Conference* (MEC) is a consultative partnership of services of Central European countries and Western European services, first established in 1994 with "club character"—openness, mutual trust, and confidence—and a secretariat as point of contact with secure communications. The nineteen participating countries hold annual plenary meetings that are chaired by a troika of the present, the former, and next chairman. It conducts seminars and forms working groups, permanent committees, and special task forces on behalf of the Troika or the MEC, with the main focus on organized crime, terrorism, illegal immigration, interception of communications, security situation, etc. It has established a MEC Code of Practice with "rules and regulations" and common proceedings. The goals of the MEC are to support further integration, contribute to European security and international cooperation, and harmonize and standardize work methods.

The *Brenner Club* is a cooperation framework of Western European security services based on periodical meetings attended by the heads of relevant services, including the security services of Germany, the United Kingdom, France, Austria, Switzerland, and some other countries. The Brenner Club deals with a range of internal security issues, including terrorism, illegal immigration, and cross-boundary forms of organized crime. It has no permanent secretariat or common offices, and operates in an informal way with meetings conducted in different locations, organized by each host country in turn.

Furthermore, numerous *special fora* exist worldwide to deal with specific subjects by bringing together the intelligence services of different countries, and which are known to a greater or lesser extent. Thus, a number of countries have agreed to set up informal groups to work together against the threat of proliferation of WMD, drawing up common lists of goods or technologies considered relevant to the activities of proliferators, and agreeing to control the exports of these, such as the *Zangger Committee*, the *Nuclear Suppliers Group*, the *Australian Group*, the *Missile Technology Control Regime*, the *Wassenaar Arrangement*, and the *Hague Code of Conduct*. In addition, there is the *Proliferation Security Initiative*, focusing on the intercepting shipments of WMD and their means of delivery, the *Container Security Initiative*, and the *Financial Intelligence Units*, which make up the Egmont Group.

The barriers to information sharing are still considerable, particularly sharing between NGOs and the military. The lack of communication means regularly constitutes a big obstacle. Other hurdles are mainly functional, political, and institutional. Connected problems include: disparate organizational cultures; mutual lack of familiarity; concerns about neutrality and impartiality, lack of incentives or ambivalence to sharing; reluctance to be perceived as associating with "intelligence" organizations; secrecy and declassification policies of nations and the military; a limited ability to plan and coordinate within NGOs; as well as varying time horizons, and competition for publicity.

Generally, sensitive operational intelligence cooperation will have to remain at the bilateral level and cannot be the subject of multilateral discussions because leaks could damage the effectiveness of such cooperation. However, in regions of pervasive suspicions about the own national aims, intelligence officers will have to work more indirectly and multilaterally through the operational channels called intelligence liaison. Since 9/11, the United States has been doing that in a major way, trading superior resources and technology for on-the-ground intelligence about the jihadist threat. The difficulty liaison relationships presents, however, is that the own intelligence service is no longer in complete control of collection. Liaison intermediaries will influence both the selection of the target and the management of the take. In many cases, the result may be bound to be a dilution of the product and diminished timeliness. The most worrisome deficiency might be a lack of confidence of getting the full picture, with the ongoing potential to leave the own nation vulnerable and the covered region instable.

Going Beyond Traditional Sharing

Since intelligence requirements of government decision makers increasingly relate to matters that are global or transnational in nature, intelligence relationships with other countries must be expanded. This is because no national intelligence agency can effectively cover all of the places where such activities may take place throughout the world. This is why, in the new threat environment, intelligence cooperation will also have to go beyond traditional partners to include new collaborators. Foreign partners can provide greater access to key areas of the world and help to identify and monitor the multiple geographic watch points that are an essential component of the response to the preeminent threats. Such cooperation can start off with information or analytic exchanges and, if successful, can provide a basis for incrementally extending cooperation.

However, it is no longer only other governments which need to be included. With the revolution in the availability of information and the kind of work that is being done in some parts of academia and by NGOs—which monitor particular kinds of activities that are directly or indirectly relevant to the preeminent threats—extending the intelligence community to incorporate these novel but highly relevant players is essential. Not only can these new participants provide new perspectives and sources of information that can help to fill gaps in "sense-making," but they can also facilitate cross-fertilization of methods. Moreover, analysis that goes beyond governments provides far greater opportunities for challenging ethnocentrism and cultural biases as well as for developing multiple alternative competing hypotheses, and for sense-making. By providing broader perspectives and alternative filters, this extended intelligence community can facilitate the development of more analytic tipping points in pattern detection, pattern discovery, and anomaly detection.

There are many obstacles to the development of a community extended to academia and NGOs. The desire to maintain high levels of secrecy, concerns over sources and methods, a lack of trust in relation to certain governments and non-traditional intelligence actors, divergent interests, parochialism, skepticism that what others might know would provide added value, along with simple resistance to change all inhibit the kind of adaptive behavior necessary for the emergence of such an enlarged community. However, if the issue of clandestine sources and information is put on one side, and if there is broad acknowledgment that transnational threats and problems are as much about mysteries as secrets, then it becomes clear that multiple inputs of information and analysis can be highly advantageous.

More Cooperation Needed

More than ever, particularly intelligence and law enforcement must find new and better ways to work together to deliver integrated results for the government, for the security and safety of the nation. Few doubt that valuable insights can derive from close correlation of information from differing intelligence, security, or law enforcement sources. However, bringing law enforcement and intelligence closer together is not without challenges. The two sets of agencies have long-established roles and missions that are separate and based on constitutional and statutory principles. Should the two communities draw too close together, there are well founded concerns that either the law enforcement effort would become increasingly inclined to incorporate intelligence sources and methods to the detriment of long-standing legal principles and constitutional rights or, alternately, that intelligence collection in-country or abroad would increasingly be hamstrung by regulations and procedural requirements, to the detriment of national security. The danger of using intelligence methods as a routine law enforcement tool is matched by the danger of regularly using law enforcement agencies as instruments of foreign policy. Thus, difficult decisions will have to be made, some affecting organizational responsibilities, and fine lines will have to be drawn. Bureaucratic overlap and conflicting roles and missions are not unknown in many government organizations, but such duplication is viewed with great concern when it affects agencies with power to arrest and charge individuals or to affect the security of the country.

A key issue is the overall direction of effort. Law enforcement may require that some information be closely held and not shared outside the organization or the ministry. If law enforcement and intelligence efforts are to work more closely in dealing with the preeminent threats, procedures will have to be in place to ensure that important information is shared. The principle of "need-to-know" thus has to give way to the principle of "need-to-share." For this to work, a seamless system must be developed that will encompass all echelons of intelligence and law enforcement agencies for storing and exchanging information in real-time. In addition, there is another problem to be solved: location.

The Case for a National Center to Handle the Preeminent Threats

The security sector lacks a place to perform all-source planning for collecting information; a place where the possible yields from efforts in overhead reconnaissance, electronic surveillance, clandestine agents, law enforcement databases and informants, and reports from foreign governments can be sifted and organized for maximum complementary effect. This is why the national intelligence effort may require a new institution to gather intelligence on the preeminent threats, with particular attention to the threat of catastrophic terrorism—a National Center for Preeminent Threats. This Center would be responsible for collection management, analysis, dissemination of information, and warning of suspected acts by networks of the unholy trinity of preeminent threats. The Center would not undertake or manage operational activities, but reconcile the practices of foreign intelligence work with the restrictions that limit domestic law enforcement. The Center would need statutory authority to:

- Monitor and provide warning of these threats to all relevant government agencies, supporting defense or intelligence operations, and law enforcement
- Set integrated collection requirements for the gathering of information for all the intelligence agencies
- Receive and store all lawfully collected, relevant information from any government agency, including law enforcement wiretaps and other information
- Analyze all forms of relevant information to produce integrated reports that could be disseminated to any agency that needs them, national or local
- Review planned collection and intelligence programs of all agencies directed toward the preeminent threats to determine the adequacy and balance among these efforts

- Facilitate international cooperation in intelligence against networks of the preeminent threats, including the bilateral efforts of individual agencies

Ultimately, to be more successful, intelligence services will require more resources, inventive technologies for collection and analysis, new procedures, new organizational structures, and the highest degree of professionalism. A cogent and well implemented full-spectrum intelligence capacity that can cope with the preeminent threats will substantially enhance national security both in the present environment and in the years ahead.

15
Conclusions

The national contribution to building a more secure world requires not only strong national leadership, but also national resources commensurate with the scale of the strategic challenges ahead. The private sector will have to contribute to these resources in its own interest. Private-public partnerships can be established for this purpose. Moreover, full cooperation and coordinated input is required from all ministries, government agencies, regional and local authorities, and their agencies, as well as from the private sector where these are essential and relevant for countering the preeminent threats.

Two inherent homeland security challenges make a risk-based approach to homeland security policymaking necessary:

1. The uncertain and complex threat environment arising from highly adaptive adversaries. Terrorists react to states' anti-terrorism and counterterrorism measures by seeking alternative state vulnerabilities. For instance, an anti-terrorism measure that works at the time of introduction may not be effective because of adversary adaptation.
2. The threatened state system comprises multiple independent subsystems like the economy, social sector, and infrastructure. Multiple vulnerabilities exist for adversaries to exploit and the consequences of a successful terrorist attack in a subsystem can have cascading effects on the other subsystems.

Without robust and coherent risk assessment, states may spend too much to protect against the threat of high consequence-low probability events, such as the terrorists attacks of 9/11, at the expense of protecting against the threat of low consequence-high probability events, like the

London bombings of July 2005. As a result, a net security effect for the state might not be created despite substantial homeland security investments.

Homeland security risk assessment is quite different from traditional risk assessment approaches because the adversary in homeland security is highly adaptive and innovative. While traditional risk assessment processes in industries—e.g., nuclear plants—focus on "what can go wrong," homeland security risk assessment focus on "how can someone make something go wrong." Thus, instead of focusing only on the possible threats, homeland security risk assessment must also identify plausible threats.

No single tool can produce a comprehensive risk assessment to cover the whole spectrum of homeland security risks. Hence, a mixture of qualitative and quantitative methods is needed. Specifically, modeling must be the basis for risk assessment because it provides a structured means to organize and analyze the problem.

In order to cope with the preeminent threats successfully, states have to establish structures for accurate risk communications. They also have to establish a sophisticated public information policy that does not feed the population's insecurities. On one hand, this is important for the public dissemination of potentially live-saving information as well as for the prevention of mass panic. On the other hand, a multidisciplinary response to terrorist incidents requires considerable coordination efforts and command structures. The interfaces between early-warning and crisis management structures are subject to particularly serious challenges in terms of coordination and communications. Transparency and rapid information exchange, from the local to the regional and national levels, are preconditions for efficient crisis management and require that roles and responsibilities be clearly delegated.

On the policy level, states are required to outline the strategic direction of the emergency preparation and response. Based on an integrated conception of the preeminent threats and risks, a strategy for protecting society must be formulated. The creation of this strategy requires a continuous process of policy formulation in the context of a comprehensive risk analysis that takes the different scenarios and challenges arising from the threats of the unholy trinity of transnational terrorism, proliferation, and organized crime into account in equal measure. This forms the basis for distributing responsibilities and resources with special attention being given to effective exploitation of the potential synergies between protective measures in the various areas between national and international efforts. Hence, a comprehensive protection concept must be regulated by the state.

Appendix A

How to systematically develop multilateral sharing?[1]

All problems connected with sharing point toward the need to adopt a careful and systematic approach to improve intelligence and information sharing. The needs of each organization and set of problems have to be assessed, because the responses are different. The subject will only be properly dealt with when it is broken down into its component parts, and each one is looked at carefully and analytically, not in a haphazard way. Success is unlikely to be found in one overarching goal to meet the vision for multilateral collaboration, but rather in small, well defined problem sets that provide a seed for broader collaboration in the future.

The first step towards successful multilateral collaboration is the decision to share. This decision needs to be driven by a compelling and clearly defined need. Four fundamental questions should be addressed:

1. Why should actors share information?[2]
2. What specific information should be shared to achieve these goals?
3. Who needs to participate in the collaboration?
4. How will the information be shared?

The basic requirements for sharing intelligence and information are decisions on:

- Principles: agreement to the ideal that an organization should in fact share
- Policy: establishing who within the organization is the contact point and communicates two-way information flow
- Procedures: how an organization processes internal data and information for sharing

- Technology: the use of technology to access, transmit, and communicate the information

There is no right or wrong approach to this. Partners may have agreed on an intelligence and information sharing protocol with each other, which is sufficient to fulfill their role in achieving their partnership's objectives. While this limited approach is acceptable, it is flawed. Advances in technology are providing an increasing range of opportunities, facilitating better analysis and coordination of interventions. Accordingly, there are positive benefits in adopting a partnership-wide approach, which will:

- Reduce unnecessary duplication of effort
- Promote greater compatibility and consistency in intelligence and information sharing arrangements
- Put an intelligence and information-led approach right at the heart of the partnership
- Discourage partners from opting out

A more centralized approach to intelligence and information sharing at partnership level, and a clear information sharing plan underpinning the overall strategy, should ensure a greater level of consistency in practice throughout the partnership. This approach also lends itself to engaging the support, encouragement, and financial backing of key decision makers.

In dealing with operations at the individual level, the partnership approach has to demonstrate the benefits of involving a number of agencies with a wide range of expertise. These will be particularly effective in reducing duplication. Protocols will therefore need to take account of the needs of agencies to share information.

In developing effective intelligence and information sharing arrangements, partnerships will need to:

1. Review strategy and its objectives
2. Examine and identify who can make a contribution to achieving the objective
3. Identify what, if any, intelligence and information would need to be exchanged in order to maximize that contribution and what effect this will have on achieving the objective
4. Consult the end users, and those within the own organization, who can make use of intelligence and information, for the specified objectives:

- What are their intelligence and information requirements?
- Do these take account of present and future information needs, utilizing future technology?
- What format should the intelligence and information be in (e.g., datasets, paper)?
- What will it be used for?
- Is personal information necessary or would depersonalized information suffice for the purpose?
- What other agencies could or should be able to benefit from the intelligence and information?
- Who will have access to the intelligence and information?
- How will it be stored (security)?
- How long will it be kept for?
- Are there any specific legal or other restrictions, preventing disclosure?
- Do any other organizations or agencies hold the same intelligence or information and if so, which is the most appropriate agency to provide it?

5. Consult your partners:
   - Are they content in principle to provide the intelligence or information?
   - How accurate is their data, intelligence, and information?
   - Can the data, intelligence or information be made more accurate, and how?
   - Has the subject of the data, intelligence or information given consent to disclosure?
   - Is disclosure without consent permissible?
   - Is the intelligence or information compatible (datasets)?
   - Do they have a fair and lawful requirement for holding it?
   - Can they meet other organizations' or agencies' intelligence and information needs?
   - Do they require the consent of an organization or an individual before exchanging it?
   - Can they depersonalize the information if necessary?
   - Are there any risk factors associated with the use of intelligence or depersonalized information that could identify an individual?
   - What procedures will they need to see in place to facilitate the intelligence and information exchange?

- Identify any reciprocal benefits: is the own organization's work likely to lead to the identification of activities that should be notified to the partner?
- What are realistic timescales for disclosing intelligence or information requested? (This may involve differing timescales for different types of intelligence or information, depending on the ease of retrieval).
- Will staff need more detailed technical or other guidance in order to comply with the requirements of the protocol?
- Is there anything that can be put in place now to take advantage of future intelligence and information requirements, and advances in technology, which will assist in future analysis?
- Should the organization collect additional data, intelligence, or information specifically to fulfill its role? If so, is that role sustainable over a relevant period, which would enable the partnership to use that intelligence or information?
- Identify any special handling requirements for sharing data, intelligence, and information

6. Consider legal and other obstacles that may prevent intelligence and information sharing.
7. Identify what format data, intelligence, or information is held in, and any resource or cost implications that may be involved in exchanging data, intelligence, and information.
8. Examine the procedures that will need to be put in place to share intelligence and information.
9. Be precise, and take care to carry decision makers with you.
10. Obtain consensus between key partners and the partnership as a whole.
11. Outline what intelligence and information sharing arrangements will be put in place, with whom, and for which objective.
12. Consider what will happen when things go wrong.
13. Is a media policy necessary to protect those involved in the intelligence and information sharing partnership, including intelligence or information owners, intelligence or information subjects, end users, and the public, when dealing with the media?
14. Appoint designated officers to authorize requests to other partners and approve disclosures of intelligence and information requested by other organizations.

15. Negotiate an intelligence and information sharing protocol with the partners.
16. Ensure that all partners understand, agree, and have signed the intelligence and information sharing protocol.
17. Revisit the strategy and protocol periodically to ensure that intelligence and information sharing arrangements are relevant and continue to meet the partnership's objectives.
18. Encourage, solicit, and monitor feedback.
19. Seek continuous improvement in the sharing arrangements.

A final note with regard to collaboration goals is that they are likely to change over time. The role of collaboration should evolve to meet the changing requirements in process, task, and organizational structure. Collaboration initiatives should include a mechanism and schedule to revisit and realign collaboration goals with inevitable changes in requirements.

What are the critical issues in intelligence and information sharing?

There are three main challenges to sharing:

- The development of a capability that allows sharing of information among disparate organizations is always a challenge.
- Information sharing is fundamentally a matter of trust, not just in the people handling it, but also in the involved systems and processes.
- Information sharing capability must include the ability to specify the classification level of information at the object level; otherwise information will ultimately be stovepiped.

Surveys done in government agencies in the United States and in Europe have resulted in lists of the following critical issues in intelligence and information sharing, ranked in order of importance:

1. Funding: Information sharing inevitably requires resources. Often there are difficulties in getting government and management to fund technology needed for sharing. One of the major costs of implementation is that of the time involved in data entry, especially for agencies in which the data entry function is assigned to a single unit.
2. Trust: Bringing agencies together to work on issues and building trust

is difficult. Trust is often lost because of misuse of information, neglect of classification, improper handling and dissemination, and lacking motivation or incentives for sharing. Demonstrations are needed to show all potential users that their information is not going to be compromised, and that the overall benefits of sharing outweigh the potential pitfalls. Inter- and intra-departmental philosophies may prevent sharing. Also, there is jurisdictional and other competition as well as a lack of ways to improve communication.

3. Willingness to share: At times, the willingness to share at the executive levels does not trickle down to the lower levels. The reverse is also quite common, where sharing occurs at the line level but receives little support from management. How can agencies be motivated to share if the more immediate gain is not for the agency itself, but the agencies it is sharing with? Willingness to share needs to be accompanied by some strong policy statements from the top. All parties need to see synergism and the value-added benefiting them as a result of sharing. Sharing has to play into the local reward system. Moreover, reluctance to share often stems from a fear that the information will be used inappropriately, resulting in legal or political liabilities for agencies.

4. Information security: Concerns are about the security of private and classified information on public networks, system protection against hackers, adequate security measures to prevent outside access to systems and databases, likelihood of being a choice target for criminals and spies, etc. Inconsistencies in handling privacy and security abound. Also, there is a need for user audits and reports: who has accessed what data, or what information has a specific user viewed? However, current encryption abilities are not a big issue.

5. Technology standards: More consensus is needed among the agencies involved. What is the right authority? Where is the right place to reach it? There are divergent views on formats, interoperability and integration, on ease of access, and on centralized versus distributed information access, use of different codes, etc. In addition, there is the problem of getting management to see the importance of technology. Other critical issues are information overload and problems with the speed of systems when fully taxed.

6. Data integrity: Differences in rules, procedures, user agreements, etc., abound. Many other concerns exist, such as is data accessed by one user editable by that user or does it appear as "read only"? Why is it

editable by the issuing agency only? Voice versus text capabilities and protection of the integrity of the database are other critical issues, along with quality control and timeliness of entry. There is the importance of making the originating agency or unit or personnel responsible for integrity and accuracy of data, and the users accountable with periodic or random audits. Another issue is the false belief that it is wrong to share partial or less than accurate information.

7. Coordination between branches of government agencies: One agency may want information from another agency. However, the other agency does not have anything to gain from giving them that information. Thus, they will be reluctant to cooperate. Where to draw the line to allow access? And there are always competing priorities—sharing often takes a back seat to more pressing issues of the moment.

8. Adequate network infrastructure: Mostly a funding and adaptability problem of programs to add new capabilities. Issues conflict over adoption of as much open architecture as possible, and vendor specific solutions. The conduct of sharing needs assessment to ensure that acquired hardware and software does not overburden existing technical infrastructure.

9. Accuracy and reliability of the intelligence and information shared: Often there is a lack of standards and a failsafe method to ensure compliance. Automated systems should be used for highlighting where data entered is abnormal or repetitive or where new data is inconsistent with other data already in the system. Just being responsible does not ensure compliance; there must be means of validating the accuracy. Oftentimes the agency that keeps the data may know how to properly interpret it but other agencies might misinterpret it. Pull down screens might not completely solve interpretation problems. Critical issues are also attributed to lack of training of personnel.

10. Insufficient staffing to support new systems: Management often does not understand the significance of additional staffing needed to support new systems. Also, there are time and other constraints.

11. User friendliness: Problems concentrate on ease of access as well as use of IT and communication equipment.

Two key aspects should be given the attention they deserve: Security and information assurance—a critical enabling capability for the sharing of sensitive information.

A high degree of interoperability of information sharing among military and civilian organizations is essential in the new security environment.

What are the principles guiding sharing, and the exchange of intelligence and information?

Sharing can only be as profitable as the information exchanged. Inspiring confidence in partners and gaining their trust is critical to information sharing. To achieve these goals, information management and exchange must be guided by the following operational principles:

ACCESSIBILITY

Intelligence, information, and data should be made accessible to all actors in need by applying easy-to-use formats, through online and offline distribution channels, and by translation into the dominant language used when necessary.

INCLUSIVENESS

Intelligence management, information management, and exchange should be based on a system of collaboration, partnership, and sharing with a high degree of participation and ownership by multiple stakeholders.

INTEROPERABILITY

All sharable intelligence, information, and data should be made available in formats that can be easily accessed, retrieved, shared, and used by all relevant participants.

RELEVANCE

Intelligence, information, and data should be practical, responsive, and driven by operational needs and priorities of requirements in support of decision making throughout all phases of a crisis or operations.

OBJECTIVITY

Information managers should consult a variety of sources when collecting and analyzing intelligence, information, and data so as to provide varied and balanced perspectives for addressing problems and recommending solutions.

QUALITY

Ensuring quality requires the development of and adherence to common standards for intelligence and information collection, exchange, security, attribution, and use. In addition, it is vital to maintain a strong sense of professional ethics at every stage of information system design, and implementation.

Timeliness

Intelligence, information, and data should be collected, analyzed, and disseminated efficiently and must be kept current.

Accountability

Users must be able to evaluate the reliability and credibility of intelligence, information, and data whenever possible by knowing its source. Moreover, information providers should be responsible to their partners and stakeholders for the content they disseminate.

Verifiability

Intelligence and information should be accurate, consistent, and based on sound methodologies, validated by other, unconnected sources, and analyzed within the proper contextual framework.

Sustainability

Intelligence, information, and data should be preserved, catalogued, and archived so that they can be retrieved for future use, such as for preparedness, analysis, lessons learned, and evaluation.

Appendix B

What are the prospects for overcoming the many obstacles to information sharing?

The technical and infrastructural problems are most likely the easiest to be solved by the progression of time. The accelerating technological innovation will also help to reduce or eliminate some of the functional and operational obstacles. While there will be little room left in the future for overcoming or reducing the many legal obstacles, there can be hope that solutions may be found to diminish rather than to augment the political and institutional obstacles. Security and classification obstacles will continue to adversely affect the sharing of information, but it will happen less often with the explosion of open source information certainly. As far as the first two categories of obstacles are concerned, some trends can be indicated, which may help to better comprehend the prospects for the future.

The trends in overcoming the technical and infrastructural obstacles

The realm of multilateral information sharing is ripe with revolutionary potential owing to recent innovations in computer-based information management. For the three problems—interoperability of systems, frequency spectrum allocation, and public networks—solutions are either already existing or foreseeable.

INTEROPERABILITY OF SYSTEMS

A deployable C4ISTAR[1] system will be available that supports advanced planning; the cooperative execution of tasks; and rapid, secure, and reliable exchange of information between armed forces, international organizations, and NGOs participating in multilateral operations. It will unify information and communications technology system interfaces deployable in field operations into a single, standardized entity, based on open, commercially available components.[2] Geographic information systems (GIS),[3] coupled with remote-sensing platforms, global positioning systems (GPS), and the Internet have the potential to serve as a catalyst for bringing military and civilian participants into a more productive partnership.

In the armed forces, advances in computer processing, precise global positioning, sensor technologies, and telecommunications will allow for accurate determination of locations of friendly and enemy forces as well as the ability to collect, process, and distribute relevant data to thousands of locations. Forces harnessing the capabilities potentially available from this "system of systems" will gain dominant battlespace awareness—an interactive picture that will yield much more accurate assessments of friendly and enemy operations. Although this interactive picture will not eliminate the fog of and friction in war, dominant battlespace awareness will improve situational awareness, decrease response time, and make the battlespace considerably more transparent. IT will improve the ability to see, prioritize, assign, and assess information. The fusion of all-source intelligence with the fluid integration of sensors, platforms, command organizations, and logistic support centers will not only allow a greater number of operational tasks to be accomplished faster, it also will enable the conduct of network centric warfare.

FREQUENCY SPECTRUM ALLOCATION

One development that will solve the problem of the now antiquated and uneconomical system of frequency allocation is the atomic clock. Using micro-electromechanical systems technology on a single chip will reduce size and power consumption of the atomic clock by factors of 200 or 300. This will greatly improve the mobility and robustness of military communication and navigation devices. Frequency references from atomic clocks will improve communications channel selectivity and density, and will also enable ultra-fast frequency hopping for improved security, jam-resistance, and data encryption. In GPS receivers, they will greatly improve the jamming margin, help track positions continuously, and quickly reacquire a GPS signal. While in surveillance, atomic clocks will improve the resolution of Doppler radars and the location of radio emitters.

Next-generation communications do not only promote more effective spectrum use, but also will effectively change the rules of the game, since it is premised on a notion that challenges the conventional wisdom about the spectrum: that the spectrum demand overwhelms the fixed supply. On average, only 2 percent of the spectrum is actually in use in the United States at any given moment, even though all of the spectrum is allocated—a percentage that may be even lower in other countries. The dynamics of how that spectrum is used or shared have not been seriously considered. Thus, the key technology question becomes whether the unused spectrum can be exploited while ensuring that foreign systems do not interfere, and that own systems do not interfere with them. To answer that question, four key technologies are in development.

The first is to embed low-power and compact spectrum sensing capability within next-generation enabled systems. Low-power use is key to highly mobile and proliferated applications. Second, the spectrum use is to be characterized by classifying the signals sensed in order to understand how to coexist with them:

1. Is it being used for military systems?
2. Is it being used for television?
3. Which cellular technology is it using?
4. Is there frequency, time, or code space available to share?

The third technology to be developed is the ability to react to the other spectrum users through selection and coordination of frequencies, bandwidths, spreading codes, and so forth. The goal is to make the next-generation systems operate without interference from, or to, other users. Media access controls are developed that support a range of physical waveforms and best exploit the features of each: looking at optimized waveforms that can best exploit next-generation capabilities through non-contiguous waveforms, highly spread water-filling underneath other signals, and other adaptive waveform technologies. Finally, the next generation needs to adapt to changes in spectrum use by developing, coordinating, and disseminating new spectrum planning. These changes could be caused by radar scanning the region, new mobile devices entering the area, or the next-generation communications network moving and encountering a new environment.

By integrating the frequency assignment function into the network operations, a battlespace can be developed where networks detect, coordinate, and manage spectrum using common protocols automatically and autonomously. Because the networks do not depend on pre-assigned spectrum, they will greatly reduce the amount of spectrum needed to operate. This will change the nature of battlespace communications.

What is envisioned is nothing less than a new generation of intelligent, situationally aware, network radio—one that takes on more and more of the resource management within itself. Today, there might be as many as 8,000 separate networks simultaneously operating, each of them needing its own, individually assigned spectrum. With the next-generation communications, there will be a generic wireless Internet that can be accessed simply by turning on a radio or communications device. The network detects other systems operating in the region. It automatically places and coordinates the network or sensor devices to appropriate frequencies. As forces move or other participants join, the system automatically adapts. When two mobile networks overlap, one automatically and seamlessly shifts to a new frequency. Also, because the next-generation communications is a dynamic system, adjusting itself to the spectrum available, it allows the priority user to adapt spectrum use as circumstances warrant.[4]

Thus, the military will be able to deploy systems without the months of meticulous planning and spectrum assignment required today. In fact, while next-generation communications will be indispensable to military applications, it has very significant advantages in civilian use. Wireless, autonomous communications networks will not only transform battlefield radios and radar, but also can transform similarly the next generation of sophisticated cell phones, digital devices, and mobile communicators that are flooding the public markets.

PUBLIC NETWORKS

The Internet has become one of the mechanisms to facilitate sharing of information as well as a medium that encourages global communications. The most commonly accessed application on the Internet is the World Wide Web. Originally developed by the European Organization for Nuclear Research (CERN) in Geneva, the Web was envisaged by its inventor as a way to help share information. The Internet continues to grow dramatically.[5] But how do actors in the peace operation environment communicate when commercial links may be compromised? How do they communicate in failed states or underdeveloped countries where telephone connections typically do not exist?

Emerging satellite technology soon may offer a solution. Already in 2000, StarBand Communications, a company based in the United States, launched a commercial two-way satellite Internet venture. The company seeks to establish satellites as the leading route for high-speed Internet connections. This technology could unleash the "telebonds" of nonsecure Internet communication and enable computers to be linked to the outside world far from telephone switches, regardless of who controls the ground-based communications hub. StarBand is still working out bugs, such as ways to make the satellite system more resistant to inclement weather. Finally, the company must decrease the operational costs of consumer satellites to become a practical application in peace operations.[6]

The trends in overcoming the functional and operational obstacles

The greatest functional and operational obstacles to information sharing arise from insufficient organization and coordination, and from an ignorance of the requirements of each stakeholder. Organizational fragmentation, compartmentalization, and stovepipes will inevitably continue to cause functional obstacles. The problem here, however, is that "sharing of information must become more than exchanges between platforms and services—it should extend to the interagency community and coalition partners."[7]

While few will disagree that sharing information is a positive development, the practical matter of getting them to agree on standard methods and processes is daunting.[8] However, the advantages of using and sharing GIS data[9] are so readily apparent that organizations will be committed to finding standards and processes on which they can all agree. While GIS is not synonymous with an information sharing regime, it does encourage actors to cooperate and lays the foundation for collaboration and much improved coordination.

Other advantages are the simplicity of use that makes GIS amenable to the often low-tech, chaotic field environment; the fact that GIS data can be recorded and manipulated on a variety of devices, including hand-held, ruggedized laptop computers that can be equipped with satellite communications capabilities; and the fact that GIS data is readily shared electronically, which allows it to be posted on a central website or shared via e-mail or CD. The Internet allows organizations to access information instantly from locations all over the world. The CD allows them to use the data without access to the Internet. It is also a suitable format for sharing information that remains relatively unchanged, such as topography.

Moreover, practitioners in the field can view and use the same information that their strategic planners at headquarters are using, and complex problems and progress in various regions can be more easily compared and assessed, hence decision makers can be better assisted.

Among the operational obstacles, one of the major challenges is that of knowledge management. Many elements of the IT revolution that have vastly increased the effectiveness, particularly of the U.S. armed forces, and transformed Western societies—time-sharing, interactive computing, the ideas behind the personal computer, and the Internet—were spurred on by the vision of scientists. In the 1970s, the vision of one of those, Joseph Carol Robnett Licklider, was of people and computers working together symbiotically. His concept was of computers seamlessly adapting to people as partners that handle routine information processing tasks. This frees people to focus on what they do best—think analytically and creatively—and, thereby, greatly extend the powers of their minds: what they can know, understand, and do.

Despite the enormous and continuing progress in IT over the years, it is clear that we are still short of this vision. Current IT-systems remain exceedingly complex, expensive to create and debug, unable to easily work together, insecure, and prone to failure. And, they still require the user to adapt to them, rather than the other way around. Computers have grown faster, but they remain fundamentally unintelligent and difficult to use. Thus, something dramatically different is needed.

In response, the U.S. Defense Advanced Research Projects Agency (DARPA)[10] is returning to Licklider's vision again in a strategic thrust called cognitive computing. Cognitive computers can be thought of as systems that know what they are doing. Cognitive computing systems will have the ability to reason about their environment, including other systems, their goals, and their own capabilities. They will be able to learn both from experience and by being taught. They will be capable of natural interactions with users, and will be able to explain their reasoning in natural terms. They will be robust in the face of surprises, and avoid the brittleness and fragility of previous expert systems.

There are a number of reasons to believe the time is ripe for a more successful attempt at completing this vision:

1. Artificial intelligence and related disciplines, such as speech processing and machine learning, have made great strides in the last twenty years.

2. Continuing rapid improvements in micro-electronics are leading to the point where circuits with the complexity of primate brains are actually foreseeable.
3. The ongoing revolution in neural and brain science should provide insights into how people actually think, which can then be applied to computers.

To meet this challenge and opportunity, DARPA will focus on five core research areas over the next few years:

1. Computational perception
2. Representation and reasoning
3. Learning, communications, and interaction
4. Dynamic coordinated teams of cognitive systems
5. Robust software and hardware infrastructure for cognitive systems

The theoretical work in these areas will be focused by emphasizing several specific, but different, applications.

A major portion of research is done in fundamentally new technologies, particularly at the component level, that historically have been the technological feedstocks enabling quantum leaps in military capabilities: materials, microsystems, IT and others, which often form enabling chains. Among the materials are:

1. Low-cost, ultra-lightweight structural materials, designed to accomplish multiple performance objectives in a single system
2. Materials with non-structural function such as for semiconductors, photonics, magnetics, and other electronic materials
3. Mesoscopic machines that can be used for air or water purification, and harvesting water from the environment
4. Smart materials and structures that can sense and respond to the environment
5. Power generation and storage materials focused on novel ways to generate and store electric power, as advanced fuel cells, and materials to extract energy from the environment

Apart from eventually leading to cognitive computing, microsystems—microelectronics, photonics, and micro-electromechanical systems—enable users to see farther with greater clarity, and better communicate information in a timely manner. Building on these accomplishments by integrating and shrinking ever more complex systems into chip-scale packages is the challenge to achieve microsystems that enable systems with enhanced radio frequency and optical sensing, more versatile signal processors for extracting signals in the face of noise and intense enemy jamming, high-performance communication links with assured bandwidth, and intelligent chips that allow a user to convert data into actionable information in near-real-time.

Quite another trend brought about by advances in information technologies, which may be helpful for diminishing organizational and institutional obstacles, is the fact that their optimal use will necessitate far-reaching organizational changes in order to take full advantage of the opportunities these advances provide. By and large, commercial organizations that have been able to fully leverage the power of information and information technologies to develop a competitive advantage have dominated their competitive domains. Those that have been slow to recognize the potential for information and IT to transform their organizations and processes, or have failed to go far enough and fast enough to change the way they do business, are being acquired by their competitors or swept away. One key concept is that effective linking can be achieved among entities in crisis management, peace operations or in the battlespace. This means that dispersed and distributed entities can generate synergy, and that responsibility and work can be dynamically reallocated to adapt to the situation. The effectiveness of linking mechanisms and processes affects the power coefficient or multiplier. Linking entities together will greatly increase productivity. The commercial experience has shown how information can substitute for material, and how to move information instead of moving people. These substitutions generate considerable savings in time and resources, and result in increased value.

Notes

Chapter 1

1. See UN Resolution of 1948, containing the first and last definition of WMD grouping all four together, thus giving each a comparable stigma, despite their different killing and destructive power. The definition accepted in 1948 stated that WMD "included atomic explosive weapons, lethal chemical and biological weapons, and any weapons developed in the future which have characteristics comparable in destructive effect to those of the atomic bomb or other weapons mentioned above." Meanwhile, radiological weapons are no longer seen as WMD proper, as there is no military interest in them.

2. Or U-235. Only 0.7 percent of naturally occurring uranium is U-235. The remainder is almost entirely the non-chain-reacting isotope U-238. Although in principle uranium with an enrichment of U-235 as low as 6 percent could sustain an explosive chain reaction, the critical mass of material required would be infinitely large. Enrichment to 20 percent U-235 is generally taken to be the lowest concentration practicable for use in a weapon. Uranium enriched to 20 percent or higher is defined as Highly Enriched Uranium (HEU). The IAEA considers such HEU a direct-use weapon material. In practice, however, in order to minimize the mass of the nuclear explosive, weapon-grade uranium is usually enriched to over 90 percent in U-235. Increasing the fraction of U-235 in uranium requires sophisticated isotope separation technology. Isotope separation on the scale required to produce nuclear weapons is not considered to be within the reach of terrorist groups.

3. Plutonium is produced in a nuclear reactor when U-238 absorbs a neutron and becomes U-239, which subsequently decays to Pu-239 via the intermediate, short-lived isotope neptunium-239. The longer an atom of Pu-239 stays in a reactor after it has been created, the greater the likelihood that it will absorb a second neutron and become Pu-240 or a third or fourth neutron and become Pu-241 or Pu-242. Plutonium therefore comes in a variety of isotopic mixtures. Weapons designers prefer to work with a mixture that is predominantly Pu-239 because of its relatively low rate of spontaneous emission of neutron and gamma rays and low generation of radioactive heat. Weapons-grade plutonium contains more than 90 percent of the isotope Pu-239.

4. Michael D. Intriligator and Abdullah Toukan, "Terrorist's Use of Weapons of Mass Destruction," in *Countering Terrorism and WMD: Creating a Global Counter-Terrorism Network*, edited by Peter Katona, Michael D. Intriligator, and John P.

Sullivan (Abingdon, UK: Routledge, 2006). Note that the data given on deaths are relative, since the lethality from a sarin attack could be reduced by antidotes and decontamination; anthrax, under certain circumstances, is curable; and both chemical and biological attacks leave some time for protective counter-measures, more time in the case of biological weapons. None of this applies to nuclear attack.

5. United Nations Security Council Resolution 1540, Non-proliferation of weapons of mass destruction. 2004.

6. European Union, Fact Sheet, *EU Strategy against the Proliferation of Weapons of Mass Destruction*, European Commission and Secretariat General of the Council of the EU, EU-U.S. Summit, Dromoland Castle, Ireland, June 26, 2004.

Chapter 2

1. Each of the bombs had an explosive yield of less than 20 kilotons of the pure fission weapons, the gun-type Hiroshima bomb contained about 60 kg of uranium enriched to about 80 percent in chain-reacting U-235. The Nagasaki bomb was an implosion device that operated on a principle that has been incorporated into most modern weapons. Chemical explosives imploded a 6 kg mass of plutonium to a higher density. Gun-type weapons are simpler than implosion devices, though they can only be constructed using HEU, not plutonium, and require at least twice as much HEU as an implosion weapon.

2. The W-76, the standard nuclear warhead used on the U.S. Trident submarine-launched ballistic missiles, has a yield of up to 100 kilotons. The USSR manufactured and tested nuclear weapons with yields over 50 megatons of TNT.

3. See Stockholm International Peace Research Institute, *SIPRI Yearbook 2007: Armaments, Disarmament and International Security* (New York: Oxford University Press Inc., 2007), 515, and Stockholm International Peace Research Institute, *SIPRI Yearbook 2008* (New York: Oxford University Press Inc., 2007), Appendix 8A.

4. This with B-61 gravity bombs under U.S. custody in Belgium, at the Kleine Brogel air base, for use by Belgian F-16s of the 10th Fighter Wing; in Germany, at the Büchel air base, for use by German Tornados of the JaboG 33; in the Netherlands, at the Volkel air base, for use by Dutch F-16s of the 1st Fighter Wing; in Italy, at Aviano air base, for use by US F-16s of the 31st Fighter Wing and at Ghedi Torre air base for use by Italian Tornados of the 6th Stormo; and in Turkey, at Incirlik air base for use by the U.S. Air Force. Meanwhile, the National Turkish nuclear strike mission has probably expired. All weapons until recently stored at RAF Lakenheath air base in the United Kingdom, and at Ramstein air base in Germany have been withdrawn. This, among other things, because most Nuclear Weapon Sites in Europe do not meet U.S. security requirements. Source: Hans M. Kristensen, "Status of U.S. Nuclear Weapons in Europe," *Federation of American Scientists* (June 2008).

5. The *Yuri Dolgoruky*, the lead boat of Russia's newest Borei-class SSBN with the Bulava missile; China's Jin-class SSBN Type 094 with the JL-2 missile; France's Triomphant Class *Le Terrible* armed with the M51.1 SLBM; the U.S. Ohio Class with the Trident II Life-Extended (D5LE) SLBM. Even Israel is said to have new nuclear warheads mounted on cruise missiles aboard its Dolphin-class submarines

6. U.S. Government Publication, *Ballistic Missiles: Delivery Systems For Weapons Of Mass Destruction*, Second Edition (Washington, DC: 2006): 1–111.

7. *Cruise Missiles: Potential Delivery Systems for Weapons of Mass Destruction* (Washington, DC: 2000): 1–53.

8. Other deployment options arose with the development of nuclear suitcase bombs, landmines, depth charges, artillery shells, and air defense systems. Space-launch vehicles could also be used to deliver nuclear weapons.

9. For a primer on ballistic missile defenses, see the Missile Defense Agency missile defense system booklet at: www.acq.osd.mil/bmdo/bmdolink/pdf/bmds book.pdf.

10. For example: Patriot; NATO's Medium Extended Air Defense; the Surface-to-Air Medium-range Air Defense System; the Theater High Altitude Air Defense system; and the Standard Missile Three system on U.S. Aegis ships.

11. The attraction of intercepting missiles in the boost phase is that they leave a clear signature of hot gases, and there are no problems in distinguishing between warhead, and decoys or chaff. But there are also many disadvantages. In particular, in order to intercept a missile during a five to eight minute section of its flight, decision making would probably need to be made automatic or delegated to the field, each option carrying a high risk of accidental or inadvertent launch of an interceptor.

12. The US *Predator B* turboprop UAV system costs $40 million, the *MQ-9 Reaper*, the most lethal UAV with twice the speed of the Predator costs $53 million, and the jet propelled *Global Hawk* costs some $64 million.

13. A Joint Declaration was issued by presidents Bush and Putin of November 13, 2001, that "neither country regards the other as an enemy or threat."

14. The Russian military started talking quietly about withdrawing from the INF treaty when it became clear that the United States would withdraw from the ABM Treaty, and more loudly, since the issue of deploying limited ABM segments in Poland (ten launchers) and the Czech Republic (radars), or eventually in a Baltic country or the United Kingdom, has come up ever since the end of 2005.

15. See: *SIPRI Yearbook 2008*, Appendix 8C, a survey of U.S. ballistic missile defence programs.

16. Israel's Prime Minister Olmert, on the occasion of his visit to Germany in early 2007, for the first time elliptically alluded to nuclear weapons Israel might have in its possession in a response to the political standoff with Iran over Tehran's nuclear program. If the statement represented a deliberate admission, however, it would signal that maintaining strategic nuclear ambiguity is no longer a major part of Israeli defense policy. This could mean Israel is willing to compromise if the international community demands that it acknowledge its nuclear weapons program, and could facilitate an international agreement supporting an Israeli civilian nuclear program.

17. French President Chirac warned in January 2006 that: "The leaders of states who would use terrorist means against us, as well as those who would consider using, in one way or another, weapons of mass destruction, must understand that they would lay themselves open to a firm and adapted response on our part. And this response could be a conventional one. It could also be of a different kind."

18. George W. Bush, *The National Security Strategy of the United States of America* (Washington, DC: The White House, September 2002). The classified version is identified jointly as National Security Presidential Directive (NSPD) 17, and Homeland Security Presidential Directive 4. This was followed by five additional National Strategies: (1) for Homeland Security; (2) for Combating Terrorism;

(3) to Combat Weapons of Mass Destruction; (4) for the Physical Protection of Critical Infrastructures and Key Assets, and (5) to Secure Cyberspace. The National Security Strategy of the United States of March 2006 confirms and refines preemption.

19. "Putin reaffirms Russia's right to preemptive strikes," Agence France-Presoe, November 4, 2003.

20. France, which not only opposed Operation Iraqi Freedom but also rejected the discussion over the principal option of preemption within the framework of NATO, explicitly mentions "capacité d'anticipation," and the necessity of the option of a preemptive strike in certain situations in its "Programmation Militaire." See: Elaine M. Bunn, "Preemptive Action: When, How and to What Effect," *Strategic Forum* 200 (Washington, DC: National Defense University, 2003): 6.

21. The then prime minister of Australia, John Howard, expressly called for a change in the UN Charter to allow for preemptive military strikes against terrorist threats. See John Shaw, "Startling His Neighbors, Australian Leader Favors First Strikes," *New York Times*, December 2, 2002.

22. General Shigeru, the Director General of the then Japanese "Defense Agency," stated in January 2003 the readiness of Japan to launch a "counterattack" should North Korea bring its missiles into a "ready for takeoff" position. See: Ishiba, "Japan to 'Counterattack' if North Korea Prepares to Attack," *Yomiuri Shimbun/Daily Yomiuri* (January 25, 2003).

23. At the Prague summit in November 2002, NATO adopted a document (MC 472) in which, at least implicitly, preemption is discussed. Though "preemption" and "anticipatory self-defense" are not explicitly quoted in the new military concept of the Alliance for the fight against terrorism (because of the insistence of Germany and France), it is clear that NATO does not fundamentally rule out preemptive strikes. See also: Adam Tanner, "NATO says could launch preemptive strikes." *Reuters*, October 31, 2002.

24. The European Union Institute for Security Studies, *A Secure Europe in a Better World: European Security Strategy*, December 12, 2003.

25. See Alan M. Dershowitz, *Preemption, The Knife That Cuts Both Ways* (New York: Norton & Company, Inc., 2006), 275; and Colin S. Gray, *The Implications of Preemptive and Preventive War Doctrines: A Reconsideration* (Carlisle Barracks, PA: Army War College, 2007).

26. There are significant dangers associated with U.S. preemption. First, it creates antagonism toward the United States and possible further terrorist attacks. Second, it sends a message to the rest of the world that they should not attempt to fight the United States with conventional weapons, leading to the proliferation of nuclear weapons. Third, this policy sets a precedent for other nations to also engage in preemption, including China in Taiwan and India in Pakistan. Fourth, it will encourage the "nations of concern," which see intervention looming, to try to protect themselves by building their own nuclear potential.

27. Addressing the Duma in February 2007, Sergei Ivanov, Russian Deputy Prime Minister and then still Defense Minister, called the 1987 Intermediate-Range Nuclear Forces (INF) Treaty between the United States and the Soviet Union—which banned short-, medium- and intermediate-range ballistic and ground-launched cruise missiles—a mistake. Ivanov first raised the midrange missile issue in August 2006, when he visited Alaska with then U.S. Defense

Secretary Rumsfeld. During the trip, Ivanov reminded Rumsfeld that a Russian withdrawal from the INF would not be unprecedented since the United States withdrew from the Anti-Ballistic Missile Treaty in 2002.

28. According to the U.S. Nuclear Posture Review of March 2002—a classified document periodically mandated by the U.S. Congress that was leaked by the *Los Angeles Times*—the United States is striving for a new triad with three components. First are offensive strike weapons, both nuclear and non-nuclear, including all three components of the old triad. Second are defenses, both active and passive, including the new national missile defense system. Third is a revitalized defense infrastructure that could design, develop, manufacture, and certify new warheads in response to new national requirements, and maintain readiness to resume underground testing if required.

29. Applies to missile forces and their early-warning and command and control systems. Hair-trigger alert is the readiness needed for a launch-on-warning posture, which is intended to ensure quick responses in the event of a missile attack detected by satellites, and reconfirmed by long-range radars.

30. Samuel Glasstone, ed., *The Effects of Nuclear Weapons*, Revised Edition, published by the U.S. Atomic Energy Commission, April 1962.

31. See Jaya Tiwari and Cleve J. Gray, *U.S. Nuclear Weapons Accidents* (Washington, DC: Center for Defense Information, 2002); http://www.cdi.org/Issues/ NukeAccidents/accidents.htm; and *Selected Accidents Involving Nuclear Weapons 1950–1993* (Washington, DC: Greenpeace, March 1996); www.user.dccnet. com/welcomewoods/Nuclear_Free_Georgia_Strait/greenacci.htm.

32. The record of these accidents is beset with mysteries and inconsistencies due to a lack of documentation available to the public. The paucity of publicly available data is largely the result of the highly classified nature of information regarding nuclear weapons and their location. To maintain this opacity, the policy of nuclear weapons' states is to *neither confirm nor deny* the presence of nuclear weapons in most accidents.

33. According to the Brookings Institution, a Washington think tank, the United States lost eleven nuclear bombs during the Cold War and, according to Greenpeace, an estimated fifty nuclear warheads, most of the former USSR, still lie on the bottom of the world's oceans,

34. October 5, 1960, Thule, Greenland; October 25, 1962, Volk Field Base, Wisconsin; June 3, 1980, and June 6, 1980, at an unknown location; and January 10, 1964, Warren AFB, Cheyenne, Wyoming. See Gregory Shaun, *The Hidden Cost of Deterrence: Nuclear Weapons Accidents* (London: Brassey's, 1990), 156, 178, 181–182; and Scott D. Sagan, *The Limits of Safety: Organizations, Accidents, and Nuclear Weapons* (Princeton: Princeton University Press, 1993), 3.

35. See Stockholm International Peace Research Institute, *SIPRI Yearbook 2007: Armaments, Disarmament and International Security* (New York: Oxford University Press Inc., 2007), 521.

36. South Africa's decision in 1993 to abandon its nuclear weapon program was historic. Belarus, Kazakhstan, and Ukraine also relinquished their physical possession of former Soviet nuclear weapons after the dissolution of the USSR Argentina, Brazil, South Korea, Sweden, Switzerland, and several other countries unilaterally chose to abandon various nuclear industrial and research pursuits that might have led to nuclear weapons, and they committed themselves to a nuclear-weapon-free status. In the case of Libya, diplomacy, supported by the

pressure of the UN, and the threat of the possible use of force, proved to be effective.

37. Weapons of Mass Destruction Commission, *Weapons of Terror: Freeing the World of Nuclear, Biological and Chemical Arms*, Final Report (Stockholm: EO Grafiska, 2006), 61. www.wmdcommission.org.

38. A shrewd businessman, Khan saw potential for financial gain between his network of clandestine suppliers and a burgeoning market for nuclear arms. North Korea, Iran, Iraq, Syria, and Libya were foremost on his list. He also met with potential customers in Egypt, Saudi Arabia, Sudan, Malaysia, Indonesia, Algeria, Kuwait, Myanmar, and Abu Dhabi. In 1997, at a series of meetings in Istanbul and Casablanca, Khan made a deal to sell Libya a complete bomb-making factory for approximately $100 million. Seif Islam, Gadhafi's elder son, approached the British SIS with the offer to talk about Libyan WMD. CIA and the British SIS held sporadic talks with the head of Libyan intelligence, Mousa Kusa. The United States and the United Kingdom wanted Libya to give up its WMD program, and Gadhafi wanted assurances that in return economic sanctions would be removed. In August 2003 SIS got a tip about a shipment leaving Khan's factory in Malaysia for Libya, and U.S. spy satellites tracked the shipment. In October 2003 the German flagged cargo vessel *BBC China* was seized by the United States and Italy.

39. An old 22 kiloton uranium implosion device. See Christoph Wirz and Emmanuel Egger, "Use of nuclear and radiological weapons by terrorists?" *International Review of the Red Cross* 859, vol. 87 (September 2005): 499.

40. A 40 MW light-water nuclear materials testing reactor was constructed in 1977 at the Al Tuwaitha Nuclear Research Center, 18 km southeast of Baghdad. It was crippled by Israeli aircraft in 1981 in a preemptive strike to prevent the regime of Saddam Hussein from using the reactor for the creation of nuclear weapons. The facility was completely destroyed by American aircraft during the 1991 Gulf War.

41. Stockholm International Peace Research Institute, *SIPRI Yearbook 2006: Armaments, Disarmament, and International Security* (New York: Oxford University Press Inc., 2006), 638

42. Weapon-grade uranium in which the percentage of fissionable isotope U-235 has been increased from the natural level of 0.7 percent to some level equal or greater to 20 percent, usually around 90 percent.

43. Plutonium can also get lost: 69 kg at the Tokai-Mura plutonium fuel production facility, Japan, in 1994, 8 kg in 1996, and 206 kg in 2003; 19 kg at Sellafield, UK, in 2004, and 29.6 kg in 2005.

44. Protection existing as in Fort Knox, the U.S. Army Armor School and training base, where the U.S. gold reserves are stored.

45. David Albright and Kimberly Kramer, "Civil HEU Watch: Tracking Inventories of Civil Highly Enriched Uranium," in *Global Stocks of Nuclear Explosive Materials* (Washington, DC: Institute for Science and International Security, 2005). http://www.isis-online.org/global_stocks/end2003/tableofcontents.html

46. Government Accountability Office, *Nuclear Nonproliferation: DOE Needs to Take Action to Further Reduce the Use of Weapons-Usable Uranium in Civilian Research Reactors* (Washington, DC: GAO, 2004).

47. IAEA states that 25 kg of HEU (U-235) or 8 kg of plutonium Pu-239 are the minimum amounts required for a 20 kiloton explosion = 20,000 tons of TNT. However, a group with more sophisticated technology could build the same

weapon with as little as 5 kg of HEU or 3 kg of plutonium—the size of a soccer ball. Uranium enrichment is a complex industrial process requiring huge facilities that house sophisticated equipment and consume large quantities of electricity. However, a nation or group that possesses an amount of HEU sufficient to make a nuclear weapon may be able to amass the engineering and scientific skills to actually build the weapon.

48. WMDC, *Weapons of Terror*, 74.

49. The plutonium obtained from spent reactor fuel can be used to make bombs though its isotopic composition is not ideal.

50. See the most recent war in Lebanon, where Iran and Syria supplied missiles to Hezbollah and Hamas.

51. Walter Laqueur, "Postmodern Terrorism," *Foreign Affairs* (September/October 1996).

52. Bin Laden has called the acquisition of WMD a "religious duty." For the best available summary of al Qaeda's nuclear efforts see David Albright, "Al Qaeda's Nuclear Program: Through the Window of Seized Documents," *Special Forum* 47 (Berkeley, CA: Nautilus Institute, November 6, 2002), and David Albright, Kathryn Buehler, and Holly Higgins, "Bin Laden and the Bomb," *Bulletin of Atomic Scientists* 1, vol. 58 (January/February 2002).

53. There is little doubt in this regard. Terrorist websites, which now number over four hundred, are overflowing with doctrine and objectives about the aim of destroying infidel populations. Were al Qaeda or some other such organization to obtain a nuclear weapon, the same doctrine that guided the 9/11 attacks would likely apply again.

54. The danger that these states would intentionally provide nuclear material to terrorists is probably far smaller than the danger of nuclear theft, for to provide the key ingredients for an act of nuclear terror would be to run the risk of being found out and facing overwhelming retaliation.

55. Pakistan's small nuclear arsenal is believed to be heavily guarded, but armed remnants of al Qaeda continue to operate in Pakistan, as do Jihadi groups with deep connections to Pakistan intelligence. Moreover, corruption and theft are endemic, including within the military establishment. Senior insiders within Pakistan's nuclear establishment have demonstrated a willingness to sell technology related to nuclear weapons.

56. Among these are: (1) inertial switches and acceleration sensors allowing priming only after a threshold level has been reached; (2) environmental sensing devices monitoring the trajectory, which switch on only at a distinct ratio of the longitudinal to lateral acceleration; (3) a barometric switch, which activates the electric circuit only at a distinct height above ground; (4) a so-called permissive-action link (PAL) is needed, consisting for instance of several number codes with up to twelve digits and allowing a limited number of tries; the code has to be entered by more than one person, i.e., each person concerned knowing only part of the entire code; (5) certain types require a high energy electrical impulse. Speculation exists about the sinking of the Soviet K-129 Golf-II-class submarine north of Hawaii because the crew must have had some confidence that it already possessed the proper disarming codes to override the fail-safe device—which apparently was not the case. See Kenneth Sewell, *Red Star Rogue: The Untold Story of a Soviet Submarine's Nuclear Strike Attempt on the U.S.* (New York, Simon & Schuster, 2005), 89–93.

57. For a discussion of the vast difference between a safe, reliable, efficient weapon that can be carried on a missile, and a crude, inefficient, unsafe terrorist bomb that might be delivered in a truck, see Matthew Bunn and Anthony Wier, "Terrorist Nuclear Weapon Construction: How Difficult?" *Annals of the American Academy of Political and Social Science* 607 (September 2006).

58. A bomb with the explosive power of 10,000 tons of TNT—half the size of the bomb that obliterated Hiroshima—if set off in midtown Manhattan on a typical workday, could kill half a million people and cause more than $1 trillion in direct economic damage. Devastating economic aftershocks would reverberate throughout the world. See John P. Holden and Matthew Bunn, "Technical Background: A Tutorial on Nuclear Weapons and Nuclear-Explosive Materials," in *Nuclear Threat Initiative Research Library: Securing the Bomb* (Washington, DC: Project on Managing the Atom, Harvard University and Nuclear Threat Initiative, 2002). http://www.nti.org/e_research/cnwm/overview/technical.asp.

59. For examples of recent assessments of the danger of nuclear terrorism, see Graham T. Allison, *Nuclear Terrorism: The Ultimate Preventable Catastrophe*, First Edition (New York: New York Times Books, 2004); and Anna M. Pluta and Peter D. Zimmerman, "Nuclear Terrorism: A Disheartening Dissent," *Survival* 2, vol. 48 (Summer 2006).

60. The critical mass of an assembly of fissile material is the amount needed for a sustained nuclear chain reaction. In a larger assembly, the reaction increases at an exponential rate—which is termed supercritical.

61. The U.S. Manhattan project to build the first nuclear weapons.

62. A man-portable low-yield nuclear device weighing less than 40 kg. A Russian commission formed on July 3, 1996, investigated reports that Chechen fighters had possibly gained access to such weapons. The United States had also developed about 300 Special Atomic Demolition Munitions "backpacks" based on its W-54 warhead.

63. See, for example, "Suitcase Nukes: A Reassessment," (Monterey, CA: Center for Nonproliferation Studies, September 12, 2002); http://cns.miis.edu/pubs/week/020923.htm. See also Nikolai Sokov, "Suitcase Nukes: Permanently Lost Luggage" (Monterey, CA: Center for Nonproliferation Studies, February 13, 2003); http://cns.miis.edu/pubs/week/040213.htm.

64. Commission on the Intelligence Capabilities of the United States Regarding Weapons of Mass Destruction, *Report to the President* (Washington, DC: WMD Commission, 2005), 276; www.wmd.gov/report.

65. See www.nti.org/db/nistraff/2006/20060210.htm.

66. See Matthew Bunn, *Securing Nuclear Warheads and Materials: Global Nuclear Security Standards* (Washington, DC, NTI Research Library, 2007). www.nti.org/e_research/cnwm/securing/standards.asp. See also Gunnar Arbman and Charles Thornton, *Russia's Tactical Nuclear Weapons, Part II: Technical Issues and Policy Recommendations* (Stockholm: Swedish Defence Research Agency, February 2005).

67. The IAEA has published some common standards contained in Information Circular 225 for the transportation of such materials, in accordance with the multilateral Convention on the Physical Protection of Nuclear Material, which has 116 state parties as of March 2006. These controls serve as a basic model for state regulatory authorities to follow in implementing their own controls.

68. See www.defenselink.mil/pubs/ctr/.

69. In a 2005 press conference Russia's chief military prosecutor reported that property crimes in the military are still increasing, including in the interior ministry forces, which guard nuclear facilities. See Colonel-General Alexander Savenkov, "Press Conference with Chief Military Prosecutor Alexander Savenkov," *RIA Novosti* (2005).

70. The head of Elron, the physical protection firm for the Russian atomic energy agency Rosatom, estimated in May 2005 that funding for nuclear security comes to only 30 percent of the need. See Nikolai N. Shemigon, remarks to "Third Russian International Conference on Nuclear Material Protection, Control, and Accountability" (May 16–20, 2005). The Commander of the Ministry of Interior (MVD) troops for the Moscow district said that only seven of the critical guarded facilities had adequately maintained security equipment, while thirty-nine had "serious shortcomings" in their physical protection. See "Over 4,000 Trespassers detained at Moscow District Restricted Access Facilities," *Interfax-Agentstvoo Voyennykh Novostey* (March 18, 2005).

71. Statement of the Director General IAEA, *Security Today: Challenges and Opportunities* (Basel: Nobel Laureate Lecture, Biozentrum, University of Basel, February 14, 2007); http://www.iaea.org/NewsCenter/Statements/2007/ebsp2007n003.html.

72. See Graham Allison, *Nuclear Terrorism: The Ultimate Preventable Catastrophe* (New York: New York Times Books, 2004); and "How to Stop Nuclear Terror," *Foreign Affairs* (January/February 2004).

Chapter 3

1. For more information on specific chemical agents, see Frederick R. Sidell, Ernest T. Takafuji, and David R. Franz, eds., *Medical Aspects of Chemical and Biological Warfare* (Bethesda, MD: Office of the Surgeon General Department of the Army, 1997), chapters 1–17. http://www.nbcmed.org/SiteContent/HomePage/WhatsNew/MedAspects/contents.html.

2. Ibid., chapters 18–29.

3. Ibid., chapters 30–34.

4. Peter Katona, John P. Sullivan, and Michael Intriligator, *Countering Terrorism and WMD: Creating a Global Counter-Terrorism Network* (Abingdon, UK: Routledge, 2006).

5. When sarin was introduced into the Tokyo subway system in 1995, over 5,500 people arrived at hospitals requesting medical treatment, but only 1,051 had medical symptoms indicative of sarin exposure.

6. Prophylaxis is generally spoken of in terms of medical or chemical treatments to protect individuals from chemical, biological, and toxin weapons. In some cases it also includes mechanical measures such as protective suits and masks.

7. Atropine and diazepam can be used to treat the effects of nerve agent exposure. In the Gulf War of 1991 the United States gave out bromide tablets that were to interfere with the firing of nerve synapses, but according to some accounts, these have never been tested for nerve agents.

Chapter 4

1. The French army used tear gas grenades in 1914 at the outbreak of WWI, but it was not until the German army used chlorine near Ypres in 1915, that the world entered the modern era of chemical warfare. Also, phosgene and mustard were

weaponized during WWI, and used by both sides. Agent development and use continued following WWI despite the signing of the 1925 Geneva Protocol, which banned the first use of chemical weapons. In the inter-war period, chemical weapons were used by Spain in Morocco, by Italy in Abyssinia, and by Japan in China. Shortly before WWII, Germans produced the first nerve agent, tabun, but neither side made use of their chemical weapons stocks. In WWII, poisonous gases and chemical weapons were used in Asia. Since the end of that war, mustard has been used by Egypt in North Yemen (1963–67), nerve and mustard, and an unknown pulmonary irritant in the Iraq–Iran War (1980–88), and by the Iraqi government against its own civilian population. In the Vietnam War, defoliants and CS gas were used by the United States. In the 1980s the United States alleged Laos and Vietnam were employing CW, as were Khmer Rouge guerillas in Cambodia. After the Soviet invasion of Afghanistan, reports of CW attacks with a mixture of fungal toxins known as trichothecene mycotoxins, which the press dubbed yellow rain, began to filter out of that country. In 1992 the Mozambican National Resistance engaged CW. Allegedly, CW were also used in the Nagorno-Karabakh conflict between Azerbaijan and Armenia, and in Angola.

2. Psikhogennyie, psikhotropnyie, and psikhomnemetnyie are the three groups of psychochemicals recognized in Russia.

3. Principal Soviet delivery means were the bombers Backfire (24 x 500 kg), Badger (18 x 500 kg), Blinder (16 x 500 kg), the fighter bombers Fitter, Flogger (20 x 100 kg), Fencer (6 x 500 kg), and Frogfoot, and the helicopters Hind and Havoc.

4. For example, the Soviet SS-23 and SS-21 missiles.

5. For example, the Soviet BM-27 and BM-21.

6. Countries that have declared abandoned weapons are China, Italy, and Panama. The countries that possess old weapons are Australia, Belgium, Canada, France, Germany, Italy, Japan, Russia, Slovenia, the United Kingdom, and the United States.

7. UNMOVIC continues to collect information on Iraq.

8. See *SIPRI Yearbook 2006*, 727–731. The U.S. State Department report on compliance with arms control agreements issued at the end of August 2005 expresses concern about possible clandestine offensive CW programs in Russia, China, Iran, and Sudan.

9. Organization for the Prohibition of Chemical Weapons, Inspection Activity, http://www.opcw.org

10. Bosnia and Herzegovina, China, France, India, Iran, Japan, South Korea, Libya, Russia, Serbia and Montenegro, the United Kingdom, and the United States.

11. Aberdeen Proving Ground, MD, Anniston Army Depot, AL., Lexington-Blue Grass Army Depot, KY., Newport Chemical Depot, Ind., Pine Bluff Army Arsenal, AR, Pueblo Chemical Depot, CO., Deseret Chemical Depot, UT, and Umatilla Chemical Depot, OR.

12. Chemical threat information has surfaced because of al Qaeda suspect debriefings, technical intercepts and analysis of al Qaeda's anticipated actions. Various seized documents demonstrate a significant interest on the part of al Qaeda planners and trainers in the potential for chemical attacks. Training manuals were found at training camps in Afghanistan indicating that the network possesses crude procedures for producing VX nerve agent, sarin,

mustard gas, and hydrogen cyanide gas. Also, some experimental training took place at camps in Chechnya and Georgia's Pankisi Gorge. Jordanian intelligence officials also claim an interdicted plot to attack intelligence service headquarters and the U.S. Embassy in Amman involved the detonation of a large "chemical bomb" that might have killed as many as 20,000 people. At least one arrested plotter backed up the chemical claims in a televised confession.

13. Ownership, sale, and rental of small aircraft are generally not well controlled, and, in the United States, they are even unregulated and unaccounted for. Getting a small plane in the United States is as easy as renting a car. Loading it with a chemical agent would present few problems for a terrorist group.

14. The judges, who all lived in the same dormitory, survived the attack when the wind blew the sarin away from the building. Seven people in the neighborhood were killed.

15. World total as of January 2006: 443 operating nuclear power reactors, 26 under construction, 35 planned, and 107 proposed; see *SIPRI Yearbook 2006*, 690.

16. P. A. D'Agostino and C. L. Chenier, *Analysis of Chemical Warfare Agents: General Overview, LC-MS Review, IN-House LC-ESI-MS Methods and Open Literature Bibliography* (Alberta, Canada: Defense Technical Information Center, March 2006).

Chapter 5

1. More than two millennia ago, Scythian archers dipped arrowheads in manure and rotting corpses to increase the deadliness of their weapons. In medieval times commanders attempted to harm their opponents by contaminating water supplies with cadavers of animals or humans that died from an infectious disease or by catapulting bodies over the walls of a besieged city. See Erhard Geissler and John Ellis van Courtland Moon, eds., "Biological Weapons: Research, Development and Use from the Middle Ages to 1845," *SIPRI Chemical and Biological Warfare Studies* 18 (Oxford: Oxford University Press, 1999).

2. Sheldon H. Harris, *Factories of Death: Japanese Biological Warfare 1932–45 and the American Cover-up* (New York: Routledge, 1994).

3. The influenza epidemic of 1918 is estimated to have killed over 20 million people worldwide, and over 500,000 in the United States. The Black Plague is estimated to have killed up to 25 percent of the total population of Europe.

4. For more on the characteristics of biological weapons, their manufacture, and delivery systems, see Frederick R. Sidell, Ernest J. Takafuji, and David R. Franz, eds., *Textbook of Military Medicine: Medical Aspects of Chemical and Biological Warfare, Part I: Warfare, Weaponry, and the Casualty* (Washington, DC: Surgeon General, U.S. Department of the Army, 1997). Also see U.S. Congress, *Technologies Underlying Weapons of Mass Destruction* (Washington, DC: U.S. Government Printing Office, 1993).

5. Departments of the Army, Navy, and Air Force, *NATO Handbook on the Medical Aspects of NBC Defensive Operations* (Washington, DC: Defense Department, 1996).

6. The Soviets had weaponized bacterial, viral, fungal organisms, biological toxins, and bio-regulators (neuro-peptide depressors), and produced genetic engineering applications for biological warfare, differentiating between weapons that kill or incapacitate, contagious or not, disseminated by aerosol or via other means, and of strategic or operational effect.

7. Peter Katona, John P. Sullivan, and Michael Intriligator, *Countering Terrorism and WMD: Creating a Global Counter-Terrorism Network* (Abingdon, UK: Routledge, 2006).

8. L. D. Rotz et al., "Public health assessment of potential biological terrorism agents," *Emerging Infectious Diseases* 2, vol. 8 (2002): 225–230.
9. For example Ebola and Lassa virus.
10. National Institute of Allergy and Infectious Diseases, *NIAID Biodefense Research Agenda for Category B and C Priority Pathogens* 03-5315 (NIH Publication, January 2003). Not all of these are deadly, but a number were weaponized in the offensive biological weapons programs of the last century.
11. Diseases that are considered for weaponization or are known to already be weaponized include anthrax, ebola, bubonic plague, cholera, tularemia, brucellosis, Q-fever, machupo, coccidioides mycosis, glanders, melioidosis, shigella, rocky mountain spotted fever, typhus, psittacosis, yellow fever, japanese B encephalitis, rift valley fever, and smallpox. Naturally occurring toxins that can be used as weapons include ricin, SEB, botulism toxin, saxitoxin, and many mycotoxins.
12. Soviet bombers or ballistic missiles using bomblets or sprayers were to deliver weaponized anthrax to deep operational or strategic targets, including the United States, in a general war. By the end of the Cold War, the Soviets viewed biological warfare solely in terms of total war with NATO and the United States.
13. Large segments of the population can be deliberately contaminated, particularly via the vast array of vitamins, health supplements, and "natural remedies," which do not need approval by the Food and Drug Administration. Producers of excipients, in particular, offer good possibilities for attack. Widely used, of which several are common to more than a hundred approved drug formulations, excipients often account for a relatively high fraction of the final dosage form, thus allowing for contamination at low concentrations. While there are multiple suppliers of excipients, already contamination of only one source could have widespread impact, including an erosion of public confidence in the safety of medicines generally.
14. Foot-and-mouth disease is a very contagious disease of cloven-hoofed animals (cattle, pigs, sheep, goats, etc.). There are seven different serotypes of the virus, and no cross immunity between these types. The disease can be highly lethal to young calves, but usually lethality is low. The problems lie in the serious production losses and, of course, in the measures that have to be taken to eradicate the outbreak. Natural infections have an incubation period of two to eight days. Infected animals release the virus in saliva, milk, feces, urine, and exhaled air. It is a hardy virus and known to have survived kilometers of airborne transmission to cause a new outbreak of disease elsewhere.
15. This is another very highly contagious viral disease and affects both domestic and wild birds. The different strains vary widely in virulence but some cause high lethality in domestic fowls, turkeys, and pheasants. Incubation time is about five days. Birds lose appetite and their egg production drops off very sharply. Profuse bright green diarrhea is common and there is extremely rapid dehydration. Many birds die within a day or two, and the mortality rate can be over 90 percent.
16 *Health Aspects of Chemical and Biological Weapons* (Geneva: World Health Organization, 1970), 93–94. See also U.S. Congress, Office of Technology Assessment, *Technologies Underlying Weapons of Mass Destruction*, OTA-BP-ISC-115 (Washington, DC: U.S. Government Printing Office, December 1993), 82, 94–96.

17. Burundi, Central African Republic, Cote d'Ivoire, Egypt, Gabon, Guyana, Haiti, Liberia, Madagascar, Malawi, Myanmar, Nepal, Somalia, Syria, United Arab Emirates, Tanzania.

18. Andorra, Angola, Cameroon, Chad, Comoros, Cook Island, Djibouti, Eritrea, Guinea, Israel, Kazakhstan, Kiribati, Marshall Islands, Mauritius, Micronesia, Mozambique, Namibia, Nauru, Niue, Samoa, Trinidad and Tobago, Tuvalu, Zambia.

19. See the achievements of the Soviet Union during the Cold War with a program called Biopreparat; Ken Alibek and Stephen Handelman, *Biohazard: The Chilling True Story of the Largest Covert Biological Weapons Program in the World—Told from Inside by the Man Who Ran it* (New York: Delta, 1999); Alexander Kouzminov, *Biological Espionage: Special Operations of the Soviet and Russian Foreign Intelligence Services in the West* (London: Greenhill Books, 2005).

20. See Judith Miller, Stephen Engelberg, and William Broad, *Germs, Biological Weapons and America's Secret War* (New York: Simon & Schuster, 2001).

21. While the United States, the United Kingdom, France, and Canada renounced biological weapons and eliminated their offensive weapons programs before the BTWC was activated, Israel, North Korea, Syria, Iran, China, and some other states are believed to have a continuing program.

22. Article III of the BTWC.

23. The Reagan administration had authorized at least forty shipments of specific biological agents to Iraq from the American Type Culture Collection, a big scientific institute that has cultures of every type of exotic disease in the world.

24. Biological weapons, which kill people but leave infrastructure intact, could become the "poor man's neutron bomb."

25. Carl W. Ford Jr. testimony, before the Senate Foreign Relations Committee. *Reducing the Threat of Chemical and Biological Weapons*, March 19, 2002; General Thomas A Schwartz testimony, before the Senate Armed Services Committee, March 5, 2002. U.S. Arms Control and Disarmament Agency, *Adherence to and Compliance with Arms Control Agreements* (Washington, DC: U.S. Department of State, 1998).

26. United Nations, *Report of the Secretary-General on the Status of the Implementation of the Special Commission's Plan for the Ongoing Monitoring and Verification of Iraq's Compliance with Relevant Parts of Section of Security Council Resolution 687 (1991)*, October 11, 1995, http://www.un.org/Depts/unscom/sres95-864.htm. Security Council Resolution 687 also called on Iraq to ratify the BTWC, which it finally did in June 1991.

27. There is a revolution in biotechnology in the sense of the revolution in computer and information processing power. The U.S. Military Critical Technology List reports technological doubling rates of six months for basic genetic engineering, the Human Genome Project, bio-regulators, and other biotechnical applications. This can result in enhanced infectivity and virulence, novel toxins and regulatory peptides, greater antibiotic resistance, and novel genetic weaponry as a distinct possibility.

28. Alibek and Handelman, *Biohazard*.

29. Though there were only a small number of cases involved in the anthrax scare—it is believed that seven letters were sent, and five people died—the incidents had a disproportionate effect on the collective American psyche. The impact was heightened by timing: the first batch of letters was postmarked

only a week after 9/11, and the second a few weeks later—during a period when American society as a whole was experiencing an unprecedented sense of vulnerability and fear. The public fears were augmented by extensive media discussions about the use of anthrax as a weapon, and further heightened by the fact that the perpetrator was never identified or apprehended. The *New York Times* published the technology behind the Daschle letter, which was very sophisticated anthrax, one trillion spores per gram, hence super-weapon grade. Tied in there was a special treatment to eliminate electrostatic charges so it would float in the air. The only people who would have the capability to do this would be individuals who are or were involved in biowarfare programs and have access to biowarfare labs.

30. For more on the toxin ricin, see Dana A. Shea and Frank Gottron, *Ricin: Technical Background and Potential Role in Terrorism*, CRS Report RS21383 (Washington, DC: Congressional Research Service, 2004).

31. Aum Shinrikyo's team of highly trained scientists worked under ideal conditions in a first-world country with a virtually unlimited budget in large, modern facilities. Despite the millions of dollars spent on its CBW program, it still faced problems in creating virulent biological agents, and it also found it difficult to dispense those agents in an effective manner. Because of these problems, the militants succeeded in killing only a few people, and they did not cause the global Armageddon they endeavored to create. The Japanese government further suspects Shinrikyo in another thirteen attacks that remain unsolved.

32. Included among the attacks were several large-scale operations. For example, in April 1990, the group used a fleet of three trucks equipped with aerosol sprayers to release liquid botulinum toxin on the Imperial Palace, the Diet, and the U.S. Embassy in Tokyo, and two U.S. naval bases and the airport in Narita. Between June and August in 1993, the group sprayed thousands of gallons of liquid anthrax in Tokyo, using sprayers mounted on the roof of their headquarters on two occasions, and conducted two attacks with sprayer trucks, one against the Diet, and the other against the Imperial Palace and the Tokyo tower.

33. Weapons of Mass Destruction Commission, *Weapons of Terror*, 42.

Chapter 6

1. "Fact Sheet on Dirty Bombs," *U.S. Air Force Counterproliferation Center*, http://www.au.af.mil/au/awc/awcgate/nrc/dirty-bombs.htm.

2. Encarta.msn.com, s.v. "Radiological weapon," http://encarta,msn.com/encyclopedia_701702435/Radiological_Weapon.html.

3. Robert Johnston, "Dirty Bombs and Other Radiological Weapons," http://www.johnstonsarchive.net/nuclear/dirtybomb.html.

4. Yield is the energy released, usually expressed in kilotons of TNT equivalent (kT); 1 kT corresponds to 10^{12} calories or 4.19×10^{12} joules.

5. 1 milliSievert (mSv) is the same as 100 mrem.

6. United Nations, *Sources and Effects of Ionizing Radiation: United Nations Scientific Committee on the Effects of Atomic Radiation to the General Assembly*, vol. 1 (Geneva: United Nations Publications, 2000).

7. Ibid.

8. Fred Burton, "Dirty Bombs: Weapons of Mass Disruption," *STRATFOR* (October 4, 2006), http://www.stratfor.com/products/premium/print.php?storyId=277090.

9. A United States survey shows that about 40 percent of the population would not follow official instructions and would attempt to flee the site as fast as possible. This, already because in 2004, six laws setting different dose limits were issued for RDD clean up.

10. This is uranium that has a reduced proportion of the isotope U-235, and is mostly made of U-238. Depleted uranium (DU) is very dense, at 19.05 g/cm^3 it is 1.7 times that of lead, and easier to work with than the slightly denser tungsten. Because of its density, it is used as kinetic energy ammunition. The weapons include 120, 105, 30, and 20 mm rounds for use by tanks, APC cannons, aircraft and naval guns, cruise missiles, and bunker-buster bombs (GBU-28, 15, 24, 27, 31 and 37, and AGM 130C with F-15, B-2, A-10, AC-130 Spooky airplanes, Apache helicopter AH-64 and cruise missiles). These range from 200 g in a 20 mm projectile, 4.5 kg in 120 mm penetrators to 1.5 tons in the BLU-109 penetrator delivered with the B-2 bomber. DU is pyrophoric and burns on impact, providing a self-sharpening penetrator through conventional armor and other target material. Three hundred and four tons of DU munitions were fired during the 1991 Gulf War, some 11 tons in the Balkans Wars, and more than these alone in Afghanistan. About 70–80 percent of all DU munitions remain buried in the soil. Up to twenty states have weapons incorporating DU in their arsenals. They include the United States, the United Kingdom, France, Russia, Greece, Turkey, Israel, Saudi Arabia, Bahrain, Egypt, Kuwait, Pakistan, Thailand, and Taiwan. DU ammunition is manufactured in eighteen countries. Because DU is radioactive, producing alpha and beta particles and gamma rays, and is chemically toxic, polluting water supplies and producing other health hazards, some states and NGOs have asked for a ban on the production and military use of DU weapons.

11. In November 1995, Chechen militants under commander Basayev placed a small quantity of cesium 137 in Moscow's Izmailovsky Park. Rather than disperse the material, however, the Chechens used the material as a psychological weapon by directing a television news crew to the location and thus creating a media storm. The material in this incident was thought to have been obtained from a nuclear waste or isotope storage facility in Grozny. In December 1998, the pro-Russian Chechen Security Service announced it had found a dirty bomb consisting of a land mine combined with radioactive materials next to a railway line. It is believed that Chechen militants planted the device.

12. Text of the memo, declassified June 5, 1974. See www.wikipedia.org, s.v. "radiological weapon," http://en.wikipedia.org/wiki/Radiological_weapon.

13. According to a declassified 1950 CIA memorandum.

14. Johnston, "Dirty Bombs."

15. www.fas.org, s.v., "Radiological Weapons," http"//www.fas.org/nuke/guide/iraq/other/radiological.htm.

16. Many in the terror universe have a strong fascination with WMD, and many jihadist websites, chat rooms, and online magazines regularly post information on how to produce RDDs and improvised nuclear weapons. Some posts provide instructions on where to obtain radioactive material and, in cases where it cannot be obtained, even purport to provide instruction on how to extract radioactive material from commercial materials, such as distilling radium from luminescent industrial paint.

17. Louise I. Shelley, "Trafficking in Nuclear Materials: Criminals and Terrorists,"

in *Global Crime* 3–4, vol. 7 (New York: Routledge, August–November 2006): 544–556.

18. Of which there are many, close to the perimeters of the former USSR, including Transdniester, Abkhazia, Ossetia, Nagorno-Karabakh, the Pankisi Gorge area of Georgia, in the Central Asian states, Afghanistan, Sri Lanka, etc.

19. L. Zaitseva, "Organized Crime, Terrorism and Nuclear Trafficking," *Strategic Insights* 5, vol. 4 (August 2007).

20. Important information rests unreported in the IAEA database, since there are many reasons for the failure to report cases to the IAEA, including the desire not to disturb the citizens of the country or that reports of nuclear seizures may discourage tourism and foreign investment. Apart for these rational disincentives for reporting incidents of nuclear smuggling, many law enforcement officials in the countries of the former USSR who have the responsibility to report or uncover the smuggling are corrupt. Therefore, it is not in their interest to find this material as they are bribed not to examine cross border contraband. Moreover, incidents of organized crime involvement in nuclear smuggling that appear in the IAEA database may be an artifact of the police clamping down on a rival crime group to that which pays them off. Other problems of relying on the IAEA, and other databases, is that they include a significant number of cases that could be called "random noise," low level movement of illicit nuclear materials by opportunists who do not have established supply or demand chains. These obscure the patterns associated with the transport of the most dangerous materials. The suppliers and potential buyers for these materials are hard to trace because they are moved by professionals who are specialists in moving high value and prohibited goods.

21. Appropriations for securing nuclear warheads and materials for fiscal years 1993–2002, and for fiscal years 2003–2006, from Anthony Wier, "Interactive Budget Database," in *Nuclear Threat Initiative Research Library: Securing the Bomb* (Washington, DC: Project on Managing the Atom, Harvard University, and Nuclear Threat Initiative, 2006), http://www.nti.org/e_research/cnwm/overview/funding.asp. This annual spending is far more than the total pledges allocated to this task for the entire decade of the Global Partnership from all other participants combined, with Germany having pledged 170 million euros by 2009, the United Kingdom 2 million euros by 2006, the EU 25 million euros, and Norway 5.3 million euros.

22. He is awaiting trial in Russia for allegedly misusing funds received from the United States to safeguard nuclear facilities. He was extradited to Russia from Switzerland even though he was wanted by the United States for money laundering and other charges.

23. Susan J. Kavan, "Viktor Mikhailov leaves MinAtom," *Executive Branch* (March 1998). http://www.bu.edu/iscip/digest/vol3/ed0304.html.

24. All these cases cited by Matthew Bunn and Anthony Wier, *Securing the Bomb 2006* (Cambridge, MA: President and Fellows of Harvard University, 2006).

25. Thomas Land, "Islamic Terrorists and the Russian Mafia, Nuclear weapons-free zone in Central Asia," *Contemporary Review* (January 2003).

26. Government Accountability Office, *U.S. and International Assistance Efforts to Control Sealed Radioactive Sources Need Strengthening*, GAO-03-638 (August 2003), 9. In July 2005 the NRC announced plans to implement a National Source Tracking System to track potentially dangerous materials, though it is unclear how quickly it will be implemented.

27. Jim Wells testimony, before the U.S. Senate, *Challenges Facing NRC in Effectively Carrying Out Its Mission: Hearing Before the Subcommittee on Clean Air, Climate Change, and Nuclear Safety, Committee on Environment and Public Works*, May 26, 2005.

28. Most of the upgrades completed thus far have been in Eastern Europe, though upgrades have also been completed at facilities in Greece and Portugal.

29. Charles D. Ferguson and William C. Potter, *The Four Faces of Nuclear Terrorism* (Washington, DC: Center for Nonproliferation Studies, 2005), 8.

30. See also Robert Wesley, "British Terrorist Dhiren Barot's Research on Radiological Weapons," *Terrorism Focus* 3, no. 44 (November 2005).

31. STRATFOR, "Dirty Bombs: Weapons of Mass Disruption" (October 2006).

32. For example, in September 1999, two Chechen militants who attempted to steal highly radioactive materials from a chemical plant in the Chechen capital of Grozny were incapacitated after carrying the container for only a few minutes each; one reportedly died. See STRATFOR, "Dirty Bombs: Weapons of Mass Disruption," STRATFOR (October 2006): 33. In the case of aerosolized plutonium, the main hazard is the dose to the lung from particles retained in the pulmonary system. If the levels are high enough, the resultant dose can lead to fibrosis and collapse of the lung with death occurring within a matter of days or weeks. Long-term lung impairment can leave people disabled and in need of intensive care for the remainder of their lifetime. Below the threshold for "early effects," alpha irradiation of the lung can lead to lung cancer. Some of the inhaled plutonium will be transferred to the blood via the lymphatic system and become deposited in other organs, notably the liver and on bone surfaces, where it will also produce a cancer risk. See International Physicians for the Prevention of Nuclear War, "Radiological Dispersion Weapons: Health, Social, and Environmental Effects," *Global Health Watch Report* (1996).

Chapter 8

1. Technically inferring a direct relationship between threat and vulnerability, and likelihood and consequences, is incorrect. Threats are measured in terms of likelihood and severity of consequence, while risk equals threat divided by vulnerability.

2. Whole-of-government denotes public service agencies working across portfolio boundaries to achieve a shared goal and an integrated government response to national security issues. Approaches can be formal and informal. They can focus on policy development, program management, and service delivery. Leadership from ministers and agency heads is a critical part of whole-of-government work.

3. Since the beginning of 2008, a reform debate has been underway. Senior officials in the U.S. executive branch, various think tanks and members of Congress are among those calling for a significant restructuring of the American security model. This group argues that today's 20th century bureaucratic superstructure is outdated, an "inadequate basis for protecting the nation from 21st century security challenges." They cite the failures of coordination and implementation in Operation Iraqi Freedom, Operation Enduring Freedom in Afghanistan, and the response to Hurricane Katrina. The process by which executive branch agencies and presidential advisers present and prioritize issues for presidential decisions has also come under criticism. These shortcomings have had a serious

effect on the results of those missions and on the reputation of the United States. There is interest in coming up with a 2009 National Security Act, which would replace the National Security Act of 1947, designed to meet the specific needs of a post–WWII, the last major organizational reform in this realm. See report of the Congressional Research Service, "Organizing the U.S. Government for National Security: Overview of the Interagency Reform Debates," at: www.fas. org/sgp/crs/natsec/RL34455.pdf.

4. European states such as Switzerland, Sweden, Germany, and Finland, having invested for years in their civil emergency and civil defense systems, are better prepared to respond to the new breed of security challenges. In the case of Finland, the state believed it would be best to be prepared for such eventualities. The approach to crisis management is based on a Total Defense Concept envisaging the mobilization of all sectors of society in case of crisis, linking all civil defense and rescue services. The system is well coordinated on the regional level, and is equipped with an efficient communication system, NBC, and radiation monitoring, and is linked to a robust border security management capability.

Chapter 9

1. See Jason D. Ellis and Geoffrey D. Kiefer, *Combating Proliferation, Strategic Intelligence and Security Policy* (Baltimore: The Johns Hopkins University Press, 2004).

2. For the many definitions see, http://intellit.muskingum.edu/whatis_folder/ wharisintelintro.html.

3. Today, most IMINT systems are digital and operate in near real time. The optical systems rely on charged couple devices, which translate the varying visible-light levels of the object viewed into numbers and immediately relay those numbers back to earth, sometimes via relay satellite and reconstructed into an image. Since radio waves are not blocked by clouds, radar imagery can be obtained not only day or night but even when clouds block the view of a satellite's visible-light and infrared sensors. Moreover, radar may also find underground installations. The infrared radiation reflected by an object can be used to produce an image during daylight and night. IMINT remains important to treaty verification, and can provide warning of events. During the Cold War, U.S. and Soviet overhead reconnaissance capabilities allowed the negotiation of arms control agreements, since each side had independent means of monitoring compliance, and providing reassurance that the other side was not in the process of preparing for a surprise attack.

4. MASINT is officially defined as "technically derived intelligence that, when collected, processed, and analyzed results in intelligence that locates, tracks, identifies, or describes the signature of fixed or dynamic target objects and sources." Numerous scientific disciplines and advanced technologies are applied in dedicated MASINT systems. Whereas SIGINT is akin to hearing, and IMINT to sight, MASINT is akin to touch, taste, and smell.

5. Seismic sensors are used to detect the signals generated by nuclear tests while acoustic sensors are used to detect the sound waves generated by atmospheric nuclear tests. Infrared sensors on satellites detect missile launches by heat signature, and optical sensors known as "bhangmeters" detect the bright flashes of light associated with nuclear explosions. Nuclear radiation sensors, largely placed on satellites like DSP, VELA, and the Global Positioning System (GPS), detect such phenomenon as X-rays and gamma rays associated with nuclear

materials. Materials sampling—the gathering and analysis of effluents, debris, and particulates—associated with WMD programs is a significant element in finding the gases emitted by plutonium production, whether plutonium or HEU is used in nuclear weapon tests, detecting precursors and chemical weapons, and materials used for building bioagents. Increasingly, MASINT sensors are designed to operate in real-time. Today, sensors are preloaded with a computerized database containing thousands of "signatures." Rather than sending the data to a lab, the sensor itself will sort through the known signatures in its database to find one that matches what has just been detected and often the results will be instantly displayed to the operator on an LCD screen. See Jeffrey T. Richelson, "MASINT: The New Kid in Town," *International Journal of Intelligence and Counterintelligence* 14, no. 2 (2001): 152, and Jeffrey T. Richelson, *Spying on the Bomb: American Nuclear Intelligence from Nazi Germany to Iran and North Korea* (New York: W. W. Norton, 2006).

6. Gregory F. Treverton, *Reshaping National Intelligence for an Age of Information* (Cambridge: Cambridge University Press, 2003), 11–13.

7. Gregory F. Treverton, "Commentary," in *Smithsonian Magazine* (June 1, 2007), www.rand.org/commentary/060107SM.html.

8. "We thought it implausible that someone like Saddam would risk the destruction of his regime over noncompliance with UN resolutions. What we did not account for was the mind-set never to show weakness in a very dangerous neighborhood—particularly in regard to a growing Iranian military capability. Relying on secrets by themselves, divorced from deep knowledge of cultural mind-sets and history, will take you only so far." George Tenet, *At the Center of the Storm, My Years at the CIA* (New York: First Harperluxe Edition, 2007), 70.

9. There was the German OTRAG, the Orbital Transport und Raketen AG, or Orbital Transport and Rockets, Inc., which in 1975 set up testing and launch facilities for missiles at Shaba, Zaïre, and later in Libya. OTRAG was accused of missile proliferation to Libya—a project stopped by the then German minister of foreign affairs under pressure from France and the Soviet Union. See http://www.univperp.fr/fuseurop/otra_e.htm.

10. See John Arquilla and David Ronfeldt, eds., *Networks and Netwars* (Santa Monica, CA: RAND Corporation, 2001). "It takes a network to defeat a network."

11. See Phil Williams, "Intelligence Requirements for Transnational Threats: New Ways of Thinking, Alternative Methods of Analysis, Innovative Organizational Structures" (paper presented at the Global Futures Partnership, University of Pittsburgh, 2006).

12. For example with steganography: the art and science of hiding information by embedding messages within others, seemingly harmless messages in such a way that no one apart from the intended recipient knows of the existence of the message. This is in contrast to cryptography, where the existence of the message itself is not disguised, but the content is obscured. Steganography works by replacing bits of useless or unused data in regular computer files (such as graphics, sound, text, HTML, or even floppy disks) with bits of different, invisible information. This hidden information can be plain text, cipher text, or even images. See http://en.wikipedia.org/wiki/Steganography.

13. The need to reorient the HUMINT collection effort to a greater reliance on non-official cover is discussed by Gregory Treverton, *Reshaping National Intelligence for an Age of Information* (New York: Cambridge University Press, 2001), 152–157.

14. Dennis Gormley, "The Limits of Intelligence: Iraq's Lessons," *Survival* 46, no. 3 (January 2004): 10.
15. Using for example TEMPEST monitoring devices.
16. Thomas L. Friedman, *The World is Flat: The Globalized World in the 21st Century,* (London: Penguin Books, 2006).
17. Ibid., 93–126.
18. Ibid., 176–186.

Chapter 10
1. Andreas Persbo and Angela Woodward, *National Measures to Implement WMD Treaties and Norms: The Need for International Standards and Technical Assistance* (Stockholm: The Weapons of Mass Destruction Commission, Verification Research. Training and Information Centre (VERTIC)), May 2005.
2. See Article 27 of the Vienna Convention on the Law of Treaties.
3. Persbo and Woodward, *National Measures*, 1.
4. For further details of common law and civil law states' obligations to adopt national implementation legislation, see Angela Woodward, "National implementing laws for arms control and disarmament treaties," *Verification Yearbook 2003* (2003), 151–167.
5. See for instance Chapter 21, § 6 of the Swedish Criminal Code, or the U.S. Code, Title 43, Chapter 23, subchapters VIII and XVII, in regard to illicit use of nuclear weapons. Compare this with the 2001 amendments to the Criminal Law of China, which considerably widened the application of the law compared to the 1997 wording.
6. See South Africa's Weapons of Mass Destruction Act of 1993.
7. See part 6 of the UK Anti-terrorism, Crime and Security Act 2001.
8. Biological Weapons Convention, V Article IV, 1972.
9. Ibid.
10. Sergey Batsanov, "Viewpoint. Approaching the 10th Anniversary of the Chemical Weapons Convention, A Plan for Future Progress," *Nonproliferation Review* 2, vol. 13 (Abingdon, UK: Routledge, July 2006): 341.
11. For those related to WMD, counterterrorism, and such things like environmental protection, human rights, and post-conflict reconstruction. Alone the 1540 Committee is not providing assistance to states. The CTBTO advises national authorities in signatory states on necessary national implementation measures. It holds seminars and workshops promoting the adoption of national implementation measures. It provides legal and technical assistance upon request and maintains a database of implementation measures taken by signatories.
12. Persbo and Woodward, *National Measures*, 8–10.
13. See also IAEA Nuclear Security Culture—Draft of Revision 8.

Chapter 11
1. See also *Backgrounder, Security Sector Governance and Reform, National Security Policy*, Geneva Centre for the Democratic Control of Armed Forces (November 2005).
2. See, for example, "National Strategy to Combat Weapons of Mass Destruction," *National Security Presidential Directive* 17 (December 2002).
3. Issued by the UN, NATO, the European Council, and other international and regional organizations as well as by individual states.

4. George W. Bush, *National Strategy For Combating Terrorism* (Washington, DC: The White House, September 2006).
5. Offensive measures taken to prevent, deter, preempt, and respond to terrorism.
6. Defensive measures taken to reduce the vulnerability of individuals and property to terrorist acts.
7. European Council, Declaration on Combating Terrorism, adopted May 2004.

Chapter 12
1. See, for example, Department for International Development, *A Beginner's Guide to Security Sector Reform* (UK: University of Birmingham, 2007), http://www.ssrnetwork.net, and: Alan Bryden and Heiner Hänggi, eds., *Security Governance in Post-Conflict Peacebuilding* (Geneva: Geneva Centre for the Democratic Control of Armed Forces, 2005); *OECD DAC Handbook on Security System Reform, Supporting Security and Justice* (Paris: OECD, 2007); and, *The Role of UN Integrated Missions in Security Sector/System Reform: Review and Recommendations* (Geneva: Geneva Centre for the Democratic Control of Armed Forces, 2007).
2. "Freedom from want, freedom from fear, and freedom to take action on one's own behalf," see UN "Human Security Now" in *Final Report of the Commission on Human Security* (New York: Commission on Human Security, 2003), and the Commission Communication on Governance and Development, COM (2003) 615 final.
3. OECD, *Security System Reform and Governance, Policy and Practice* (Paris: OECD, 2004).
4. A strategy is a statement of fundamental values, highest priorities, and orientation toward the future, but it is an action document as well.
5. Mission objectives relate to efforts to predict, prevent, counteract and preempt threats to national security, and to assist all who make and implement national security policy, fight the preeminent threats, protect the nation, and enforce the laws in the implementation of national policy goals. Enterprise objectives relate to the capacity to maintain competitive advantages over all actors and forces that threaten the security of the nation.
6. Transformation must be driven by the doctrinal principle of security sector integration, and must be centered on a high-performing workforce that is: (1) results focused; (2) collaborative; (3) bold; (4) future oriented; (5) self-evaluating; and (6) innovative. These six characteristics are interdependent and mutually reinforcing. They will shape the organization's internal policies, programs, and technologies.
7. For IT and communications, education and training, internal cooperation, international cooperation, and anti-corruption.
8. For a comprehensive analysis of the Code, see Victor-Yves Ghebali and Alexander Lambert, *The OSCE Code of Conduct on Politico-Military Aspects of Security: Anatomy and Implementation* (Leiden: Martinus Nijhoff Publishers, 2005), xxi–428.
9. North Atlantic Treaty Organization, "Partnership Action Plan for Defence Institute Building," http://www.nato.int/ducu/basictxt/b040607e.htm.
10. Adopted by the General Assembly in its resolution 34/169 of December 17, 1979.
11. "Recommendation Rec (2001)10 of the Committee of Ministers to member states on the European Code of Police Ethics," adopted September 19, 2001, by the Committee of Ministers.

12. MC.DOC/2/05 of December 6, 2005. See also: Marina Caparini and Otwin Marenin, eds., *Borders and Security Governance* (Geneva: Geneva Centre for the Democratic Control of Armed Forces, 2006), 315.
13. In its current version it contains 239 pages of practical instructions and numerous specimens of travel documents and visas.
14. The text is expressly labeled as "explanatory and having no legally binding status"; see Council of the European Union, "Catalogue of Best Practices on External Borders Control, Removal and Readmission: Recommendations and Best Practices of February 2002" (2002).
15. "Council Regulation No. 2007/2004, OJL349," *Official Journal of the European Council* 47 (November 25, 2004): 1.
16. See Resolution 1166 on human rights of conscripts, Resolutions 903 and 1572 on the right to association for members of the armed forces, Recommendation 1402 and 1713, and the "European Code of Police Ethics."
17. See OECD, *Security System Reform and Governance, Policy and Practice* (Paris: OECD, 2004).
18. Communication from the Commission to the Council and the European Parliament, A Concept for European Community Support for Security Sector Reform.
19. OECD, *2004 Guidelines on Security System Reform and Governance* (Paris: OECD, 2004), http://www.oecd.org/dataoecd/8/39/31785288.pdf; and *2007 Handbook on Security System Reform: Supporting Security Justice* (Paris: OECD, 2007), http://www.oecd.org/dataoecd/43/25/38406485.pdf.
20. The police are primarily responsible for: (1) identification of criminal offenders and criminal activity and, when appropriate, apprehension of offenders and participating in subsequent court proceedings; (2) reducing the opportunities for the commission of crimes through preventive measures; (3) creating and maintaining a feeling of security in the community; (4) promoting and protecting the laws of the state; and (5) providing other services on a emergency basis.
21. David H. Bayley, *Democratizing the Police Abroad: What to Do and How to Do It* (Washington, DC: National Institute of Justice, 2001), 13–15.
22. Police are the most public manifestation of government authority. When they use that authority primarily to serve the interests of government, they belie the democratic promise of government for the people. The most dramatic contribution police can make to democracy is to become responsive to the needs of individual citizens. This is what the various emergency telephone systems have achieved in developed democracies. Most of the work done by the police in developed democracies is instigated by individual members of the public rather than by orders issued by government. A police force whose primary business is serving the disaggregate public supports democracy in two ways. First, it becomes accountable to the most diverse set of interests possible. Second, it enhances the legitimacy of government by demonstrating daily and practically that the authority of the state will be used in the interest of the people.
23. These activities are freedom of speech, association, and movement; freedom from arbitrary arrest, detention, and exile; and impartiality in the administration of law.
24. The most relevant international agreements and code of conducts are: (1) Council of Europe, *European Code of Police Ethics*; (2) *UN Code of Conduct for Law*

Enforcement Officials; (3) *UN Civilian Police Principles and Guidelines*; and (4) *OSCE Code of Conduct on Politico-Military Aspects of Security.*

25. Anita Hazenburg, "Target Areas of Police Reform," in *Police in Transition*, Kadar Andras, ed. (Budapest: Central European University Press, 2001), 177–186.

26. Gary T. Marx, "Police and Democracy," in *Policing, Security and Democracy: Theory and Practice*, Menachim Amir and Stanley Einstein, eds. (Chicago: Office of International Criminal Justice, 2001), http://www.mit.edu/gtmarx/www/dempol.html

27. Council of the European Union Presidency, "Integrated Border Management, Strategy Deliberations, Brussels," (Brussels: CEPS, 2006).

28. Peter Hobbing, *Integrated Border Management at the EU Level* (Brussels: CEPS, 2005).

29. It amends the earlier 1991 Directive in two main respects: (1) it widens the definition of criminal activity giving rise to money laundering to include all serious crimes, including offenses related to terrorism, and (2) it applies to activities and professions beyond credit and financial institutions, such as accountants, lawyers, notaries, real estate agents, casinos, and dealers in high value goods. They are now subject to the same obligations as regards customer identification, record keeping, and reporting of suspicious transactions.

30. Directive 2005/60/EC of the European Parliament and of the Council of October 26, 2005, which replaced Directive 91/308/EEC.

31. For more information, see: http://ec.europa.eu/justice_home/fsj/customs/fsj_customs_intro_en.htm.

32. COM/2005/608 and COM/2005/609 of November 30, 2005.

33. Regulation (EC) No 648/2005 of the European Parliament and of the Council of April 13, 2005, amending Council Regulation (EEC) No 2913/92 establishing the Community Customs Code.

34. Medicines such as Viagra, Cialis, and Levitra are the most popular counterfeit. However, medicines such as anti-cholesterol, anti-osteoporosis or medicines to control hypertension are also found as counterfeit.

35. In WWII an average of eighteen rounds was needed to destroy a tank at a range of 800 yards. In the 1973 Arab-Israeli War the average was two rounds at 1,200 yards, and in Desert Storm the average was two rounds at 400 yards. See Robert H. Scales, *Future Warfare Anthology* (Carlisle Barracks, PA: Strategic Studies Institute, 1999), 6.

36. Steven Metz, *Armed Conflict in the 21st Century: The Information Revolution and Post-Modern Warfare* (Carlisle Barracks, PA: Strategic Studies Institute, 2000), 81.

37. John Arquilla and David Ronfeldt, *Swarming and the Future of Conflict* (Santa Monica: RAND, 2000), and Sean J. A. Edwards, *Swarming on the Battlefield: Past, Present, and Future* (Santa Monica: RAND, 2000).

38. Joint Vision 2020 states, "Joint force headquarters will be dispersed and survivable and capable of coordinating dispersed units and operations. Subordinate headquarters will be small, agile, mobile, dispersed, and networked." *Joint Vision 2020* (Washington, DC: Joint Staff, June 2000): 32.

39. Deployable forces required for maintaining the rotation needed in long-term, high-intensity operations: 1/3 on deployment; 1/3 on training; 1/3 resting and refurbishing.

40. Rupert Smith, *The Utility of Force: The Art of War in the Modern World* (New York: Alfred A. Knopf, 2007), 448.

41. Gordon A. Craig, "Delbrück: The Military Historian," in *Makers of Modern Strategy*, Peter Paret, ed. (Princeton: Princeton University Press,1986), 314–342. Delbrück. building on Clausewitz's concept of total and limited war, used the terms *Niederwerfungsstrategie* (the strategy of annihilation) and *Ermattungsstrategie* (the strategy of exhaustion).
42. See Timothy Edmunds, "Security Sector Reform: Concepts and Implementation" (Paper presented for Workshop on the Workshop, November 20–22, 2001).
43. Arthur K. Cebrowski, *Military Transformation—a Strategic Approach* (Washington, DC: Department of Defense, 2003). See also William J. Haynes, letter to the House of Representatives J. Dennis Hastert, April 10, 2003, http://www.govexec.com/pdfs/transformation.pdf; and James J. Carafano, "A Congressional Guide to Defense Transformation: Issues and Answers," *Heritage Foundation Backgrounder* 1847 (Washington, DC: Heritage Foundation, 2005); U.S. Congress, House, Committee on Armed Services, *Army Transformation* (Washington, DC: GPO, 2005); and David E. Chesser, *Transformational Leadership: An Imperative for Army Reserve Readiness in the 21st Century* (Carlisle Barracks, PA: Army War College, 2006).

Chapter 13

1. Much of this chapter is based on the superb work: National Research Council, *Making the Nation Safer: The Role of Science and Technology in Countering Terrorism*, (Washington, DC: The National Academies Press, 2002), http://www.nap.edu/catalog/10415.html
2. Consequence management is a capacity to deal with the aftermath of an attack. The nation, at all levels of government, must develop the ability to respond effectively within hours, if not minutes, to any use of WMD on its territory with appropriate and specific measures to mitigate casualties and damage. This is a tall order. The needed capabilities include emergency medical care, distribution of protective gear or medications, including vaccines for those not yet exposed to a pathogen, evacuations, and area quarantines, among other measures. Since these capabilities need to be on a large scale, extensive preparations are needed to ready them in central locations, be able to mobilize them on sudden notice, be able to transport them where needed, and expect local authorities, first responders, and caregivers to be ready to receive and use them. The nation must also have emergency plans readied, including redundant or alternative control systems, for sustaining the operation of critical infrastructure that provides the necessities of life, if this infrastructure comes under attack.
3. Red teaming and blue teaming is an approach to defining the weaknesses of a system and devising ways to mitigate the resulting vulnerabilities. The red team tries to devise attack tactics, and the blue team tries to design counter-measures.
4. However, very difficult to achieve for explosives of the SEMTEX type.
5. The most influential regulator of food safety in the United States is not the Food and Drug Administration, nor is it the Department of Agriculture. In fact, it is not a government agency at all. It is the retailers, the end-of-the-line sellers who have learned by experience that consumers will blame them if something goes wrong. Public attention likely will also focus on a little-known body that establishes global food safety standards: the Codex Alimentarius Commission. Known as Codex, it is a joint project of the UN Food and Agricultural Organization (FAO) and the World Health Organization (WHO).

6. See the excellent work of Sergio Bonin, *International Biodefense Handbook 2007: An Inventory of National and International Biodefense Practices and Policies* (Zürich: ETH, Center for Security Studies, 2007), http://www.crn.ethz.ch.

7. Elizabeth L. Stone Bahr, "Biological Weapons Attribution: A Primer" (master's thesis, Monterey Naval Postgraduate School, 2007).

8. www.wikipedia.org, s.v. "Container Security Initiative," http://en.wikipedia.org/wiki/Container_Security_Initiative.

9. See Brian M. Jenkins, *Protecting Public Surface Transportation Against Terrorism and Serious Crime: An Executive Overview*, Report No. MTI-01-14 (San Jose: San Jose State University, 2001).

Chapter 14

1. UN Security Council Resolution 1373 (2001), adopted September 28, 2001. In particular, it called for states to "find ways of intensifying and accelerating the exchange of operational information, especially regarding actions or movements of terrorist persons or networks," and to cooperate more generally to "prevent and suppress terrorist attacks and take action against perpetrators of such acts."

2. Infrastructure is used with different contextual meanings. Infrastructure most generally relates to and has a hardware orientation, but note that it is frequently more comprehensive and includes software and communications. Collectively, the structure must meet the performance requirements of, and capacity for, data and application requirements. But just citing standards for designing an architecture or infrastructure does not include functional and mission area requirements for performance. Performance requirement metrics must be an inherent part of overall infrastructure to provide performance interoperability and compatibility. It identifies the top-level design of communications, processing, and operating system software. It describes the performance characteristics needed to meet database and application requirements. It provides a geographic distribution of components to locations. The service provider for these capabilities defines the infrastructure architecture. It includes processors, operating systems, service software, and standard profiles that include network diagrams showing communication links with bandwidth, processor locations, and capacities to include hardware builds versus schedule and cost. See: DoD 8020.1-M.

3. See similarity: Standardization within NATO; NATO AAP-6; INT DEF STAN 00-00 (Part 1)/3.

4. Sue A. Payton, Deputy Under Secretary of Defense for Advanced Systems and Concepts, "Technological Innovations. The ACTD Program," *Joint Force Quarterly* (Summer 2002): 71–76.

5. C4ISR: Command, Control, Communications, Computers, Intelligence, Surveillance, and Reconnaissance.

6. Many other ACTD program have been realized: Extending the Littoral Battlespace ACTD; the C4I for Coalition Warfare ACTD; the Language and Speech Exploitation ACTD; the Commander in Chief for the 21st Century ACTD; the Information Assurance Automated Intrusion Detection Environment ACTD; the Active Network Intrusion Defense ACTD; the Content-Based Information Security ACTD; the Information Operations Planning Tool ACTD; the Space Surveillance Operations ACTD; the Compact Environmental Anomaly Sensor

ACTD; the Communication/Navigation Outage Forecasting ACTD; the Navigation Warfare ACTD; etc.

7. RC-135V/W Rivet Joint detects, identifies, and geolocates signals throughout the electromagnetic spectrum; the E-8 JSTARS is an aircraft doing ground surveillance of moving targets by radar; the E-3 is an airborne warning and control system for surveillance, command and control, and battle management function; Global Hawk and Predator are UAVs (Unmanned Aerial Vehicles); the U-2 is a reconnaissance aircraft with electro-optic sensors; and the EP-3E ARIES II is an electronic warfare and reconnaissance aircraft.

8. See Geneva International Centre for Humanitarian Demining, *Willing to Listen: An Evaluation of the United Nations Mine Action Programme in Kosovo 1999–2001* (Geneva: The Praxis Group, Ltd., 2002).

9. Interoperability here meaning: "The ability of alliance forces, and when appropriate, forces of partner and other nations, to train, exercise, and operate effectively together in the execution of assigned missions and tasks." See AAP-6, *NATO Glossary of Terms and Definitions.*

10. A system, often dedicated or proprietary, that operates independently of other systems. The stovepipe system often has unique, non-standard characteristics.

11. Establishment and management of an organization so that information about the personnel, internal organization, or activities of one component is made available to any other component only to the extent required for the performance of assigned duties.

12. Knowledge management caters to the critical issues of organizational adaptation, survival, and competence in the face of increasingly discontinuous environmental change. Essentially, it embodies organizational processes that seek synergistic combination of data and information-processing capacity of IT, and the creative and innovative capacity of human beings.

13. See William J. Krouse and Raphael F. Perl, *Terrorism: Automated Lookout Systems and Border Security: Options and Issues,* Report RL31019 (Washington, DC: Congressional Research Service, 2001).

14. Intelligence services in democracies normally have no police, subpoena, law enforcement powers, and are barred from domestic spying.

15. This sometimes has tragic consequences for public safety. For example, a sheriff in Broward County, Florida stopped Mohamed Atta, one of the men responsible for the 9/11 terrorists attacks, issued him a ticket for driving without a license, and ordered him to appear in court. Because many federal, state, and local databases are not integrated, authorities in Broward County never had access to information indicating that Atta was on a U.S. Government "watch list" for terrorist activities.

16. For example, the British Rehabilitation of Offenders Act of 1975.

17. Among others, the following U.S. websites have all been withdrawn: Department of Transport—documents on pipeline mapping; risk profiles of various chemicals. Environmental Protection Agency—risk management program. Department of Energy—transportation of radioactive materials. International Nuclear Safety Center—information to learn more about nuclear power plants. Federal Energy Regulatory Commission—specifications for energy facilities. Center for Disease Control and Prevention—Report on Chemical Terrorism. U.S. Geological Survey—characteristics of large public surface water supplies, etc.

18. Attorney General John Ashcroft, Attorney General testimony, before the U.S. Senate Committee on the Judiciary, Oversight of the Department of Justice, July 25, 2002, http://www.fas.org/irp/congress/2002_hr/072502ashcroft.html

19. See David M. Walker testimony, before the Senate Select Committee on Intelligence and the House Permanent Select Committee on Intelligence, *Homeland Security: Information Sharing Activities Face Continued Management Challenges*, October 1, 2002.

20. Jeffrey T. Richelson, *The U.S. Intelligence Community: Exchange and Liaison Arrangements*, Fourth Edition (Boulder: Westview Press, 1999).

21. See for example Micheal Herman, *Intelligence Services in the Information Age: Norway as an Intelligence Ally* (London: Frank Cass Publishers, 2001), 139–146.

22. U.S. intelligence is the main contributor to UN and to NATO operations. During IFOR/SFOR and the Kosovo operations in the former Republic of Yugoslavia, the United States provided by far the largest part of necessary intelligence.

23. Many failures in the history of UN field operations might have been avoided if the UN had taken a more forthright approach to intelligence, and if it had possessed a stronger mandate to collect information. Though an enlightened view would see international security as an essential prerequisite to national security, and the UN as an international institution that needs to be strengthened, including by increasing its capacity to gather and analyze intelligence, major states have been reluctant to give the UN a greater intelligence mandate. Many of them hold this belief because intelligence is power, and because they feel that their own power would be threatened by a UN that possessed real intelligence, especially intelligence they may themselves not have. See: Walter A. Dom, "The Cloak and the Blue Beret: The Limits of Intelligence-Gathering in UN Peacekeeping" *The Pearson Paper*, vol. 4 (Ottowa: Pearson Peacekeeping Centre, 1999).

24. It was national intelligence services' concern over document security that obliged NATO to abandon any idea of creating an integrated intelligence body within the NATO Alliance.

25. France, Germany, Italy, the Netherlands, Spain, Sweden, and the United Kingdom.

26. The SAR-Lupe high-resolution radar system comprises five satellites of some 720 kg, two of which are already in space, and a ground segment for controlling the satellites and for receiving and processing image data. This ground segment and the French optical reconnaissance system Helios II are to be used jointly as the core element of European-wide strategic reconnaissance operations.

27. TREVI ceased to exist in 1992 when it was integrated into the Justice and Home Affairs pillar of the EC.

Appendix A

1. This *systematic approach* is taken in adapted form from *Crime Reduction Toolkits. Using Intelligence and Information,* a document focused on internal and criminal intelligence supporting the fight against local crime and disorder, at: www.crimereduction.co.uk/toolkits/ui0402.htm.

2. The expected value added of collaboration to specific activities has to be articulated.

Appendix B

1. C4ISTAR = Command, Control, Communications, Computers, Intelligence, Surveillance, Target Acquisition, and Reconnaissance.

2. Multiple efforts are underway. One project is the ITCM which aims to enhance the interoperability of systems between organizations involved in crisis response, humanitarian emergencies, and peace support operations. The ITCM program is a joint venture of Tampere University, the Defense Forces, the Ministry of Defense, and the Ministry of Foreign Affairs of Finland, and Crisis Management Initiative. Seminar on Crisis Management and Information Technology, *Seminar Report*, Crisis Management Initiative, Office of the President Ahtisaari, Helsinki, September 29 to October 1, 2002.

3. See: Linda D. Koontz testimony, *Geographic Information Systems: Challenges to Effective Data Sharing*, before the Subcommittee on Technology, Information Policy, Intergovernmental Relations and the Census, Committee on Government Reform, House of Representatives, June 10, 2003.

4. Preston Marshall, "*Next-Generation Communications* Briefing" (Washington, DC: February 2001).

5. See Global Reach for update, at: http://glreach.com/globstats/index.php3.

6. Peter S. Goodman, "Dishing up a New Link to the Internet," *Washington Post*, November 6, 2000.

7. Richard B. Myers, Chairman of the Joint Chiefs of Staff, "A Word from the Chairman," *Joint Forces Quarterly* (Summer 2002): 7.

8. David M. Walker testimony, before the Senate Select Committee on Intelligence and the House Permanent Select Committee on Intelligence, *Homeland Security: Information Sharing Activities Face Continued Management Challenges*, October 1, 2002.

9. See Geneva International Centre for Humanitarian Demining, *Willing to Listen: An Evaluation of the United Nations Mine Action Programme in Kosovo 1999–2001* (Geneva: The Praxis Group, Ltd., 2002).

10. See: Strategic Plan, DARPA, February 2003, at: www.fas.org/irp/agency/nima/commission/article20.htm.

Selected Bibliography

Armed Forces

Arquilla, John, and David Ronfeldt. *Networks and Netwars*. Santa Monica: RAND Corporation, 2001.

Arquilla, John, and David Ronfeldt. *Swarming and the Future of Conflict*. Santa Monica: RAND, 2000.

Carafano, James J., Jack Spencer, and Kathy Gudgel. "A Congressional Guide to Defense Transformation: Issues and Answers." *Heritage Foundation Backgrounder* 1847 (April 25, 2005).

Chesser, David E. *Transformational Leadership: An Imperative for Army Reserve Readiness in the 21st Century*. Carlisle Barracks, PA: Army War College, 2006.

Dershowitz, Alan M. *Preemption: A Knife That Cuts Both Ways*. New York: W.W. Norton & Company, Inc., 2006.

Edwards, Sean J. A. *Swarming on the Battlefield: Past, Present, and Future*. Santa Monica: RAND, 2000.

Gray, Colin S. *The Implications of Preemptive and Preventive War Doctrines: A Reconsideration*. Carlisle Barracks, PA: US Army War College, 2007.

National Defense Panel. *Transforming Defense. National Security in the 21st Century. A Transformation Strategy, Report of the National Defense Panel*. December 1997.

Smith, Rupert. *The Utility of Force: The Art of War in the Modern World*. New York: Alfred A. Knopf, 2007.

Biological Weapons and Warfare

Ainscough, Michael J. "Next Generation Bioweapons: Genetic Engineering and Biological Warfare." In *The Gathering Biological Warfare Storm*, edited by Jim A. Davis and Barry R. Schneider. Westport, CT: Praeger, 2004.

Alibek, Ken, and Stephen Handelman. *Biohazard: The Chilling True Story of the Largest Covert Biological Weapons Program in the World—Told from Inside by the Man Who Ran it*. New York: Delta, 1999.

Bernett, Brian. "U.S. Biodefense and Homeland Security: Toward Detection and Attribution." Masters thesis, Naval Postgraduate School, December 2006.

Bonin, Sergio. *International Biodefense Handbook 2007*. Zürich: Center for Security Studies, 2007.

Geissler, Erhard, and John Ellis van Courtland Moon, eds. "Biological Weapons: Research, Development and Use from the Middle Ages to 1845." *SIPRI Chemical and Biological Warfare Studies* 18. Oxford: Oxford University Press, 1999.

Harris, Sheldon H. *Factories of Death: Japanese Biological Warfare 1932-45 and the American Cover-up.* New York: Routledge, 1994.

Health Aspects of Chemical and Biological Weapons. Geneva: World Health Organization, 1970.

Leitenberg, Milton. *The Problem with Biological Weapons.* Stockholm: The Swedish National Defence College, 2004.

Martinez, Coleen K. *Biodefense Research Supporting the DoD: A new Strategic Vision.* Carlisle, PA: U.S. Army War College, 2007.

Meier, Oliver. "Aerial Surveillance and BWC Compliance Monitoring." *Research Group for Biological Arms Control* (November 2006).

Miller, Judith. Stephen Engelberg, and William Broad. *Germs, Biological Weapons and America's Secret War.* New York: Simon & Schuster, 2001.

National Institute of Allergy and Infectious Diseases. *NIAID Biodefense Research Agenda for Category B and C Priority Pathogens* 03-5315. NIH Publication, January 2003.

Rotz L. D., et al. "Public health assessment of potential biological terrorism agents." *Emerging Infectious Diseases* 2, vol. 8 (2002): 225–230.

Steinbruner, John, Elisa D. Harris, Nancy Gallagher, and Stay Okutani. *Controlling Dangerous Pathogens: A Prototype Protective Oversight System.* Center for International and Security Studies at Maryland (December 2005).

Stone Bahr, Elizabeth L. "Biological Weapons Attribution: A Primer." Masters thesis, Naval Postgraduate School, June 2007.

Webb, G. F. "A Silent Bomb: The Risk of Anthrax as a Weapon of Mass Destruction." *Proceedings of the National Academy of Sciences of the United States of America* 8, vol. 100 (April 2003).

Border Guards
Anthony, Ian, Aline Dewaele, Rory Keane, and Anna Wetter. "Strengthening WMD-related Border Security Management Assistance." Stockholm International Peace Research Institute, *Background Paper* 7 (September 2005).

Hobbing, Peter. "Integrated Border Management at the EU Level." Centre for European Policy Studies, *CEPS Working Document* 227 (August 2005).

Krouse William J., and Raphael F. Perl. *Terrorism: Automated Lookout Systems and Border Security: Options and Issues.* Washington, DC: Congressional Research Service, 2001.

Chemical and Biological Weapons and Warfare
Kosal, Margaret E. "The Basics Of Biological and Chemical Weapons Detectors." *Center for Nonproliferation Studies.* November 23, 2003.

Sidell, Frederick R., Ernest T. Takafuji, and David R. Franz, eds. *Medical Aspects of Chemical and Biological Warfare.* Bethesda, MD: Office of the Surgeon General, Department of the Army, 1997.

———. *Textbook of Military Medicine: Medical Aspects of Chemical and Biological Warfare, Part I: Warfare, Weaponry, and the Casualty.* Washington, DC: Surgeon General, U.S. Department of the Army, 1997.

Chemical Weapons and Warfare
Batsanov, Sergey. "Viewpoint. Approaching the 10th Anniversary of the Chemical Weapons Convention: A Plan for Future Progress." *Nonproliferation Review* 2, vol. 13 (July 2006): 341.

D'Agostino, P. A., and C. L. Chenier, *Analysis of Chemical Warfare Agents: General Overview, LC-MS Review, IN-House LC-ESI-MS Methods and Open Literature Bibliography.* Alberta, Canada: Defense Technical Information Center, 2006.

European Union
Commission of the European Communities. *Commission Staff Working Paper: Report of the R&D Expert Group on Countering the Effects of Biological and Chemical Terrorism.* Brussels: June 3, 2002.
———. *Communication from the Commission to the Council and the European Parliament on Cooperation in the European Union on Preparedness and Response to Biological and Chemical Agent Attacks.* Brussels: June 2, 2003.
———. *Communications from the Commission to the Council: Reinforcing the Management of the European Union's Southern Maritime Borders.* November 30, 2006.
Council of the European Union. *Integrated Border Management: Strategy Deliberations.* Brussels: November 21, 2006.
Council of the European Union. "Removal and Re-admission: Recommendations and Best Practices." In *Schengen Catalogue of Best Practices on External Borders Control.* Brussels: February 2002.
The European Union Institute for Security Studies. *A Secure Europe in a Better World: European Security Strategy.* Brussels: December 12, 2003.

Export Controls
Beck, Michael, Cassidy Craft, Seema Gahlaut, and Scott Jones. *Strengthening Multilateral Export Controls: A Nonproliferation Priority.* Athens: Center for International Trade and Security, 2002.

G8
G8. *G8 Action Plan on Nonproliferation.* June 9, 2004.
G8. *Gleneagles Statement on Non-Proliferation.* July 8, 2005.

Germany
Deutscher Bundestag. *Ausrüstung und Vorbereitung für einen Grossschadensfall mit biologischen und chemischen Schadstoffen.* June 20, 2005.
———. *Entwicklung eines Gesamtkonzepts zur Abwehr bioterroristischer Gefahren.* October 16, 2003.
———. *Organisation des Katastrophenschutzes im Grossschadensfall mit biologischen oder chemischen Schadstoffen.* May 6, 2005.

ICRC
Harland, Christopher B., and Angela Woodward. "A Model Law: The Biological and Toxin Weapons Crimes Act." *International Review of the Red Cross* 859 (September 30, 2005).
ICRC. *Appeal on Biotechnology, Weapons and Humanity.* Geneva: ICRC Publications, 2002.
Wirz, Christoph, and Emmanuel Egger. "Use of nuclear and radiological weapons by terrorists?" *International Review of the Red Cross* 859, vol. 87 (September 2005): 499.

Intelligence
Ellis, Jason D., and Geoffrey D. Kiefer. *Combating Proliferation, Strategic Intelligence and Security Policy.* London: The Johns Hopkins University Press, 2004.

Gormley, Dennis. "The Limits of Intelligence: Iraq's Lessons." *Survival* 3, vol. 46 (Autumn 2004).

Kouzminov, Alexander. *Biological Espionage: Special Operations of the Soviet and Russian Foreign Intelligence Services in the West.* London: Greenhill Books, 2005.

Richelson, Jeffrey T. "MASINT: The New Kid in Town." *International Journal of Intelligence and Counterintelligence* 2, vol. 14 (2001).

———. *Spying on the Bomb: American Nuclear Intelligence from Nazi Germany to Iran and North Korea.* New York: W.W. Norton, 2006.

Tenet, George. *At the Center of the Storm: My Years at the CIA.* New York: Harper Collins, 2007.

Treverton, Gregory. *Reshaping National Intelligence for an Age of Information.* New York: Cambridge University Press, 2001.

Williams, Phil. "Intelligence Requirements for Transnational Threats: New Ways of Thinking, Alternative Methods of Analysis, Innovative Organizational Structures." Paper presented at the University of Pittsburgh, 2006.

NATO

Departments of the Army, Navy, and Air Force. *NATO Handbook on the Medical Aspects of NBC Defensive Operations.* Washington, DC: Defense Department, 1996.

NATO. *The NATO Nuclear, Biological, and Chemical Defence Initiatives.* 2002.

Pilat, Joseph F, and David S. Yost, eds. *NATO and the Future of the Nuclear Non-Proliferation Treaty.* Rome: NATO Defense College, 2007.

New Zealand

Arotake, Tumuaki o te Mana. *Managing Threats to Domestic Security, Report of the Controller and Auditor-General.* Wellington, NZ: The Audit Office, 2003.

Nuclear Weapons and Warfare

Albright, David, Kathryn Buehler, and Holly Higgins. "Bin Laden and the Bomb." *Bulletin of Atomic Scientists* 1, vol. 58 (January/February 2002).

Albright, David, and Kimberly Kramer. *Civil HEU Watch: Tracking Inventories of Civil Highly Enriched Uranium.* Washington, DC: Institute for Science and International Security, 2005.

Albright, David. "Al Qaeda's Nuclear Program: Through the Window of Seized Documents." *Special Forum* 47 (November 6, 2002).

Allison, Graham T. "How to Stop Nuclear Terror." *Foreign Affairs* (January/February 2004).

———. *Nuclear Terrorism: The Ultimate Preventable Catastrophe,* First Edition. New York: Times Books/Henry Holt, 2004.

Arbman, Gunnar and Charles Thornton. *Russia's Tactical Nuclear Weapons, Part II: Technical Issues and Policy Recommendations.* Stockholm: Swedish Defence Research Agency, 2005.

Bunn, Matthew and Anthony Wier. *Securing the Bomb.* Washington, DC: Project on Managing the Atom, Harvard University and Nuclear Threat Initiative, 2002.

Holden, John P. and Matthew Bunn. *Technical Background: A Tutorial on Nuclear Weapons and Nuclear-Explosive Materials.* Washington, DC: Project on Managing the Atom, Harvard University and Nuclear Threat Initiative, 2002.

Pluta Anna M. and Peter D. Zimmerman. "Nuclear Terrorism: A Disheartening Dissent." *Survival* 2, vol. 48 (Summer 2006).

Wier, Anthony. *Interactive Budget Database.* Washington, DC: Project on Managing the Atom, Harvard University, and Nuclear Threat Initiative, 2006.

OECD

OECD. *DAC Handbook on Security System Reform: Supporting Security and Justice.* Paris: OECD Publishing, 2007.

Organized Crime

Lampe, Klaus von. "The Use of Models in the Study of Organized Crime." Paper presented at the 2003 Conference of the European Consortium for Political Research, Marburg, September 19, 2003.

Land, Thomas. "Islamic terrorists and the Russian Mafia, Nuclear weapons-free zone in Central Asia." *Contemporary Review* (January 2003).

Shelley, Louise I. "Trafficking in Nuclear Materials: Criminals and Terrorists." *Global Crime* 3–4, vol. 7 (August–November 2006): 544–556.

Williams, Phil, and Roy Godson. "Anticipating Organized and Transnational Crime." *Crime, Law and Social Change* 4, vol. 37 (June 2002): 311–355.

Zaitseva, Lyudmila. "Organized Crime, Terrorism and Nuclear Trafficking." *Strategic Insights* 5, vol. 6 (August 2007).

OSCE

Ghebali, Victor-Yves, and Alexander Lambert. *The OSCE Code of Conduct on Politico-Military Aspects of Security: Anatomy and Implementation.* Leiden: Martinus Nijhoff Publishers, 2005.

OSCE. *Guidebook on Democratic Policing,* Second Edition. Vienna: OSCE Publishing, 2008.

Police

Bayley, David H. *Democratizing the Police Abroad: What to Do and How to Do It.* Washington, DC: National Institute of Justice, 2001.

Gregory, Frank. *The UK's Domestic Response to Global Terrorism: Strategy, Structure and Implementation with Special Reference to the Role of Police.* Madrid: Real Instituto Elcano, 2007.

Hazenburg, Anita. "Target Areas of Police Reform." In *Police in Transition,* edited by Andras Kadar. Budapest: Central European University Press, 2001.

Marx, Gary T. "Police and Democracy." In *Policing, Security and Democracy: Theory and Practice,* edited by Menachim Amir and Stanley Einstein. Chicago: Office of International Criminal Justice, 2001.

Radiological Weapons

"British Terrorist Dhiren Barot's Research on Radiological Weapons." *Terrorism Focus* 44, vol. 3 (November 15, 2006).

Burton, Fred. "Dirty Bombs: Weapons of Mass Disruption." www.stratfor.com/products/premium/print.php?storyId=277090

Cordesman, Anthony H. *Radiological Weapons as Means of Attack.* Center for Strategic and International Studies (November 8, 2001).

Eraker, Elizabeth. "Cleanup After a Radiological Attack: U.S. Prepares Guidance." *NonProliferation Review* 3, vol. 11 (Fall/Winter 2004).

Ferguson, Charles D, Tahseen Kazi, and Judith Perera. *Commercial Radioactive Sources:*

Surveying the Security Sources. Monterey: Monterey Institute of International Studies, 2003.

Johnston, Robert. "Dirty Bombs and Other Radiological Weapons." http://www.johnstonarchive.net/nuclear/dirtybomb.html

Physicians for the Prevention of Nuclear War. "Radiological Dispersion Weapons: Health, Social, and Environmental Effects." *Global Health Watch Report* (1996).

U.S. Nuclear Regulatory Commission. *Fact Sheet on Dirty Bombs.* July 2002.

Russia

Committee on Future Contributions of the Biosciences to Public Health, Agriculture, Basic Research, Counter-Terrorism, and Non-Proliferation Activities in Russia; Office for Central European and Eurasia; National Research Council. *Biological Science and Biotechnology in Russia: Controlling Diseases and Enhancing Security.* Washington, DC: National Academies Press, 2005.

Security Sector Reform

A Beginner's Guide to Security Sector Reform. Birmingham: Department for International Development, 2007.

Bryden, Alan, and Heiner Hänggi, eds. *Security Governance in Post-Conflict Peacebuilding.* London: Transaction Publishers, 2005.

Terrorism

Booth, Ken, and Tim Dunne, eds. *Worlds in Collision: Terror and the Future of Global Order.* New York: Palgrave, 2002.

Ferguson, Charles D., and William C. Potter, *The Four Faces of Nuclear Terrorism.* Washington, DC: Center for Nonproliferation Studies, 2005.

Friedman, Lawrence, ed. *Superterrorism: Policy Responses.* Oxford: Blackwell Publishing, 2002.

Jenkins, Brian. "Protecting Public Surface Transportation Against Terrorism and Serious Crime: An Executive Overview, Report No. MTI-01-14." *Norman Y. Mineta Institute for Surface Transportation Policy Studies* (2001).

———. *Terrorism: Current and Long-Term Threats.* Santa Monica: Rand, 2001.

Laqueur, Walter. "Postmodern Terrorism," *Foreign Affairs* (September/October 1996).

United Kingdom

Foreign Affairs Committee. *The Biological Weapons Green Paper.* London: Stationery Office, Ltd., 2002.

United Nations

Deliberate Use of Biological and Chemical Agents to Cause Harm. Geneva: World Health Organization, 2002.

Department of Communicable Disease, Surveillance and Response. *Strengthening national preparedness & response to biological weapons: Report of a WHO consultation with the participation of the Food and Agricultural Organization of the UN and the Office International des Epizooties.* Rome: World Health Organization, 2002.

Implementation of resolution WHA55.16 on global public health response to natural occurrence, accidental release or deliberate use of biological and chemical agents or radio-nuclear material that affect health. Geneva: World Health Organization, 2005.

Laboratory Biosafety Manual, Third Edition. Geneva: World Health Organization, 2004.

United Nations. *A More Secure World: Our Shared Responsibility—Report of the Secretary-General's High-level Panel on Threats, Challenges and Change.* New York: United Nations Publications, 2004.

———. *Report of the Secretary-General on the Status of the Implementation of the Special Commission's Plan for the Ongoing Monitoring and Verification of Iraq's Compliance with Relevant Parts of Section of Security Council Resolution 687(1991).* New York: United Nations Publications, 1995.

———. *Report of the United Nations Scientific Committee on the Effects of Atomic Radiation to the General Assembly.* New York: United Nations Publications, 2000.

World Health Organization. *Public Health response to Biological and Chemical Weapons: WHO Guidance.* http://www.who.int/csr/delibepidemics/biochemguide/en/print.html

United States

Ballistic Missiles: Delivery Systems For Weapons Of Mass Destruction, Second Edition. Washington, DC: U.S. Government Publication, 2006.

Bush, George W. *The National Security Strategy of the United States of America of 2002.* Washington, DC: The White House, 2002.

———. *The National Security Strategy of the United States of America of 2006.* Washington, DC: The White House, 2006.

Chairman of the Joint Chiefs of Staff. *National Military Strategy to Combat Weapons of Mass Destruction* (February 13, 2006).

Commission on the Intelligence Capabilities of the United States Regarding Weapons of Mass Destruction. *Report to the President.* Washington, DC: WMD Commission, 2005.

Cruise Missiles: Potential Delivery Systems for Weapons of Mass Destruction. Washington, DC: U.S. Government Publication, 2000.

Government Accountability Office. *Homeland Security: Information Sharing Activities Face Continued Management Challenges.* Washington, DC: GAO, 2002.

———. *Nuclear Nonproliferation: DOE Needs to Take Action to Further Reduce the Use of Weapons-Usable Uranium in Civilian Research Reactors.* Washington, DC: GAO, 2004.

———. *U.S. and International Assistance Efforts to Control Sealed Radioactive Sources Need Strengthening.* Washington, DC: GAO, 2003.

Joint Vision 2020. Washington, DC: U.S. Department of Defense, 2000.

Military Transformation: A Strategic Approach. Washington, DC: U.S. Department of Defense, 2003.

"National Strategy to Combat Weapons of Mass Destruction." *National Security Presidential Directive* 17 (December 2002).

"National Strategy For Combating Terrorism." *National Security Presidential Directive* 8 (September 2003).

Office of the Director of National Intelligence. *The National Intelligence Strategy of the United States of America: Transformation through Integration and Innovation.* October 2005.

The National Counterintelligence Policy Board. *The National Counterintelligence Strategy of the United States of America.* 2007.

The White House. "Biodefense for the 21st Century," press statement, April 28, 2004. http://www.whitehouse.gov/homeland/20040430.html.

U.S. Congress. House, Committee on Armed Services. *Army Transformation.* Washington, DC: GPO, 2005.

————. *Technologies Underlying Weapons of Mass Destruction.* Washington, DC: GPO, 1993.

WMD

Committee on Science and Technology for Countering Terrorism, and National Research Council. *Making the Nation Safer: The Role of Science and Technology in Countering Terrorism.* Washington, DC: The National Academies Press, 2002.

Persbo, Andreas, and Angela Woodward. *National Measures to Implement WMD; Threats and Norms: The Need for International Standards and Technical Assistance.* WMDC. Stockholm: The Weapons of Mass Destruction Commission, 2005.

Smith, Derek D. "Establishing a Global Quarantine Against Weapons of Mass Destruction." Paper 1 of the Yale Law School Scholarship Series, February 2, 2005.

Stockholm International Peace Research Institute. *SIPRI Yearbook 2006: Armaments, Disarmament and International Security.* New York: Oxford University Press Inc., 2006.

————. *SIPRI Yearbook 2007: Armaments, Disarmament and International Security.* New York, Oxford University Press Inc., 2007.

Weapons of Mass Destruction Commission. *Weapons of Terror: Freeing the World of Nuclear, Biological and Chemical Arms.* Stockholm, EO Grafiska, 2006.

Websites

www.zanggercommittee.org
www.nuclearsuppliersgroup.org
www.australiagroup.net
www.mtcr.info/english/press.htm
www.wassenaar.org
www.un.org
www.state.gov
www.wikipedia.org
www.globalpartnership.gc.ca
www.legislationonline.org
www.osce.org
www.stabilitypact.org
http://register.consilium.europa.eu
http://eur-lex.europa.eu
www.opcw.org
http://ue.eu.int
www.government.ru
http://untreaty.un.org/English/overview.asp

Index

About the Author

Fred Schreier is a consultant with the Geneva Centre for the Democratic Control of Armed Forces. A retired colonel, he has served in various command and general staff positions and in different functions in the Swiss Ministry of Defense as a senior civil servant. He is a graduate in international relations of the Institut Universitaire de Hautes Etudes Internationals, Geneva, and in strategic studies of the Fletcher School of Law and Diplomacy.